HANDBOOK ON RESEARCH IN RELATIONSHIP MARKETING

T0329674

Handbook on Research in Relationship Marketing

Edited by

Robert M. Morgan
University of Alabama, USA

Janet Turner Parish
Texas A&M University, USA

George Deitz
University of Memphis, USA

Cheltenham, UK • Northampton, MA, USA

Published by
Edward Elgar Publishing Limited
The Lypiatts
15 Lansdown Road
Cheltenham
Glos GL50 2JA
UK

Edward Elgar Publishing, Inc.
William Pratt House
9 Dewey Court
Northampton
Massachusetts 01060
USA

Paperback edition 2016

A catalogue record for this book
is available from the British Library

Library of Congress Control Number: 2014950741

This book is available electronically in the **Elgar**online
Business subject collection
DOI 10.4337/9781783478637

ISBN 978 1 84844 368 6 (cased)
ISBN 978 1 78347 863 7 (eBook)
ISBN 978 1 78347 940 5 (paperback)

Typeset by Servis Filmsetting Ltd, Stockport, Cheshire
Printed and bound in Great Britain by TJ International Ltd, Padstow

Contents

Contributors

Mousumi Bose, Montclair State University

Tom Boyd, Kaplan University

Susan Cadwallader, California State University, Fullerton

George Deitz, University of Memphis

Judith Anne Garretson Folse, Louisiana State University

Dwayne D. Gremler, Bowling Green State University

Thomas W. Gruen, University of New Hampshire

Evert Gummesson, Stockholm University School of Business

Kevin P. Gwinner, Kansas State University

John D. Hansen, University of Alabama at Birmingham

Betsy Bugg Holloway, Samford University

Michael J. Howley, Jr., Drexel University

Russell Lacey, Xavier University

Sandi Lampo, Christopher's World Grille

Kristin Landua, The Maryborough Hotel and Spa, Ireland

Katherine N. Lemon, Boston College

Hufrish Majra, SVKM's NMIMS University

Robert W. Palmatier, University of Washington

Janet Turner Parish, Texas A&M University

Randle D. Raggio, University of Richmond

Stephen A. Samaha, California State University, Northridge

Rajan Saxena, SVKM's NMIMS University

Jagdish N. Sheth, Emory University

Mona Sinha, Southern Polytechnic State University

Aaron Thomas, Safeway, Inc.

Peter C. Verhoef, University of Groningen

Anna Green Walz, Grand Valley State University

Sijun Wang, Loyola Marymount University

1. The future evolution of relationship marketing
Jagdish N. Sheth

INTRODUCTION

The purpose of this chapter is to review the forces that led to the spectacular rise of relationship marketing both as a marketing practice and as a discipline. More importantly, I will suggest how relationship marketing is likely to evolve in the future.

The fundamental force behind the rise of relationship marketing was the economic recession of the early 1980s caused by the first energy crisis of the 1970s (1974–78). This is often referred to as stagflation (inflation without economic growth). Both the monetary policy of high interest rates to curb inflation and the fiscal policy of wholesale deregulation of infrastructure industries such as airlines and trucking to stimulate growth during the Carter administration failed.

This was followed by the Reagan administration's focus on the global competitiveness of U.S. industries. It led to lowering the corporate tax rate and establishing the Malcolm Baldrige Quality Awards in manufacturing and services industries. The Reagan administration also allowed megamergers of directly competitive businesses. For example, General Electric (GE) was allowed to buy RCA in the consumer electronics industry, and similar mergers and acquisitions were allowed in the beer, soft drinks, aviation, and defense industries. The fundamental impact of this exogenous macro-economic reality was to shift the marketing objective from organically gaining market share to acquiring market share through mergers and acquisitions. The vast amount of prior research which empirically validated the prevailing view (on what was referred to as PIMS database research) that the financial performance of a product or a company was directly related to its marketing plans, including segmentation, positioning, and targeting (SPT) to gain market share, was now questioned. Return on marketing investment (RoMI) could not be justified, especially based on economic value added (EVA) and activity based costing (ABC).

The best ways, therefore, to gain market share were inorganic growth such as mergers, acquisitions, and alliances. This was further reinforced with the growth of private equity companies such as KKR and

Berkshire Hathaway. Hostile takeovers became more prevalent, including the famous takeover of RJR Nabisco by KKR, as well as more long term investment by Berkshire Hathaway in the Coca-Cola Company. Similarly, massive wholesale deregulation of the airline industry resulted in meg-amergers as airlines raced to survive from regional regulated monopolies to nationally deregulated competitive businesses.

A final factor responsible for the growth of relationship marketing was computerization in the services sectors such as airlines, banks, utilities, and telephone services, all directly marketed to end users, unlike the con-sumer packaged goods (CPG) companies and industries. This generated enormous amounts of data on usage at the individual customer level, pro-viding significant opportunity for analytic research, including data mining and consumer insights.

Airlines such as United, American, and Delta survived the wholesale deregulation by massively investing in computerized reservation systems (CRS), which provided them with the opportunity to develop and suc-cessfully promote loyalty programs such as frequent flyer miles. Industry after industry went into a defensive posture of protecting their existing customers by establishing key account management (KAM) (Shapiro and Moriarty 1980; Shapiro 1988; Anderson and Narus 1991) and at the same time reducing the number of suppliers, using transaction cost economics (TCE) (Williamson 1979). Also, as part of total quality management (TQM) (Crosby 1979; Deming 1986), industrial customers began to reduce the number of suppliers and establish partnerships with their strategic suppliers.

Relationship marketing changed the marketing paradigm from a trans-actional to a relational perspective, and from a market share to share of wallet objective in marketing. This led to understanding the lifetime value (LTV) of customers, the bundling of offerings, customer profitability analysis, and strategic partnering with customers (Sheth and Parvatiyar 2000). The discipline began to shift from theories of competition and com-petitive advantage to theories of cooperation and transaction cost eco-nomics. Instead of empirically testing low cost or differentiation strategies, scholars began to examine the role of trust, commitment, and interorgani-zational alignment (Morgan and Hunt 1994; Sheth and Parvatiyar 2000).

In contrast to other schools of marketing thought, relationship market-ing became a global phenomenon all at once. Scholars from Scandinavia, the United Kingdom, and Australia began to offer their perspectives and conduct empirical research at about the same time as scholars from North America (Hakansson 1982; Gronroos 1995, 2000; Payne 1995, 2000; Hakansson and Snehota 2000). The diffusion of the relationship market-ing school of thought was more exponential than the traditional S-shaped curve.

EXTANT RESEARCH

I have classified most of the empirical research and academic perspectives into the following five areas:

a. Loyalty programs
    These began in the 1980s with the airline industry, as mentioned before. Today, they are virtually everywhere, ranging from hospitality to grocery, department stores to pet stores, and hair salons to doctors and dentists. With the growth of the Internet, loyalty programs have exploded in the world of online marketing and especially so with virtual communities (Rosenberg and Czepiel 1984; Dick and Basu 1994; Raphel 1995; Reichheld 1996). Groupon's tri-pronged loyalty program has "Daily Deals" for customer acquisition, "Groupon Now" for businesses to manage demand during the day, and "Groupon Rewards," its most recent foray aimed at retention rather than acquisition, for frequent visitors (Wong 2011). We are at the cusp of a virtual revolution that straddles both reality and imagination, where real money buys virtual currency for trading in virtual clothes, furniture, animals, and even land, such as on *Second Life, Habbo Hotel,* and *Farmville* (Keegan 2010). The potential for companies to draw in loyal customers via these virtual realities and alternate economies is immense, but only just being explored.
b. Customer satisfaction, customer lifetime value, and net promoter score
    A second area of research and practice has been measuring customer satisfaction, lifetime value of a customer, and word of mouth influence of customers (Payne 2000). Measurement of customer satisfaction was led by J.D. Power and Associates ratings of brands and companies across virtually all industries. It was supplemented by more aggregate industry level indices by the University of Michigan's American Customer Satisfaction Index (ACSI) (Fornell et al. 1996). At the same time, a number of practitioner books were written, such as *Moments of Truth* (Carlzon 1987), *Aftermarketing* (Vavra 1992), and *The Loyalty Effect* (Reichheld 1996). Quantification of customer retention (Pfeifer and Farris 2004) began along with quantification of customer lifetime value (CLV) (Shapiro et al. 1987; Venkatesan and Kumar 2004; Kumar and Rajan 2009). It also led to research on customer profitability, with a discovery that profitability is even more skewed than revenues and, therefore, it is better to withdraw from unprofitable customers and concentrate marketing efforts toward profitable customers (Halinen and Tahtinen 2002; Helm et al. 2006).

Word of mouth has always been a very powerful form of communication in marketing. It began to be formally introduced as a metric for management compensation into what is referred to as Net Promoter Score (NPS) (Reichheld 2006) (http://www.netpromoter. com). Companies rose to the challenge of creating marketing programs that   formally galvanized positive word of mouth from loyal customers and made them the company's brand ambassadors. With the eruption of blogging, online reviews, and social media, word of mouth marketing has become a significant part of marketing by virtually all companies (Kozinets et al. 2010; O'Brien 2011).

c.   Bundling and share of wallet research

A significant amount of research also took place on multiple offerings to individual customers, especially in financial services (e.g., banking, brokerage, insurance, mortgage) and in telecommunication (e.g., triple play of telephone, Internet, and cable). More recent research cautions against indiscriminate cross-selling, because one in five cross-buying customers may be unprofitable (Shah and Kumar 2012).

As the cost of storing and analyzing customer information became cheaper, companies began to focus on utilizing what came to be known as customer relationship management (CRM) or database marketing (Peppers and Rogers 1995, 2004; Reinartz et al. 2004; Bohling et al. 2006). There was now a direct measure of how marketing efforts led to purchase behavior, including effectiveness of cross-selling other products and services, as well as upselling. Target marketing was no longer a shotgun approach. It was now segment-of-one marketing or what came to be known as one-to-one marketing (Peppers and Rogers 1993). Mass customization and personalized offerings were all cost effective as a result of direct access to end customers, especially in services industries. This complemented the stronger shift of the U.S. economy toward services as American households began to outsource traditional homemaker activities such as cooking, cleaning, and child care. By now, a majority of households had become dual income wage earners. Working outside the family was not just a discretionary activity by the homemaker; it became a necessity even among college educated families. Time shift and time poverty became equally important resource constraints, resulting in the growth of services industries (Sheth and Sisodia 1999).

d.   Key account management

A fourth area of research was the establishment of key accounts in business to business marketing (Shapiro and Moriarty 1982; Cannon and Narayandas 2000; Homburg et al. 2002). It was no longer sufficient to segment business customers into vertical markets organized by standard industrial classification (SIC). Companies began to fully understand the implications of the 80/20 rule (80 percent of the revenue is concentrated in the top 20 percent of the accounts). Retaining these key accounts was not just the responsibility of the sales executive. It needed cross-functional support as well as direct involvement by the supplier company. In fact, it became important to recognize that one-on-one CEO meetings facilitated by the key account managers were critical to negotiating strategic partnerships with customers to become sole source suppliers, if possible. This evolved into strategic account management (SAM) (Spekman 1988) and also into global account management (GAM) (Yip and Madsen 1996). Indeed, as a consequence of reengineering the corporation (which led to downsizing, outsourcing noncore functions, and leveraged buyouts (LBOs) of noncore businesses), customer–supplier relationships were elevated as strategic and collaborative partnerships (Mentzer 2000). Sometimes it led to the creation of joint ventures between a supplier and a customer. For example, Sears and IBM created a separate joint venture company which managed Sears data processing centers. Similarly, General Electric outsourced and spun off its call center and business process outsourcing (BPO) into a separate entity called Genpact. Finally, Citibank did the same with its internal software department into a standalone company called iFlex.

e.   Industrial marketing and purchasing (IMP) research
The fifth area of research emerged from Scandinavia, where industrial marketing has historically been a large component of the economy. The focus was to understand industrial buying behavior and the strategic importance of the procurement department. How do customers engage with their suppliers, and what type of relationship is appropriate for developing strong supplier networks and creating supplier ecosystems? Similar to Japan, Scandinavia has a high concentration of the economy in the hands of a few large conglomerates, which made this research unique (Hakansson and Snehota 2000).

The Proverbial Five Blind Men and the Elephant

Over the years, relationship marketing began to diverge rather than converge into a cohesive marketing practice or discipline. While there were several efforts to identify key constructs such as trust and commitment, it did not evolve into a theory with propositions to be empirically testable in contrast to the market orientation perspective in managerial marketing.

Research in relationship marketing today resembles the proverbial five blind men and the elephant. It means different things to different scholars and practitioners. To some, it means CRM and it is a part of the CIO organization focused on database integration and management, for example predictive modeling and yield management in the airline industry. To others, it means post-sales marketing, including customer support and what is referred to as "aftermarketing." To most practitioners and scholars, it still means managing loyalty programs and segmenting the market based on customer profitability analysis. In my view, it represents a great opportunity for someone to synthesize the divergent practices and perspective into a comprehensive theory of relationship marketing. The notable exception is Shelby Hunt (2010). However, he has expanded his general theory of marketing anchored to resource advantage and suggests that relationship strength is one of the many resource advantages.

THE FUTURE EVOLUTION

In the meanwhile, relationship marketing as a dynamically evolving practice is likely to shift on two dimensions, as depicted in Figure 1.1. It will shift from share of wallet to share of heart as the purpose of relationship

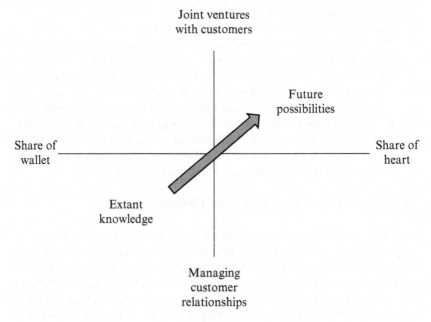

Figure 1.1   The future evolution of relationship marketing

marketing and from managing relationships with customers to managing contractual or virtual joint ventures with customers.

Share of Heart

As existing relationship marketing practices, including loyalty programs, bundled offerings, personalized services, key account management, and CRM efforts, all become universal and therefore commoditized, marketing strategies and tactics designed to gain the share of wallet of customers as a key metric for relationship marketing will give way to what I refer to as winning the "share of heart" as the new metric.

Share of heart, as the name implies, is bonding with customers on an emotional plane and goes beyond offering just economic or functional value of the product or service. The relationship transcends from business to friendship with customers. It also transcends measuring the strength of the relationship by numerical and financial outcomes both for the company and for its customers. It therefore transcends beyond trust and commitment, the twin foundations of relationship marketing. It also transcends transaction cost economics as the basis of developing and maintaining the relationship. Finally, it transcends from an explicit contractual relationship governed by laws to an implicit friendship governed by passion, purpose, and mutual respect. This will result in at least three new areas of research and practice in relationship marketing:

a. Emotive feedback
    Past practice and research in measuring relationship marketing, such as customer satisfaction and lifetime value of customers, have been numerical, mechanistic, and impersonal. Even though we have databases on both attitudinal and behavioral dimensions of individual customers, especially in the services industries, customers are still ID numbers to the company. We still don't know who is behind the ID number: what makes them tick and what are their feelings, thoughts, and prejudices about the company and its offerings. This will require restoring the emotive research techniques of the 1970s, such as motivation research (cf. Levy 1985; Zaltman 2003; Zaltman and Zaltman 2008), immersion into the life of customers, and nonintrusive customer safaris – employees and executives visiting customers. It will also require use of brain research (Chamberlain and Broderick 2007; Kenning et al. 2007), storytelling (Brown 2005), metaphor elicitation (Zaltman 1996; see also http://www.olsonzaltman.com/), and science fiction, as depicted in movies like *Back to the Future* and *Minority Report*. Finally, it will require more holistic understanding

of customers. Just as we went from analytic to odyssey research in consumer behavior, we will have to learn how to collect, analyze, and interpret conversations and conscious (and unconscious) streams of thoughts. Unfortunately, so far, we have neither the expertise nor the training to analyze video and voice data for scientific research.

b. Being purpose driven

A second major way to win the share of heart of customers is to make products and brands more meaningful to them above and beyond ingredients and benefits. In other words, how can we market the product or the brand so as to make customers feel that they are serving a higher purpose in life when they procure, consume, and dispose of the product or brand? Companies have often attempted to win the share of heart by sponsoring social causes such as breast cancer research, diabetes awareness, obesity reduction, and economic development. They have also encouraged their employees to volunteer their time and talent to serve local social issues. More recently, many companies are proactively engaging in what is referred to as strategic philanthropy or corporate social responsibility (CSR). Retired chairman of Coca-Cola Neville Isdell has even started a connected capitalism initiative, as has founder and chairman of Whole Foods John Mackey. A purpose driven relationship, however, is much deeper and quite different. It is to enable customers to achieve a meaningful life through consumption of a product or brand. In other words, how can a marketer make its brand or product more meaningful through consumption by bonding it with customers at a deeper emotive level? In short, how can customers achieve self-actualization through consumption behavior? This may mean encouraging reduced consumption as opposed to encouraging and enabling mindless consumption; it may mean informing and educating customers about the impact of their choices on society and community; it may mean linking the product or service to spirituality; it may mean informing and educating the consumer about the moral and ethical dilemmas involved in choosing products and brands; and, finally, it may mean the brand itself acts as a moral compass.

c. Brand communities through social media

A third area of future research in relationship marketing is the use of social media in developing and nurturing brand communities. Brand communities are not new. In the business to business markets, companies often organized user groups by vertical market segments. Similarly, Harley-Davidson has organized and nurtured the Harley Owners Group (HOG), and most recently Apple has developed very loyal brand cults. This is also true for some consumer packaged goods companies and brands, for example Betty Crocker in cake mixes and Bisquick for making biscuits. In most cases, it has been the users who have bonded with the brand at an emotional level; and, once the companies recognized it, they have organized and enabled the users to form communities around the brand. The impact of social media in the development of brand communities has been dramatic even at a nascent stage (Muniz and O'Guinn 2001; Kaplan and Haenlein 2010). First, social media are interactive and allow users to be both consumers and producers of information about the brand or the company. This means not only user generated reviews and comments about the brand or the company but also taking liberties with the brand asset or corporate reputation. The dark side of both unintended and intended consequences is so critical that the marketer must channel the emotive moods of the customer–company relationship. Social media are analogous to a potent drug which has great efficacy but also significant side effects.

Second, social media have enormous reach with lightning speed. It can catch like wildfire. In a dry, brittle season, an accidental fire (usually started by human mistake) can get out of hand and result in disastrous consequences. Therefore, it is best to prevent the fire. And, if it does happen, the local community must be ready for crisis management and allow others to provide resources and capabilities to mitigate the disaster. This analog is critical in managing customer relationships in the age of social media. Unfortunately, all of us are now fish in a digital aquarium. Everyone is curious about everything we do, and they are constantly watching us through the glass. Customers are becoming either vigilantes or ambassadors of brands, products, and corporations. Often, the stakeholding transcends beyond their role as customers (users, payers, and buyers).

Given this reality, traditional concepts and tactics of relationship management will be limiting, and there is an analogy with what the law enforcement agencies are learning: that it takes more than enforcement to be useful to the community. Developing and nurturing brand communities through social media will require a more holistic approach, and the skill sets of sensing, intervention, and mentoring the brand community.

Joint Venturing with Customers

A second dimension of the shift in the evolution of relationship marketing is the formation and governance of what I refer to as joint venturing with customers. A joint venture is a collaborative co-creation of value by mutual commitment of resources and complementary capabilities by all parties to the venture. In a joint venture, the foundation of the relationship is anchored in mutual interdependence, mutual commitment, and shared mission.

In traditional relationship marketing, it is usually the supplier that commits resources by investing in key accounts or in relationship managers. Customers are free to walk away from the relationship, almost at will, unless they are bound by contracts, such as in cell phone services, or unless there are non-contractual exit barriers, such as in installed technology, machines, processes, or people.

In joint venturing, customers must commit resources (time, money, and capabilities). Also, both parties must accept interdependence instead of dependence in the relationship. Finally, joint venturing with customers does not require formation of a legal entity; it is often governed by contracts. In many traditional cultures, it is also governed by the silent languages of doing business or by social norms.

There are three new areas of research opportunities related to the shift from managing relationships with customers to joint venturing with customers:

a. Co-creation of value for end users
    Sheth et al. (2000) and Vargo and Lusch (2004) have suggested why and how co-creating value with customers will be both desirable and necessary as marketing becomes more customer-centric. Prahalad and Rangaswamy (2004) even wrote a whole book on how to create a competitive advantage through co-creation of value. From the perspective of joint venturing with customers, co-creation of value becomes the mission or the goal of the joint venture. Therefore, it requires formal metrics to measure the outcome of co-creation. For example, the co-creation's objective may be cost reduction, quality improvement, or creating value for end users (both internal and external). Alternatively, it can be financial, such as greater revenues and profits. Finally, some goals of co-creation of value may be more intangible, such as co-branding, co-marketing, co-learning, and co-sharing of resources. No matter what, there is a need to define the goals and develop mission driven outcomes for co-creation of value with mutual accountability.
    One key perspective in co-creating value is to focus on the customer's customer or the ultimate end users. End users have three different customer roles. They are users, payers, and buyers. As users, they look for performance value; as payers, they look for price value; and as buyers they look for service value. Mittal and Sheth (2001) have

suggested a number of ways a company creates value for end users. For example, performance value is created by quality, innovation, and customization. Price value is created by target costing and lean operations. Service value is created by easy access, rapid response, and relational nurture. In my view, co-creating value for end users with respect to performance, price, and personalization is a useful framework.

b.   Cross-functional collaboration

Co-creating value for end users requires both internal and external cross-functional collaboration. Therefore, the traditional approach to relationship marketing, where the key account manager and customer support are the only two touch points with the customer, transcends to where all functions, such as legal, finance, IT, operations, engineering, human resources, and supply chain, learn to collaborate with each other and across customer and supplier organizations. This was a key transformation in Procter & Gamble (P&G)'s relationship with its customers, including Wal-Mart. More than 200 full time P&G employees and managers are embedded in Wal-Mart, and more than 100 full time Wal-Mart employees and managers are embedded in P&G. This is all glued together by the IT systems of both companies, which are also operating in tandem on a global basis.

While P&G and Wal-Mart partnering is well known, it is not unique. This has been the key competitive advantage for Coca-Cola in its Foundation Division with customers such as McDonald's. It has also been the foundation of a long term relationship between Whirlpool and Sears in manufacturing the Kenmore brand of appliances.

The transformation from the traditional key account or relationship management to joint venturing with customers is depicted in Figure 1.2.

What it requires is coordination and communication by the joint venture leadership team of two dedicated executives, one from the supplier and the other from the customer. Their job is to act as relationship ombudsmen and streamline their companies' bureaucracy as well as lead a team of dedicated functional employees from both organizations, ranging from frontline factory workers to top engineering and corporate staff people. The team's performance is measured by the objectives of the joint venture above and beyond performance appraisal by the functional supervisors. As with any joint venture, it requires long term commitment by both the supplier and the customer. As I mentioned before, in many cultures the non-contractual relationship between a supplier and a customer often transcends several generations, especially among family owned businesses.

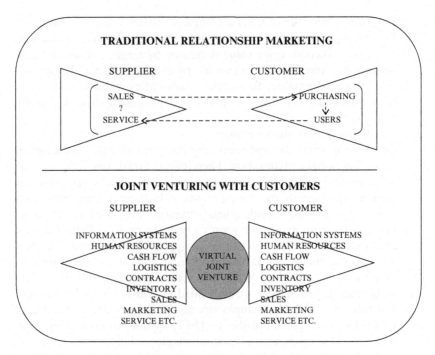

Figure 1.2   Joint venturing with customers

c. Strategic philanthropy and public private partnership
    A third major area of research opportunity is corporate social
    responsibility and economic development (Porter and Kramer 2006).
    Through public private partnership, this ranges from sustainability
    to micro-financing and from nutrition, education, and public health
    to eradication of poverty and diseases. Large corporate and personal
    foundations such as the Bill and Melinda Gates Foundation, the
    MacArthur Foundation, and the Azim Premji Foundation are learn-
    ing to partner with governments and world agencies such as the World
    Bank and IMF to contribute toward economic development, espe-
    cially in emerging markets such as India, Africa, and Latin America.
    Corporate social responsibility and public private partnership will
    require understanding public policy, and managing inherent differ-
    ences in both the goals and the approaches between the capitalistic
    private sector and the political public sector to serve a common cause.
    It will require a joint venture perspective.

CONCLUDING REMARKS

In the past 20 years, relationship marketing both as a practice and as a discipline has grown spectacularly. It has definitely become a major school of thought in marketing. Unfortunately, it has also become synonymous with CRM and database marketing. The focus on "relationship" in relationship marketing is relegated to "marketing." However, I strongly believe that relationship marketing will be revitalized as the discipline begins to shift from the "share of wallet" to the "share of heart" objective, and from managing customer relationships to joint venturing with customers.

REFERENCES

Anderson, James C. and James A. Narus (1991), "Partnering as a Focused Market Strategy," *California Management Review*, Spring, 95–113.

Bohling, Timothy, Douglas Bowman, Steve LaValle, Vikas Mittal, Das Narayandas, Girish Ramani and Rajan Varadarajan (2006), "CRM Implementation: Effectiveness, Issues and Insights," *Journal of Service Research*, 9(2), 184–93.

Brown, Stephen (2005), "I Can Read You like a Book! Novel Thoughts on Consumer Behavior," *Qualitative Market Research*, 8(2), 219–37.

Cannon, Joseph P. and Narakesari Narayandas (2000), "Relationship Marketing and Key Account Management," in Jagdish N. Sheth and Atul Parvatiyar (eds.), *Handbook of Relationship Marketing*, Thousand Oaks, CA: Sage, pp. 407–29.

Carlzon, Jan (1987), *Moments of Truth*, New York: Ballinger.

Chamberlain, Laura and Amanda J. Broderick (2007), "The Application of Physiological Observation Methods to Emotion Research," *Qualitative Market Research*, 10(2), 199–216.

Crosby, P.B. (1979), *Quality Is Free: The Art of Making Quality Certain*, New York: McGraw-Hill.

Deming, W. Edwards (1986), *Out of the Crisis*, Cambridge, MA: MIT Press.

Dick, Alan S. and Kunal Basu (1994), "Customer Loyalty: Toward an Integrated Conceptual Framework," *Journal of the Academy of Marketing Science*, 22 (Spring), 99–113.

Fornell, Claes, Michael D. Johnson, Eugene W. Anderson, Jaesung Cha and Barbara Everitt Bryant (1996), "The American Customer Satisfaction Index: Nature, Purpose, and Findings," *Journal of Marketing*, 60 (October), 7–18.

Gronroos, Christian (1995), "Relationship Marketing: The Strategy Continuum," *Journal of the Academy of Marketing Science*, 23, 252–4.

Gronroos, Christian (2000), "Relationship Marketing: The Nordic Perspective," in Jagdish N. Sheth and Atul Parvatiyar (eds.), *Handbook of Relationship Marketing*, Thousand Oaks, CA: Sage, pp. 95–117.

Hakansson, Hakan (1982), *International Marketing and Purchasing of Industrial Goods: An Interactive Approach*, New York: John Wiley.

Hakansson, Hakan and Ivan J. Snehota (2000), "The IMP Perspective: Assets and Liabilities of Business Relationships," in Jagdish N. Sheth and Atul Parvatiyar (eds.), *Handbook of Relationship Marketing*, Thousand Oaks, CA: Sage, pp. 69–93.

Halinen, Aino and Jaana Tahtinen (2002), "A Process Theory of Relationship Ending," *International Journal of Service Industry Management*, 13(2), 163–80.

Helm, Sabrina, Ludger Rolfes and Gunter Bernd (2006), "Suppliers' Willingness to End Unprofitable Customer Relationships," *European Journal of Marketing*, 40(3/4), 366–83.

Homburg, Christian, John P. Workman, Jr. and Ove Jensen (2002), "A Configurational Perspective on Key Account Management," *Journal of Marketing*, 66(2), 38–60.

Hunt, Shelby (2010), *Marketing Theory: Foundations, Controversy, Strategy and Resource Advantage Theory*, Armonk, NY: M.E. Sharpe.

Kaplan, Andreas M. and Michael Haenlein (2010), "Users of the World, Unite! The Challenges and Opportunities of Social Media," *Business Horizons*, 53, 59–68.

Keegan, Victor (2010), "Virtual Worlds: Is This Where Real Life Is Heading?," *Guardian*, August 22.

Kenning, Peter, Hilke Plassmann and Dieter Ahlert (2007), "Applications of Functional Magnetic Resonance Imaging for Market Research," *Qualitative Market Research*, 10(2), 135–52.

Kozinets, Robert V., Kristine de Valck, Andrea C. Wojnicki and Sarah J.S. Wilner (2010), "Networked Narratives: Understanding Word-of-Mouth Marketing in Online Communities," *Journal of Marketing*, 74(2), 71.

Kumar, V. and Bharath Rajan (2009), "Profitable Customer Management: Measuring and Maximizing Customer Lifetime Value," *Management Accounting Quarterly*, 10(3), 1–18.

Levy, Sidney J. (1985), "Dreams, Fairy Tales, Animals and Cars," *Psychology and Marketing*, 2(2), 67–82.

Mentzer, John T. (2000), "Supplier Partnering," in Jagdish N. Sheth and Atul Parvatiyar (eds.), *Handbook of Relationship Marketing*, Thousand Oaks, CA: Sage, pp. 457–77.

Mittal, Banwari and Jagdish N. Sheth (2001), *Value Space: Winning the Battle for Market Leadership*, New York: McGraw-Hill.

Morgan, Robert M. and Shelby Hunt (1994), "The Commitment-Trust Theory of Relationship Marketing," *Journal of Marketing*, 58(3), 20–38.

Muniz, A.M. and T.C. O'Guinn (2001), "Brand Community," *Journal of Consumer Research*, 27(4), 412–32.

O'Brien, Clodagh (2011), "The Emergence of the Social Media Empowered Consumer," *Irish Marketing Review*, 21(1&2), 32–40.

Payne, Adrian (1995) (ed.), *Advances in Relationship Marketing*, London: Kogan Page.

Payne, Adrian (2000), "Relationship Marketing: The U.K. Perspective," in Jagdish N. Sheth and Atul Parvatiyar (eds.), *Handbook of Relationship Marketing*, Thousand Oaks, CA: Sage, pp. 39–67.

Peppers, Don and Martha Rogers (1993), *The One to One Future: Building Relationships One Customer at a Time*, New York: Doubleday.

Peppers, Don and Martha Rogers (1995), "A New Marketing Paradigm: Share of Customer, Not Market Share," *Managing Service Quality*, 5(3), 48–51.

Peppers, Don and Martha Rogers (2004), *Managing Customer Relationship: A Strategic Framework*, Hoboken, NJ: John Wiley.

Pfeifer, Phillip E. and Paul W. Farris (2004), "The Elasticity of Customer Value to Retention: The Duration of a Customer Relationship," *Journal of Interactive Marketing*, 18(2), 20–31.

Porter, Michael E. and Mark R. Kramer (2006), "Strategy and Society: The Link between Competitive Advantage and Corporate Social Responsibility," *Harvard Business Review*, December, 1–15.

Prahalad, C.K. and Venkat Rangaswamy (2004), *The Future of Competition: Co-Creating Unique Value with Customers*, Boston, MA: Harvard Business School.

Raphel, Murray (1995), "The Art of Direct Marketing: Upgrading Prospects to Advocates," *Direct Marketing*, 58 (June), 34–7.

Reichheld, Frederick F. with Thomas Teal (1996), *The Loyalty Effect*, Boston, MA: Harvard Business School Press.

Reichheld, Frederick F. (2006), "The Microeconomics of Customer Relationships," *MIT Sloan Management Review*, Winter, 73–8.

Reinartz, Werner, Manfred Krafft and Wayne D. Hoyer (2004), "The Customer Relationship Management Process: Its Measurement and Impact on Performance," *Journal of Marketing Research*, 41(3), 293–305.

Rosenberg, Larry and John Czepiel (1984), "A Marketing Approach to Customer Retention," *Journal of Consumer Marketing*, Spring, 45–51.

Shah, Denish and V. Kumar (2012), "The Dark Side of Cross-Selling," *Harvard Business Review*, December, 21–3.

Shapiro, Benson P. (1988), *Close Encounters of the Four Kinds: Managing Customers in a Rapidly Changing Environment*, Industry and Background Note No. 589015, Boston, MA: Harvard Business School.

Shapiro, Benson P. and Ronald T. Moriarty, Jr. (1980), *National Account Management*, Cambridge, MA: Marketing Science Institute.

Shapiro, Benson P. and Rowland T. Moriarty (1982), "National Account Management: Emerging Insights," *Marketing Science Institute*, March.

Shapiro, B.P., V.K. Rangan, R.T. Moriarty and E.B. Ross (1987), "Manage Customers for Profits (Not Just Sales)," *Harvard Business Review*, 63(5) (September–October), 101–08.

Sheth, Jagdish N. and Atul Parvatiyar (eds.) (2000), *Handbook of Relationship Marketing*, Thousand Oaks, CA: Sage.

Sheth, Jagdish N. and Rajendra S. Sisodia (1999), "Outsourcing Comes Home," *Wall Street Journal* (Eastern edn.), June 28, A.26.

Sheth, Jagdish N., Rajendra S. Sisodia and Arun Sharma (2000), "The Antecedents and Consequences of Customer-Centric Marketing," *Academy of Marketing Science*, 28(1), 55–66.

Spekman, Robert.E (1988), "Strategic Supplier Selection: Understanding Long-Term Buyer Relationships," *Business Horizons*, July–August, 75–81.

Vargo, S.L. and Robert F. Lusch (2004), "Evolving to a New Dominant Logic for Marketing," *Journal of Marketing*, 68(1), 1–17.

Vavra, Terry G. (1992), *Aftermarketing: How to Keep Customers for Life through Relationship Marketing*, Burr Ridge, IL: Irwin.

Venkatesan, Rajkumar and V. Kumar (2004), "A Customer Lifetime Value Framework for Customer Selection and Resource Allocation Strategy," *Journal of Marketing*, 68(4), 106–25.

Williamson, Oliver E. (1979), "Transaction-Cost Economics: The Governance of Contractual Relations," *Journal of Law and Economics*, 22(2), 233–61.

Wong, Wailin (2011), "Groupon Rolls Out Loyalty Program to Help Businesses Keep Daily Deal Customers," *Chicago Tribune*, http://articles.chicagotribune.com/2011-09-27/news/ct-biz-0928-groupon-loyalty-20110928_1_daily-deal-loyalty-program-merchant (accessed February 10, 2013).

Yip, George S. and Tammy L. Madsen (1996), "Global Account Management: The New Frontier in Relationship Marketing," *International Marketing Review*, 13(3), 24–42.

Zaltman, Gerald (1996), "Metaphorically Speaking," *Marketing Research*, 8(2), 13–20.

Zaltman, Gerald (2003), *How Customers Think: Essential Insights into the Mind of the Market*, Boston, MA: Harvard Business Publishing.

Zaltman, Gerald and Lindsay Zaltman (2008), *Marketing Metaphoria: What Deep Metaphors Reveal about the Minds of Consumers*, Boston, MA: Harvard Business School Publishing.

2. Relationship marketing: Berry's insights from the past and for the future
Janet Turner Parish, Sandi Lampo and Kristin Landua

In 1983, Leonard L. Berry introduced the term "relationship marketing" to the services marketing literature (Berry 1983). He defined relationship marketing as "attracting, maintaining, and – in multi-service organizations – enhancing customer relationships" (1983: 25). While acknowledging the attraction of new customers as an important step in the marketing process, Berry emphasized that "cementing the relationship, transforming indifferent customers into loyal ones, [and] serving customers as clients" (1983: 25) was also an integral part of marketing and should not be overlooked or underestimated. Encouraging both marketing academics and practitioners to take note, Berry called for a strategic focus on how to retain, not just acquire, customers.

Following that call, research into relationship marketing (RM) has grown and flourished over the past three decades. In fact, by 1999, over 26 definitions of RM had been identified in the literature (Harker 1999). Relationship marketing has become a prevalent term in the marketing field and is growing in importance to marketers as they try to win over consumers in an increasingly competitive environment.

The purpose of this chapter is to discuss the emergence of RM into the marketing literature and identify fertile areas of future research to stimulate knowledge and understanding of this potentially powerful marketing tool. The chapter begins with a discussion of how Dr. Leonard L. Berry's exploration of RM emerged since the concept's inception in 1983. It provides a look back at Berry's research on RM, along with a look forward identifying his suggestions for the future. The authors of this chapter interviewed Dr. Leonard L. Berry to discuss RM topics he feels warrant future research. A brief discussion of what research has been done in each of seven key areas, as well as specific questions that need to be answered, follows. This chapter is not meant to be all inclusive of the research conducted on relationship marketing. Rather, it is meant to serve as a synopsis of Leonard Berry's research on relationship marketing and as an agenda outlining where research should be directed in the future. For other authors' contributions, see such work as Turnbull and Wilson

(1989), Gummesson (1994), Morgan and Hunt (1994), Harker (1999) and Hennig-Thurau et al. (2002).

THE INTRODUCTION OF RELATIONSHIP MARKETING

In his seminal presentation introducing the term "relationship marketing" to the marketing literature, Dr. Leonard L. Berry presents five RM strategies, captured in Table 2.1, to be considered in the development of a relationship marketing plan (Berry 1983).

Berry explains that these RM strategies are not mutually exclusive and a firm can choose to use all five simultaneously. They do share a common element – "the incentive a customer is given to remain a customer" (1983: 28). Almost 20 years later, in 2002, Berry confirmed the relevance of these strategies and prioritized them according to relative importance (Berry 2002). He reiterated that a well-designed core service is essential to relationship marketing. Relationship customization, service augmentation, relationship pricing and internal marketing revolve around this central construct. However, the right service must be delivered excellently to reinforce trust and build commitment. Core services, service quality, trust and commitment are the center of relationship marketing (e.g., Morgan and Hunt 1994; Hennig-Thurau et al. 2002).

LEVERAGING AN OLD-FASHIONED IDEA – TRUST

Expanding on this view of trust serving as a fundamental component of relationship marketing (Crosby et al. 1990; Czepiel 1990; Parasuraman et al. 1991; Morgan and Hunt 1994; Berry 2002), Berry, in 1995, identified three strategies for firms to use to demonstrate their trustworthiness to customers (Berry 1995):

- Firms must open lines of communication between themselves and customers. "Regular, open, two-way, communication conveys the firm's interest in the customer's welfare" (Berry 1995: 243). How do firms effectively create two-way communication between the firm and the customer? Marketers must have an organizational structure in place to encourage and manage this flow of information. Firms should develop employee incentive systems to encourage and reward consistent two-way communication. Organizations should create cross-functional teams to serve customers, foster service continuity

Table 2.1   Berry's five relationship marketing strategies

Core services marketing *The foundation*	Develop a "core service" that attracts new customers by meeting their needs, provides quality, offers multiple parts or choices, is long-term in nature and provides a base for selling additional services to those customers over time. This type of core service should be the foundation for building customer relationships.
Relationship customization *Not mass marketing*	Custom-fit the service offering to create relationships. Learn about specific characteristics and requirements of individual customers, capture the individual data, and ultimately create unique, personalized service experiences for each individual customer.
Service augmentation *The extras*	Augment the core service offering with "extras" to encourage customer loyalty and develop relationships. "Extras" can be anything, ranging from preferred customer programs to free gifts, as long as they are valued by the target market and not easily matched by competitors.
Relationship pricing *A better price for better customers*	Give customers quantity discounts or price incentives to consolidate much or all of their business with one supplier (e.g., frequent flyer programs). Customer loyalty should be encouraged with rewards.
Internal marketing *View the employee as the customer, and the job as the product*	Use marketing activities to develop relationships with the internal customer or employees. Marketers should encourage external customers to buy; however, they should also encourage internal customers to perform. Good employee performance increases the likelihood of external customer buying.

Source: Berry (1983).

and communicate with customers. Open communication leads to trust, and trust leads to committed relationships (Morgan and Hunt 1994).

- Firms should consider guaranteeing the service to build trust. "When executed well, service guarantees can symbolize a company's commitment to fair play with customers and facilitate competitive differentiation" (Berry 1995: 243). However, firms with poor service quality should never implement a guarantee. Service quality comes first, followed by a possible guarantee to help facilitate further improvement.

● Firms must be willing to operate with a higher standard of conduct than just legality. Doing what is right, not just what is required, builds trust with the customer. Asking "Is it right?" instead of "Is it legal?" builds trust, and consequently the potential for a relationship (Berry and Parasuraman 1991: 145; Berry 1995).

In 1999, Berry interviewed more than 250 people from 14 outstanding labor-intensive service companies (the average age of these companies as of 1999 was 31 years) and discovered that trust-based relationships characterize the sustained success of these sample companies (Berry 1999). In fact, companies cannot build true relationships without trust. Customers must trust a company to keep its promises and conduct itself honorably. Employees and partners must also trust a company to keep its promises, or they will physically abandon the relationship or, worse, simply quit emotionally. "Keeping promises . . . is at the heart of business partnerships" (1999: 124). Without trust, relationships cannot work.

In Berry's (1999) model of trust-based relationships (see Figure 2.1), perceptions of a company's competence and fairness are instrumental in establishing customer trust. This sense of trust serves as the foundation for *all* company relationships – customer, employee and partner relationships. A company's relationships with its employees and partners contribute to its efforts to build strong customer relationships. "The greater the trust in these relationships, the greater the commitment to them" (1999: 125).

Berry identifies seven levels of relationship commitment, with each level depending upon the extent to which the commitment to the relationship derives from dedication as opposed to constraint. Dedication derives from trust-based relationships. In the first level, *interest in alternatives*, customers feel constrained to a relationship because there are no other appealing options. The relationship is necessary but not valued – and consequently interest outside of the relationship is high. The second level, *acquiescence*, implies passive agreement to maintain a relationship, while the third level, *cooperation*, involves parties in a relationship actually working together to achieve mutual goals. In fact, cooperation naturally flourishes from trust-based relationships. The fourth level, *enhancement*, refers to investing in strengthening the relationship beyond its current status and can lead to the fifth commitment level of *identity*, where one party thinks of the relationship as a team. The sixth level, *advocacy*, exists when one party of the relationship is willing to advocate, promote and defend, if necessary, the other party. This ultimately leads to the strongest level of commitment, *ownership*, which embodies trust based on dedication to one another.

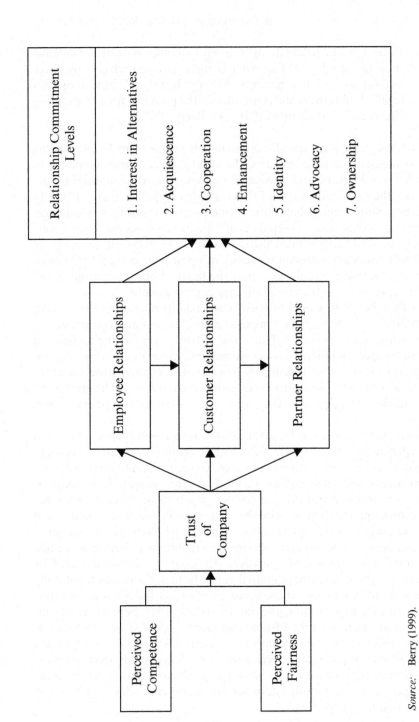

Relationship Commitment Levels

1. Interest in Alternatives

2. Acquiescence

3. Cooperation

4. Enhancement

5. Identity

6. Advocacy

7. Ownership

Employee Relationships

Customer Relationships

Partner Relationships

Trust of Company

Perceived Competence

Perceived Fairness

Source: Berry (1999).

Figure 2.1 Berry's model of trust-based relationships

Trust is powerful. It is so powerful that companies relying on human performance to create value cannot achieve sustained success without it. Trust
provides the foundation for service companies' efforts to establish enduring,
commitment-rich relationships with customers and with employees and partners who perform for customers . . . Great service companies by definition are
high trust companies. (Berry 1999: 154–5)

PRACTICING RELATIONSHIP MARKETING SUCCESSFULLY

After encouraging marketers to move beyond customer acquisition in his
seminal 1983 article, Berry offers marketers guidance for implementing
relationship marketing successfully (Berry 1995). He recommends that
firms target profitable customers, practice different levels of relationship
marketing, and utilize technology as an alternative to mass marketing.

Target Profitable Customers

Marketers should mount dual strategies: relationship marketing for some
customer groups, transactional marketing for other customer groups
(Reichheld 1993; Berry 1995). "Relationship marketing is not an appropriate strategy for all customers" (Berry 1995: 239). A more profitable
approach is for firms to analyze their customers and identify who is loyal
as opposed to defection-prone, understand why they stay or leave, and discover what creates value for them. After deciding which types of customer
defectors they wish to save, firms should target value-creating strategies
at these select defectors and the loyalty-prone customers. The remaining
customers should be reached on a transactional basis.

Practice Multiple Levels of Relationship Marketing

Relationship marketing should be practiced on multiple levels, depending
on the types of linkages or bonds (i.e., financial, social, structural) firms
use to create customer loyalty (Turnbull and Wilson 1989; Berry and
Parasuraman 1991; Berry 1995). *Level 1* relationship marketing relies on
pricing incentives to secure customer loyalty. However, it is important to
note that firms trying to develop strong relationships with customers must
not compete solely on price; they must perform at a higher level. *Level 2*
relationship marketing involves not only aggressive pricing, but also the
development of social bonds with the customers. Social bonding involves
personalization and customization of the relationship between the firm
and customer (e.g., recognizing customers by name, communicating

regularly with customers through multiple means, and enabling customers to interact with the same employees transaction after transaction). While social bonding cannot overcome a noncompetitive core product (Crosby and Stephens 1987), it can create customer loyalty in situations where competitive differences are not strong. Also, creating social relationships with customers may make them more tolerant of service failures. *Level 3* relationship marketing binds the customer to the firm through the structural design of the service and product itself. The solution to the customer's problem is designed into the actual delivery and consumption of the product or service rather than tied to a specific employee. The result is a relationship bound to the company rather than to an individual employee who may leave the firm.

Utilize Technology as an Alternative to Mass Marketing

Instead of viewing relationship marketing as an expensive alternative to mass marketing, marketers should take advantage of rapid advances in technology to decrease the costs and increase the practicality of relationship marketing. Information technology actually enhances the practical value of relationship marketing by "efficient performance of key tasks" such as:

- tracking buying patterns;
- customizing services;
- promotions and pricing;
- coordinating or integrating the delivery of multiple services to the same customer;
- enhancing two-way communication between the customer and company;
- decreasing service errors;
- augmenting core service offerings with valued extras; and
- personalizing service experiences (Berry 1995: 238).

With the advancement of technology, the implication of relationship marketing is increasingly more cost efficient and effective, eliminating many obstacles formerly perceived by companies.

THE CENTRAL PURPOSE OF RELATIONSHIP MARKETING

Berry, in his original relationship marketing thoughts in 1983, addresses the importance of marketing to internal customers or employees to ultimately improve service to the customer (Berry 1983). Years later, he broadened his scope of relationship marketing to include the development of relationships with other non-customer stakeholders, such as the vendors, buyers and integral lateral partners (Gronroos 1990; Gummesson 1994; Morgan and Hunt 1994; Berry 1995, 2002). It is important to note that, while he broadened his view on the *scope* of relationship marketing over time, he has never changed his perspective on the central purpose of these non-customer relationships. "The purpose of non-customer relationships ultimately is to strengthen customer relationships" (Berry 2002: 76). "Companies must establish successful relationships with noncustomer groups (the means) to establish successful relationships with customers (the end)" (Berry 1995: 242).

While recognizing the benefits of relationship marketing from the firm's perspective (Berry 1983), Berry feels that the ultimate outcome of relationship marketing is how relationship marketing is good for the customers (Berry 1995, 2002; Bendapudi and Berry 1997). Relationship marketing benefits customers by reducing their risks associated with purchasing and consuming high involvement services (Berry 1995, 2002), creating social benefits such as friendships with employees (Price and Arnould 1999), meeting the basic human need of feeling important (Jackson 1993), and receiving more precise service customization (Berry 1995, 2002). In fact, customers often desire personalized, close relationships with firms (Parasuraman et al. 1991). In situations where the product or service is personally important, varies in quality and is complex, customers often desire to be "relationship customers" (Berry 1995: 237).

Relationship Marketing Is a Philosophy

Relationship marketing is not just a strategy; it is a philosophy (Berry 2002). It is an integrative approach to marketing for creating lifetime customers. Relationship marketing is about creating an "unthinkability of switching" in the minds of the consumer by coordinating all pieces of the marketing puzzle into "a compelling customer experience and solution" (2002: 74). In his meticulous study of 14 successful service companies presented in his book *Discovering the Soul of Service* (1999), Berry uncovered considerable evidence that this level of relationship marketing not only is possible, but does exist and truly helps companies achieve sustained excellence and success.

Berry has stated that he never intended to start a new field of inquiry with his original paper in 1983 (Berry 1995). He just could not understand why so many marketing resources were being spent to attract new customers, only to ignore them once they became customers. Today, it is hard to imagine a marketing plan based solely on attracting new customers. Relationship marketing is not a choice; it is often a requisite. Born from a conference paper over 30 years ago, the power of relationship marketing is just beginning to be unleashed.

FUTURE RESEARCH IN RELATIONSHIP MARKETING

The authors of this chapter interviewed Dr. Leonard L. Berry on the past, present and future of RM. In this interview, Berry identified seven key areas of RM that warrant further exploration and understanding.

1. Profitability of Relationship Marketing

Understanding the profitability aspect of relationship marketing may provide the incentive companies require to believe in the necessity and impact of implementing such a strategy. The Reichheld and Sasser (1990) study, for example, identifies the profit implications of reducing customer defections by 5 percent. They report a range of 25–85 percent improvement in profits depending upon the industry (Reichheld and Sasser 1990). This research demonstrates the profit impact of reducing customer defections. This widely cited study has not been replicated. Now, over 20 years later, a replication study could prove to be very valuable to reinforce the initial findings. Along these lines, there is also a need to study the inter-industry profit potential of relationship marketing. Owing to changing market conditions it would be helpful to have answers to the following questions:

- Is the impact of customer retention reported by Reichheld and Sasser still accurate today?
- Is the variation by industry still as dramatic?
- What are the characteristics of industries that increase or decrease their profit potential?

2. Relationship Commitment

Examining customer commitment from a social psychology perspective, Bugel et al. (2010) develop a model of commitment where commitment is a function of satisfaction level, alternative quality and investment size. They compare commitment to companies using this model across five industries: banking, health insurance, supermarkets, mobile telecommunications and automotive. The authors conclude that the model is applicable across all sectors; however, it is most relevant in the banking sector and to a lesser extent in the automotive and supermarket segments. In addition, they find that satisfaction plays a particularly important role in commitment determination in both banking and health insurance. Ultimately, their results indicate that investing in relationship commitment is primarily valuable in markets that are extremely competitive.

Evanschitzky et al. (2006) researched commitment from the perspective of how affective commitment and continuance commitment impacts attitudinal and behavioral loyalty in the context of European mass transit. Results from this study suggest that "emotional bonds with customers provide a more enduring source of loyalty as compared to economic incentives and switching costs" (2006: 1207). Customers who have an emotional connection with, and trust in, a company develop strong commitments. While "continuance commitment could arise from a lack of alternatives, the presence of a rebate loyalty card, or external incentives or pressures," affective commitment "influences loyalty to a much higher degree" (2006: 1207).

There remains much to learn about relationship commitment and its different levels. Commitment is defined as "an enduring desire to maintain a valued relationship" (Moorman et al. 1992: 316). A three-component model of commitment (affective, continuance and normative) is widely studied in the organization behavior literature (Meyer and Allen 1991). In the marketing literature, the distinction between commitment, loyalty and behavioral intentions is not always clear. Additionally, definitions of commitment need to be expanded. Therefore, further research is needed to clarify the following issues:

● What is the difference between commitment and loyalty?
● How do levels of commitment differ in their effects on marketing outcomes (e.g., customer retention and repurchase intentions)?
● How can companies nurture customers and different levels (e.g., advocacy)?

3.   Role of Price in Relationship Marketing

Price is often used to encourage a relationship by offering price incentives to customers purchasing a predetermined number of products in one transaction or for multiple transactions over a specified time period. However, it is important to note that price is the easiest marketing variable to imitate. While price cuts may be a temporary solution for increased profits, this action may not add customers in the long term or develop strong relationships between the company and customers.

Currently, research is not clear as to whether loyal customers become less price-sensitive or feel they should be rewarded for their loyalty with price breaks. One recent study by Dawes (2009) examines how price increases affect different consumer groups in the domestic insurance industry. Empirical evidence from this study shows that "the effect of a price increase is moderated by both tenure and breadth of the customer's relationship" (2009: 232). Customers engaged in a long-standing relationship with a company seem to be "less sensitive to price increases" (2009: 240). However, customers "with multiple product holdings appear to be more price sensitive" (2009: 241).

A study by Kaltcheva et al. (2010) investigates the types of relationships that should be developed depending on price competition. These authors determine that companies participating in markets with extreme price competition may have to invest a higher level of resources in relational strategies to retain customers (Kaltcheva et al. 2010). In situations with moderate price competition, it is recommended that companies develop an equality-matching relationship which requires companies to convey respect for their customers (Kaltcheva et al. 2010).

Because price is more easily manipulated than other marketing mix variables, more research could be conducted to provide companies with conclusive findings to the following questions:

- What is the true role of price in relationship marketing?
- What does loyalty really mean when price competition is involved (i.e., does loyalty imply a greater share of wallet)?

4.   Relationship Customer Segmentation

"Consumer relationship proneness" (CRP) was introduced as a term in 2001 by De Wulf et al. to describe a consumer's tendency to engage in relationships with retailers. It is argued that companies may need to engage simultaneously in transactional and relational marketing because consumers have different responses to "the same working relationship"

(Parish and Holloway 2010: 63). CRP may be one way to determine how consumer responses will differ. Parish and Holloway (2010: 65) suggest that "CRP positively and directly influences trust in service providers and trust is positively related to commitment" across research collected from call center data, insurance data and health care data. The authors' results did not find an association between CRP and intention to remain with the firm. However, identifying CRP consumers adds to managerial understanding of individual consumers and allows for better customer relationship management. Thus, it is possible to segment customers according to their level of relationship proneness.

Garbarino and Johnson (1999) segment customers based on relational exchange behaviors with a local theatre company to understand the primary mediating construct(s) between the component attitudes and future intentions. The mediator for low relational customers is overall satisfaction; however, the mediator for high relational customers is trust and commitment (Garbarino and Johnson 1999). The authors suggest that future research to determine whether developing trust and commitment can move customers from low to high relational interactions could have important implications for companies (Garbarino and Johnson 1999).

Again, consumers have different needs and desires in their relationships with service firms, and not every consumer may be willing to engage in close commercial relationships in the same manner (Parish and Holloway 2010). Mende et al. (2009) predict that recognition of relational preferences can be understood through customers' attachment style. Their study determined that customers with attachment anxiety prefer closeness with the firm, and customers exhibiting attachment avoidance shun closeness (Mende et al. 2009). By including questions on "both customers' desire for closeness and attachment styles" (2009: 42) in their market research efforts, companies can use the information collected to segment customer groups. This allows companies to "tailor relationship marketing activities and more effectively allocate CRM resources" (2009: 23).

Progress has been made, but customer segments need to be further defined and profiled based on the concept of relationship marketing. Answers to the following questions could have valuable implications for managers:

- What is the role of relationship proneness? Does it vary over the length of the relationship?
- Does CRP vary by industry?
- Are there demographic differences?
- What about non-loyalists – those who mistrust?

5.   Want Services versus Need Services

Want services have been and are continually studied extensively in marketing. However, there is not as much knowledge and research available about need services. In need services, consumers may be forced into the relationship against their will, such as being hospitalized, and not be interested in developing relationships with service providers. It is hypothesized that the conventional ways of measuring service quality may be different for need services. Additionally:

- Are relationship commitment levels different for want versus need services?
- Should relationships be developed differently?

6.   Characteristics of Services

Future research identifying the specific characteristics of services that lend themselves to relationship marketing would also prove helpful. For example, commodities are hard to differentiate in terms of function or pricing and thus require frequent contact. Owing to the format of some services, customers may be required to take a more active role in the consumption and production of the service. One study focusing on health services recommends empowering customers in these types of situations in order to develop relationships (Ouschan et al. 2006). Relationship development through customer empowerment "is most relevant to professional services that require a collaborative customer–service provider relationship, a significant amount of customer self-service (self-care), customer input, customer cooperation, and customer competence to achieve desirable service outcomes" (2006: 1070–71). Different aspects of services may have diverse implications; therefore, further questions need to be investigated, such as:

- What are the implications of personal versus remote contact?
- What are the relational differences between services designed for a person versus services designed for a person's property?
- Are there specific service characteristics that have implications for relationship building and maintenance?

7.   Do the Primary Drivers of Strong Relationships Vary by Industry?

An investigation of the Greek retail banking industry suggests that loyalty is the outcome of a cognitive rather than an affective process and is subject to situational changes (Lewis and Soureli 2006). Through their research, the authors identify the main antecedents of bank loyalty to be "perceived value, service quality, service attributes, satisfaction, image and trust" (2006: 27). In a study of health care service providers, "patient empowerment dimensions (patient control, patient participation and physician support) have a positive impact on both patient trust and patient commitment to the physician" (Ouschan et al. 2006: 1080).

A research study conducted in the restaurant industry concludes that intangible "antecedents (customer orientation, communication, relationship benefits, and price fairness) prove to be stronger predictors of relationship quality than those of the two tangible antecedents (physical environment and food quality)" (Kim et al. 2006: 161). Therefore, the authors suggest that social benefits are more desirable to loyal customers than functional benefits. In fact, employees' customer orientation was established to be the factor with the strongest influence on relationship quality (Kim et al. 2006).

Other opportunities for exploration across industries could include studies to investigate the following questions:

- Are some drivers of strong relationships consistent across industries?
- Can we identify industries where price versus quality is a primary driver?
- Do intangible attributes outweigh tangible ones in some (or most) service industries?

CONCLUDING REMARKS

With some of the most highly cited work on relationship marketing, Dr. Leonard L. Berry identifies the areas of profitability of relationship marketing, relationship commitment exploration, the role of price in RM, the utilization of customer segmentation in RM, understanding want versus need services, and relationship building from an industry-specific perspective as key areas for future research. These suggestions, along with the discussion of current research beginning to address each of these issues, represent Berry's new call for research into relationship marketing.

Although this chapter covers only a small portion of research conducted on relationship marketing concepts, it demonstrates that opportunities remain for researchers to help guide marketers in RM strategy and implementation. Many of the completed studies on RM tend to be definitional, and there is a need for empirical studies to guide conceptual work and vice versa. Additionally, many studies have been conducted in only one service area, service industry or cultural context, limiting marketers' ability to apply RM effectively to all areas of business.

There is much about relationship marketing that is still unknown. Thirty years after the introduction of the term into the literature, there is much more to uncover to truly unleash the power of this marketing tool. There are too many companies today not taking part in relationship marketing strategies from which they could benefit. RM in theory seems like common sense. RM in practice is much more complex.

REFERENCES

Bendapudi, N. and L.L. Berry (1997), "Customers' Motivations for Maintaining Relationships with Service Providers," *Journal of Retailing*, 73(1), 15–37.

Berry, L.L. (1983), "Relationship Marketing," in L.L. Berry, G.L. Shostak and G.D. Upah (eds.), *Emerging Perspectives on Services Marketing*, Chicago: American Marketing Association, pp. 25–38.

Berry, L.L. (1995), "Relationship Marketing of Services – Growing Interest, Emerging Perspectives," *Journal of the Academy of Marketing Science*, 23(4), 236–45.

Berry, L.L. (1999), *Discovering the Soul of Service: The Nine Drivers of Sustainable Business Success*, New York: Free Press.

Berry, Leonard L. (2002), "Commentary on Relationship Marketing," *Journal of Relationship Marketing*, 1(1), 71–7.

Berry, L.L. and A. Parasuraman (1991), *Marketing Services: Competing through Quality*, New York: Free Press.

Bugel, M., A. Buunk and P. Verhoef (2010), "A Comparison of Customer Commitment in Five Sectors Using the Psychological Investment Model," *Journal of Relationship Marketing*, 9, 2–29.

Crosby, L.A. and N. Stephens (1987), "Effects of Relationship Marketing and Satisfaction, Retention, and Prices in the Life Insurance Industry," *Journal of Marketing Research*, 24, 404–11.

Crosby, L.A., K.R. Evans and D. Cowles (1990), "Relationship Quality in Services Selling: An Interpersonal Influence Perspective," *Journal of Marketing*, 54(3), 68–81.

Czepiel, J. (1990), "Service Encounters and Service Relationships: Implications for Research," *Journal of Business Research*, 20, 13–21.

Dawes, J. (2009), "The Effect of Service Price Increases on Customer Retention," *Journal of Service Research*, 11, 232–45.

De Wulf, K., G. Odekerken-Schroder and D. Iacobucci (2001), "Investments in Consumer Relationships: A Cross-Country and Cross-Industry Exploration," *Journal of Marketing*, 65, 33–50.

Evanschitzky, H., G. Iyer, H. Plassmann, J. Niessing and H. Meffert (2006), "The Relative Strength of Affective Commitment in Securing Loyalty in Service Relationships," *Journal of Business Research*, 59, 1207–13.

Garbarino, E. and M.S. Johnson (1999), "The Different Roles of Satisfaction, Trust, and Commitment in Customer Relationships," *Journal of Marketing*, 63(2), 70–87.

Gronroos, C. (1990), *Service Management and Marketing: Managing the Moments of Truth in Service Competition*, Lexington, MA: Lexington.

Gummesson, E. (1994), "Is Relationship Marketing Operational?," paper presented at the annual European Marketing Academy Conference, May, Maastricht, Netherlands.

Harker, M. (1999), "Relationship Marketing Defined? An Examination of Current Relationship Marketing Definitions," *Marketing Intelligence and Planning*, 17, 13–20.

Hennig-Thurau, T., K.P. Gwinner and D.D. Gremler (2002), "Understanding Relationship Marketing Outcomes: An Integration of Relational Benefits and Relationship Quality," *Journal of Service Research*, 4(3), 230–47.

Jackson, D. (1993), "The Seven Deadly Sins of Financial Services Marketing . . . and the Road to Redemption," *Direct Marketing*, 55 (March), 43–5.

Kaltcheva, V., R. Winsor and A. Parasuraman (2010), "The Impact of Customers' Relational Models on Price-Based Defection," *Journal of Marketing Theory and Practice*, 18, 5–22.

Kim, W., Y. Lee and Y. Yoo (2006), "Predictors of Relationship Quality and Relationship Outcomes in Luxury Restaurants," *Journal of Hospitality and Tourism Research*, 30(2), 143–69.

Lewis, B. and M. Soureli (2006), "The Antecedents of Consumer Loyalty in Retail Banking," *Journal of Consumer Behavior*, 5, 15–31.

Mende, M., R.N. Bolton and M. Bitner (2009), "Relationships Take Two: Customer Attachment Styles' Influence on Consumers' Desire for Close Relationships and Loyalty to the Firm," *MSI Reports*, 3, 23–49.

Meyer, J.P. and N.J. Allen (1991), "A Three-Component Conceptualization of Organizational Commitment," *Human Resource Management Review*, 1, 61–89.

Moorman, C., G. Zaltman and R. Deshpande (1992), "Relationships between Providers and Users of Market Research: The Dynamics of Trust within and between Organizations," *Journal of Marketing Research*, 29(3), 314–29.

Morgan, R.M. and S.D. Hunt (1994), "The Commitment-Trust Theory of Relationship Marketing," *Journal of Marketing*, 58(3), 20–38.

Ouschan, R., J. Sweeney and L. Johnson (2006), "Customer Empowerment and Relationship Outcomes in Healthcare Consultations," *European Journal of Marketing*, 40, 1068–86.

Parasuraman, A., L.L. Berry and V.A. Zeithaml (1991), "Understanding Customer Expectations of Service," *Sloan Management Review*, 32(3), 39–48.

Parish, J. and B. Holloway (2010), "Consumer Relationship Proneness: a Reexamination and Extension across Service Exchanges," *Journal of Services Marketing*, 24, 61–73.

Price, L.L. and E. Arnould (1999), "Commercial Friendships: Service Provider–Client Relationships in Context," *Journal of Marketing*, 63(4), 38–56.

Reichheld, F.F. (1993), "Loyalty-Based Management," *Harvard Business Review*, 74(4), 64–73.

Reichheld, F. and W.E. Sasser, Jr. (1990), "Zero Defections: Quality Comes to Services," *Harvard Business Review*, September–October, 105–11.

Turnbull, P.W. and D.T. Wilson (1989), "Developing and Protecting Profitable Customer Relationships," *Industrial Marketing Management*, 18, 233–8.

3. Relational benefits research: a synthesis
Dwayne D. Gremler and Kevin P. Gwinner

The publication of a book on relationship marketing attests to the immense interest, among academics and practitioners alike, in various facets of the relationships between commercial exchange partners. Our particular interest in this topic stems from our research into the benefits that accrue to customers when they engage in long-term relationships with companies. These customer *relational benefits* (RBs), in our research, consist of "those benefits customers receive from long-term relationships above and beyond the core service performance" (Gwinner et al. 1998: 102). For example, in an overnight delivery context, the on-time delivery of a package by a package delivery service represents the core service provision. Repeated usage of the firm that has resulted in many successful, on-time deliveries should lead a customer to feel confidence and reduced anxiety about the next package arriving on time; confidence and reduced anxiety represent the RB.

Building on our interest in RBs, we pursue two primary goals in this chapter. First, we seek to review and categorize extant literature that explores RBs from the customer's perspective. We also compare and contrast RBs with switching costs in the course of making the observation that these two constructs actually may describe the same phenomena. Second, on the basis of our review and observations, we offer a variety of suggestions for further academic inquiry within the RB domain. In suggesting a research agenda, we hope to spark additional exploration into this research topic that is both managerially relevant and theoretically grounded.

RELATIONAL BENEFITS

At its core, a customer–service provider relationship must be characterized by repeated interactions over some period of time. As with any interpersonal relationship, one can think of commercial relationships on a continuum from weak or nonexistent to very strong. Because research examining RBs has not really advanced beyond "repeated patronage" as a definition of commercial relationships, there is certainly an opportunity to expand our understanding of relationships in commercial settings. For example, issues such as commitment to the relationship, familiarity between participants, and even levels of friendship might be useful for describing commercial relationships more fully. Regardless of how we define or operationalize "relationship," both parties should receive benefits if that relationship is to be considered "healthy." Our research into RBs thus began with the goal of understanding the reasons customers might want to form (or maintain) relationships with firms. Prior to 1998, the reasons that *firms* would want to form relationships with customers had been fairly well documented (e.g., Danaher et al. 2008), but the reasons *customers* might want to do so, and the benefits that they might gain from it, were not as well articulated. Since 1998, research focused on the relational benefits received by consumers has provided a better understanding of this second side of healthy commercial relationships.

Using a mix of qualitative and quantitative methods, our 1998 study (Gwinner et al. 1998) identifies three core RBs that consumers receive as a consequence of engaging in a long-term relationship with a service provider, above and beyond the delivery of the core service. The most important RB that the respondents to our study identified pertained to *confidence benefits*, or 1) feelings of reduced anxiety and risk in purchasing the service that accrue as a result of having developed a relationship with the provider, along with 2) a sense of knowing what to expect. To illustrate, in the qualitative portion of our study, one respondent described the benefits of a relationship with a service provider as follows: "You don't have as much anxiety, and you have a higher confidence level in being a loyal customer. You know it is going to be good in advance, or if something is wrong it will be taken care of." This confidence in the service and familiarity with the process may serve to offset negative attributes of a particular service provider, such as an inconvenient location or higher prices.

Social benefits, the second most important RB to emerge across a wide range of services, are those associated with personal recognition by employees, familiarity, or friendship – all gained as a consequence of cultivating a relationship with the firm. Another quote from our original study effectively summarizes this idea: "The relationship [with employees at the grocery store] built up over time and has become a more important factor over time. The people know us [the entire family] there. They make a big deal over the kids. They would miss us if we didn't go one Saturday morning." Customers often value the social relationship that develops with frontline service providers as a critical element of their social support network that allows for a more customized and personalized interaction.

The third RB, *special treatment benefits*, occurs when customers who have developed a relationship with the service provider get better deals, faster service, or more offers than other consumers as a result of the long-term nature of their relationship. The following quote from our interviews is typical of this type of benefit: "I think you get special treatment [when you have an established relationship]. My pediatrician allowed me to use the back door to the office so my daughter could avoid contact with other sick children." Such special treatment can be a structured (e.g., loyalty reward programs) or unstructured (e.g., an occasional price break, receiving special services) element of the service offering. Generally, RB research shows that special treatment benefits are less important than confidence or social benefits in terms of customers' perceptions of value.

In the period since our study was published, the notion of RBs for customers has received significant attention. A 2005 editorial in the *Journal of the Academy of Marketing Science* even recognized our article (Gwinner et al. 1998) as the most cited among those published in the journal for the period 1998–2004 (Zinkhan 2005). While the concept was somewhat novel at the time, knowledge advances in this area have been natural outgrowths of the relationship marketing movement in general. We feel that at least a portion of the attention paid to RBs derives from their practical application for service managers. Specifically, RBs provide operationally concrete guidance for implementing programs that may increase important outcomes, such as customer satisfaction, loyalty, and commitment. Furthermore, as we discuss subsequently in this chapter, RBs can serve as a barrier to switching (i.e., by inducing switching costs), which thus reinforces their importance for customer retention.

CUSTOMER RELATIONAL BENEFIT RESEARCH

Our 1998 article was one of the first to explore RBs from the perspective of the consumer. Prior to that point, most work on the benefits of commercial exchange relationships examined benefits to the *firm*, typically in a business-to-business setting. Certainly customers received benefits prior to that time, but the nature of those benefits and their relative importance had not been studied in any systematic manner. Considering the dual nature of exchange relationships, this dearth of research from a *customer* perspective seemed problematic, as well as a good opportunity to identify important RBs. Many researchers since have examined this topic. In a review of more than two dozen articles focused on RBs since 1998, we can identify three broad areas: 1) *context-related research*, which seeks to identify situations and contexts in which customer RBs are most valued; 2) *additional RBs*, or studies that propose additional benefits that accrue to customers beyond the original three RBs that we identified; and 3) relational benefit *outcomes*, which pertain to the relationships between RBs and outcomes that are important to companies. In Table 3.1, we

Table 3.1 Studies focused on relational benefits

Studies (year)	Relational benefits studied	Antecedents of relational benefits	Consequences of relational benefits	Context	Key findings
Gwinner et al. (1998)	Confidence benefits. Special treatment benefits. Social benefits.	None.	Loyalty. Word-of-mouth communication. Continue in relationship. Satisfaction.	21 customer interviews for qualitative analysis and 299 customers across a variety of services in the United States.	In the original study on relational benefits, confidence, special treatment, and social benefits emerge as key relational benefits received by consumers in long-term relationships with service providers. Across three different service types, the three relational benefits rank 1) confidence benefits, 2) social benefits, and 3) special treatment benefits in terms both of benefits most frequently received and of the importance of those benefits.
Reynolds and Beatty (1999)	Time saving benefits. Social benefits. Relief from shopping benefits. Advice benefits.	None.	None.	364 upscale retailing clothing shoppers in the United States.	The benefits customers receive from having maintained relationships with employees include time savings, social benefits, relief from shopping, receiving good advice, and convenience.

Table 3.1 (continued)

Studies (year)	Relational benefits studied	Antecedents of relational benefits	Consequences of relational benefits	Context	Key findings
	Convenience benefits.				Six relationship customer segments are identified, using time poverty, shopping enjoyment, shopping confidence, and social needs as variables. Each segment is "profiled on levels of . . . relationship benefits valued (received)."
Hennig-Thurau et al. (2000)	Confidence benefits. Special treatment benefits. Social benefits. Identity-related benefits.	None.	None.	344 customers from a variety of service providers in the United States.	Responses to customer's preferences for confidence, special treatment, and social benefits are used to create four customer segments. Identity-related benefits are conceptualized but not empirically tested.
Patterson and Smith (2001)	Confidence benefits. Special treatment benefits. Social benefits.	Switching costs. Attractiveness of alternatives.	Satisfaction. Repurchase intent.	155 customers across a variety of services in Thailand.	Regardless of culture, relational benefits are highly valued, above and beyond satisfaction with the core service. However, some differences in the relative importance of benefits

Study				Sample	Findings
Hennig-Thurau et al. (2002)	Confidence benefits. Special treatment benefits. Social benefits.	None.	Satisfaction. Loyalty. Commitment. Word-of-mouth communication.	336 consumers who have a relationship with a specific service provider (selected from a list of various types of services) in the United States.	are attributed to cultural differences. In particular, Thai consumers place a higher value on special treatment benefits, whereas their U.S. counterparts value confidence benefits. Satisfaction and commitment partially mediate the impact of RBs on loyalty and word-of-mouth communication. Special treatment benefits have limited impact on word-of-mouth communication and loyalty.
Lin et al. (2003)	Structural benefits. Economic benefits. Social benefits.	None.	Trust. Commitment.	364 financial services consumers in Taiwan.	Relational benefits (bonds) consist of economic (e.g., money or time savings), social (e.g., genuine concern, friendship), and structural (e.g., convenience, customization) benefits. All three types of relational benefits have positive impacts on customer relationship performance (i.e., commitment and trust), with structural

Table 3.1 (continued)

Studies (year)	Relational benefits studied	Antecedents of relational benefits	Consequences of relational benefits	Context	Key findings
					benefits having the strongest influence. Economic benefits and structural benefits have a stronger relationship with trust and commitment among those who use the Internet for purchases, whereas social benefits have a stronger relationship with trust and commitment for face-to-face customers.
Spake et al. (2003)	Comfort.	None.	Satisfaction. Trust. Commitment. Active voice.	National sample of 508 consumers of hair care and physicians in the United States.	Consumer comfort is defined (similarly to confidence benefits) as a "psychological state wherein a customer's anxiety concerning a service has been eased, and he or she enjoys peace of mind and is calm and worry free concerning service encounters with this provider." This construct has a direct and positive impact on satisfaction, trust, commitment, and complaints to provider.

Yen and Gwinner (2003)	Confidence benefits. Special treatment benefits.	Perceived control. Performance of technology. Convenience. Efficiency (reduced transaction times).	Satisfaction. Loyalty.	459 online bookstore and online travel customers in Taiwan.	An eight-item consumer comfort scale is developed. Relational benefits mediate the relationship between selected Internet self-serve technology attribute variables (perceived control, technology performance, convenience, and efficiency) and the satisfaction and loyalty outcomes. RB constructs are relevant in non-face-to-face online environments.
Marzo-Navarro et al. (2004)	Functional benefits. Social benefits.	None.	Customer satisfaction. Loyalty.	228 retail clothing customers in Spain.	Persons who have greater perceptions of functional benefits (e.g., time savings, convenience, making the best purchase decision) and social benefits (e.g., a pleasant and comfortable relationship), derived from maintaining a stable relationship with a service provider, express greater satisfaction and loyalty.
Colgate et al. (2005)	Confidence benefits. Special treatment benefits.	None.	Satisfaction.	120 Internet banking customers and 122 "traditional"	For "traditional" customers, history (which relates to long-term association and familiarity) emerges as a new RB dimension.

Table 3.1 (continued)

Studies (year)	Relational benefits studied	Antecedents of relational benefits	Consequences of relational benefits	Context	Key findings
	Social benefits. History benefits. Personal service.			banking customers in New Zealand.	For Internet customers, in addition to history benefits, personal service benefits (receiving the highest service, personalized service, and quick problem handling) are an additional RB. In this context, the personal service dimension may serve to replace the social benefits dimension. Confidence benefits seem to play a less significant role in Internet-based relationships. Special treatment benefits are not received in either context.
Hennig-Thurau et al. (2005)	Social benefits. Confidence benefits. Economic benefits. Customization benefits.	None.	Loyalty.	Conceptual article.	Two new RBs are proposed. Identity-related benefits refer to positive additions or reinforcement to one's self-concept as a result of being in a relationship with a particular service provider. Quality improvement benefits result

	Identity-related benefits. Quality improvement benefits.				from the service provider learning about a customer's preferences and improving on the core service provided. National culture dimensions (power distance, individualism/collectivism, masculinity/femininity, and uncertainty avoidance) may moderate the relationship between the expanded list of RBs and loyalty.
Kinard and Capella (2006)	Confidence benefits. Special treatment benefits. Social benefits.	Customized service offering. Personal involvement.	Loyalty. Word-of-mouth communication. Customer satisfaction.	91 fast-food consumers and hairdresser/barber consumers in the United States.	Consumers purchasing high-contact, customized services perceive greater relational benefits than do consumers engaged in a standardized, moderate-contact service. Confidence benefits are the sole predictor variable, among the RBs examined, of customer loyalty, word-of-mouth communication, and satisfaction across two service categories (fast food, hairdressers). There is a significant difference between perceived RBs for different levels of involvement for high-contact services.

Table 3.1 (continued)

Studies (year)	Relational benefits studied	Antecedents of relational benefits	Consequences of relational benefits	Context	Key findings
Martín-Consuegra et al. (2006)	Confidence benefits. Special treatment benefits. Social benefits.	None.	None.	561 banking customers in Spain.	Banking consumers receive all three types of benefits, but special treatment benefits are received with less frequency than social or confidence benefits. Three customer segments are developed from a cluster analysis based on how much the groups value each of the RBs.
Xu et al. (2006)	Confidence benefits. Special treatment benefits. Social benefits.	None.	Satisfaction.	476 bank customers in China.	Relational benefits have a positive impact on satisfaction. Consistent with other research, the importance levels of relational benefits are as follows (most to least important): 1) confidence benefits, 2) social benefits, and 3) special treatment benefits.
Lacey et al. (2007)	Special treatment benefits.	None.	Relationship commitment. Increased purchases.	2591 upscale department store customers in the United States.	Preferential treatment (special treatment benefits) has a direct influence on each of several outcome variables (relationship

Study	Relational benefits	Mediators	Outcomes	Sample	Key findings
			Share of customer. Word-of-mouth communication. Customer feedback.		commitment, increased purchases, share of customer, word-of-mouth communication, and feedback). Relationship commitment plays a partial mediating role between preferential treatment (special treatment benefits) and the remaining four outcomes (increased purchases, share of customer, word-of-mouth communication, and feedback).
Martín-Ruiz et al. (2007)	Confidence benefits. Social benefits.	None.	Customer value clusters.	877 wireless communication customers in Spain.	Customer value is operationalized as a multidimensional construct with five formative components; one of these value components is confidence benefits. Confidence benefits and service quality are the strongest determinants of customer value. Social benefits are a (relatively weak) predictor of customer value clusters.
Molina et al. (2007)	Confidence benefits. Special treatment benefits. Social benefits.	None.	Satisfaction.	204 retail bank customers in Spain.	Although all three RBs are present in a banking context, only confidence benefits affect customer satisfaction.

Table 3.1 (continued)

Studies (year)	Relational benefits studied	Antecedents of relational benefits	Consequences of relational benefits	Context	Key findings
Berenguer-Contrí et al. (2009)	Confidence benefits. Special treatment benefits. Social benefits.	None.	None.	400 customers from four retail industries (groceries, clothing, electronics, furniture) in Spain.	Confidence benefits are more present for electronics retail consumers than for grocery store consumers. Social benefits are present in electronics retailing but not very common in furniture stores. Special treatment benefits are common in electronics retailers but are rarely present in grocery and furniture stores.
Paul et al. (2009)	Functional benefits. Psychological benefits.	Service product. Service delivery. Service environment. Service location.	Individual motivational values. Mixed motivational values.	Study 1 includes 188 consumers in the United States and Germany; Study 2	Applying means–end theory, a unifying framework for understanding how relational benefits affect the core values held by consumers is presented. Three primary "relationship-driving" benefits are identified: functional benefits, psychological benefits, and social benefits. These higher-order benefits refer to the advantages (beyond the

Social benefits.

Relationship characteristics.
Company characteristics.

Collective motivational values.

includes 618 German service consumers across a variety of service contexts.

core service) customers receive from being in a relationship that leads them to repurchase. 28 different service attributes are identified that lead to these relationship-driving benefits. The relationship-driving benefits predict ten distinct customer values (or desired end states).

summarize RB research since 1998; we next illustrate each of these areas with representative research studies.

Context-Related Research on Relational Benefits

Several studies seek, whether as a primary objective or a secondary finding, to discover the extent to which RBs developed in prior research remain relevant to consumers in different contexts (e.g., Berenguer-Contrí et al. 2009). Although our initial work to develop the three RBs considered a wide variety of service types, subsequent research examining context-based issues has sought a better understanding of if and how these three benefits might be valid in different contexts and whether they maintain the same level of importance (i.e., if RBs are particularly well suited, or ill suited, for specific contexts).

The contexts studied vary widely, including grocery stores, clothing retailers, electronics retailers, furniture stores, online and traditional banks, fast-food restaurants, hair salons, financial services, upscale department stores, cellular phone service providers, online retail, travel agencies, health care, and bookstores. Because of the varying operationalizations of RBs among these studies, though, it is not easy to develop a definitive list of contexts in which specific RBs appear particularly useful. However, the three principal RBs seem present and influential across most contexts. Such context-oriented RB research is especially important from an applied standpoint, because the results can provide managers who operate in different environments with the necessary guidance to implement their own RB strategies.

In our opinion, some of the most interesting research examining RBs deals with comparing the delivery of face-to-face and online services. Colgate et al. (2005) contrast the RBs that customers receive in traditional face-to-face relationships with the benefits received in Internet-based relationships. In an Internet context, they find that *personal service*, which is characterized by superior customer service, quick problem resolution, and service options tailored to unique needs, does not tend to exist in traditional face-to-face contexts. Thus, personal service benefits might serve as replacements for social benefits for Internet customers. Furthermore, they find evidence that confidence benefits, which have been found to be the most important benefit in face-to-face contexts, are much less valued in an online environment. In a study of online bookstores and travel agencies, Yen and Gwinner (2003) examine the impact of the confidence and special treatment RBs on customer satisfaction and loyalty and find significant positive influences on these two outcome variables. As a result, they conclude that these two RB constructs remain relevant in non-face-to-face, online environments. Overall, then, support emerges for two of the three RBs in online settings, and further evidence suggests additional RBs may exist in non-face-to-face contexts.

National culture provides another interesting contextual variable, with RBs appearing relevant in such diverse countries as Canada, Germany, Korea, Spain, Taiwan, and the United States (Park and Kim 2003; Colgate et al. 2005; Chang and Chen 2007; Berenguer-Contrí et al. 2009; Paul et al. 2009). However, studies that take national culture into account also find some differences. For example, Patterson and Smith (2001) reveal that consumers in Thailand, similar to those in the United States, place a high value on all three of the consumer RBs, over and above the satisfactory provision of the core service. Yet Thai consumers place a higher value on special treatment benefits, whereas U.S. consumers most highly value confidence benefits. In examining the reasons that consumers tend to stay with a service provider – several of which parallel the three RBs we identified – Colgate and colleagues (2005) discover nearly identical factor structures across Chinese and New Zealand consumers but find differences with respect to the importance of the reasons to stay: New Zealand consumers are much more focused on the importance of confidence benefits as a reason to stay than are Chinese customers. In a conceptual paper, Hennig-Thurau and colleagues (2005) propose that the national culture dimensions of power distance, individualism/collectivism, masculinity/femininity, and uncertainty avoidance moderate the relationship between various RBs and loyalty. Together, these studies caution RB strategists that they should consider how cultural differences may influence customers' perceptions of benefits.

Additional Relational Benefits

Some RB research identifies additional benefits beyond the original three we listed (Gwinner et al. 1998). This line of research represents an important contribution, because it may be able to discern benefits that evolve over time or emerge in different contexts. The identification of new benefits also enables managers to develop their own relationship management programs by prioritizing the RB areas that their customers perceive as most important.

For example, another identified RB is *respect benefits*, cited by Chang and Chen (2007) as an important RB in non-Western cultures. They construe these benefits in terms of "saving face" in interactions – a very important issue in Eastern cultures – and contend it is especially important in relationships marked by a high level of social interaction. Saving face through respect benefits reportedly encourages the development of emotional attachment with an organization and thus greater customer commitment and loyalty. According to Chang and Chen, respect benefits have the greatest direct and total effects on customer loyalty, exceeding even confidence benefits.

Colgate et al. (2005) also find *history benefits*, which relate to the service provider's extensive knowledge about and familiarity with the customer as a consequence of their long-term association, to be present in both face-to-face and online contexts. In the qualitative part of our 1998 study, we found a history component, which we considered a feature of a customization benefit, but we did not find enough empirical support in our quantitative study to suggest it as a separate benefit. The notion of history benefits is interesting, because a customer might enjoy familiarity with a provider and the comfort of a long-term association as a benefit of the relationship. However, this history actually may enable other RBs, such as confidence, social, and special treatment benefits, to develop. That is, customers are more likely to receive superior service when employees have knowledge about them and their needs (i.e., employees know the history of the customers). Thus, it remains an open question if history benefits should be construed as an additional RB construct or an antecedent to RBs.

As mentioned previously, *personal service*, as identified by Colgate et al. (2005), in an online context includes superior customer service, quick resolution of problems, personal advice, and tailor-made service options. Colgate et al. (2005: 434) suggest that this RB "may be the replacement [for] the social benefits dimension" in services that get provided online. Although social benefits may be difficult to achieve in online contexts, online customers still enjoy personal service. Further study is needed to discover if personal service should be considered a salient RB construct in face-to-face encounters as well.

Another pioneering RB study (Reynolds and Beatty 1999) suggests several RBs that consumers might receive in a retail shopping context, including *time savings, convenience, advice, shopping assistance*, and *personal relationships*. Reynolds and Beatty find that different customer segments (defined by their level of shopping enjoyment, shopping confidence, social needs, and time poverty) have unique preferences for these RBs. For example, their "happy busy shoppers" segment (high on time poverty and shopping enjoyment) values time savings as an RB, whereas "challenged shopping lovers" (high in shopping enjoyment, low on shopping confidence) are most interested in advice. Their research therefore emphasizes the notion that RB attractiveness might be not only context specific, as discussed in the prior subsection, but also customer segment specific.

Marzo-Navarro et al. (2004) explore consumer benefits and, like Reynolds and Beatty (1999), find that time savings and convenience benefits accrue to consumers in longer-term relationships. Their study also suggests the concept of *making the best purchase* as a benefit consumers receive from relationships. This benefit corresponds somewhat with our confidence RB and also relates to the consumer comfort construct developed by Spake and colleagues (2003). Consumer comfort is defined as a "psychological state wherein a customer's anxiety concerning a service has been eased, and he or she enjoys peace of mind and is calm and worry free concerning service encounters with this provider" (Spake et al. 2003: 321). Although some previously identified RBs seem similar to the confidence, special treatment, or social benefits, others, including advice and convenience, clearly are unique.

Being in a relationship with a specific provider might add meaning to the consumer's self-concept, a notion that has been termed *identity-related relational benefits* (Hennig-Thurau et al. 2000, 2005). This concept is based in the consumer–brand relationship research done by Fournier (1998) in the context of consumer goods. Identity-related benefits may lead to greater levels of customer loyalty and be influenced by Hofstede's individualism/collectivism national culture dimension.

Hennig-Thurau and colleagues (2005) also discuss the idea of *quality improvement benefits*, derived from the qualitative analysis of professional service relationships performed by Sweeney and Webb (2002), who instead use the term "symbiotic benefits." Quality improvement benefits reflect the idea that service employees learn customer preferences through repeated interactions, which enables them to provide improved levels of service. Similar to special treatment benefits, which encompass doing out-of-the-ordinary things for only relational customers, quality improvement benefits differ in that they adjust the core service (e.g., adapting a meal at a restaurant to meet the dietary needs of the customer).

In considering these studies together, we find that the list of RBs might be expanded to include several constructs, beyond confidence, social, and special treatment benefits. Respect, history, personal service, advice giving, convenience, comfort, and time savings are all benefits, beyond the core service, that may accrue to consumers who have developed relationships with service firms. As scholars continue to identify and expand the list of RBs that consumers receive, service firms should be able to take better-informed actions that may improve the value that they offer to customers.

Yet an ever-expanding list of RBs could quickly get out of hand without some form of structure. In a study, Paul and colleagues (2009) offer an integrative, comprehensive framework of the benefits that a customer receives from the service provider – beyond the advantages derived from the core service – that should prompt repeat purchase. The result is a hierarchical classification scheme that organizes benefits into three areas: functional, psychological, and social. These three categories comprise 12 subfactors: 1) *functional benefits* entail customer benefits of a utilitarian nature and include convenience, money savings, and knowledge accumulation (i.e., information acquired during repeat purchases); 2) *psychological benefits* describe those customer benefits that satisfy important intrinsic, self-oriented goals of the customer and include autonomy, comfort, confidence, privilege, and welcomeness benefits; and 3) *social benefits* make people feel closer to one another or portray a desired image to others, and include communication, affiliation, altruism, and community benefits.

A key advantage of an elaborate, hierarchal RB classification scheme is that it allows service firms to segment their markets according to customers' desired RBs. Several studies (e.g., Reynolds and Beatty 1999; Hennig-Thurau et al. 2000; Coulter and Ligas 2004; Danaher et al. 2008) offer typologies for segmenting customers on the basis of RBs; these segments can help organizations position their service offerings uniquely to appeal to their targeted segments (e.g., those that want confidence benefits, or segments with a keen interest in receiving social benefits). Paul and colleagues (2009) find that attributes of service offerings, such as the amount of customer–employee contact or the level of service customization, can accurately predict which benefits will be most desired by the different segments of consumers.

Relational Benefit Outcomes

The constructs influenced by consumer RBs represent the focus of the third area of past RB research. Outcome-focused research should be of particular interest to managers who want to execute RB strategies, because it provides a justification (or lack of one) for the pursuit of such strategies. Understanding that outcomes such as satisfaction, loyalty, and commitment (to name just a few of the outcomes explored) can be influenced by customers' receipt of RBs enables management to consider the costs versus benefits of implementing RB programs in their organizations.

Two of the most studied outcomes of RBs are customer satisfaction and loyalty to the provider. Because research consistently shows that these two constructs can be predicted by the RBs that customers receive across a wide range of contexts (e.g., Patterson and Smith 2001, 2003; Yen and Gwinner 2003; Marzo-Navarro et al. 2004; Colgate et al. 2005; Kinard and Capella 2006; Vázquez-Carrasco and Foxall 2006; Xu et al. 2006; Chang and Chen 2007; Molina et al. 2007), it seems safe to say that the links between RBs and customer satisfaction and loyalty are well established.

In extant literature pertaining to individual RB constructs and their impact on satisfaction and loyalty outcomes, confidence benefits consistently appear strongly correlated with both outcome variables (e.g., Hennig-Thurau et al. 2002; Colgate et al. 2005; Kinard and Capella 2006; Xu et al. 2006). Perhaps this strong linkage is not surprising; confidence benefits typically emerge as the most important RB for consumers. Just as reliability (i.e., the ability to provide a promised service consistently and accurately) often ranks as the most important service quality dimension (Parasuraman et al. 1988), confidence benefits (i.e., feeling of reduced anxiety and trust in the service provider) consistently appear as the most valued RB. According to Paul and colleagues (2009), confidence benefits are a key dimension of the higher-order psychological benefits construct. This proposition underscores the critical role of confidence benefits, because these authors also find that psychological benefits are a key rationale for consumers' repatronage decisions.

Social benefits appear to have a fairly consistent positive influence on loyalty across studies, though their influence on customer satisfaction is mixed; several studies report a significant relationship (e.g., Patterson and Smith 2001; Marzo-Navarro et al. 2004; Colgate et al. 2005; Xu et al. 2006), whereas others do not (e.g., Hennig-Thurau et al. 2002; Kinard and Capella 2006; Molina et al. 2007). For social benefits, some contexts may be more conducive to their establishment and importance than are others (Gwinner et al. 1998). That is, context may partially explain the inconsistent relationship between social benefits and customer satisfaction, in that research which identifies no relationship between social RBs and satisfaction may simply reflect the difficulty of establishing social RBs in that particular study context. For example, our results indicate that social benefits are much less likely to be received in moderate-contact, standardized services (e.g., airlines) than in high-contact, customized personal services (e.g., hair care) (Gwinner et al. 1998).

Special treatment benefits may have significant impacts on satisfaction (e.g., Patterson and Smith 2001), but researchers more commonly find that the special treatment benefit–satisfaction relationship is weak or nonexistent (e.g., Hennig-Thurau et al. 2002; Colgate et al. 2005; Kinard and Capella 2006; Molina et al. 2007). In studies that examine the role of special treatment for predicting loyalty (i.e., repatronage behavior), we find some reports of a significant positive relationship (e.g., Patterson and Smith 2001, 2003; Xu et al. 2006), but again others offer no such evidence (e.g., Hennig-Thurau et al. 2002; Kinard and Capella 2006). Therefore, special treatment RBs do not appear to be as critical compared with the other two RBs in leading to greater levels of satisfaction and loyalty.

Finally, researchers have explored some other outcomes that may be important to managers. For example, word-of-mouth communication

(Kinard and Capella 2006; Lacey et al. 2007), trust in the company (Lin et al. 2003), commitment (Hennig-Thurau et al. 2002), and customer feedback to the firm (Lacey et al. 2007) are highly correlated with at least some RBs. Confidence benefits, according to Kinard and Capella (2006), are the only RB that significantly predicts word-of-mouth communication. Hennig-Thurau et al. (2002) find a significant causal relationship from both social benefits and special treatment benefits to commitment. In examining several outcomes that occur when consumers receive RBs, Lacey et al. (2007) find that preferential treatment (or special treatment, in our terminology) leads to higher levels of relationship commitment (i.e., repatronage attitude), increased purchases, and higher share of wallet. This variety of outcomes provides evidence of the importance of RBs for service firms – especially confidence RBs. Therefore, companies that hope to improve on important outcome measures can rest assured that improving their RBs provides a sound path toward that ultimate goal.

RELATIONAL BENEFITS AND SWITCHING COSTS

Originally, RBs were conceived as customers' perceptions of the benefits that accrue to them as a result of staying or remaining in a relationship with a service provider. Of course, customers who decide not to continue to patronize a service firm must forgo whatever RBs they may be receiving from that firm. Thus, the presence of RBs may make it costly for a customer to switch to a new firm.

Switching barriers and switching costs have received considerable attention in the past 15 years. The two terms tend to describe similar phenomena: *switching barriers* refer to "any factor which makes it more difficult or costly for consumers to change providers" (Jones et al. 2000: 261), whereas *switching costs* are generally described as the "costs customers associate with the process of switching from one provider to another" (Burnham et al. 2003: 110). Although some research operationalizes switching costs as a type of switching barrier (e.g., Jones et al. 2000; Vázquez-Carrasco and Foxall 2006), we agree with Colgate and colleagues (2007) about the confusion associated with how these concepts differ. (Table 3.2 offers a summary of representative studies.) As Colgate and colleagues (2007) point out, these two terms often appear interchangeably; we regard them as conceptually equivalent and use the term "switching costs" to represent both concepts.

From the preceding discussion, we can infer conceptual similarity between customers receiving benefits while staying with a service provider and experiencing costs when they leave that service provider. Thus,

Table 3.2   Studies focused on switching costs

Studies (year)	Switching costs studied	Antecedents of switching costs	Consequences of switching costs	Context	Key findings
Jones et al. (2000)	Switching barriers: – interpersonal relationships; – perceived switching costs; – attractiveness of competing alternatives.	N/A.	Satisfaction. Repurchase intentions.	228 banking services customers and 206 hairstyling/barber services customers in the United States.	All three switching barriers are critical determinants of retention, even when customer satisfaction is included in the model. The effect of satisfaction on repurchase intentions declines when customers perceive high switching barriers. The relationship between satisfaction and retention varies somewhat as a function of the magnitude of switching barriers present in a given service context.
Jones et al. (2002)	Switching costs: – lost performance costs; – uncertainty costs; – pre-switching search and evaluation costs;	N/A.	Repurchase intentions. Perceived service quality. Interpersonal relationships.	228 banking services customers and 206 hairstyling/barber services customers in the United States.	Six empirically distinct switching costs are confirmed: lost performance costs, uncertainty costs, pre-switching search and evaluation costs,

Table 3.2 (continued)

Studies (year)	Switching costs studied	Antecedents of switching costs	Consequences of switching costs	Context	Key findings
	– post-switching behavioral and cognitive costs; – setup costs. – sunk costs.				post-switching behavioral and cognitive costs, setup costs, and sunk costs. All switching costs dimensions are positively and significantly associated with repurchase intentions, with lost performance costs having the strongest association. The data suggest industry differences in the mean level of perceptions across the switching cost dimensions.
Burnham et al. (2003)	Switching costs: – procedural switching costs (economic risk costs, evaluation costs, learning costs, setup costs); – financial	Market characteristics (product complexity, provider heterogeneity). Consumer investments (breadth of	Intention to stay with the incumbent provider.	158 credit card consumers and 144 long-distance consumers in the United States.	A three-factor, higher-order conceptualization of switching costs receives support, and eight distinct dimensions (facets) of switching costs are empirically confirmed. Switching costs account for nearly double the variance

Author	Constructs	Measurement	Dependent variable	Context	Findings
	switching costs (benefit loss costs, monetary loss costs); – relational switching costs (personal relationships loss costs, brand relationship loss costs).	use, extent of modification). Domain expertise (alterative experience, switching experience).			in customer retention (i.e., intention to stay with the provider) compared with satisfaction. All three switching costs drive consumers' intentions to stay with their current provider, with financial switching costs having the weakest impact.
Patterson and Smith (2003)	Switching barriers: – search costs; – loss of social bonds; – setup costs; – functional risk; – attractiveness of alternatives; – loss of special treatment benefits.	N/A.	Propensity to stay with a focal service provider.	Travel agencies, medical services, and hairdressers in Australia and Thailand	Switching barriers explain a large amount of variance in the "propensity to stay with the present service provider," even when satisfaction is included in the model. Two of the switching barriers, namely loss of special treatment benefits and loss of social bonds – both relational benefits – have an especially strong impact on behavioral intentions (i.e., the decision to stay with a service provider).

55

Table 3.2 (continued)

Studies (year)	Switching costs studied	Antecedents of switching costs	Consequences of switching costs	Context	Key findings
					The major switching barriers differ for each type of service studied (travel agencies, medical services, and hairdressers).
Vázquez-Carrasco and Foxall (2006)	Switching barriers: – relational benefits (including confidence benefits, special treatment benefits, and social benefits); – switching costs; – availability and attractiveness of alternatives.	Need for variety.	Satisfaction. Customer retention.	754 hairdresser consumers in Spain.	Positive switching barriers (those "naturally created" in any relationship or based on a customer's own initiative) differ from negative barriers (perceived as coercive and "locking" the customer in the relationship). Relational benefits are positive switching barriers. Relational benefits correlate strongly with (contribute to the explained variance of) satisfaction, switching costs, and customer retention. As RBs increase, customers perceive higher switching costs and

Author	Switching barriers	Relational benefits	Dependent variable	Sample	Findings
Chang and Chen (2007)	Switching barriers (unidimensional construct with the following items): – lost personal relationships; – perceived risk of switching; – uncertainty of competitors' offerings).	Confidence benefits. Special treatment benefits. Social benefits. Respect benefits.	Customer loyalty.	326 airline passengers in Taiwan.	have lower perceptions of the availability and attractiveness of alternatives. Positive switching barriers [RBs] play a more important role in satisfaction and customer retention than do negative switching barriers. Confidence benefits and social benefits are strongly correlated with switching barriers. Switching barriers have a significant and positive influence on customer loyalty.
Colgate et al. (2007)	Switching barriers: – time and effort; – lack of perceived alternatives; – emotional bonds; – other types of switching costs.	N/A.	N/A.	343 service customers (across a wide variety of services) in New Zealand and 350 service customers in China.	Seven categories of factors, organized around two main themes, are identified and confirmed regarding why customers stay in relationships. The

Table 3.2 (continued)

Studies (year)	Switching costs studied	Antecedents of switching costs	Consequences of switching costs	Context	Key findings
	Affirmatory factors: – confidence; – social bonds; – well-handled service recovery.				first – switching barriers – includes time and effort, lack of perceived alternatives, emotional bonds, and other types of switching costs. The remaining three categories, labeled affirmatory factors (as they affirm to the customers that staying with their current service provider is the right thing to do), include confidence, social bonds, and (well-handled) service recovery.
Jones et al. (2007)	Switching costs: – social switching costs (positive switching costs); – lost benefits costs (positive switching costs);	N/A.	Affective commitment. Calculative commitment. Positive emotions (indirectly).	484 consumers across a variety of services (banks, cable television, cell phone, physicians, hairstylists, retail stores) in the United States.	Negative switching costs (procedural costs) are distinguished from positive switching costs (social switching costs and lost benefits costs). Social switching costs and lost benefits costs increase

– procedural costs (negative switching costs).	Negative emotions (indirectly) Repurchase intentions (indirectly). Negative word of mouth (indirectly).	affective commitment, which subsequently increases positive emotions and repurchase intentions and decreases negative word of mouth. Procedural switching costs bolster calculative commitment, which subsequently increases repurchase intentions but also increases negative emotions and negative word of mouth.

Notes: Switching barriers and switching costs describe similar phenomena in the literature. We regard these terms as conceptually equivalent and use "switching costs" to represent both ideas, both in the table title and in the column headings. However, in the cells of the table we include the specific term used by each set of authors to describe each study.

might switching costs and RBs be the same construct, but looked at (and defined) from different perspectives? That is, are RBs and switching costs simply opposite sides of the same coin? Chang and Chen (2007: 105) even assert: "Customer relational benefits constitute switching barriers because when people switch to new service providers, all benefits accruing to them for being loyal to the original provider diminish."

In a comprehensive investigation of switching costs, Burnham et al. (2003) propose a typology that includes three distinct types. *Procedural switching costs* primarily involve the expenditure of time and effort, including economic risk costs, evaluation costs, learning costs, and setup costs. Their second type, *financial switching costs*, involve the loss of "financially quantifiable resources" and consist of the costs of losing benefits (e.g., unused frequent flyer miles) or finances. Finally, *relational switching costs* include psychological or emotional discomfort due to the loss of identity and the breaking of bonds; they consist of personal and brand relationship loss costs. Jones and colleagues (2002, 2007) examine switching costs and generally agree with these three major types, though they label them somewhat differently. In their terminology, *procedural switching costs* involve increased time, effort, and inconvenience associated with finding and adapting to a new provider; *lost benefits switching costs* pertain to the loss of special deals or concessions received from the service provider; and *social switching costs* are the loss of a personal bond or friendship with the service provider when the consumer switches (Jones et al. 2007).

Many of the RBs that have been articulated appear to be mirrored by specific types of switching costs identified in switching costs studies. For example, we originally described *confidence benefits* as feelings of reduced anxiety and risk in making a purchase decision that accrue as a result of having developed a relationship with a firm (Gwinner et al. 1998). To exit the relationship, a customer must forgo this benefit; in effect, the customer incurs the *economic risk (switching) cost* of "accepting uncertainty with the potential for a negative outcome when adopting a new service provider" (Burnham et al. 2003: 111). Similarly, *social benefits* – which include personal recognition by employees, familiarity, and friendship – seem to address the same issue that Burnham et al.'s (2003) personal relationship loss costs entail, or what Jones and colleagues (2007) call social switching costs. History benefits (Colgate et al. 2005; Paul et al. 2009), which relate to the service provider's extensive knowledge of and familiarity with the customer, also are very similar to Burnham et al.'s (2003) learning costs and setup costs.

Jones and colleagues (2002, 2007) also distinguish between positive switching costs (social and lost benefits costs) and negative switching costs (e.g., procedural switching costs), which derive primarily from negative sources of constraint (e.g., the time and effort needed to find a new provider). In a similar line of research, Colgate and colleagues (2007) suggest seven categories, organized around two main themes, of the factors that explain why customers stay in relationships. The first theme – which they call switching barriers – fits very closely with previous research on switching costs and includes 1) time and effort, 2) lack of perceived alternatives, 3) emotional bonds, and 4) other types of switching costs. These four factors are barriers in the true sense of the word; they prohibit (mainly in a negative sense) a customer from leaving. In effect, RBs serve the same purpose, except that their presence provides a positive incentive for customers to stay in a relationship. The remaining three categories from Colgate and colleagues' (2007) study consist of factors that encourage customers to stay in a relationship, which they label affirmatory factors (i.e., they affirm to the customers that staying with the current service provider is the right thing to do): confidence, social bonds, and (well-handled) service recovery. Vázquez-Carrasco and Foxall (2006) contend that RBs constitute what they call "positive" switching barriers. Their study provides evidence that RBs (i.e., positive switching barriers) play a greater role in determining customer satisfaction and retention than do negative switching barriers (i.e., switching costs).

The seemingly parallel nature of RBs and switching costs leads us to wonder: Are switching costs simply the cost that customers perceive when they lose RBs? Does the presence of RBs naturally imply a switching cost? If the answers to these questions are "yes," then perhaps each literature stream can inform the other. For example, perhaps the drivers of RBs and switching costs, as well as the consequences of each, are the same. Alternatively, maybe RBs need to be present to create a switching cost. A study by Chang and Chen (2007) suggests that RBs lead to switching costs in an airline service context. However, more research is needed to tease out the conceptual and empirical differences and relationships between RBs and switching costs.

RESEARCH QUESTIONS TO ADVANCE RB KNOWLEDGE AND PRACTICE

Although we have learned much about RBs, there is room for more work on this topic. In the sections that follow, we suggest some specific areas that may have potential to add insight to this topic. We organize these areas into four categories: contextual, financial, conceptual, and nomological.

Contextual Issues

How do RBs evolve over time?
As we mentioned previously, we originally conceptualized RBs as a consequence of customers staying in a relationship with a firm. This conceptualization, by its very nature, implies a temporal dimension, because a relationship (as least as we perceive it) does not appear instantaneously; rather, it must be cultivated over time. Yet virtually no research on RBs is longitudinal in nature, and one study (Berenguer-Contrí et al. 2009) finds no relationship between the assessments of RBs and the length of patronage, which often serves as a proxy for the presence of a relationship. Thus, we wonder if (or how) RBs might change and/or evolve over time:

- How do RBs evolve over time?
- Are some RBs more prevalent early in a relationship?
- Are some RBs more prevalent later in a relationship?
- Does the salience of the various RBs change over time?
- As a relationship progresses, does one type of RB (e.g., confidence benefits) get taken for granted as other RBs (e.g., social benefits, special treatment benefits) become more important?

What influence can or does the environment (i.e., servicescape) have on the development of RBs?
Previous research indicates that RBs and their importance can vary by the service context. For example, Chang and Chen's (2007) respect benefit appears particularly salient in settings characterized by high levels of personal interaction. Might part of this variation across contexts be due to the nature of the environment in which the service is delivered? Considerable evidence implies that physical elements (what some have labeled atmospherics) can substantially influence consumer behavior in service settings (Turley and Milliman 2000), and it seems reasonable to assume that the servicescape (Bitner 1992) might lead to the creation of RBs. For example, some banks have removed traditional teller windows and replaced them with small, office-like cubicles that allow customers to sit comfortably across the desk from an employee and encourage a slower-paced interaction – which promotes social bonds and perhaps presents the possibility of special treatment – without the pressure of having to hurry through a transaction because of a queue of customers waiting for service. A study by Parish et al. (2008) suggests that the servicescape also can affect employees' ability to serve and interact effectively with customers. Perhaps servicescape issues, such as atmosphere, physical layout, or store design,

should be included in future RB studies. Some research questions involving RBs and the servicescape include:

- To what extent might the servicescape influence the development of RBs?
- Does atmosphere, physical layout, or store design have an impact on the firm's ability to cultivate RBs with customers?
- What specific elements of physical evidence are instrumental in conveying confidence benefits or facilitating the creation of social benefits?
- What impact might physical evidence have on a firm's ability to provide special treatment benefits?
- In online service environments, such as hotel reservation Web sites or airline travel portals, can Web page design features (e.g., color, movement, navigation, images) influence perceptions of RBs?

Tombs and McColl-Kennedy (2003) argue that the social environment in which a service is delivered, which they term the *social servicescape*, significantly influences customers' affective and cognitive responses to the environment. That is, in addition to atmospherics, Tombs and McColl-Kennedy contend that social aspects of the service environment – including customer–employee interactions and customer-to-customer interactions – may influence customers' perceptions of what they receive in the exchange. It is easy to imagine how social servicescape issues could affect RBs; for example, a provider's employees clearly influence how customers perceive the social benefits they receive from the firm. Social benefits also may come from fellow customers – especially in "third places" – who provide companionship and emotional support (Oldenburg 1991; Rosenbaum 2006). Thus, pertinent research questions involving both RBs and the social servicescape include:

- Are RBs perceived to come from the firm or from the employee? If they are perceived to come from the employee, what happens when that employee leaves the organization?
- Can employees be trained, selected, or rewarded for delivering RBs?
- Can RBs be provided, at least in part, by other customers?
- As technology evolves, might service delivery in an online setting generate social RBs (e.g., virtual worlds of e-commerce, complete with avatar personifications of employees and customers)?

Are RBs applicable to mass marketing?

Logically, RBs should work particularly well in situations in which the firm has an opportunity to develop a relationship with selected customers (e.g., hair salons, health care). Social and special treatment benefits may be difficult to achieve in mass markets, especially if no extensive one-to-one interaction occurs or at least is not possible on a regular basis (e.g., fast-food restaurants, video rentals, grocery stores, airlines). Colgate et al. (2005) find that special treatment and social RBs do not predict customer satisfaction in an online context, where one-to-one relationships are difficult to form. Similarly, Berenguer-Contrí et al. (2009) find that all three RBs are absent in a large-scale grocery store context, whereas they are very important in an electronics retailing context, for which one-on-one interactions are the norm. Therefore, we wonder how RBs might work in mass market contexts:

- Can RBs be provided in mass marketing (large-scale) situations?
- Can social benefits be provided, or provided effectively, by firms serving large numbers of customers?
- Is it possible, or even desirable, for a firm to develop personal relationships with all of its customers in order to provide social benefits?
- Can firms provide confidence benefits when they serve large numbers of customers?
- In mass market contexts, in which conditions might firms want to develop RBs with customers?
- In mass market contexts, in which conditions might firms *not* want to develop RBs with customers?
- In mass market contexts, how might customer databases and customer relationship management (CRM) systems help increase (or manage) RBs?
- In mass market contexts, how might the desired level of RBs be used to segment customers?
- Can loyalty programs be used to provide RBs successfully in mass market contexts?

Is there a dark side to providing RBs?

Perhaps in some situations RBs are not appropriate or relevant. For example, Noble and Phillips (2004) suggest drawbacks of relationships to the consumer; in their study of why consumers avoid or disengage from loyalty and relationship-building programs, they find four factors that hinder relationship formation: *upkeep* refers to the (unpleasant) tasks in which consumers must engage to keep up with or maintain a relational exchange; *time* reflects consumers' concerns that relational programs require some sort of unappealing time commitment; *benefit* illustrates that retailers often offer unappealing relational program benefits; and *personal loss* involves some sort of perceived personal loss by the consumer, such as a loss of social status or privacy. In a study of commercial friendships (e.g., social benefits) in a business-to-business setting, Grayson (2007) discovers that the role of friendship can lead to negative outcomes for the customer. These findings suggest a potential dark side to the offering of RBs:

- Are there drawbacks for the company in offering RBs to customers?
- Are there drawbacks for the customer to the offering of RBs?
- In which conditions might consumers choose not to patronize a service provider that offers RBs?
- When might consumers perceive the offering of RBs as negative (e.g., relationship-avoiding customers, customers with privacy concerns)?

In addition to these potentially negative consequences for customers, firms may experience drawbacks, even beyond the additional costs we discussed previously. For example, social RBs result in greater levels of friendship, so firms might experience negative repercussions if the employee acts in the best interest of the customer/friend but at the expense of the firm. Negative responses seem likely when the firm stops providing RBs to its customers; Wagner et al. (2009) find that, when special treatment benefits (e.g., "elite membership" in a loyalty program) end, customers may decide to stop doing business altogether with the firm. Thus, the following questions come to mind:

- How is business affected if the provision of RBs declines or disappears?
- As social benefits increase, will employees take actions that are advantageous for the customer but disadvantageous for the company?
- Are there inequity issues when some consumers perceive they are not receiving the same level of RBs as other customers?

Financial Issues

What is the relationship between RBs and profitability?
Our review of RB literature reveals that financial issues have not been investigated sufficiently in RB studies. Yet over the past 15 years we find an increased emphasis in marketing literature on the financial returns generated as a result of marketing programs and investments (e.g., Rust et al. 2004; Rao and Bharadwaj 2008). A Marketing Science Institute Research Priorities publication calls for even more research on the returns

on marketing investments (MSI 2008). However, to our knowledge, no published research addresses returns on RB investments (i.e., financial rewards that accrue to the firm when it offers RBs). Therefore, another research challenge involves analyzing the monetary consequences of the implementation of RB offerings. Researchers might explore the relationships between RBs and a variety of financial outcomes, as follows:

- What is the relationship between RBs and sales?
- What is the relationship between RBs and the ability to charge a price premium?
- What is the relationship between RBs and firm profitability?
- Do RBs lead to increased purchases by a consumer?
- Do RBs lead to an increased share of wallet from individual customers?

Such insights are needed because current research provides minimal information about the measurable (financial) benefits of RBs.

What are the costs associated with RBs?
A related financial issue pertains to the cost of offering RBs. Service firms need to understand that, before implementing RB programs, they may need to adjust their processes, set quality standards, and train employees in how to reach the standards expected for the implementation. These activities have (time and monetary) costs. For example, to increase social RBs a firm might change its service delivery process to increase the time available for employee–customer interactions, which increases the number of contact employees needed and their space requirements, both of which likely have significant cost implications for the firm. Assessing the costs of the implementation of an RB program therefore is essential for evaluating the potential impact on firm profitability and demands research attention. Our review of RB literature reveals that the costs of offering RBs have not been examined, so we suggest the following research questions:

- What are the costs associated with offering specific RBs?
- Which RBs are the most costly to implement?
- Which RBs are the most costly to maintain?
- Does the firm's cost, in the form of time or money, of delivering RBs to a given consumer decrease as the relationship continues? Is there an experience curve effect when it comes to learning about and delivering RBs?

To assess the payback of offering RBs, perhaps we need a metric, such as RB equity. Data about the (financial) performance of RBs would enable firms to understand the extent to which RB strategies work well, relative to other strategies. Such empirical evidence may assist managerial decision makers in refining their RB strategies. Thus, research should develop effective metrics to evaluate RB performance and then analyze the relationship between different RBs and the financial performance of the firm.

Conceptual Issues

Relationship quality and RBs: which is the chicken and which is the egg?
Descriptions of relationship quality generally include customer satisfaction with the service provider's performance, trust in the service provider, and commitment to the relationship with the firm (Crosby et al. 1990; Palmer and Bejou 1994; Dorsch et al. 1998; Smith 1998; Baker et al. 1999; Garbarino and Johnson 1999). Most RB research we have reviewed suggests, or at least implies, that customers perceive the presence of a large number (and amount) of RBs in a very positive light. The greater the number of RBs customers receive, the more likely they are to perceive the relationship as high quality (Hennig-Thurau et al. 2002). We originally conceptualized RBs as a consequence of a customer's relationship with a firm, though no empirical examination has confirmed whether this assumption is valid. That is, are RBs really a consequence of relationship quality, or is relationship quality a consequence of receiving RBs? This challenge leads to the following questions:

- Are RBs drivers of relationship quality, or does relationship quality drive RBs?
- Might RBs be considered formative indicators of relationship quality?
- Alternatively, is relationship quality needed before RBs can be delivered?

Should RBs appear in examinations of customer perceived value?
The concept of customer value attracts considerable research attention, and several studies suggest that RBs should be included in measures of customer value. Sweeney and Soutar (2001) feature the equivalents of both emotional and social benefits in their operationalization of customer value, which is generally defined in the literature as "consumers' overall assessment of the utility of a product based on perceptions of what is received and what is given" (Zeithaml 1988: 14). For many service purchases, RBs represent an important portion of that which is received from the service offering. Therefore, Xu et al. (2006) include RBs as part

of their operationalization of service value; Martín-Ruiz and colleagues (2007, 2008) similarly suggest that confidence benefits derived from an ongoing relationship with the service provider entail part of the value that customers evaluate when they receive service. These studies raise key questions:

- Are RBs part of a higher-order construct (e.g., customer value)?
- Should customer value be conceptualized to include various RB components?
- Alternatively, do RBs predict customer value?

Nomological Issues

What influence do the various RBs have on one another?

Although previous research suggests a variety of RBs that customers receive as a result of having developed a relationship with a service provider, academic research has generally examined these benefits in isolation from each other. Yet it is easy to imagine some RBs influencing others, which prompts the following questions for further research:

- What influence do the various RBs have on one another?
- Is there a (natural) sequential order of RBs? For example, do social benefits precede confidence benefits?
- Do the various RBs develop independently of one another? Do they develop in parallel?
- Are there interaction effects among the various RBs?
- Is there a "snowball" effect of RBs? That is, does the receipt of one RB (or a few RBs) lead to more RBs, which lead to even more RBs?
- Is there a "halo effect" of RBs? Does the presence of an RB lead customers to believe they are receiving several other RBs?

Are RBs antecedents to, or consequences of, customer–firm relationships?

Our original conceptualization suggests RBs are a consequence of the relationship that a customer has with a service firm. We define RBs as "those benefits customers receive *from* long-term relationships above and beyond the core service performance" (Gwinner et al. 1998: 102, emphasis added). That is, we envisioned RBs as accruing *after* a customer–firm relationship had been established. However, some subsequent RB literature conceptualizes RBs as antecedents of customer–firm relationships. For example, Lin et al. (2003) recast RBs as relational bonds and then conceptualize them as drivers, rather than consequences, of ongoing relationships. These studies raise questions:

- Are RBs consequences of customer–firm relationships or drivers of such relationships?
- Is there a connection between the strength of the relationship and the amount of RBs received?

Are RBs dependent on ongoing customer–firm relationships?
An underresearched issue focuses on the assumed *ongoing* nature of the customer–provider relationship (Gwinner et al. 1998). Originally RBs were derived in contexts in which customers were directed to identify a service provider with which they had an established relationship. What happens if this constraint is lifted? That is:

- Are RBs dependent on ongoing customer–firm relationships?
- Can RBs be received without the requirement of an ongoing customer–provider relationship?
- Can RBs be provided by transaction-oriented (one-time usage) services?
- Do different RBs emerge in transaction-oriented services?

For example, Park and Kim (2003) suggest that the benefits customers receive from shopping online regularly with a particular firm may not necessarily require the customer to maintain much of an ongoing relationship. Similarly, Paul and colleagues (2009) relax the relationship constraint by examining all contexts from which customers repeatedly purchased services – whether or not they professed to having a relationship with the firm. Their findings suggest a host of relationship-driving factors, several of which include RBs identified in previous studies, which appear when the nature of the relationship is simply ongoing. On the other end of the relationship spectrum is the idea of a single encounter. In another study (Gremler and Gwinner 2008), we examine the relational construct of rapport and suggest that it may occur even in a single encounter. Might the same be true for RBs? That is:

- At what point in the relationship can RBs be provided (or received)?
- Can RBs be received during the first customer–company encounter, when no prior relationship exists, or is an ongoing relationship a requirement to receive RBs?

How should RBs be conceptualized – formatively or reflectively?
If the various RB components we have described are first-order factors of a second-order construct, as some have suggested (e.g., Park and Kim 2003; Paul et al. 2009), the question arises about whether these first-order factors

(e.g., confidence benefits, social benefits) are formative or reflective indicators of a higher-order factor. When making this determination, there are several issues to keep in mind. First, a reflective approach suggests that each component is (or should be) highly correlated with the others, because changes in the underlying construct cause changes in the components (Martín-Ruiz et al. 2008); however, previous research suggests that the different RB components may not necessarily be highly correlated (Hennig-Thurau et al. 2002; Molina et al. 2007). Second, a reflective approach indicates that the various components are not independent but rather result from the underlying construct (Jarvis et al. 2003; MacKenzie et al. 2005); most RB research generally posits that RBs are independent. Third, a reflective approach suggests that the components are interchangeable (Jarvis et al. 2003); clearly, many of the RB components that have been identified are not interchangeable. In light of these issues, perhaps the best way to capture the essence of RBs is by constructing a formative index. However, the best way to settle the argument would be to build a theory, and then find empirical evidence to address these questions:

- Is there a higher-order RB construct? If so, how should it be conceptualized?
- Should the RB components be conceptualized formatively or reflectively?

What more can we learn about the additional RBs that have been identified?

The prevalence of the original three RBs has been empirically confirmed in many studies over the past 15 years. Although we strongly believe in the three original RBs we identified, we also concede (and subsequent research suggests) that customers may receive other RBs. As we indicated previously, these other benefits might include respect, history, personal service, comfort, time savings, convenience, advice, shopping assistance, reduced effort, and credible customer service (Reynolds and Beatty 1999; Park and Kim 2003; Colgate et al. 2005; Chang and Chen 2007; Paul et al. 2009). The identification of these new benefits leads to the following questions:

- To what extent is each additional RB present?
- Are these additional RBs generalizable across contexts and cultures?
- What are the relationships among all of the RBs that have been identified in the literature?
- Are there interaction effects among the various RBs?
- Do these additional RBs exist only after the original RBs have been established?

- Is there a hierarchy among the RBs?
- What other RBs exist that have not yet been identified?

One drawback of research on this topic as a whole is the lack of an underlying framework that might be used to organize RBs in a coherent fashion. Perhaps what we need is a relational benefits typology. Paul and colleagues (2009) explicitly study relationship drivers, but they also present a hierarchical classification scheme that could be used to organize RBs into an integrative, comprehensive framework that relies on means–end theory. Other theories and approaches for organizing and understanding RBs should also be explored.

FINAL THOUGHTS

We posit that the strong causal relationship between RBs and outcomes that are critical for companies is a central reason that the RB concept has gained widespread acceptance. Furthermore, though increasing loyalty or satisfaction is a good goal for an organization, that alone cannot provide the type of "street-level" guidance that service managers need. As constructs that operate at the operational level, RBs appeal more to managers than do abstract constructs, such as customer satisfaction, in terms of their implementation on the firm's front line.

Our review of RB literature also leads us to believe that, though researchers have gained substantial knowledge on this topic during the past 15 years, much remains to be learned. The intent of this review has been to describe the state of our knowledge on the topic and provide some thoughts as to what paths further research on this topic might take. We hope this examination of RBs piques the interest of additional researchers who will pursue further knowledge of these issues in their research efforts.

REFERENCES

Baker, Thomas L., Penny M. Simpson and Judy A. Siguaw (1999), "The Impact of Suppliers' Perceptions of Reseller Market Orientation on Key Relationship Constructs," *Journal of the Academy of Marketing Science*, 27 (Winter), 50–57.

Berenguer-Contrí, Gloria, María-Eugenia Ruiz-Molina and Irene Gil-Saura (2009), "Relationship Benefits and Costs in Retailing: A Cross-Industry Comparison," *Journal of Retail and Leisure Property*, 8(1), 57–66.

Bitner, Mary J. (1992), "Servicescapes: The Impact of Physical Surroundings on Customers and Employees," *Journal of Marketing*, 56 (April), 57–71.

Burnham, Thomas A., Judy K. Frels and Vijay Mahajan (2003), "Consumer Switching Costs:

A Typology, Antecedents, and Consequences," *Journal of the Academy of Marketing Science*, 31 (Spring), 109–26.

Chang, Yu-Hern and Fang-Yuan Chen (2007), "Relational Benefits, Switching Barriers and Loyalty: A Study of Airline Customers in Taiwan," *Journal of Air Transport Management*, 13, 104–09.

Colgate, Mark, Margo Buchanan-Oliver and Ross Elmsly (2005), "Relationship Benefits in an Internet Environment," *Managing Service Quality*, 15(5), 426–36.

Colgate, Mark, Vicky Thuy-Uyen Tong, Christina Kwai-Choi Lee and John U. Farley (2007), "Back from the Brink – Why Customers Stay," *Journal of Service Research*, 9 (February), 211–28.

Coulter, Robin A. and Mark Ligas (2004), "A Typology of Customer–Service Provider Relationships: The Role of Relational Factors in Classifying Customers," *Journal of Services Marketing*, 18(6), 482–93.

Crosby, Lawrence A., Kenneth R. Evans and Deborah Cowles (1990), "Relationship Quality in Services Selling: An Interpersonal Influence Perspective," *Journal of Marketing*, 54 (July), 68–81.

Danaher, Peter J., Denise M. Conroy and Janet R. McColl-Kennedy (2008), "Who Wants a Relationship Anyway? Conditions When Consumers Expect a Relationship with Their Provider," *Journal of Service Research*, 11 (August), 43–62.

Dorsch, Michael J., Scott R. Swanson and Scott W. Kelley (1998), "The Role of Relationship Quality in the Stratification of Vendors as Perceived by Customers," *Journal of the Academy of Marketing Science*, 26 (Spring), 128–42.

Fournier, Susan (1998), "Consumers and Their Brands: Developing Relationship Theory in Consumer Research," *Journal of Consumer Research*, 24 (March), 343–73.

Garbarino, Ellen and Mark S. Johnson (1999), "The Different Roles of Satisfaction, Trust, and Commitment in Customer Relationships," *Journal of Marketing*, 63 (April), 70–87.

Grayson, Kent (2007), "Friendship versus Business in Marketing Relationships," *Journal of Marketing*, 71 (October), 121–39.

Gwinner, Kevin, Dwayne D. Gremler and Mary Jo Bitner (1998), "Relational Benefits in Services Industries: The Customer's Perspective," *Journal of the Academy of Marketing Science*, 26 (Spring), 101–14.

Hennig-Thurau, Thorsten, Kevin P. Gwinner and Dwayne D. Gremler (2000), "Why Customers Build Relationships with Companies – and Why Not," in Thorsten Hennig-Thurau and Ursula Hansen (eds.), *Relationship Marketing: Gaining Competitive Advantage through Customer Satisfaction and Customer Retention*, Berlin: Springer, pp. 369–91.

Hennig-Thurau, Thorsten, Kevin P. Gwinner and Dwayne D. Gremler (2002), "Understanding Relationship Marketing Outcomes: An Integration of Relational Benefits and Relationship Quality," *Journal of Service Research*, 4 (February), 230–47.

Hennig-Thurau, Thorsten, Kevin P. Gwinner, Dwayne D. Gremler and Michael Paul (2005), "Managing Service Relationships in a Global Economy: Exploring the Impact of National Culture on the Relevance of Customer Relational Benefits for Gaining Loyal Customers," *Advances in International Marketing: Research on International Service Marketing – a State of the Art*, 15, 11–31.

Jarvis, Cheryl Burke, Scott B. MacKenzie and Philip M. Podsakoff (2003), "A Critical Review of Construct Indicators and Measurement Model Misspecification in Marketing and Consumer Research," *Journal of Consumer Research*, 30 (September), 199–218.

Jones, Michael A., David L. Mothersbaugh and Sharon E. Beatty (2000), "Switching Barriers and Repurchase Intentions in Services," *Journal of Retailing*, 76 (Summer), 259–74.

Jones, Michael A., David L. Mothersbaugh and Sharon E. Beatty (2002), "Why Customers Stay: Measuring the Underlying Dimensions of Services Switching Costs and Managing Their Differential Strategic Outcomes," *Journal of Business Research*, 55, 441–50.

Jones, Michael A., Kristy E. Reynolds, David L. Mothersbaugh and Sharon E. Beatty (2007), "The Positive and Negative Effects of Switching Costs on Relational Outcomes," *Journal of Service Research*, 9 (May), 335–55.

Kinard, Brian R. and Michael L. Capella (2006), "Relationship Marketing: The Influence of Consumer Involvement on Perceived Service Benefits," *Journal of Services Marketing*, 20(6), 359–68.

Lacey, Russell, Jaebeom Suh and Robert M. Morgan (2007), "Differential Effects of Preferential Treatment Levels on Relational Outcomes," *Journal of Service Research*, 9 (February), 241–56.

Lin, Neng-Pai, James C.M. Weng and Yi-Ching Hsieh (2003), "Relational Bonds and Customer's Trust and Commitment – a Study on the Moderating Effects of Web Site Usage," *Service Industries Journal*, 23 (May), 103–24.

MacKenzie, Scott B., Philip M. Podsakoff and Cheryl Burke Jarvis (2005), "The Problem of Measurement Model Misspecification in Behavioral and Organizational Research and Some Recommended Solutions," *Journal of Applied Psychology*, 90(4), 710–30.

Martín-Consuegra, David, Arturo Molina and Agueda Esteban (2006), "The Customers' Perspective on Relational Benefits in Banking Activities," *Journal of Financial Services Marketing*, 10(4), 98–108.

Martín-Ruiz, David, Carmen Barroso Castro and Enrique Martín Armario (2007), "Explaining Market Heterogeneity in Terms of Value Perceptions," *Service Industries Journal*, 27(8), 1–24.

Martín-Ruiz, David, Dwayne D. Gremler, Judith H. Washburn and Gabriel Cepeda Carrión (2008), "Service Value Revisited: Specifying a Higher-Order, Formative Measure," *Journal of Business Research*, 61(12), 1278–91.

Marzo-Navarro, Mercedes, Marta Pedraja-Iglesias and Ma Pilar Rivera-Torres (2004), "The Benefits of Relationship Marketing for the Consumer and for the Fashion Retailers," *Journal of Fashion Marketing and Management*, 8(4), 425–36.

Molina, Arturo, David Martín-Consuegra and Águeda Esteban (2007), "Relational Benefits and Customer Satisfaction in Retail Banking," *International Journal of Bank Marketing*, 25(4), 253–71.

MSI (Marketing Science Institute) (2008), "MSI Research Priorities 2008–2010," http://www.msi.org/pdf/MSI_RP08–10.pdf (accessed August 15, 2009).

Noble, Stephanie M. and Joanna Phillips (2004), "Relationship Hindrance: Why Would Consumers Not Want a Relationship with a Retailer?," *Journal of Retailing*, 80 (Winter), 289–303.

Oldenburg, Ray (1991), *The Great Good Place*, New York: Paragon House.

Palmer, Adrian and David Bejou (1994), "Buyer–Seller Relationships: A Conceptual Model and Empirical Investigation," *Journal of Marketing Management*, 10(6), 495–512.

Parasuraman, A., Valarie A. Zeithaml and Leonard L. Berry (1988), "SERVQUAL: A Multiple-Item Scale for Measuring Consumer Perceptions of Service Quality," *Journal of Retailing*, 64 (Spring), 12–40.

Parish, Janet Turner, Leonard L. Berry and Shun Yin Lam (2008), "The Effect of the Servicescape on Service Workers," *Journal of Service Research*, 10 (February), 220–38.

Park, Chung-Hoon and Young-Gul Kim (2003), "Identifying Key Factors Affecting Consumer Purchase Behavior in an Online Shopping Context," *International Journal of Retail and Distribution Management*, 31(1), 16–29.

Patterson, Paul G. and Tasman Smith (2001), "Relationship Benefits in Service Industries: A Replication in a Southeast Asian Context," *Journal of Services Marketing*, 16(6), 425–43.

Patterson, Paul G. and Tasman Smith (2003), "A Cross-Cultural Study of Switching Barriers and Propensity to Stay with Service Providers," *Journal of Retailing*, 79 (Summer), 107–20.

Paul, Michael, Thorsten Hennig-Thurau, Dwayne D. Gremler, Kevin P. Gwinner and Caroline Wiertz (2009), "Toward a Theory of Repeated Purchase Drivers for Consumer Services," *Journal of the Academy of Marketing Science*, 37(2), 215–37.

Rao, Ramesh K.S. and Neeraj Bharadwaj (2008), "Marketing Initiatives, Expected Cash Flows, and Shareholders' Wealth," *Journal of Marketing*, 72 (January), 16–26.

Reynolds, Kristy E. and Sharon E. Beatty (1999), "Customer Benefits and Company Consequences of Customer–Salesperson Relationships in Retailing," *Journal of Retailing*, 75 (Spring), 11–32.

Rosenbaum, Mark (2006), "Exploring the Social Supportive Role of Third Places in Consumers' Lives," *Journal of Service Research*, 9 (August), 1–14.

Rust, Roland T., Katherine N. Lemon and Valarie A. Zeithaml (2004), "Return on Marketing: Using Customer Equity to Focus Marketing Strategy," *Journal of Marketing*, 68 (January), 109–27.

Smith, J. Brock (1998), "Buyer–Seller Relationships: Similarity, Relationship Management, and Quality," *Psychology and Marketing*, 15(1), 3–21.

Spake, Deborah F., Sharon E. Beatty, Beverly K. Brockman and Tammy Neal Crutchfield (2003), "Consumer Comfort in Service Relationships: Measurement and Importance," *Journal of Service Research*, 5 (May), 316–32.

Sweeney, Jillian C. and Geoffrey N. Soutar (2001), "Consumer Perceived Value: The Development of a Multiple Item Scale," *Journal of Retailing*, 77 (Summer), 203–20.

Sweeney, Jillian C. and Dave Webb (2002), "Relationship Benefits: An Exploration of Buyer–Supplier Dyads," *Journal of Relationship Marketing*, 1(2), 77–92.

Tombs, Alastair and Janet R. McColl-Kennedy (2003), "Social-Servicescape Conceptual Model," *Marketing Theory*, 3(4), 447–75.

Turley, L.W. and Ronald E. Milliman (2000), "Atmospheric Effects on Shopping Behavior: A Review of the Experimental Evidence," *Journal of Business Research*, 49, 193–211.

Vázquez-Carrasco, Rosario and Gordon R. Foxall (2006), "Positive vs. Negative Switching Barriers: The Influence of Service Consumers' Need for Variety," *Journal of Consumer Behavior*, 5 (July–August), 367–79.

Wagner, Tillmann, Thorsten Hennig-Thurau and Thomas Rudolph (2009), "Does Customer Demotion Jeopardize Loyalty?," *Journal of Marketing*, 73 (May), 69–85.

Xu, Yingzi, Robert Goedegebuure and Beatrice van der Heijden (2006), "Customer Perception, Customer Satisfaction, and Customer Loyalty within Chinese Securities Business: Towards a Mediation Model for Predicting Customer Behavior," *Journal of Relationship Marketing*, 5(4), 79–104.

Yen, Hsiu Ju Rebecca and Kevin P. Gwinner (2003), "Internet Retail Customer Loyalty: The Mediating Role of Relational Benefits," *International Journal of Service Industry Management*, 14(5), 483–500.

Zeithaml, Valarie A. (1988), "Consumer Perceptions of Price, Quality, and Value: A Means–End Model and Synthesis of Evidence," *Journal of Marketing*, 52 (July), 2–22.

Zinkhan, George M. (2005), "Scientific Status and Knowledge Use: Two Perspectives," *Journal of the Academy of Marketing Science*, 33 (Summer), 251–3.

4. Advances in customer value management
Peter C. Verhoef and Katherine N. Lemon

INTRODUCTION

One of the key developments in marketing and management practice in the last decade has been the growth of customer relationship management (CRM). Many firms have invested in large customer databases to understand, monitor and influence customer behavior (Boulding et al. 2005). "CRM is defined as the practice of analyzing and utilizing marketing databases and leveraging communication technologies to determine corporate practices and methods that will maximize the lifetime value of each individual customer" (Kumar and Reinartz 2005: 5). One of the critical aspects in this definition is the role of customer value, which is the economic value of the customer relationship for the firm. Therefore, other researchers also use the term "customer value management" (CVM), which:

> entails the optimization of the value of a company's customer base. CVM focuses on the analysis of individual data on prospects and customers. The resulting information is used to acquire and retain customers, and to drive customer behavior with the developed marketing strategies in such a way that the value of all current and future customers is optimized. (Verhoef, van Doorn et al. 2007)

CVM conceptually has its roots within relationship marketing. Relationship marketing has mainly focused on measuring constructs, such as commitment and trust, which create successful relationships with customers (R.M. Morgan and Hunt 1994). Customer data are not essential within relationship marketing. In that sense CVM enriches relationship marketing, with its primary focus on the analysis of customer data and explicitly seeking data-driven ways to enhance customer value. Important developments in information and communication technology – allowing firms to build large customer databases with real-time access at customer touch points – and the development of strong software packages for analyzing these data have accelerated interest in and application of CVM. Companies such as Capital One, Harrah's Entertainment, UK-based retailer Tesco and the Dutch mobile phone operator KPN have as a consequence heavily invested in CVM.

In this chapter we first aim to discuss the CVM process. Next, we elaborate on some important issues within CVM, which include customer-centric management, customer data, customer intelligence as the backbone of successful CVM, customer metrics, and CVM and performance. Subsequently, we discuss some important new directions in CVM, such as going beyond current customer metrics, engaging customers in relationships and the dynamics of these relationships, and customer networks.

THE CVM PROCESS

In CVM, understanding and optimizing the value of a firm's customer base is one of the core goals. Companies can increase the value of their customer base by 1) attracting new customers, 2) increasing customer retention, 3) creating customer expansion, 4) winning back old customers, 5) (active) relationship termination and 6) effective resource allocation among customers (Bolton et al. 2004; Reinartz et al. 2004; Venkatesan and Kumar 2004). This should occur in a balanced and coordinated manner. Firms focusing too much on customer retention and neglecting customer acquisition will at some point face difficulties because their customer base becomes too "old."

The CVM process is displayed in Figure 4.1. One central element of CVM is customer data analysis. Customer strategies flow out of the data analysis. These strategies may concern acquisition activities, marketing campaigns, customer service plans and multi-channel management. The customer strategies influence customer acquisition and the behavior of current customers. These strategies come at a cost. Activities are formulated so that scarce marketing resources are allocated to customers in such a way that more value is created (Venkatesan and Kumar 2004). The net end result is thus that the customer lifetime value (CLV) should increase, which should finally be translated to increased firm value (Gupta et al. 2004).

FROM PRODUCT-CENTRIC TO CUSTOMER-CENTRIC

A crucial element of CVM is that it assumes a customer-centric approach. Although focusing on customers and creating value for customers have been a central element of marketing, many firms still have a product-centric orientation.

Product-centric approaches are commonly found in manufacturer-based businesses, where the main activities are to sell branded prod-

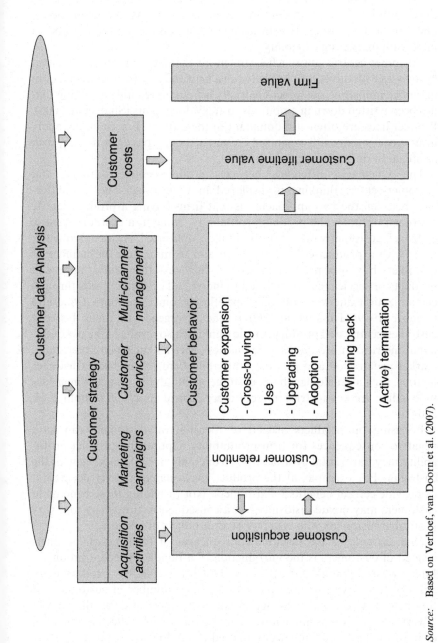

Source: Based on Verhoef, van Doorn et al. (2007).

Figure 4.1   The CVM process

ucts through intermediary channels, such as retailers. Examples include global companies, such as Procter & Gamble, Nestlé and Unilever. In these industries the product-centric approach remains dominant; developing innovative products with distinctive brands will continue to be an important marketing capability.

Customer-centric approaches are more common in service-oriented businesses with direct contacts between a firm and its customers. Still, even in service industries, customer-centricity is frequently only something that has been written down in ambitious strategy documents (Shah et al. 2006). Product lines are often still dominant in these firms. For example, many insurance firms are still organized around distinct types of insurance, such as life, auto or health insurance.

The schematic difference between product-centric thinking and customer-centric thinking is displayed in Figure 4.2. The key difference between the two approaches is that firms having a product-centric approach optimize the product profitability, while in a customer-centric approach customer value or profitability is optimized. As a consequence, firms with a product-centric approach aim to maximize the number of customers buying a product or service. In a customer-centric approach products or services can be tailored to individual customer needs through customization and/or developing specific customer solutions (Pine and Gilmore 1999; Tuhli et al. 2007). The divergence in focus between customer-centric and product-centric thinking also results in the use of different metrics. In product-centric business, metrics such as market share, market penetration and product profitability are key metrics. Customer metrics, such as customer share, customer profitability and customer lifetime value, are key metrics in a customer-centric approach (Gupta et al. 2004).

Focusing on products instead of focusing on customers can have negative consequences for firm profitability. Optimizing product profitability may harm total profitability, as one only has a limited view of the customer. For example, at the product level, managers may decide not to provide certain benefits to customers. Not providing these benefits to customers may create disloyalty. As a consequence, firms may lose very profitable customers who also buy other products or services.

One example of the negative consequences of focusing on products instead of customers is the introduction of a bundled telecom product – Internet (broadband) and calls – by Dutch-based KPN. Product managers of this service focused on getting a large number of customers for this new service. The introduction was very successful, as the heavily advertised service was much lower priced than an unbundled combination of both Internet and calls (using the old technology). As a consequence,

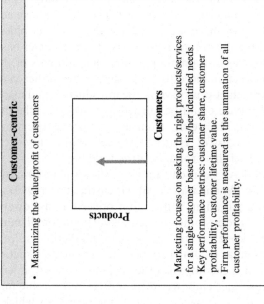

Product-centric	Customer-centric
• Maximizing the value/profit of products and services	• Maximizing the value/profit of customers

Product-centric

Products → Customers

• Marketing is focused on seeking the maximum number of customers for a single product/service.
• Key performance metrics: market share, product penetration, product profitability.
• Firm performance is measured as the summation of product/service profitability.

Customer-centric

Customers ← Products

• Marketing focuses on seeking the right products/services for a single customer based on his/her identified needs.
• Key performance metrics: customer share, customer profitability, customer lifetime value.
• Firm performance is measured as the summation of all customer profitability.

Source: Adapted from Bügel (2006).

Figure 4.2   From product-centric to customer-centric

operations could not handle the demand, owing to a lack of capacity, and customer service problems arose. However, this strategy also meant that many current customers who were using old technology calls were stimulated to move to a much cheaper service. They would have adopted this new service at some point anyway, but probably in a later phase. The net result was dissatisfaction among large parts of the customer base, and customer profitability was lost among potential late adopters of the new service who were, in effect, induced to adopt this service earlier in its life-cycle. Hence, from a product-centric view, the introduction and marketing of this new bundled service could be labeled as a success – the product manager reached targets. However, from a customer-centric view, this introduction was not successful. Hence, customer profitability decreased substantially as a result of this product-centric thinking.

Scientifically, there have been enormous pledges for more customer-centric approaches (e.g., Shah et al. 2006). Hoekstra et al. (1999) argued that there should be a paradigm shift within organizations towards the customer concept, with the customer as the starting point for all marketing actions. Empirical evidence on customer-centric marketing is, however, scarce. Ramani and Kumar (2008) introduce the customer interaction orientation construct, which encompasses the customer concept, interaction response capacity, customer empowerment and customer value management. Interaction response capacity involves the degree to which firms offer successive products, services and relationship experiences to each customer by dynamically incorporating feedback from previous behavioral responses of that customer and other customers collectively. Customer empowerment is defined as the extent to which a firm provides its customers with avenues 1) to connect with the firm and actively shape the nature of transactions and 2) to connect and collaborate with each other by sharing information, praise, criticism, suggestions and ideas about its products and services (Ramani and Kumar 2008: 28–9). They empirically demonstrate the existence of this construct and they also show that firms having a high interaction orientation tend to have a higher customer performance (i.e., satisfaction, positive word of mouth), which is positively related to firm performance. This especially holds in markets where the customer initiates more contacts with a firm. They also show that interaction orientation is higher when 1) firms rely more on customer metrics for evaluating and rewarding customers, 2) firms do more outsourcing and 3) firms feel more institutional pressures to adopt interactive technologies (i.e., the Internet). Interaction orientation is lower when firms depend more on trademark and patent protection. The latter suggests that, for firms emphasizing brand management, customer interaction orientation will be lower.

In sum, there is some evidence that a customer-centric approach increases business performance. However, given that the reported study uses cross-sectional data, this evidence is not conclusive, as only conclusions regarding associations (and not causation) can be drawn. Essentially, surveyed customer-centric firms have a higher performance than firms having no customer-centric focus. There is no research suggesting that firms moving from a more product-centric approach to a customer-centric approach indeed start to increase their performance. This would be an important future research issue. We also do not know much about which factors drive a successful transformation towards customer-centricity. Finally, despite some initial evidence on moderating factors of the relationship between customer-centricity and performance (Ramani and Kumar 2008), there is a lack of research on the circumstances under which firms should make this transformation.

CUSTOMER DATA

CVM requires customer data. We broadly distinguish between the following data types: 1) customer descriptors, 2) transaction data, 3) customer contact data, 4) marketing contact data, 5) customer characteristics, 6) customer attitudes and 7) derived customer data.

Customer descriptors involve all characteristics required for contacting customers. These data involve: name, address, zip code, phone number and e-mail address. Transaction data concern all data on customers' transactions with the firm and may involve variables such as the last time of purchase, the type of product purchased, the monetary value of the purchase, the transaction channel and product returns. Customer contact data involve data on the customer-initiated contact history, such as information requests, website visits and so on. Marketing contacts are firm-initiated contacts and may involve the number of mailings sent, timing of mailings and loyalty program membership. Customer characteristics concern additional information on the customer on socio-demographics, psychographics, lifestyle and so on. Some of these data may arise from internal sources. External data suppliers also provide this information at different levels of aggregation. Customer attitude data concern data on customer satisfaction and other attitudes such as commitment. These data are usually not present for all customers. Finally, firms can derive data, such as share of wallet and total monetary value of a customer (based on all past values of transactions, e.g., Du et al. 2007).

Verhoef et al. (2003) and a replication study (Hoekstra et al. 2008) have investigated the presence of data types for Dutch firms. Customer descriptors and transaction data are the most frequently stored in customer databases. Between 2003 and 2008, a strong increase in the presence of all types of variables was observed. This reflects the fact that firms had been successful in setting up complete data warehouses, in which information for all kinds of databases were being integrated.

Data quality is important for shaping performance in CVM strategies (Zahay and Griffin 2002; Jayachandran et al. 2005). However, the question is whether firms should have an extremely high level of data quality with perfectly complete data, no data mistakes and 100 percent up-to-date data. Neslin et al. (2006) propose that there might an optimum level (see Figure 4.3). Achieving good data quality comes at a cost. However, these costs may rise in a non-linear fashion when higher levels of data quality are achieved, while the return in terms of increased customer value from this data quality may actually decrease in a non-linear fashion. This implies that firms should assess the optimum level of data quality and not necessarily pursue a 100 percent score.

Related to the issue of data quality is the provision of customer data. Individual data are collected in different ways. The direct nature of the business models of cataloguers and online retailers allows them to associate transactions with customers in their databases. Most firms, however, face difficulties linking transactions to individual customers unless they have a loyalty program or a specific CRM system designed to track and link such data. Several issues then become prevalent. First, are customers willing to provide the data, as customers may have privacy concerns? A few studies in the direct marketing and public policy literature have investigated privacy issues (e.g., see Peltier et al. 2009). One general finding is that only a limited percentage of customers – privacy activists – tend to worry about their privacy (e.g., Fletcher, 2003; van Doorn, Verhoef, & Bijmolt, 2007). Despite the existence of privacy concerns, their effect on the provision of data (e.g., participating in loyalty programs) is not strong (van Doorn et al. 2007).

On customer data, important research issues remain prevalent. First, there is still a lack of empirical research on the data quality and data integration. So far, only conceptual insights are present, but can we infer an optimal level that may be contingent on customer strategies, customer behavior and competition? Furthermore, the rich data availability on websites and resulting behavioral targeting may create worries about privacy and potentially may cause customer reactance (White et al. 2008). We believe that, owing to the noted developments in retail practice, privacy should gain more attention in the general marketing literature.

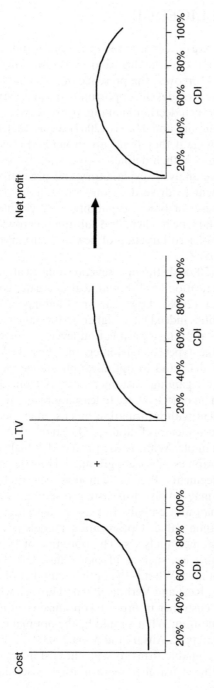

Note: LTV: lifetime value; CDI: customer data information.

Source: Neslin et al. (2006).

Figure 4.3   Net benefits of investing in data quality

CUSTOMER INTELLIGENCE

Managers often tend to make decisions based on intuition and experience. However, in a more complex world this kind of decision making may lead to wrong decisions. Moreover, the presence of more data on many processes within a business provides the opportunity for more intelligence-based decision making. In such decision making, firms heavily rely on the analytical function. Davenport and Harris (2007) argue that firms can gain a competitive advantage if they build up strong and effective analytical capabilities. Analytics is then defined as the extensive use of data, statistical and quantitative analysis, explanatory and predictive models, and fact-based management to drive decisions and actions (Davenport and Harris 2005: 7). These analytical capabilities are essential within CVM. For example, Capital One has achieved substantial growth through a more effective analytical-based targeting of new and current customers (Kumar and Reinartz 2005).

Davenport and Harris (2005) distinguish several sophistication levels of analytics. A higher sophistication level should lead to greater competitive advantage. Hoekstra et al. (2008) show that firms having superior customer intelligence capabilities indeed have higher performance. Following the above general classification in sophistication levels of customer analytics, we distinguish three types of customer analytics: 1) knowledge creation; 2) predictive models; and 3) optimization models. Knowledge creation mainly focuses on gaining customer insights from descriptive statistical analyses. The main objectives are to learn more about customers and to provide management with information on customer metrics, such as retention rates and customer profitability. Questions that are being answered concern, for example: What is the profile of a high-value customer in terms of demographics or psychographics? How do churn rates differ between customer segments? Predictive models focus on forecasting customer behavior. This may involve forecasting response to marketing actions, such as direct mail and e-mails, but also forecasting of churn, product returns and lifetime value. Optimization models are the most sophisticated level of customer analytics. The objective of these models is to optimize customer metrics, such as lifetime value. Questions to be answered concern, for example: What is the optimal number of mailers to be sent to a customer (e.g., Rust and Verhoef 2005)? Through which channels should we contact a customer in order to optimize customer value? It may also involve the question: What should be the optimal customized offer in a customized e-mail (e.g., Ansari and Mela 2003)?

Customer analytics also enable firms to segment customers effectively based upon customer value. Customer segmentation based upon CLV and/or customer profitability is being used in many industries. Firms are expanding on traditional bases of segmentation (e.g., demographic, socio-economic, psychographic) to incorporate customer purchase data into such segmentation models (Johnson and Selnes 2004, 2005). Lemon and Mark (2006) define CLV-based segmentation as "a segmentation approach used by a firm that groups customers into meaningful segments based upon customer lifetime value and potentially other factors" (2006: 58). They suggest that this process typically includes the following steps:

1. Gather data to analyze current and potential profitability of existing customers.
2. Develop a firm-specific model for CLV.
3. Categorize customers based upon CLV, and use these groups, along with other factors, as the segmentation scheme.
4. Develop segment-specific marketing approaches, allocating additional resources to segments with high CLV, and fewer resources to low or negative CLV segments.

Future research may conceptually and empirically provide more insights on the important role of customer analytics and how customer analytics is actually used within marketing. It is especially important to investigate the interface between the customer analytics department and the marketing department. Marketers must become adjusted to more analytic- and fact-based decision making. Similarly, customer analysts are required to understand marketing problems.

CUSTOMER METRICS

Customer metrics are of essential importance within CVM, as use of these metrics allows customers to be evaluated and the success of customer strategies to be determined. Firms are interested in several customer metrics. In general, one distinguishes between attitudinal metrics and behavioral/ financial customer metrics (see Table 4.1). Attitudinal customer metrics involve metrics such as customer satisfaction, likelihood to recommend and payment equity. These metrics are positively related to customer behavior and business performance (see Gupta and Zeithaml 2006 for an overview). Links with performance metrics can be non-linear, and in some industries (i.e., with high switching costs) they might be absent. Rust et al. (2004) distinguish between value equity, relationship equity and brand equity. Whereas value equity focuses on the objective value of the service through its delivered quality, price and convenience, brand equity focuses

Table 4.1   Overview of customer metrics

Type	Metric	Definition
Attitudinal metrics	Satisfaction	An overall evaluation based on the customers' total purchase and consumption experience within the relationship (Anderson et al. 1994).
	Trust	Customers' confidence in the quality and reliability of the services provided (Garbarino and Johnson 1999).
	Payment equity	Customers' perceived fairness of the price paid for their consumed products or services (Bolton and Lemon 1999).
	Commitment	The extent to which a customer believes that an ongoing relationship with the company is so important as to warrant maximum efforts at maintaining it (R.M. Morgan and Hunt 1994).
	Value equity	The customer's objective assessment of the utility of a brand based on perceptions of what is given up for what is received. Sub-drivers of value equity include quality, price and convenience.
	Brand equity	The customer's subjective and intangible assessment of the brand, above and beyond its objectively perceived value. Sub-drivers of brand equity include brand awareness, customer brand perceptions and brand associations, and perceptions of brand ethics.
	Relationship equity	The customer's assessment of interactions with the brand, above and beyond objective and subjective assessments of the brand. Sub-drivers of relationship equity include salesperson and serviceperson relationships, loyalty programs, customer communities and knowledge of the customer.
	Net promoter score	The percentage of promoters minus the percentage of detractors.
	Loyalty intentions	The extent to which customers intend to remain loyal to a firm.
Behavioral metrics	Churn or defection rate	The percentage of customers leaving a firm (Neslin et al. 2006).
	Retention rate	The percentage of customers remaining customers of a firm (1 less the churn rate) (Verhoef 2003).
	Relationship duration	The time since the start of the relationship (Bolton 1998).

Table 4.1   (continued)

Type	Metric	Definition
	Cross-buying	The amount of additional products or services a customer purchases in a specific time period (Verhoef et al. 2001).
	Service usage	The customers' usage level of a specific service (i.e. number of calling minutes) (Bolton and Lemon 1999).
	Upgrade	The extent to which a customer upgrades current products or services to higher levels (Bolton et al. 2008).
	Customer share	The percentage of products or services of his or her total purchase that a customer purchases at a specific firm in a specific category (Verhoef 2003).
	Purchase recency	The time since last purchase.
	Purchase frequency	The number of purchases or transactions in a specific time period (i.e., year).
Financial metrics	Customer revenue	The total customers' monetary revenue in a specific time period (i.e., year).
	Customer profitability	The total customers' net revenue (revenue less costs) in a specific time period (i.e., year).
	Customer lifetime value	The expected net present value of all customers' future profits or earnings (Bolton et al. 2004).
	Customer equity	The sum of all current customers' and future customers' (prospects) customer lifetime values (Rust et al. 2004).

on the mere emotional value delivered through the brand. Relationship equity focuses on the customers' evaluation of the relationship and specific interactions that the customer has with the firm and the brand. Empirically, these metrics have been linked to loyalty intentions, customer choice, customer lifetime value and overall customer equity (e.g., Rust et al. 2004; Verhoef, Langerak et al. 2007; Vogel et al. 2008).

Another frequently discussed attitudinal metric is likelihood to recommend and more specifically the net promoter score (NPS; Reichheld 2003). To measure NPS, customers are asked to what extent they would recommend a firm to other customers. Based on these questions, customers are grouped into three segments: promoters, neutral consumers and detractors. NPS is then calculated by subtracting the percentage of detractors from percentage of promoters. In today's networked society, NPS is believed to be a crucial metric, as customers interact frequently with each other through social communities (e.g., Kozinets 1999; de Valck 2005). Bain Consulting especially has marketed this metric successfully in practice (e.g., Reichheld 2003). It advocated that NPS is the "one number a firm needs to grow." Companies around the globe, such as Philips and GE, have embraced this metric.

Within the academic literature there has been an extensive discussion on whether this metric is indeed superior to traditional customer satisfaction metrics (N.A. Morgan and Rego 2006). Keiningham et al. (2007) executed a study in which they compare the predictive performance of these two metrics for business performance. Their conclusion is that NPS cannot be considered a superior metric and thus that the claims of Reichheld (2003) that NPS is the "ultimate metric" required in business are at least exaggerated. Though this might academically be true, large multinationals are still adopting this metric. An important issue, however, is whether the NPS metric can be compared across countries, industries and so on. Methodological cross-cultural research has emphasized the existence of differences in the prevalence of response styles (e.g., yea-saying) around the globe (e.g., Steenkamp and de Jong 2010). Despite these methodological concerns, NPS may still be a metric of importance for firms, especially in business-to-business relationships. For example, a large American construction management firm, Gilbane, utilizes NPS as a key metric. As it is a project-based firm, recommendations are critical, because it may complete only a single project for a client, and yet over 70 percent of its new business comes from recommendations and referrals (Gilbane 2009). It is clearly a metric with some initial face validity. Moreover, adopting this metric within different layers of the firm might enhance a firm's customer-centricity (e.g., Shah et al. 2006).

Behavioral metrics can be retrieved from the customer database. These metrics concern actual behavioral outcomes of a customer relationship and may involve the length (i.e., retention), breadth (i.e., cross-buying) and depth (i.e., usage) of the relationship (Bolton et al. 2004). Firms might also be more interested in traditional direct marketing metrics, such as recency of last purchase and purchase frequency (e.g., Reinartz and Kumar 2000; Venkatesan and Kumar 2004). The advantage of behavioral metrics is that these metrics do not suffer from measurement error. However, one disadvantage is that a mere focus on behavioral outcomes may detract attention away from the underlying customers' motives. Therefore, authors have proposed frameworks linking attitudinal metrics to behavioral metrics (e.g., Bolton et al. 2004; Vogel et al. 2008). One important question is whether behavioral metrics indeed measure loyalty.

In this respect, authors have proposed combining behavioral metrics with attitudinal metrics to distinguish between true and spurious loyalty (Dick and Basu 1994), where truly loyal customers score high on behavioral and attitudinal customer metrics.

The focus on accountability within firms has urged marketers to search for more metrics that can be linked to financial performance metrics and shareholder value (Lehmann 2004; Verhoef and Leeflang 2009). This might explain the increasing importance of financial customer metrics. Customer lifetime value especially has received considerable attention in the academic literature. CLV is defined as the discounted value of all expected future customer profits in a determined time period (Bolton et al. 2004). The underlying idea is that customers can be considered to be important assets of the company, who should be cultivated and activated (Srivastava et al. 1998; Hogan et al. 2002). CLV is thus calculated based on future expectations of customers' profit margins, retention rate, cross-buying behavior and so on.

Several authors have proposed methods to calculate and predict CLV (Berger and Nasr 1998). Donkers et al. (2007) compare different econometric models to predict CLV in the insurance industry and, remarkably, report that a simple model assuming constant customer profits over time predicts as well as more advanced models accounting for retention and cross-buying behavior. Multiple other researchers who have aimed to build advanced models to predict CLV have experienced difficulties providing an exact, individual CLV prediction (e.g., Rust et al. 2007). However, researchers have shown that using CLV as an optimization metric leads to more effective allocation of marketing resources across customers, which improves financial performance (Venkatesan and Kumar 2004). This suggests that knowing the exact CLV is not that important, but that an approximation of CLV can enable firms to allocate marketing resources in a more effective way.

CLV has also been linked to shareholder value. Gupta et al. (2004) have shown that, for specific firms (e.g., Capital One), the total customer equity for a customer base is close to the actual value of the firm at the stock market. However, for certain firms, such as eBay, this did not hold. One potential reason is that CLV calculations do not take network effects into account. Actual insights from their calculations also show that improving churn has the strongest impact on CLV. However, insights on CLV and shareholder value are still very limited. There is clearly more research required on this topic.

One important issue with regard to CLV predictions and their link with shareholder value is environmental turbulence. Models are always based on past data, which may only slightly reflect changes in the environment.

Risselada et al. (2010) show that churn prediction models – frequently used as input for CLV predictions – have only limited staying power. In today's turbulent economic times, CLV predictions might be an uncertain exercise, while linking them to shareholder value might be even more ambitious in volatile financial markets. From a future research perspective, clearly more insights are required on how models can be adapted to account for environmental turbulence. For this purpose, data covering longer time horizons could be used that take into account the possibility that model parameters might vary over time and might be affected by environmental developments.

CVM AND PERFORMANCE

CVM can improve business performance in three ways: 1) CVM is a market-based resource for a competitive advantage; 2) CVM increases a firm's customer-centric orientation; and 3) CVM leads to more accountable marketing (see Figure 4.4).

CVM provides firms with sustainable competitive advantage. Firms constantly seek competitive advantages. The customer database and existing customer relationships are considered to be important market-based resources (Srivastava et al. 1998). These relationships are hard to develop and difficult to copy. Research shows that a database focusing on customer acquisition and customer retention improves business performance (Reinartz et al. 2004; Jayachandran et al. 2005).

CVM creates a stronger focus on the customer, as CVM requires a customer-centric focus. Moreover, CVM provides firms with extensive customer knowledge. There is extensive research showing that firms with a customer-oriented focus tend to have a higher performance than firms without such a focus (Kirca et al. 2005). Moreover, as discussed previously, Ramani and Kumar (2008) show a positive relationship between a customer-centric focus and performance.

CVM leads to more analytical and fact-based decision making within firms and a stronger focus on the return on investment (ROI) of marketing decisions. As a consequence, marketing becomes more accountable. Such marketing causes less waste of marketing spending and more effective allocation of the marketing budget over customers and marketing instruments (e.g., Rust et al. 2004; Venkatesan and Kumar 2004). Accountable marketing strategies also improve firm performance (O'Sullivan and Abela 2007).

Future research might aim to integrate the above insights from different studies and test the existence of the model shown below. The shown path

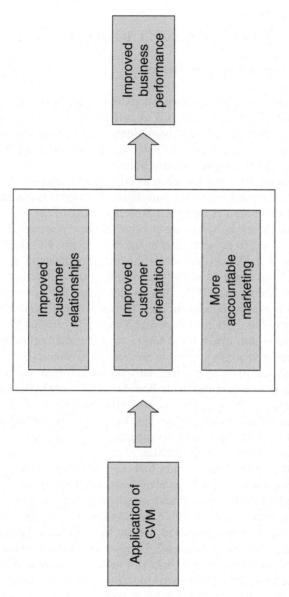

Figure 4.4   Mechanisms through which CVM improves business performance

to improved business performance is based purely on theory. Empirical research should aim to establish the existence of such a path.

NEW DIRECTIONS FOR FUTURE RESEARCH

Going Beyond Present Customer Metrics

In the prior discussion we focused on existing customer metrics. We, however, believe that research in CVM might benefit from theoretical developments in economics and psychology (Zeithaml et al. 2006), in which researchers have developed new insights on the importance of extending the utility paradigm and emotions.

To explain customer behavior, such as customer retention, researchers have frequently adopted the utility paradigm, in which it is assumed that customers maximize their (subjective) expected utility of the relationship. Expected utility theory has a strong background in economics. Expected utility theory started to get criticized in the early 1950s, and there is now an abundance of evidence demonstrating that people tend to deviate systematically from expected utility theory owing to bounded rationality (Starmer 2000; Kahneman 2003). This evidence has led to the development of new non-expected utility models. The most famous and influential model is prospect theory (Kahneman and Tversky 1979). The key insight from this model is that losses loom larger than gains. Insights from this model have been frequently applied in behavioral economics and marketing research in areas such as pricing, satisfaction and customer relationships (e.g., Kalwani and Yim 1992; Boulding et al. 1993; Bolton 1998; Wedel and Leeflang 1998; Verhoef et al. 2001). Beyond the development of non-expected utility models, researchers have suggested broadening the utility concept by including other constructs such as emotions and goal completion (e.g., Frey and Stutzer 2002).

Within the (behavioral) economics literature several other variables as predictors of human behavior have been discussed. They include fairness, happiness, regret and disappointment, goal completion, and status (e.g., Elster 1998; Loewenstein 1999, 2000; Frey and Stutzer 2002). Happiness especially has gained much attention. Regret has also been the subject of multiple investigations (e.g., Bell 1982; Loomes and Sudgen 1982).

Descriptive models for customer behavior have, to some extent, included additional measures already discussed in this section under utility in economics. Customer happiness has not been studied as a specific antecedent of customer behavior. However, if one closely considers specific questions used in economic research, these questions sometimes resemble questions to measure customer satisfaction. For example, the Eurobarometer surveys ask the following question to European citizens: "On the whole, are you very satisfied, fairly satisfied, not very satisfied, or not at all satisfied with the life you lead?" Or questions specifically focus on happiness. Moreover, being happy versus unhappy is sometimes used as an item in multi-item scales to measure satisfaction (e.g., Oliver and Westbrook 1993).

Some studies have included the concept of (anticipated) regret and/ or disappointment as a predictor of customer behavior (Zeelenberg and Pieters 2007). Inman et al. (1997) show the importance of regret as a determinant of post-choice valuation. In an experimental study Lemon et al. (2002) show that anticipated regret influences customer retention so that, when customers are primed to consider the anticipated regret of dropping a service, they are more likely to keep the service. Zeelenberg and Pieters (2004) relate regret, disappointment and (dis)satisfaction to several stated behavioral outcomes, such as customer switching and word of mouth. They report that regret and disappointment have an effect on these behaviors beyond the effect of satisfaction and argue that regret and disappointment should be considered as separate determinants of customer behavior.

Emotion research originated in psychology (e.g. Frijda 1986; Tagney and Fisher 1995) and emotions have been considered in several studies. Already in early satisfaction studies it was considered that satisfaction has both an affective and a cognitive component (e.g., Oliver 1993). Oliver et al. (1997) introduce customer delight as an emotional component of customer satisfaction, which is based on feelings of arousal and surprise (see also Rust and Oliver 2000). They show that customer delight is related to repurchase intentions in a specific service context. This notion has also been used to explain why only high satisfaction scores impact customer behavior (i.e., non-linear effect) (Verhoef and Langerak 2003; Gupta and Zeithaml 2006). At this point it is also not clear how the notion of customer delight differs from customer happiness, as happiness is one of the items used to measure delight. In some recent studies authors have studied the impact of more social emotions, such as pride and anger. Studies have mainly provided evidence for the existence of positive and negative (service) consumption emotions. Positive emotions include aspects such as hope, happiness, joy and surprise, while negative emotions include aspects such as anger, depressiveness and guilt (see Nyer 2007 for an overview). Bougie et al. (2003) report that anger occurring after a service failure is positively related to self-reported customer behavior, such as switching. Moreover, they show that anger mediates the effect of dissatisfaction.

Customer goals and goal completion have gained little attention in studying customer value management. Louro et al. (2005) is one of the few exceptions. Pride can be regarded as an emotional consequence of goal completion. This study experimentally investigates how two types of goal-related pride – *prevention pride* arising from avoiding negative outcomes and *promotion pride* arising from achieving ideals – impact repurchase intentions differently. Their study suggests that (prevention) pride may function as an additional variable for explaining customer behavior. Heitmann et al. (2007) considered how customer goals drive customer satisfaction, which in turn is related to stated customer loyalty (i.e., word of mouth, customer switching). Still, the attention on customer goals in customer value management research is limited. In addition, perceived status as a separate antecedent of customer behavior has gained little attention.

Beyond the adoption of the utility paradigm, researchers in the relationship marketing tradition have considered a mere relational perspective in which they include variables from psychology (Rusbult 1980), such as trust and commitment, as determinants of customer behavior (e.g., De Wulf et al. 2001). Yim et al. (2008) have gone beyond these variables and show the existence of love components (such as intimacy, passion and commitment) in customer relationships (Sternberg 1986). Bügel et al. (2009) show that intimacy and passion can be considered as one construct. Moreover, they show that intimacy is not frequently present in most customer-to-firm relationships in consumer markets.

The above overview of variables is graphically summarized in Figure 4.5. In this figure we distinguish between the discussed relational variables and utility indicators. The utility indicators are classified as traditional cognitive and attribute-based indicators versus extended more emotional and experience-based indicators. The overview suggests that the extended utility indicators potentially could have a stronger predictive power. However, these variables are also less frequently studied. Hence, we believe that future research within CVM should aim to integrate the suggested additional metrics in studies explaining customer behavior.

Dynamic Customer Management

One of the crucial characteristics of customer relationships is that relationships evolve over time. Hence it is important to consider the dynamics of an exchange when studying customer relationships. Within the scientific literature, several researchers have acknowledged that past behaviors at time t will influence both subsequent attitudes and subsequent behaviors (in time t+1) (Bolton and Lemon 1999). Others have reflected on the dynamic development of customer attitudes over time (Bolton and Drew 1991). Van Doorn and Verhoef (2008) showed a strong relationship between customer behavior and satisfaction scores over time. However,

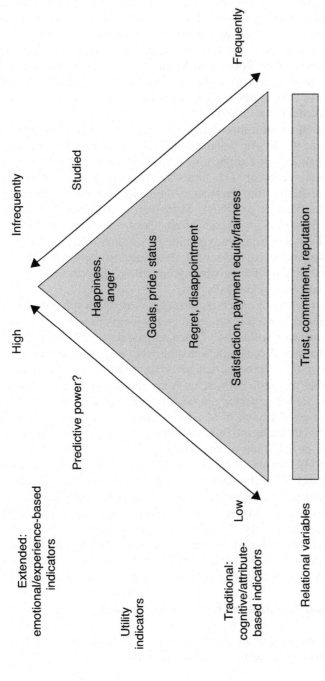

Figure 4.5 Graphical representation of the discussed antecedents of customer behavior

these relationships are less strong when a negative critical incident occurs. This suggests that the positive effects of relationship development over time (path dependence) are at risk when new (negative) events occur in a relationship. This does not have to be negative for relationship development, however. Van Doorn and Verhoef (2008) show that a negative incident can be used to revive the customer relationship. The discussed research shows that understanding customer relationships over time is important (Verhoef et al. 2009).

A recognition of customer dynamics is also required when analyzing and calculating CLV. As noted above, most current CLV models are based on estimations of a single time period, which are subsequently used to project future behavior. This limits the dynamic nature of models and ignores the possibility that parameters (and customer behavior) may vary over time (Leeflang et al. 2009). Moreover, a customer's profitability may change over time as a result of changes in the relationship. Netzer et al. (2008) have modeled the dynamics of customer relationships using a hidden Markov model. In this model, the transitions between relationship states are a function of time-varying covariates. Importantly, dynamic segments of customers can be derived.

Yet another aspect of understanding customer relationship dynamics is the recognition of a need for more forward-looking models. The above-described models are still heavily based on past data, reflecting the future in a limited manner. As customers change over time, their current and past behavior may not be the best predictor of future behavior. Understanding and being able to predict future customer needs (and customer value) are therefore needed, especially in situations and context with significant uncertainty (e.g., Zeithaml et al. 2006). Future research should aim to develop models that take into account this uncertainty. Probably Bayesian models might be helpful in this respect.

Current models within CVM also do not account for the role of important developments in the macro and micro environment. Important external economic developments, such as recessions, may have a strong impact on customer behavior within relationships, owing for example to increased price sensitivity. Moreover, dramatic events within markets, such as the credit crisis, may strongly impact relationships and create for example distrust. There is a lack of research studying customer relationships over longer time periods and relating them to external developments.

Customer Communication and Customer Engagement

In analyzing the value of a customer it is also important to understand the level and extent of customer engagement with the firm. Current models of CVM do not examine this issue. Future research needs to address the extent to which the firm's interaction with the customer is one-way (firm-to-customer) or bidirectional (customer-to-firm and firm-to-customer). Customers with higher levels of engagement may be of higher value to the firm because they might have a higher likelihood of 1) being retained by the firm, 2) having stronger attitudinal loyalty to the firm and 3) spreading more positive word of mouth about the firm to others. Venkatesan and Kumar (2004) indeed show that bidirectional communication positively influences purchase frequency. However, so far research has mainly focused on firm-initiated communication (e.g., Verhoef 2003).

Customer engagement is potentially enriched as a result of the development of new technologies and media. Customers can post messages on their experiences with firms on the Internet (e.g., through blogs, reviews, discussion boards or social networking platforms such as Twitter). These new technologies also enable firms to capture and measure much of the interaction between customers and firms. For example, web-based metrics provided by (sometimes free) software, such as Google Analytics, enable a firm to track where a customer goes on a firm's website, what is viewed, how long it is viewed and so on. These metrics show great promise for measuring customer engagement (Bucklin and Sismeiro 2009; Rangaswamy et al. 2009). The effect of social media on customer behavior can also be measured. Firms such as TNS cymfony (www.cymfony.com) measure and monitor social media for firms and brands. In recent case studies, they show that the extent of social media (e.g., blog postings) can influence brand perceptions and may influence market share, and that active monitoring of social media can be a significant source of consumer insight, enabling firms to react quickly to negative events as well (www.cymfony.com; Anonymous 2009).

Research on customer engagement is, however, still in the infant stage. We need to know an exact definition of the customer engagement construct. Furthermore, measures should be developed. An important issue is whether it should be measured with actual data (i.e., number of contacts, duration of visits to websites) or with more attitudinal-based measures. Furthermore, we need to know how firms can turn customer engagement into a driver of performance. We believe this is a promising area of research.

Customer Networks

Today it is claimed that we live in a networked society. Consumers are networked to each other through real and virtual communities (Algesheimer and Dholakia 2006). Recently, much attention has been devoted to networks in the marketing literature. In the last decade Internet usage has increased enormously, and consumers use it to search for information, to buy products and to communicate. This trend of digital communication, and the increased availability of data that comes with it, encourages marketing scholars to analyze the role of networks in the decision-making process of consumers (e.g., Iacobucci 1996; Chevalier and Mayzlin, 2006; Hill et al. 2006; Van den Bulte and Wuyts 2007).

Remarkably, there has been less attention on customer networks within CVM. The only related research issue concerns word of mouth as a customer metric (Verhoef et al. 2002; Reichheld 2003; Hogan et al. 2004). However, networks may be very important for creating customer value. This especially holds for the adoption of new services (Hogan et al. 2003). We believe that new data will become available to researchers in which the network structures of customers can be detected and can be linked to customer behavior and value. Future research should focus on how they can use these new data for an enrichment of CVM. It potentially can help in more complete models for customer valuation. Hopefully, this new direction in CVM will be fully explored in the next decade.

CONCLUSION

In the past decade much progress has been made on studying customer relationships and the application of customer value management. It has been one of the most studied topics within marketing science. This research has provided insights into how CVM affects firm performance and how the application of CVM can be improved. Furthermore, knowledge has been developed on the influence of different marketing mix instruments and attitudes affecting customer behavior within a relationship. Within the CVM literature, the development of new prediction methods has also gained enormous attention. An important contribution of the CVM literature is the introduction of customer metrics, of which CLV is clearly the most important. Moreover, this metric has also gained increasing attention and popularity in marketing practice (e.g., Kumar et al. 2008). In this chapter we provided an overview of this literature and the most significant findings. Beyond this, we also extensively discussed important areas for pursuing future research. An important area concerns a re-examination of customer attitudinal metrics, inspired by the increasing attention in economics and psychology to new predictors of customer behavior. Furthermore, important developments include the dynamics of customer relationships, customer engagement and customer networks. In sum, we believe that CVM remains a fruitful area for research.

REFERENCES

Algesheimer, René and Paul M. Dholakia (2006), "Do Customer Communities Pay Off?," *Harvard Business Review*, 84(11), 26–30.

Anderson, Eugene W., Claes Fornell and Donald R. Lehmann (1994), "Customer Satisfaction, Market Share, and Profitability: Findings from Sweden," *Journal of Marketing*, 58(3), 53–66.

Anonymous (2009), "Real-Time Crisis Response in a Consumer-Controlled World: A TNS Cymfony Influence 2.0™ Case Study," www.cymfony.com (accessed April 16, 2009).

Ansari, Asim and Carl F. Mela (2003), "E-Customization," *Journal of Marketing Research*, 40(2), 131–45.

Bell, David E. (1982), "Regret in Decision Making under Uncertainty," *Operations Research*, 30, 961–81.

Berger, Paul D. and Nada I. Nasr (1998), "Customer Lifetime Value: Marketing Models and Applications," *Journal of Interactive Marketing*, 12(1), 17–30.

Bolton, Ruth N. (1998), "A Dynamic Model of the Duration of the Customer's Relationship with a Continuous Service Provider: The Role of Satisfaction," *Marketing Science*, 17(1), 45–65.

Bolton, Ruth N. and James H. Drew (1991), "A Longitudinal Analysis of the Impact of Service Changes on Customer Attitudes," *Journal of Marketing*, 55 (January), 1–9.

Bolton, Ruth N. and Katherine N. Lemon (1999), "A Dynamic Model of Customers' Usage of Services: Usage as an Antecedent and Consequence of Satisfaction," *Journal of Marketing Research*, 36(2), 171–86.

Bolton, Ruth N., Katherine N. Lemon and Peter C. Verhoef (2004), "The Theoretical Underpinnings of Customer Asset Management: A Framework and Propositions for Future Research," *Journal of the Academy of Marketing Science*, 32(3), 271–92.

Bolton, Ruth N., Katherine N. Lemon and Peter C. Verhoef (2008), "Expanding Business-to-Business Customer Relationships: Modeling the Customer's Upgrade Decision," *Journal of Marketing*, 72(1), 46–64.

Bougie, J. Roger G., Rik Pieters and Marcel Zeelenberg (2003), "Angry Customers Don't Come Back, They Get Back: The Experience and Behavioral Implications of Anger and Dissatisfaction in Services," *Journal of the Academy of Marketing Science*, 31(4), 377–93.

Boulding, William, Ajay Kalra, Richard Staelin and Valarie A. Zeithaml (1993), "A Dynamic Process Model of Service Quality: From Expectations to Behavioral Intentions," *Journal of Marketing Research*, 30 (February), 7–27.

Boulding, William, Richard Staelin, Michael Ehret and Wesley J. Johnston (2005), "A Customer Relationship Management Roadmap: What Is Known, Potential Pitfalls, and Where to Go," *Journal of Marketing*, 69 (October), 155–66.

Bucklin, Randolph E. and Catarina Sismeiro (2009), "Click Here for Internet Insight: Advances in Clickstream Data Analysis in Marketing," *Journal of Interactive Marketing*, 23(1), 35–48.

Bügel, Marnix (2006), Presentation for Customer Value Management Master Course, University of Groningen.

Bügel, Marnix, Peter C. Verhoef and Abraham P. Buunk (2009), "The Role of Intimacy in Customer-to-Firm Relationships during the Customer Lifecycle," working paper, University of Groningen.

Chevalier, Judith A. and Dina Mayzlin (2006), "The Effect of Word of Mouth on Sales: Online Book Reviews," *Journal of Marketing Research*, 43(3), 345–54.

Davenport, Thomas H. and Jeanne G. Harris (2005), "Automated Decision Making Comes of Age," *MIT Sloan Management Review*, 46(4), 83–9.

Davenport, Thomas H. and Jeanne C. Harris (2007), *Competing on Analytics: The New Science of Winning*, Boston, MA: Harvard Business School Press.

de Valck, Kristine (2005), "Virtual Communities of Consumption: Networks of Consumer Knowledge and Companionship," dissertation, Erasmus Research Institute in Management.

De Wulf, Kristof, Gaby Odekerken-Schröder and Dawn Iacobucci (2001), "Investments in Consumer Relationships: A Cross-Country and Cross-Industry Exploration," *Journal of Marketing*, 65, 33–50.

Dick, Alan S. and Kunal Basu (1994), "Customer Loyalty: Toward an Integrated Conceptual Framework," *Journal of the Academy of Marketing Science*, 22(2), 99–113.

Donkers, Bas, Peter C. Verhoef and Martijn de Jong (2007), "Modeling CLV: A Test of Competing Models in the Insurance Industry," *Quantitative Marketing and Economics*, 5(2), 163–90.

Du, Rex Y., Wagner A. Kamakura and Carl F. Mela (2007), "Size and Share of Customer Wallet," *Journal of Marketing*, 71(2), 94–113.

Elster, Jon (1998), "Emotions and Economic Theory," *Journal of Economic Literature*, 36(1), 47–74.

Fletcher, Keith (2003), "Consumer Power and Privacy: The Changing Nature of CRM," *International Journal of Advertising*, 22, 249–72.

Frey, Bruno S. and Alois Stutzer (2002), "What Can Economists Learn from Happiness Research?," *Journal of Economic Literature*, 40(2), 402–35.

Frijda, Nico H. (1986), *The Emotions*, Cambridge: Cambridge University Press.

Garbarino, Ellen and Mark S. Johnson (1999), "The Different Roles of Satisfaction, Trust, and Commitment in Customer Relationships," *Journal of Marketing*, 63(2), 70–87.

Gilbane Construction (2009), "Customer Satisfaction at Gilbane," presentation at Boston College, Carroll School of Management, April 7.

Gupta, Sunil and Valarie Zeithaml (2006), "Customer Metrics and Their Impact on Financial Performance," *Marketing Science*, 25(6), 718–39.

Gupta, Sunil, Donald R. Lehmann and Jennifer A. Stuart (2004), "Valuing Customers," *Journal of Marketing Research*, 41(1), 7–18.

Heitmann, Mark, Donald R. Lehmann and Andreas Herrmann (2007), "Choice Goal Attainment and Decision and Consumption Satisfaction," *Journal of Marketing Research*, 44(2), 234–50.

Hill, Shawndra, Foster Provost and Chris Volinsky (2006), "Network-Based Marketing: Identifying Likely Adopters via Consumer Networks," *Statistical Science*, 21(2), 256–76.

Hoekstra, Janny C., Peter S.H. Leeflang and Dick R. Wittink (1999), "The Customer Concept: The Basis for a New Marketing Paradigm," *Journal of Market-Focused Management*, 4(1), 43–76.

Hoekstra, Janny C., Peter C. Verhoef and Hiek van der Scheer (2008), "State-of-the-Art Use of Customer Intelligence in the Netherlands," presentation at Customer Insights Center/ VODW Seminar on Customer Intelligence, November.

Hogan, John E., Donald R. Lehmann, Maria Merino, Rajendra K. Srivastava, Jacquelyn S. Thomas and Peter C. Verhoef (2002), "Linking Customer Assets to Financial Performance," *Journal of Service Research*, 5(1), 26–38.

Hogan, John E., Katherine N. Lemon and Barak Libai (2003), "What Is the True Value of a Lost Customer?," *Journal of Service Research*, 5(3), 196–208.

Hogan, John E., Katherine N. Lemon and Barak Libai (2004), "Quantifying the Ripple: Word-of-Mouth and Advertising Effectiveness," *Journal of Advertising Research*, 44 (September/October), 271–80.

Iacobucci, Dawn (1996), *Networks in Marketing*, Thousand Oaks, CA: Sage.

Inman, J. Jeffrey, James S. Dyer and Jianmin Jia (1997), "A Generalized Utility Model of Disappointment and Regret Effects on Post-Choice Valuation," *Marketing Science*, 16(2), 97–111.

Jayachandran, Satish, Subhash Sharma, Peter Kaufman and Pushkala Raman (2005), "The Role of Relational Information Processes and Technology Use in Customer Relationship Management," *Journal of Marketing*, 69(4), 177–92.

Johnson, Michael D. and Fred Selnes (2004), "Customer Portfolio Management: Toward a Dynamic Theory of Exchange Relationships," *Journal of Marketing*, 68(2), 1–17.

Johnson, Michael D. and Fred Selnes (2005), "Diversifying Your Customer Portfolio," *MIT Sloan Management Review*, 46(3), 11–14.

Kahneman, Daniel (2003), "Maps of Bounded Rationality: Psychology for Behavioral Economics," *American Economic Review*, 93(5), 1449–75.

Kahneman, Daniel and Amos Tversky (1979), "Prospect Theory: An Analysis of Decision under Risk," *Econometrica*, 47(2), 237–51.

Kalwani, Manohar and Chin Kin Yim (1992), "Consumer Price and Promotion Expectations: An Experimental Study," *Journal of Marketing Research*, 29(1), 90–100.

Keiningham, Timothy L., Bruce Cooil, Tor W. Andreassen and Lerzan Aksoy (2007), "A Longitudinal Examination of Net Promoter and Firm Revenue Growth," *Journal of Marketing*, 71(3), 39–51.

Kirca, Ahmet H., Satish Jayachandran and William O. Bearden (2005), "Market Orientation: A Meta-Analytic Review and Assessment of Its Antecedents and Impact on Performance," *Journal of Marketing*, 69(2), 24–41.

Kozinets, Robert V. (1999), "E-Tribalized Marketing? The Strategic Implications of Virtual Communities of Consumption," *European Management Journal*, 17(3), 252–64.

Kumar, V. and Werner Reinartz (2005), *Customer Relationship Management: A Databased Approach*, Hoboken, NJ: John Wiley.

Kumar, V., Rajkumar Venkatesan, Dennis Beckman and T. Bohling (2008), "The Power of CLV: Managing Customer Lifetime Value at IBM," *Marketing Science*, 27(4), 585–99.

Leeflang, Peter S.H., Tammo H.A. Bijmolt, Jenny van Doorn, Dominique H. Hanssens, Harald J. van Heerde, Peter C. Verhoef and Jaap E. Wieringa (2009), "Creating Lift versus Building the Base: Current Trends in Marketing Dynamics," *International Journal of Research in Marketing*, 26(1), 13–20.

Lehmann, Donald R. (2004), "Metrics for Making Marketing Matter," *Journal of Marketing*, 68(4), 73–5.

Lemon, Katherine N. and Tanya Mark (2006), "Customer Lifetime Value as the Basis of Customer Segmentation: Issues and Challenges," *Journal of Relationship Marketing*, 5 (October), 55–69.

Lemon, Katherine N., Tiffany B. White and Russell S. Winer (2002), "Dynamic Customer Relationship Management: Incorporating Future Considerations into the Service Retention Decision," *Journal of Marketing*, 66(1), 1–14.

Loewenstein, George J. (1999), "Because It Is There: The Challenge of Mountaineering . . . for Utility Theory," *Kyklos*, 52(3), 315–43.

Loewenstein, George J. (2000), "Emotions in Economic Theory and Economic Behavior," *American Economic Review*, 90(2), 426–32.

Loomes, Graham and Robert Sugden (1982), "Regret Theory: An Alternative Theory of Rational Choice under Uncertainty," *Economic Journal*, 92, 805–24.

Louro, Maria J., Rik Pieters and Marcel Zeelenberg (2005), "Negative Returns on Positive Emotions: The Influence of Pride and Self-Regulatory Goals on Repurchase Decisions," *Journal of Consumer Research*, 31 (March), 833–40.

Morgan, Neil A. and Lopo Leotte Rego (2006), "The Value of Different Customer Satisfaction and Loyalty Metrics in Predicting Business Performance," *Marketing Science*, 25(5), 426–39.

Morgan, Robert M. and Shelby D. Hunt (1994), "The Commitment-Trust Theory of Relationship Marketing," *Journal of Marketing*, 58(3), 20–38.

Neslin, Scott A., Sunil Gupta, Wagner Kamakura, J.X. Lu and Charlotte Mason (2006), "Defection Detection: Measuring and Understanding the Predictive Accuracy of Customer Churn Models," *Journal of Marketing Research*, 43(2), 204–11.

Netzer, Oded, James M. Lattin and V. Srinivasan (2008), "A Hidden Markov Model of Customer Relationship Dynamics," *Marketing Science*, 27(2), 185–204.

Nyer, Raidh (2007), "The Effect of Consumption Emotions on Satisfaction and Word-of-Mouth Communications," *Psychology and Marketing*, 24(12), 1085–1108.

Oliver, Richard L. (1993), "Cognitive, Affective, and Attribute Bases for Satisfaction," *Journal of Consumer Research*, 20 (December), 418–29.

Oliver, Richard L. and Robert A. Westbrook (1993), "Profiles of Consumer Emotions and

Satisfaction in Ownership and Usage," *Journal of Consumer Satisfaction, Dissatisfaction and Complaining Behavior*, 6, 12–27.

Oliver, Richard L., Roland T. Rust and Sajeev Varki (1997), "Customer Delight: Foundations, Findings, and Managerial Insights," *Journal of Retailing*, 73(4), 311–36.

O'Sullivan, Don and Andrew V. Abela (2007), "Marketing Performance Measurement Ability and Firm Performance," *Journal of Marketing*, 71(2), 79–83.

Peltier, James W., George Milne and Joseph E. Phelps (2009), "Information Privacy Research: Framework for Integrating Multiple Publics, Information Channels, and Responses," *Journal of Interactive Marketing*, 23(2), 191–205.

Pine, B. Joseph and James H. Gilmore (1999), *The Experience Economy: Work Is Theatre and Every Business a Stage*, Boston, MA: Harvard Business School Press.

Ramani, Girish and V. Kumar (2008), "Interaction Orientation and Firm Performance," *Journal of Marketing*, 72(1), 27–45.

Rangaswamy, Arvind, C. Lee Giles and Silvija Seres (2009), "A Strategic Perspective on Search Engines: Thought Candies for Practitioners and Researchers," *Journal of Interactive Marketing*, 23(1), 49–60.

Reichheld, Frederick F. (2003), "The One Number You Need to Grow," *Harvard Business Review*, 81(12), 46–57.

Reinartz, Werner J. and V. Kumar (2000), "On the Profitability of Long-Life Customers in a Noncontractual Setting: An Empirical Investigation and Implications for Marketing," *Journal of Marketing*, 64(4), 17–35.

Reinartz, Werner J., Manfred Krafft and Wayne D. Hoyer (2004), "The Customer Relationship Management Process: Its Measurement and Impact on Performance," *Journal of Marketing*, 41(3), 293–305.

Risselada, Hans, Peter C. Verhoef and Tammo H.A. Bijmolt (2010), "Staying Power of Churn Prediction Models," *Journal of Interactive Marketing*, 24(3), 198–208.

Rusbult, Caryl E. (1980), "Commitment and Satisfaction in Romantic Associations: A Test of the Investment Model," *Journal of Experimental Social Psychology*, 16(2), 172–86.

Rust, Roland T. and Richard L. Oliver (2000), "Should We Delight the Customer?," *Journal of the Academy of Marketing Science*, 28(1), 86–94.

Rust, Roland T. and Peter C. Verhoef (2005), "Optimizing Marketing Interventions Mix in Intermediate CRM," *Marketing Science*, 24(3), 477–89.

Rust, Roland T., Katherine N. Lemon and Valarie A. Zeithaml (2004), *Driving Customer Equity: How Customer Lifetime Value Is Reshaping Corporate Strategy*, New York: Free Press.

Rust, Roland T., V. Kumar and Rajkumar Venkatesan (2007), "Will the Frog Change into a Prince? Predicting Future Customer Profitability," *MSI Reports*, 07–205.

Shah, Denish, Roland T. Rust, A. Parasuraman, Richard Staelin and George S. Day (2006), "The Path to Customer Centricity," *Journal of Service Research*, 9(2), 113–24.

Srivastava, Rajendra K., Tasadduq A. Shervani and Liam Fahey (1998), "Market-Based Assets and Shareholder Value: A Framework for Analysis," *Journal of Marketing*, 62(1), 2–18.

Starmer, Chris (2000), "Developments in Non-Expected Utility Theory: The Hunt for a Descriptive Theory of Choice under Risk," *Journal of Economic Literature*, 38(2), 332–82.

Steenkamp, Jan Benedict E.M. and Martijn G. de Jong (2010), "A Global Investigation into the Constellation of Consumer Attitudes toward Global and Local Products," *Journal of Marketing*, 74(6), 18–40.

Sternberg, Robert J. (1986), "A Triangular Theory of Love," *Psychological Review*, 93(2), 119–35.

Tagney, June P. and Kurt Fisher (1995), *Self-Conscious Emotions: The Psychology of Shame, Guilt, Embarrassment and Pride*, New York: Guilford Press.

Tuhli, Kapil R., Ajay K. Kohli and Sundar G. Baradwaij (2007), "Rethinking Customer Solutions: From Product Bundles to Relational Processes," *Journal of Marketing*, 71(3), 1–17.

Van den Bulte, Christophe and Stefan Wuyts (2007), *Social Networks and Marketing*, Cambridge, MA: Marketing Science Institute.

van Doorn, Jenny and Peter C. Verhoef (2008), "Critical Incidents and the Impact of Satisfaction on Customer Share," *Journal of Marketing*, 72(4), 123–42.

van Doorn, Jenny, Peter C. Verhoef and Tammo H.A. Bijmolt (2007), "The Importance of Non-Linear Relationships between Attitude and Behaviour in Policy Research," *Journal of Consumer Policy*, 30, 75–90.

Venkatesan, Raijkumar and V. Kumar (2004), "A Customer Lifetime Value Framework for Customer Selection and Resource Allocation Strategy," *Journal of Marketing*, 68(4), 106–25.

Verhoef, Peter C. (2003), "Understanding the Effect of Customer Relationship Management Efforts on Customer Retention and Customer Share Development," *Journal of Marketing*, 67(4), 30–45.

Verhoef, Peter C. and Fred Langerak (2003), "Eleven Misconceptions about Customer Relationship Management," *Business Strategy Review*, 13(4), 70–76.

Verhoef, Peter C. and Peter S.H. Leeflang (2009), "Understanding the Marketing Department's Influence within the Firm," *Journal of Marketing*, 73(2), 14–37.

Verhoef, Peter C., Philip H. Franses and Janny C. Hoekstra (2001), "The Effect of Satisfaction and Payment Equity on Cross Buying: A Dynamic Model for a Multi-Service Provider," *Journal of Retailing*, 77(3), 359–78.

Verhoef, Peter C., Philip H. Franses and Janny C. Hoekstra (2002), "The Effect of Relational Constructs on Customer Referrals and Number of Services Purchased from a Multi-Service Provider: Does Age of Relationship Matter?," *Journal of the Academy of Marketing Science*, 30(3), 202–16.

Verhoef, Peter C., Penny N. Spring, Janny C. Hoekstra and Peter S.H. Leeflang (2003), "The Commercial Use of Segmentation and Predictive Modeling Techniques for Database Marketing in the Netherlands," *Decision Support Systems*, 34(4), 471–81.

Verhoef, Peter C., Fred Langerak and Bas Donkers (2007), "Understanding Brand and Dealer Retention in the New Car Market: The Moderating Role of Brand Tier," *Journal of Retailing*, 83(1), 97–113.

Verhoef, Peter C., Jenny van Doorn and Mathilda Dorotic (2007), "Customer Value Management: An Overview and Research Agenda," *Marketing: Journal of Research in Management*, 2, 51–69.

Verhoef, Peter C., Katherine N. Lemon, A. Parasuraman, Anne Roggeveen, Michael Tsiros and Leonard A. Schlessinger (2009), "Customer Experience Creation: Determinants, Dynamics and Management Strategies," *Journal of Retailing*, 85(1), 31–41.

Vogel, Verena, Heiner Evanschitzky and B. Ramaseshan (2008), "Customer Equity Drivers and Future Sales," *Journal of Marketing*, 72(6), 98–108.

Wedel, Michel and Peter S.H. Leeflang (1998), "A Model for the Effects of Psychological Pricing in Gabor–Granger Price Studies," *Journal of Economic Psychology*, 19(2), 237–60.

White, Tiffany B., Debra L. Zahay, Helge Thorbjørnsen and Sharon Shavitt (2008), "Getting Too Personal: Reactance to Highly Personalized Email Solicitations," *Marketing Letters*, 19(1), 39–50.

Yim, Chi K., David K. Tse and Kimmy W. Chan (2008), "Strengthening Customer Loyalty through Intimacy and Passion: Roles of Customer–Firm Affection and Customer–Staff Relationships in Services," *Journal of Marketing Research*, 45(6), 741–56.

Zahay, Debra and Abbie Griffin (2002), "Are Customer Information Systems Worth It? Results from B2B Services," *Marketing Science Institute*, 02–113.

Zeelenberg, Marcel and Rik Pieters (2004), "Beyond Valence in Customer Dissatisfaction: A Review and New Findings on Behavioral Responses to Regret and Disappointment in Failed Services," *Journal of Business Research*, 57(4), 445–55.

Zeelenberg, Marcel and Rik Pieters (2007), "A Theory of Regret Regulation 1.0," *Journal of Consumer Psychology*, 17(1), 3–18.

Zeithaml, Valarie A., Ruth N. Bolton, John Deighton, Timothy L. Keiningham, Katherine N. Lemon and J. Andrew Petersen (2006), "Forward-Looking Focus: Can Firms Have Adaptive Foresight?," *Journal of Service Research*, 9(2), 168–83.

5. Relationship marketing tools: understanding the value of loyalty programs
Russell Lacey

INTRODUCTION

Loyalty programs have emerged as the most commonly utilized marketing tool for developing and preserving valued customer relationships. According to a 2007 Colloquy survey, the average American household is a member of 12 different loyalty programs and is active in 4.7 loyalty programs (Ferguson and Hlavinka 2007). Other countries where loyalty programs are prevalent include the United Kingdom, Canada, Germany, India, Switzerland, and Australia. Loyalty programs are considered standard in many industries. Current examples of leading firms across a broad spectrum of vertical consumer markets employing proprietary loyalty programs include airlines (e.g., American, Delta, United, British Airways), car rental companies (e.g., Enterprise, Budget, Dollar, Thrifty, Hertz), hotels (e.g., Hilton, Hyatt, Marriott), financial services companies (e.g., American Express, Citibank), and supermarkets and drugstores (e.g., Kroger, Tesco, CVS, Eckerds, Boots), as well as an array of specialty retailers (e.g., Best Buy, Barnes & Noble, Hallmark, Nordstrom).

The wide proliferation of loyalty programs has led to increasingly widespread attention among marketing scholars (e.g., Kivetz and Simonson, 2002; Roehm et al. 2002; Keh and Lee 2006; Nunes and Dreze 2006; Liu and Yang 2009). Amidst mixed theoretical and empirical support for how firms and customers, alike, benefit from loyalty programs, they remain a controversial relationship marketing tool. Marketing scholars have questioned the value of loyalty programs, including such charges that they serve only as ubiquitous discount mechanisms, are motivated by competitive parity, require costly administrative support, and drive loyal behaviors in relation to the program rather than to the firm (e.g., Dowling 2002; Uncles et al. 2003; Kumar and Shah 2004; Noble and Phillips 2004; Meyer-Waarden and Benavent 2006). Shugan (2005) argues that many loyalty programs are shams because they create liabilities rather than customer assets by generating short-term revenue from customers while producing considerable impending cumbersome obligations to the customers.

"With limited research on loyalty programs, it is still unclear to what extent loyalty programs are effective and, more important, what induces the success and failure of different programs" (Liu and Yang 2009: 97).

The objective of this chapter is to address how loyalty programs can be effectively utilized as a relationship marketing component that produces valued reciprocal benefits for the firm and its customers. In doing so, this chapter promises to deliver important insights to both academic and managerial audiences. For scholars, the discussion is aimed at expanding our collective understanding of the conceptual contributions of loyalty programs toward building and sustaining customer relationships. For managers, this work provides instruction for how to employ different combinations of customer relational benefits to strengthen the impact of loyalty programs and how to further leverage the firm's benefits of loyalty programs.

This chapter is organized as follows. First, loyalty programs are distinguished from reward programs. Second, loyalty programs are examined as a conduit for value proposition segmentation. Third, a framework is developed to describe an array of economic, social, and resource benefits customers may gain by participating in loyalty programs. Finally, a corresponding framework is developed to assess the value of loyalty programs from the firm's perspective. In addition to repatronage, loyalty programs can help the firm strengthen customer advocacy behaviors and secure otherwise elusive customer-specific information.

LOYALTY PROGRAMS

Figure 5.1 depicts the conceptual framework of loyalty programs. Loyalty programs are coordinated, membership-based marketing activities designed to enhance the building of cooperative marketing relationships among pre-identified customers toward the sponsoring brand(s). Given that many firms consider customers to be their most valuable asset, loyalty programs provide a more strategic marketing component for attracting and retaining valued customers. Through proprietary, partnership, or coalition models, loyalty programs work to build expeditiously and preserve stronger customer relationships with the firm than would likely result without these programs.

Multiple brand loyalty programs can occur between firms or within a corporate conglomerate (e.g., Starwood Hotels and Resorts, InterContinental Group), with the latter serving as an enterprise-wide program of a customer's total marketing relationship with a firm. Coalition-style programs (e.g., Airmiles, Nectar, Payback) supported by multiple participants offer

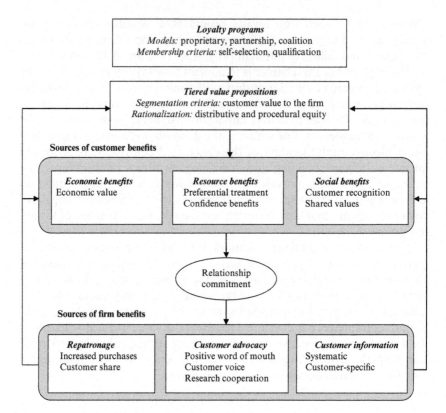

Figure 5.1   The conceptual framework of loyalty programs

greater customer value and flexibility in loyalty program redemption for customers. Partnerships and coalitions also accommodate a broader scope of business and raise brand visibility while reducing the costs for individual firm participants. Effective coalition programs offer the ability to leverage customers' daily spending in high-frequency categories in order to realize more attainable rewards as well as reach members with joint-branded marketing communications. Participants of multiple branded programs typically align themselves with strategic partners that are perceived to possess complementary brand images.

Depending on a loyalty program's structure and design, cooperative marketing relationships may already be well established before customers are enrolled in a particular loyalty program (Kivetz and Simonson 2002). One firm may use loyalty programs to focus directly on loyalty building activities, whereas another may seek to cultivate higher retention among its most valuable customers. Loyalty programs use targeted communications in an effort to customize more relevant offerings. Loyalty programs differ from other forms of marketing communications by their longer-term orientation and deliberate emphasis on preserving customer retention and intensifying purchase frequency (Sharp and Sharp 1997; Liu and Yang 2009). Based on cumulative brand purchases, loyalty programs enhance the firm's value proposition offerings to attract new customers and retain customers.

Loyalty programs and reward programs are similar but different relationship marketing tools, despite scholars' frequent usage of "loyalty programs" and "reward programs" as synonymous terms (e.g., Hennig-Thurau et al. 2002; Kivetz and Simonson 2002; Dreze and Nunes 2004; Shugan 2005; Dholakia 2006). Reward programs are more simplistic in design and narrower in scope, as they depend exclusively on economic-based benefits, which loyalty or reward program marketing managers commonly refer to as "hard benefits" in exchange for continued patronage once such behaviors are revealed. Found in both loyalty and reward programs, hard benefits are composed of tangible rewards that represent economic value and savings to customers, such as price reductions, cash incentives, and rebates in the form of free or discounted merchandise.

A key distinction between loyalty programs and rewards programs is the former's more deliberate and extensive use of so-called "soft benefits." Successful loyalty programs are composed of a blend of hard and soft benefits. Hard benefits are tangible rewards with direct monetary value. Soft benefits are intangible and relationship-oriented, such as expedited customer service, special access to property amenities, invitations to special members-only events, complimentary product and service upgrades, preferred seating, and communication offers designed to build emotional connections with members. Such intangible benefits may hold greater potential for competitive advantage than hard benefits for firm sponsors (Hennig-Thurau et al. 2002). Compared to rewards programs, loyalty programs often engage in recognition and personalization through extensive communications to their participating members.

Another distinction can be made between those loyalty programs that serve to reward and retain already committed customers and loyalty programs that help to create and build relationship commitment (Daams et al. 2008). Relationship commitment reflects an enduring attitude or desire for a particular firm or brand. Committed customers are motivated to maintain the relationship because of attachment feelings and sincerity in their personal attitudes (Moorman et al. 1992). As a psychological construct, relationship commitment may be discernible by repatronage behaviors, yet such manifestations do not ensure its presence.

To determine whether customers are already committed to the firm at the time they are enrolled in the loyalty program and that their commitment is indeed strengthened by their participation in the program, firms must capture the motivations behind customers' enrollment and participation in loyalty programs. Depending on the firm's philosophy and goals of the program, loyalty program membership can be automatically offered to all customers or by invitation only to certain customers who qualify for membership (Liu and Yang 2009). When loyalty programs are offered to customers for attaining certain spending levels with the firm through automatic enrollment, it is the firm (not the customer) that determines loyalty program membership. Dholakia (2006) suggests that customers who perceive that a firm's marketing initiatives are "self-determined" (i.e., they believe they join through their own initiative) are more likely to engage in behaviors that benefit the firm than will those customers who perceive their joining as "firm-determined."

In non-contractual relationships, loyalty programs can be used to lock customers in and thus make it more costly for customers to purchase substitute brands (Kim et al. 2001). In addition to generating additional revenue, some firms (e.g., Starbucks, Barnes & Noble) employ membership fees for joining their loyalty program to create a switching cost barrier. Not only do switching costs serve as a means to stop customer attrition, but they also make it more costly for another firm to acquire the customer (Sharp and Sharp 1997). The next section describes how loyalty programs support value proposition segmentation strategies.

TIERED VALUE PROPOSITIONS

In a general sense, relationship marketing involves treating individual customers differently. The relationship marketing perspective is actually part of a broader service-centered view in which firms strive to cultivate relationships through differentiated and customized value propositions (Vargo and Lusch 2004). By being adaptive to the individual and dynamic service needs of customers, customized value propositions allow firms to build more sustainable marketing relationships. In an age in which many competitors are increasingly offering comparable products, shared distribution systems, and emulated price promotions, firms are encouraged to direct more of their focus on developing and implementing relationship efforts to improving customer value to gain competitive advantage (De Wulf and Odekerken-Schröder 2003).

Aided by sophisticated segmentation modeling, firms use loyalty programs explicitly to reward their most valuable customers by creating tiered levels of customer benefits based on the customer's value to the firm. Marketers are challenged with the desire to serve their most valuable customers better without overtly discriminating against less valuable customers. Scholars contend that it is neither economically nor operationally wise for a firm to expand its value proposition to all its customers (O'Brien and Jones 1995; Sheth and Parvatiyar 1995), especially in cases where there is significant heterogeneity in annual spending and profitability between customer tiers. Failure to consider customer value may result in the firm wasting resources over-satisfying less valuable customers, while under-satisfying those with greater value. Loyalty programs can be designed to realign the firm's core value proposition around a subset of customers and accommodate individual customers in the form of added products or enhanced service options not generally presented to all of the firm's customers. Tiered value propositions result from the firm focusing its resources on high-value customers and awarding select customers with elevated social status recognition and/or enhanced products above and beyond what is normally offered to customers.

Customers may rationalize differentiation of firm value propositions using equity theory (Huppertz et al. 1978). According to equity theory, customers form perceptions of the inputs (i.e., money, time, effort, opportunity costs) and outputs (e.g., hard and soft benefits) that are associated with an exchange. *Distributive equity* is the extent to which customers perceive that they are equitably rewarded for their input (Oliver and Swan 1989). Customers' perceptions of distributive equity increase when it is perceived that the firm is exerting extra effort through enhanced value propositions. Customers will consider the balance of their own inputs and outcomes compared to those received by other customers who are deemed to be of similar stature (Xia et al. 2004). Tiered value propositions are awarded on the basis of proportionate customer inputs.

Through the separation of value proposition variables, firms are essentially transferring value from non-participants to program participants and rewarding loyalty program members at the expense of non-member customers. Though the biggest increases in spending and purchase frequency occur among lighter user segments (Liu 2007), loyalty programs are targeted towards the firm's heavier user segment of a particular product or service, and heavy users stand to gain the most from these programs (Meyer-Waarden and Benavent 2006). To ensure customer perceptions of distributive equity, the firm should clearly communicate the loyalty program criteria used to determine different tiers of value propositions and program rewards. The criteria should be straightforward, unbiased, and consistently administered (Lacey and Sneath 2006).

Processes used to determine distributive equity can be as significant as the output of loyalty programs. Specifically, *procedural equity* involves the fairness of the process or means by which reward allocation decisions are derived. It represents the fairness of the process that leads to the outcome (Thibaut and Walker 1975), including consistency of application in policies, procedures, and other criteria used to determine the results (Smith et al. 1999). Customers are more likely to be dissatisfied with loyalty programs when they are difficult to evaluate, have changing rules and regulations, and lack portability (Shugan 2005). For example, airlines frequently disappoint customers who want to travel to popular destinations at peak times, because of lack of program redemption availability or higher mileage requirements. Equity for one customer segment resulting from loyalty program participation may create sentiments of inequity among other customers. In response, some researchers have advised marketers to use caution in exercising their flexibility to individual requests to ensure that such actions do not create feelings of inequity for other customers (Tax and Brown 1998). If non-member customers perceive that tiered value propositions to qualifying members are unbiased, impartially delivered, and consistently administered, they are likely to perceive procedural equity (Lacey and Sneath 2006).

Consistent with relationship marketing theory, for supporting relationship marketing initiatives to be effective there must be value for both parties. In the next section, we examine the various benefits customers may reap from participating in loyalty programs.

HOW CUSTOMERS BENEFIT FROM LOYALTY PROGRAMS

Relationship marketing suggests that the development of customer relationships can be predicted by examining the benefits sought by customers (Hennig-Thurau et al. 2002). In this section, a framework is presented for how combinations of customer benefits for engaging in marketing relationships can be effectively enhanced through loyalty programs. This discussion expands the previously highlighted separation of hard benefits and soft benefits into three distinct multi-dimensional customer relational benefits: economic, resource, and social. The major basis of this relationship marketing framework is that, to the extent that the firm fulfills each of these categories, the firm will be more successful in building and sustaining valued customer relationships.

Economic Benefits

The first category of the relational benefits framework is economic benefits. Economic benefits are viewed as those "hard benefits" used by the firm to influence consumers' perceptions of the rewards they receive from their participation in the loyalty program. Loyalty programs raise economic value through a convergence of rewards. Often based on cumulative purchases and a menu of tiered level benefits and redemption packages, loyalty programs typically provide customers with added value and beyond-customary firm offerings.

Economic value via loyalty programs is delivered in many forms, including product offerings and gifts, reward cards, gift cards, cash rebates, in-kind merchandise, special deals, price discounts, extended warranties, and concessions and waivers from standard fees. All are designed to serve as tactical levers to influence customer behaviors favorably. Since non-competing firms share many of the same customers, loyalty programs frequently adopt multiple branding schemes, where customers are able to combine and transfer economic-based benefits, and provide a richer reward structure to enhance the program's overall value proposition. Recent research shows that consumers became more responsive to rewards offered via a retailer's loyalty program versus conventional discounts of equal economic value in their store visit decisions (Zhang and Breugelmans 2012).

Since customers have unequal value, many firms aggressively employ segmentation to direct greater economic value toward their more valuable customer base. Through loyalty programs, firms are essentially transferring economic benefits from non-participants to loyalty program participants as they give enhanced value propositions to selected customers. Loyalty programs are chiefly aimed at the biggest spenders, and it is these customers who stand to benefit most from a loyalty program. By default those customers who do not participate in loyalty programs receive comparably fewer economic-based enhancements and incentives than loyalty program members (Kim et al. 2001; Shugan 2005).

Resource Benefits

A second category of benefits to customers from loyalty programs is resource benefits. As a source of "soft benefits," resource benefits offer reassurance and conviction, and enhance the services customers gain by engaging in marketing relationships. Two specific components of resource benefits are preferential treatment and confidence benefits.

Preferential treatment reflects the practice of giving selected customers elevated social status and enhanced services beyond the firm's standard value proposition and customer service practice. The notion of preferential treatment is consistent with the relationship marketing perspective, because it recognizes the special status of preferred customers (Czepiel

1990). Examples of loyalty program-based preferential treatment include members-only access to ancillary facilities and concierge services, special service arrangements, special access to dedicated customer service personnel, use of private tours, invitations to exclusive events, early check-ins and late check-outs, expedited repairs, reservations at short notice, and express service lines for program members. Primarily through loyalty programs, a wide variety of firms appear to be deliberating enhancing value propositions for their more valuable customer segments by explicitly shifting resources in their direction. When customers perceive themselves as benefactors of preferential treatment, their level of emotional attachment and desire to maintain the marketing relationship is strengthened (Lacey et al. 2007).

Because marketing relationships involve potential vulnerability, customers are more likely to be committed to the firm that delivers reliable goods and services. *Confidence benefits* describe the resource relief experienced by customers in established marketing relationships as a result of higher conviction in correct product or service performance, lower purchasing anxiety, and knowing what to expect (Gwinner et al. 1998). Customers engage in marketing relationships because they want to simplify information processing and buying behaviors, reduce perceived risks, and enjoy a state of resource comfort (Sheth and Parvatiyar 1995). Loyalty programs can help simplify the purchasing decision process, and therefore provide relief for customers, because the perceived risk of making a wrong decision is lower when returning to established relationships. Loyalty programs may experience fewer problems, because the firm is paying more attention to meeting the customers' needs. For example, firms may use their loyalty programs to notify members about urgent issues such as service delays, safety notifications, and product recalls. Loyalty programs favorably impact confidence benefits, because participating members receive explicit assurance from the program sponsor that they will benefit by their active participation.

Social Benefits

Social benefits are an additional source of soft benefits. Loyalty programs create a more extensive connection between the sponsoring firm and its customers. Customer recognition and shared values exemplify social benefits that may be enhanced by way of loyalty programs.

Customers base their level of commitment, in part, on the degree of recognition received as a result of their status as contributing customers (Gruen et al. 2000). *Customer recognition* is the level of individual identification a customer receives from the sponsoring brand. With increased customer familiarity, there emerges a greater desire by customers to maintain a marketing relationship with the firm. In addition, by individually recognizing its customers, the firm is positioned to customize its value propositions to match idiosyncratic customer needs. In the absence of frequent interpersonal contact between employees and customers, firms can use loyalty programs to build a sense of community with their customers. Loyalty programs can lend depth and uniqueness to targeted customer segments (Bolton et al. 2000). Previous research has shown that loyalty program members perceive that the sponsoring brand is more familiar to them than to their non-member customer counterparts (Lacey 2007).

Shared values are in place when a customer perceives that the values being practiced by the firm are consistent with his or her own personal values. A bond is created between an individual customer and a firm's employees by their joint appreciation of the welfare for society (Sirdeshmukh et al. 2002). Firms increasingly use their loyalty programs to signal shared values through a variety of social responsibility initiatives, such as donations in support of green marketing (e.g., carbon-reduction projects) and not-for-profit organizations (e.g., the American Cancer Society, Special Olympics). To the extent that such initiatives indicate to customers over time that the firm has characteristics that are compatible with their own personal values, customers are more likely to identify with the sponsoring firm and consequently are more likely to support the firm (Lichtenstein et al. 2004).

Differential Impact of Customer Relational Benefits

While this section has identified key building blocks of customer relationships and how loyalty programs can be used to enhance customer relational benefits, all individual relational benefits will not yield equal impact to the firm. Depending on the industry, firm, and loyalty program characteristics, the direct and indirect effects of various economic, resource, and social benefits will vary. Understanding the relative impact of individual customer benefits is of particular interest to marketers who are charged with building customer relationships and maximizing customer lifetime value. While the cumulative effect of all relational benefits may be necessary to produce optimal impact from the customer's perspective, marketers must recognize the inherent limitations of relying on economic benefits alone in loyalty program design and are advised to consider social and resource benefits as more instrumental for building customer relationships. Research has shown that investing in resource and social benefits more favorably influences customer relationships than those investments and activities geared toward improving economic benefits (Lacey 2007).

The focus of this chapter now shifts to discussing the benefits that firms may gain from offering loyalty programs to their customers. The next section describes how loyalty programs contribute to distinct types of firm benefits.

HOW FIRMS BENEFIT FROM LOYALTY PROGRAMS

Given the ongoing challenges of connecting a firm's marketing activities with its bottom line, scholars have argued for firms to increase customer equity by building and sustaining customer relationships (e.g., Blattberg et al. 2001; Kamakura et al. 2002; Rust et al. 2004). The ultimate success of a loyalty program should be assessed by its financial contribution (Kopalle and Neslin 2003). Drawing from previous research, three broad categories have emerged which capture the major avenues from which firms stand to benefit from offering loyalty programs by increasing the value of customer relationships and associated revenues and profits for the firm. First, loyalty programs can be used to preserve and strengthen active customer spending status. Second, loyalty programs can help firms build stronger customer advocacy behaviors. Third, loyalty programs provide a wealth of individualized customer information that can be used to facilitate improved marketing performance.

Increasing Repatronage

In the marketing literature, there is wide agreement on the crucial role of repatronage as a key behavioral outcome for measuring relationship marketing success (e.g., Crosby and Stephens 1987; Reichheld 1996). Relationship commitment has been shown to have a significant, direct effect on repeat customer purchases (Gruen et al. 2000; Lacey and Morgan 2007). Loyalty programs not only are linked to preserving current customer status, but play an instrumental role in increasing the magnitude and volume of customers' repatronage over time. Separate closely related repatronage metrics are increased purchases and customer share.

Increased purchases display the customer's desire to do more business with the firm over a period of time into the future, depending on the repurchasing cycle of the product category. Customers who are repeat buyers of a brand are more likely to increase business volume in the future (Mattila 2001; Verhoef 2003). Loyalty programs are distinguished by their emphasis on lifting average purchase frequency by offering incrementally higher incentives to customers on the basis of frequency and dollar value of purchases over a specified time period (Dowling and Uncles 1997). Loyalty programs are structured to ensure that the highest spending customers receive the greatest rewards. Owing to higher tiered value propositions, loyalty program members are more willing to increase their overall volume of purchasing activities than are non-member customers (Zhang and Breugelmans 2012).

Customer share represents the percentage of the volume of the customer's total spending in a product category devoted to a particular brand over a fixed time period. Though a limitation of customer share is its ceiling effect, proportion of purchases devoted to a customer's most purchased brand or service firm remains a frequently used operational measure of customer loyalty (Bowman and Narayandas 2004). Customer share portrays a stronger relational measure than the absolute volume of increased customer spending because it captures the firm's market share of individual customers in a particular product category (Jones and Sasser 1995). Loyalty programs have been shown to have a positive impact on encouraging participating customers to make a higher share of their product category purchases from the sponsoring brand as opposed to competing brands (Lewis 2004; Leenheer et al. 2007).

Customer Advocacy

Past studies tend to base the effectiveness of loyalty programs to the firm solely on purchase frequency and value of transactions (e.g., Sharp and Sharp 1997; Bolton et al. 2000; Kivetz and Simonson 2002; Lewis 2004). However, repatronage purchases alone provide a narrow view of how loyalty programs contribute to a firm's marketing performance. As a multi-dimensional construct, customer advocacy reflects combinations of marketing resources that contribute to a more efficient and effective marketing enterprise (Lacey and Morgan 2009), including positive word of mouth, customer voice, and marketing research cooperation.

Positive word of mouth describes favorable communications regarding a specific brand or firm that a customer is willing to share with others. While the critical role that positive word of mouth plays in helping firms attract new customers is well established (e.g., Day 1971; Richins 1983; Furse et al. 1984), the importance of word of mouth is further magnified by the ever-increasing speed and scale of online communications, including email, blogs, message boards, social networks, and video or photo sharing sites. Loyalty programs provide added leverage to a brand's word of mouth marketing when the members play a more instrumental role in new customer acquisitions than non-member counterparts (Dowling and Uncles 1997).

Customer feedback is fundamental to the marketing concept, and active customer participation is necessary for collaborative marketing relationships. One particularly critical aspect of customer feedback is customer voice. *Customer voice* refers to the general level of comfort that a customer experiences in the complaining process to the firm when problems arise (Crutchfield 2007). Customer voice reflects the customer's feelings of ease with a specific firm rather than the individual customer's general predisposition to express or not express his or her complaint. Fornell and Wernerfelt (1987) show that, as a defensive strategy, customer complaints should be encouraged, because complaints provide the firm with opportunities to appease and retain dissatisfied customers. Encouraging customers to voice their complaints directly to the firm can be used to modify the brand to better match customer preferences (Maxham and Netemeyer 2003).

Customers with loyalty program ties to a firm are more apt to view customer voice as an opportunity to notify management of a problem needing attention and perhaps as a reflection of their continued support of the firm. A customer who has a relationship with the firm chooses to voice complaints to the firm when dissatisfaction arises rather than defecting, in part because he or she believes that the complaint will be handled appropriately (A.O. Hirschman 1970). Customer voice not only protects against customer defection but also contributes to customer relationship building (Lacey 2012).

Loyalty programs can provide a valuable dialogue channel through which the firm can secure marketing research cooperation from its customers. *Marketing research cooperation* describes the customer's desire to provide input that can be used for improving the firm's marketing performance, including by participating in new product development testing, evaluating advertising campaigns, giving opinions on service quality, and sharing insights about unfulfilled customer needs (Bettencourt 1997). Mixed results have been reported on the influence of loyalty program membership on raising the level of cooperative customer feedback by means of marketing research requests (Lacey et al. 2007; Lacey and Morgan 2009). One explanation for the occurrence of higher levels of cooperation is that customers in loyalty programs have more invested in the brand's success and stand to realize greater benefits for staying in the relationship (Keh and Lee 2006).

Customer Information

To practice relationship marketing, it is imperative for firms to collect and manage an ongoing flow of customer information. Furthermore, tiered value propositions require customer-specific information. So, while the benefits of loyalty programs for strengthening customer repatronage and advocacy behaviors can be substantial for the firm, perhaps loyalty programs' greatest asset is systematically collecting essential customer information that might be otherwise unobtainable (Liu and Yang 2009).

Customer information represents the firm's accessibility to proprietary and individualized customer information. Loyalty programs can provide the most complete source for capturing purchase-related customer information over time. When this is combined with pertinent demographic information, firms are positioned to have a more complete view of their customer relationships. Value in use of loyalty program generated customer-specific information can be instrumental in how firms adapt to the individual and dynamic product needs of their customers as well as how firms design customized value propositions in order to build more sustainable marketing relationships (Leenheer and Bijmolt 2008).

Aided by increasingly sophisticated customer relationship management technologies and analytics, firms can systematically maintain organizational memory on specific customers, including their preferences and behavior patterns, and apply that knowledge to develop statistical models to predict the propensity to increase frequency of spending and segment by risk of attrition, thereby reducing customer defections and increasing customer lifetime values (Nunes and Dreze 2006). In addition, customer information gleaned from loyalty programs can be used to reduce promotion expenses through the combination of 1) identifying unprofitable customers and 2) raising such customers to profitable status (or no longer pursuing their business).

On the strength of accurate and relevant individualized customer information, loyalty programs can also serve to facilitate personalized communications and enable the firm to target brand offerings more accurately based on individual interests (Liu and Yang 2009). Loyalty programs can be used as an alternative to mass-market promotion by enhancing the firm's ability to target more precisely a fragmented customer base and engage them with relevant and timely communications that reinforce the firm's brand(s) and provide value to the customer. Loyalty programs often serve as the primary vehicle used by firms to communicate regularly with their customers and share loyalty program account information for members to track, buy, earn, and redeem loyalty currency (e.g., airline miles, loyalty points) online. Using permission-based email marketing support, it is often through loyalty program-sponsored websites that the firm has its best opportunity to connect with its best customers and engage in interactive dialogue through customized content (McCartney 2009).

Marketers face an often tenuous balancing act of taking advantage of the abundance of individual customer information while preserving customer privacy protection safeguards. Meanwhile, the collection and use of customer information can favorably impact the longevity and profitability of customer relationships and depend upon customers' participation in loyalty programs. Information privacy exists when individuals can limit accessibility to and control the release of information about themselves (Westin 1967). Individual information disclosure has been linked to exchange theory (E.C. Hirschman 1980), whereby customers are willing to exchange their personal information in order to obtain other resources. Consumers must receive perceived value and incentives as a trade-off to share personal information (IBM Institute 2009).

With a few notable exceptions in the U.S. (e.g., healthcare, financial services), the information a customer provides a firm is considered the property of the firm unless the customer expresses explicit objections through available "opt-out" mechanisms. U.S. "opt-out" standards are in sharp contrast to the European Union's Data Protection Directive, which requires that consumer information remain private unless the customer gives permission to utilize his or her personal information. In effect, in the U.S., loyalty programs can serve as an opt-in program that allows firms to collect customer-specific information. By way of loyalty programs, the firm gains the customer's permission to collect and utilize personal information and receives compensation for the information through enhanced value proposition benefits (Lacey and Sneath 2006).

SUMMARY

As a hallmark of relationship marketing, mutual benefits can be realized through loyalty programs. Loyalty programs continue to be used by firms as marketing tools to support their relationship marketing strategies. Despite major criticisms received from marketing scholars (e.g., Dowling 2002; Kumar and Shah 2004; Noble and Phillips 2004; Shugan 2005), loyalty programs have achieved unprecedented popularity in the U.S. and abroad. On the basis of relationship marketing theory, this chapter has evaluated potential loyalty program benefits from two perspectives: from the perspective of the customer and from the perspective of the firm.

This chapter has examined how loyalty programs can be used by firms to shift greater marketing resource allocations toward selected customers and thereby achieve higher customer retention among their most valuable customers. Much of the discussion has centered on how firms use loyalty programs to collect specific consumer information and differentiate value propositions among customer segments, whereby firms can more effectively recognize and reward more valuable customers without alienating less valuable customers. Moreover, firms can determine customer value and define marketing strategies for specific customers or narrow customer segments as well as model customer attrition and intervention strategies.

From a theoretical standpoint, the proposed customer relational framework offers scholars an outline for elaboration of drivers of relationship commitment and how loyalty programs can contribute to building and maintaining the requisite convergence of economic, social, and resource benefits. Understanding the magnitude of how a loyalty program contributes to strengthening various customer benefits and their respective impact on building and sustaining customer relationships offers both theoretical and practice insights for prioritizing firm resources to support loyalty program components.

The expanded sources of firm benefits include a mixture of repatronage and other supporting behaviors, highlighting the potentially value-added role of customers as advocates to the firm. By considering more than purchasing activities in this assessment, the model provides a broader view of potential contributions of loyalty programs to the firm that may contribute toward improving the efficiency and effectiveness of marketing performance. Customers' desire to serve as advocates depends on the degree to which marketing relationships with the firm already exist. Finally, through loyalty programs, firms can secure authorization to collect and use valued (and, in some cases, elusive) individual customer information in exchange for enhanced value proposition offerings. Marketers use enhanced levels of benefits available through loyalty programs that customers would not otherwise receive as a form of compensation to customers to gain greater access to their personal information. Using sophisticated segmentation modeling, firms can use individualized customer data that can be used to further refine relationship marketing strategies and tactics.

REFERENCES

Bettencourt, Lance A. (1997), "Customer Voluntary Performance: Customers as Partners in Service Delivery," *Journal of Retailing*, 73(3), 383–406.

Blattberg, Robert C., Gary Getz and Jacquelyn S. Thomas (2001), *Customer Equity: Building and Managing Relationships as Valuable Assets*, Boston, MA: Harvard Business School Press.

Bolton, Ruth N., P.K. Kannan and Matthew D. Bramlett (2000), "Implications of Loyalty Program Membership and Service Experiences for Customer Retention and Value," *Journal of the Academy of Marketing Science*, 28(1), 95–108.

Bowman, Douglas and Das Narayandas (2004), "Linking Customer Measurement Effort to Customer Profitability in Business Markets," *Journal of Marketing Research*, 41 (November), 433–47.

Crosby, Lawrence A. and Nancy Stephens (1987), "Effects of Relationship Marketing on Satisfaction, Retention, and Prices in the Life Insurance Industry," *Journal of Marketing Research*, 24 (November), 404–11.

Crutchfield, Tammy Neal (2007), "Individual Service Providers versus the Firm: Where Do Customer Loyalties Lie?," *Service Marketing Quarterly*, 29(2), 19–44.

Czepiel, John A. (1990), "Service Encounters and Service Relationships: Implications for Research," *Journal of Business Research*, 20 (January), 13–21.

Daams, Peter, Kees Gelderman and Jos Schijns (2008), "The Impact of Loyalty Programmes in a B-to-B Context: Results of an Experimental Design," *Journal of Targeting, Measurement and Analysis for Marketing*, 16(4), 274–84.

Day, George S. (1971), "Attitude Change, Media, and Word of Mouth," *Journal of Advertising Research*, 11(6), 31–40.

De Wulf, Kristof and Gaby Odekerken-Schröder (2003), "Assessing the Impact of a Retailer's Relationship Efforts on Consumers' Attitudes and Behavior," *Journal of Retailing and Consumer Services*, 10, 95–108.

Dholakia, Utpal M. (2006), "How Customer Self-Determination Influences Relational Marketing Outcomes: Evidence from Longitudinal Field Studies," *Journal of Marketing Research*, 43(1), 109–20.

Dowling, Grahame R. (2002), "Customer Relationship Management: In B2C Markets, Often Less Is More," *California Management Review*, 44 (Spring), 87–104.

Dowling, Grahame and Mark Uncles (1997), "Do Customer Loyalty Programs Really Work?," *Sloan Management Review*, 38 (Summer), 71–82.

Dreze, Xavier and Joseph C. Nunes (2004), "Using Combined-Currency Prices to Lower Consumers' Perceived Cost," *Journal of Marketing Research*, 41(1), 59–72.

Ferguson, Rick and Kelly Hlavinka (2007), "The Colloquy Loyalty Marketing Census: Sizing Up the US Loyalty Marketing Industry," *Journal of Consumer Marketing*, 24(5), 313–21.

Fornell, Claes and Birger Wernerfelt (1987), "Defensive Marketing Strategy by Customer Complaint Behavior: A Theoretical Analysis," *Journal of Marketing Research*, 24 (November), 337–46.

Furse, David H., Girish N. Punj and David W. Stewart (1984), "A Typology of Individual Search Strategies among Purchasers of New Automobiles," *Journal of Consumer Research*, March 10, 417–23.

Gruen, Thomas W., John O. Summers and Frank Acito (2000), "Relationship Marketing Activities, Commitment, and Membership Behaviors in Professional Associations," *Journal of Marketing*, 64 (July), 34–49.

Gwinner, Kevin P., Dwayne D. Gremler and Mary Jo Bitner (1998), "Relational Benefits in Services Industries: The Customer's Perspective," *Journal of the Academy of Marketing Science*, 26 (Spring), 101–14.

Hennig-Thurau, Thorsten, Kevin P. Gwinner and Dwayne D. Gremler (2002), "Understanding Relationship Marketing Outcomes: An Integration of Relational Benefits and Relationship Quality," *Journal of Service Research*, 4 (February), 230–47.

Hirschman, Albert O. (1970), *Exit, Voice and Loyalty: Responses to Decline in Firms, Organizations and States*, Cambridge, MA: Harvard University Press.

Hirschman, Elizabeth C. (1980), "Innovativeness, Novelty Seeking, and Consumer Creativity," *Journal of Consumer Research*, 7(3), 283–95.

Huppertz, John, Sidney J. Arenson and Richard H. Evans (1978), "An Application of Equity Theory to Buyer–Seller Exchange Situations," *Journal of Marketing*, 15(2), 250–60.

IBM Institute (2009), "Beyond Advertising: Fact or Fiction," www.ibm.com/media/beyondadverting (accessed April 18, 2009).

Jones, Thomas O. and W. Earl Sasser, Jr. (1995), "Why Satisfied Customers Defect," *Harvard Business Review*, 73 (November–December), 88–99.

Kamakura, Wagner A., Vikas Mittal, Fernando de Rosa and Jose Afonso Mazzon (2002), "Assessing the Service Profit Chain," *Marketing Science*, 21(3), 294–317.

Keh, Hean Tat and Yih Hwai Lee (2006), "Do Reward Programs Build Loyalty for Services?

The Moderating Effect of Satisfaction on Type and Timing of Rewards," *Journal of Retailing*, 82(2), 127–36.

Kim, Byung-Do, Mengze Shi and Kannan Srinivasan (2001), "Reward Programs and Tacit Collusion," *Marketing Science*, 20 (Spring), 99–120.

Kivetz, Ran and Itamar Simonson (2002), "Earning the Right to Indulge: Effort as a Determinant of Customer Preferences toward Frequency Program Rewards," *Journal of Marketing Research*, 39 (May), 155–70.

Kopalle, Praveen K. and Scott Neslin (2003), "The Economic Viability of Frequency Reward Programs in a Strategic Competitive Environment," *Review of Marketing Science*, 1(1), 1–39.

Kumar, V. and Denish Shah (2004), "Building and Sustaining Profitable Customer Loyalty for the 21st Century," *Journal of Retailing*, 80(4), 317–30.

Lacey, Russell (2007), "Relational Drivers of Customer Commitment," *Journal of Marketing Theory and Practice*, 15(4), 313–31.

Lacey, Russell (2012), "How Customer Voice Contributes to Stronger Service Provider Relationships," *Journal of Services Marketing*, 26(2), 137–44.

Lacey, Russell and Robert M. Morgan (2007), "Committed Customers as Strategic Marketing Resources," *Journal of Relationship Marketing*, 6(2), 51–66.

Lacey, Russell and Robert M. Morgan (2009), "Customer Advocacy and the Impact of B2B Loyalty Programs," *Journal of Business and Industrial Marketing*, 24(1), 3–13.

Lacey, Russell and Julie Z. Sneath (2006), "Customer Loyalty Programs: Are They Fair to Consumers?," *Journal of Consumer Marketing*, 23(7), 464–70.

Lacey, Russell, Jae Suh and Robert M. Morgan (2007), "Differential Effects of Preferential Treatment Levels on Relational Outcomes," *Journal of Service Research*, 9 (February), 241–56.

Leenheer, Jorna and Tammo H.A. Bijmolt (2008), "Which Retailers Adopt a Loyalty Program? An Empirical Study," *Journal of Retailing and Consumer Services*, 1(2), 429–42.

Leenheer, Jorna, Harald J. van Heerde, Tammo H.A. Bijmolt and Ale Smidts (2007), "Do Loyalty Programs Really Enhance Behavioral Loyalty? An Empirical Analysis Accounting for Self-Selecting Members," *International Journal of Research in Marketing*, 24(1), 31–47.

Lewis, Michael (2004), "The Influence of Loyalty Programs and Short-Term Promotions on Customer Retention," *Journal of Marketing Research*, 41 (August), 281–92.

Lichtenstein, Donald R., Minette E. Drumwright and Bridgette M. Braig (2004), "The Effect of Corporate Social Responsibility on Customer Donations to Corporate-Supported Nonprofits," *Journal of Marketing*, 68 (October), 16–32.

Liu, Yuping (2007), "The Long-Term Impact of Loyalty Programs on Consumer Purchase Behavior and Loyalty," *Journal of Marketing*, 71 (October), 19–35.

Liu, Yuping and Rong Yang (2009), "Competing Loyalty Programs: Impact of Market Saturation, Market Share, and Category Expandability," *Journal of Marketing*, 73 (January), 93–108.

Mattila, Anna S. (2001), "The Impact of Relationship Type on Customer Loyalty in a Context of Service Failures," *Journal of Service Research*, 4 (November), 91–103.

Maxham, James G., III and Richard G. Netemeyer (2003), "Firms Reap What They Sow: The Effects of Shared Values and Perceived Organizational Justice on Customers' Evaluations of Complaint Handling," *Journal of Marketing*, 67(1), 46–62.

McCartney, Scott (2009), "Your Airline Wants to Get to Know You," *Wall Street Journal*, March 24, http://online.wsj.com/article/SB12378524295689529.html (accessed March 27, 2009).

Meyer-Waarden, Lars and Christophe Benavent (2006), "The Impact of Loyalty Programmes on Repeat Purchase Behavior," *Journal of Marketing Management*, 22(1–2), 61–88.

Moorman, Christine, George Zaltman and Robit Deshpande (1992), "Relationships between Providers and Users of Market Research: The Dynamics of Trust within and between Organizations," *Journal of Marketing Research*, 29, 314–28.

Noble, Stephanie M. and Joanna Phillips (2004), "Relationship Hindrance: Why Would

Consumers Not Want a Relationship with a Retailer?," *Journal of Retailing*, 80(4), 289–303.

Nunes, Joseph and Xavier Dreze (2006), "Your Loyalty Program Is Betraying You," *Harvard Business Review*, 84 (April), 124–31.

O'Brien, Louise and Charles Jones (1995), "Do Rewards Really Create Loyalty?," *Harvard Business Review*, 73 (May–June), 75–82.

Oliver, Richard and John E. Swan (1989), "Consumer Perceptions of Interpersonal Equity and Satisfaction in Transactions: A Field Survey Approach," *Journal of Marketing*, 53 (July), 21–35.

Reichheld, Frederick F. (1996), *The Loyalty Effect*, Boston, MA: Harvard Business School Press.

Richins, Martha (1983), "Negative Word-of-Mouth by Dissatisfied Consumers: A Pilot Study," *Journal of Marketing*, 47 (Winter), 68–78.

Roehm, Michelle, Ellen Bolman Pullins and Harper A. Roehm, Jr. (2002), "Designing Loyalty-Building Programs for Packaged Goods Brands," *Journal of Marketing Research*, 39 (May), 202–13.

Rust, Roland T., Katherine N. Lemon and Valarie A. Zeithaml (2004), "Return on Marketing: Using Customer Equity to Focus Marketing Strategy," *Journal of Marketing*, 68 (January), 109–27.

Sharp, Byron and Anne Sharp (1997), "Loyalty Programs and Their Impact on Repeat-Purchase Loyalty Patterns," *International Journal of Research in Marketing*, 14(5), 473–86.

Sheth, Jagdish N. and Atul Parvatiyar (1995), "Relationship Marketing in Consumer Markets: Antecedents and Consequences," *Journal of the Academy of Marketing Science*, 23 (Fall), 255–71.

Shugan, Steven (2005), "Brand Loyalty Programs: Are They Shams?," *Marketing Science*, 24(2), 185–93.

Sirdeshmukh, Deepak, Jagdip Singh and Barry Sabol (2002), "Consumer Trust, Value, and Loyalty in Relational Exchanges," *Journal of Marketing*, 66 (January), 15–37.

Smith, Amy K., Ruth N. Bolton and Janet Wagner (1999), "A Model of Customer Satisfaction with Service Encounters Involving Failure and Recovery," *Journal of Marketing Research*, 36 (August), 356–73.

Tax, Stephen and Stephen Brown (1998), "Recovering and Learning from Service Failure," *Sloan Management Review*, 40(1), 75–88.

Thibaut, John W. and Laurens Walker (1975), *Procedural Justice*, Hillsdale, NJ: Erlbaum.

Uncles, Mark D., Grahame R. Dowling and Kathy Hammond (2003), "Customer Loyalty and Customer Loyalty Programs?," *Journal of Consumer Marketing*, 20(4), 294–316.

Vargo, Stephen L. and Robert F. Lusch (2004), "Evolving to a New Dominant Logic for Marketing," *Journal of Marketing*, 68 (January), 1–17.

Verhoef, Peter C. (2003), "Understanding the Effect of Customer Relationship Management Efforts on Customer Retention and Customer Share Development," *Journal of Marketing*, 67 (October), 30–45.

Westin, Alan F. (1967), *Privacy and Freedom*, New York: Atheneum.

Xia, Lan, Kent B. Monroe and Jennifer L. Cox (2004), "The Price Is Unfair! A Conceptual Framework of Price Fairness Perceptions," *Journal of Marketing*, 68 (October), 1–15.

Zhang, Jie and Els Breugelmans (2012), "The Impact of an Item-Based Loyalty Program on Consumer Purchase Behavior," *Journal of Marketing Research*, 49(1), 50–65.

6. Service failure and recovery: implications for relationship marketing
Betsy Bugg Holloway and Sijun Wang

INTRODUCTION

Relationship marketing is built on the premise that building and maintaining relationships with customers leads to long-term retention, which in turn results in higher firm profitability. Service failure and recovery management is a key driver of customer relationship quality and ultimately customer retention (Hoffman, Kelley and Soulage 1995; Roos 1999). Research investigating why customers choose to remain with a firm indicates the most important reason, out of all the reasons identified, is "lack of a critical incident," or the lack of a memorable service failure (Colgate et al. 2007). Given the nature of services, however, some degree of failure is inevitable. Thus, firms must have well-planned processes and systems in place to identify failures when they occur, to learn from failures by improving service delivery, and to manage recoveries effectively, thereby restoring satisfaction, trust, and loyalty to the firm (J.S. Smith et al. 2009; J.S. Smith and Karwan 2010).

Service failure involves activities that occur as a result of customer perceptions of initial service delivery performance falling below the customer's expectations, or "zone of tolerance" (see Zeithaml et al. 1993). Service recovery involves the actions taken by an organization in response to a service failure (Grönroos 1988), presenting a critical opportunity by which the company may not only restore satisfaction but potentially even delight the customer with its efforts. Research indicates a good recovery has the potential to create more goodwill than if the failure had not happened in the first place (Hart et al. 1990). Service recovery is typically deemed to involve a wider set of activities than mere complaint handling, as it may include those situations in which a recovery is initiated by the service firm or employee without a complaint being made by the consumer (A.K. Smith et al. 1999). In such cases, the consumer may be unable or unwilling to complain, or the service personnel may acknowledge the failure before the consumer initiates a formal complaint.

There are two distinct dimensions of the service recovery, outcome and process. The outcome involves what is done (e.g., tangible compensation), while the process entails how it is done (e.g., employee interaction with the customer), and both influence customer perceptions of the service recovery. When failures occur, the service provider's recovery effort offers the potential either to reinforce a strong customer bond or to exacerbate the situation and potentially drive the customer to a competitor. Because customers are often more observant of the recovery effort than a routine or first-time service experience, they may be more dissatisfied by an organization's failure to recover than by the service failure itself (Bitner et al. 1990; A.K. Smith et al. 1999). The service quality literature suggests that a poor recovery after a service failure – a failed service recovery – presents a double deviation from customer expectations (Bitner et al. 1990); both the perceived service encounter and the company's incommensurate response may fail to meet the customer's expectations. Therefore, in attempting to respond to a service failure, organizations should carefully implement a systematic recovery strategy (J.S. Smith et al. 2009; J.S. Smith and Karwan 2010), taking into consideration factors unique to both the situation and the consumer.

Service failure and recovery issues have been the focus of considerable research throughout the past 15 years, and during this time we have achieved considerable understanding of the topic. Table 6.1 provides a comprehensive overview of the empirical service failure or recovery-focused research published in nine premier academic marketing journals during the time period 1990–2009, with the volume of research clearly increasing over this time. These nine journals were selected based on their frequency of publishing empirical studies on service failure and recovery as well as their impact factors. The following sections will elaborate on the main findings of our overview. Figure 6.1 presents a comprehensive illustration of the research findings related to the service failure and recovery process.

THE SERVICE FAILURE AND RECOVERY PROCESS

In the past decade, research has focused extensively on the characteristics of the service failure (e.g., type) and associated recovery strategies (e.g., employee responsiveness) in various contexts. In addition, substantial research has examined various outcomes of a service failure and recovery encounter, including cognitive reactions (e.g., justice), affective responses (e.g., post-recovery satisfaction), and behaviors or behavioral intentions (e.g., word of mouth). More recent research has focused on a wide range of variables that serve to moderate consumer perceptions of and reactions to a service failure and recovery experience, including the nature of the consumer–firm relationship (e.g., prior experience), individual variables (e.g., gender), and contextual variables relevant to the experience (e.g., presence of other customers). Further, as the interaction between consumers and organizations increasingly moves online, research has also begun to consider the complexity that technology adds to service failure and recovery experiences.

Service Failure and Service Recovery Encounters

Research indicates that it is possible to recover from almost any service failure, regardless of its type or magnitude, as long as the recovery is perceived to be commensurate with the failure experienced (Hoffman, Kelley and Rotalsky 1995; A.K. Smith et al. 1999). The nature, magnitude, and criticality of the service failure together determine the level of recovery required to recover justice. Research shows that customer perceptions of the service failure will vary, depending on the nature of the failure (outcome versus process), the severity of the failure, and the criticality of the consumption or service context (i.e., the importance of the service to the customer) (Ostrom and Iacobucci 1995). Further, attribution of the service failure, whereby the customer judges who is responsible for the failure (i.e., who should be blamed) and the magnitude of blame, is important as well (Maxham and Netemeyer 2002). For instance, A.K. Smith et al. (1999) found that, in the case of face-to-face encounters, when the service failure is clearly attributable to the service provider, customers were more dissatisfied than if the failure was attributable to a process that was not observable by the customers. Similarly, research has examined the impact of perceived controllability over service failures and service quality expectations on customer reactions to those failures, finding customers react negatively when they believe the service firm could have easily prevented the failure. However, when customers feel at least partly responsible for the failure or are uncertain about its cause, the negative effects of poor performance are somewhat lessened (Choi and Mattila 2008).

The service recovery literature has focused on justice theory as a meaningful way to explain consumers' perceptions of a service failure and subsequent recovery efforts, and the critical link between the service recovery and post-recovery satisfaction (Goodwin and Ross 1992; Tax et al. 1998; A.K. Smith et al. 1999). Once a consumer has voiced a complaint to a retailer, the complainant's subsequent attitudes and behaviors are largely determined by his or her perceptions of justice (Blodgett and Anderson 2000). A three-dimensional perspective of justice has evolved, including distributive justice (i.e., decision outcomes), procedural justice (i.e., decision-making procedures), and interactional justice (i.e., interpersonal

Table 6.1   Empirical studies on service failure and service recovery

Studies	Characteristics of failures	Recovery strategies	Post-recovery
			Affective
McColl-Kennedy and Sparks (2003)		Employee effort.	Anger. Contentment. Delight.
McColl-Kennedy et al. (2003)		Allow voice. Display of concern. Compensation. Employee effort.	Satisfaction.
Priluck (2003)	Product/service failure.		Trust. Commitment. Satisfaction.
Verma (2003)	Outcome vs. process.		Outrage. Delight.
Mattila and Patterson (2004)		Causal explanation. Compensation.	Satisfaction.
Weun et al. (2004)	Severity.	Compensation (distributive justice). Employee effort (interactional justice).	Satisfaction. Trust. Commitment.
Wong (2004)		Compensation. Apology.	Satisfaction.
Forbes et al. (2005)	Types of e-tail failures.	Discount. Correction. Correction plus. Replacement. Apology. Refund. Store credit. Replace at bricks-and-mortar store.	Satisfaction.

(failure) outcomes		Moderators		
Cognitive	Behavioral/ intentional	Relationship variables	Individual variables	Contextual variables
Justice (distributive, procedural, interactional).				
	Repurchase intention.		Gender.	
		Prior relationship quality.		
Attribution.			Cultural orientation.	
	Word of mouth.			
	Repurchase intention. Word of mouth.		Cultural orientation.	
	Switching.			

Table 6.1   (continued)

Studies	Characteristics of failures	Recovery strategies	Post-recovery Affective
Homburg and Furst (2005)		Mechanistic vs. organic approaches.	Satisfaction.
Schoefer and Ennew (2005)			Positive/negative emotions.
Harris et al. (2006)	Attribution of blame.	High/low recovery.	Satisfaction.
Hocutt et al. (2006)		Redress responsiveness. Empathy responsiveness.	Satisfaction.
Kau and Loh (2006)			Satisfaction. Trust.
Mattila (2006)		Explanation. Compensation.	
Patterson et al. (2006)		Apology. Cognitive control initiation.	Satisfaction.
Dallimore et al. (2007)		Provider facial expression. Provider affective state.	Anger.
Hedrick et al. (2007)			Pride. Faith. Trust.

(failure) outcomes		Moderators		
Cognitive	Behavioral/ intentional	Relationship variables	Individual variables	Contextual variables
Justice.	Loyalty.			B2B vs. B2C.
Justice (interactional procedural, distributive).				
Recovery expectation.	Repurchase intention.			Online/ offline shopping medium.
	Word of mouth.			
Justice.	Word of mouth. Loyalty.			
Justice (distributive, information).	Tipping.			
Justice (distributive, procedural, interactional).			Power distance. Uncertainty avoidance. Collectivism.	
			Gender.	
		Types of relationship (satisfaction- as-love,		

Table 6.1   (continued)

Studies	Characteristics of failures	Recovery strategies	Post-recovery
			Affective
Hedrick et al. (2007)			Love. Defensiveness. Power.
Hess et al. (2007)	Severity. Process (interactional) failure.		Dissatisfaction.
Karande et al. (2007)		Voice.	Satisfaction.
Magnini et al. (2007)	Attribution of blame (stability, control). Severity.		Satisfaction.
Matos et al. (2007)			Satisfaction.
Ringberg et al. (2007)	Situational vs. self-relevant breaches.		
Baker et al. (2008)		Apology. Discount.	Anger.

(failure) outcomes		Moderators		
Cognitive	Behavioral/ intentional	Relationship variables	Individual variables	Contextual variables
		satisfaction-as-trust, and satisfaction-as-control).		
Organization/ employee globality attribution.		Quality of past experience. Type of relationships.		
Justice (procedural).		Transaction history.	Gender.	
		History with the firm.		
	Repurchase intention. Word of mouth. Corporate image.		Subjects in the study.	Service contexts.
			Cultural models (relational, utilitarian, and opposi-tional).	
Perceived discri-mination. Perceived severity.	Word of mouth. Repurchase intention.		Race.	Presence of other customers.

Table 6.1   (continued)

Studies	Characteristics of failures	Recovery strategies	Post-recovery
			Affective
Bonifield and Cole (2008)		Compensation. Social comparison.	Anger.
Bunker and Ball (2008)		Compensation. Speed. Apology. Recovery initiation.	Relationship quality. Grudge.
Choi and Mattila (2008)	Attribution of blame.		Satisfaction.
DeWitt et al. (2008)			Positive/ negative emotions. Trust.
Dong et al. (2008)			Satisfaction.
Forbes (2008)	Self-serving-technology failures.		
Grégoire and Fisher (2008)			Betrayal.
Grewal et al. (2008)	Attribution of blame.	Compensation.	
Hess (2008)	Severity.		Satisfaction.

(failure) outcomes		Moderators		
Cognitive	Behavioral/ intentional	Relationship variables	Individual variables	Contextual variables
	Exit. Word of mouth. Complaint to management. Complaint to third party.			
	Retaliation desire. Communication avoidance.			
	Return intention. Word of mouth.			
Perceived value.	Repurchase intention.			
	Switching.			
Justice (distributive, procedural, interactional).	Retaliation. Demands for reparation.			
	Repurchase intention.			
	Repurchase intention. Word of mouth.	Firm reputation.		

Table 6.1   (continued)

Studies	Characteristics of failures	Recovery strategies	Post-recovery
			Affective
Kalamas et al. (2008)			Anger. Satisfaction.
Mittal et al. (2008)			Satisfaction.
Park et al. (2008)			
Raimondo et al. (2008)			Satisfaction. Trust.
Schoefer and Diamant-opoulos (2008)			Emotions.
Grégoire et al. (2009)			Negative emotions.
Matos et al. (2009)	Severity.		Satisfaction.
McColl-Kennedy et al. (2009)			Rancorous rage. Retaliatory rage.

(failure) outcomes		Moderators		
Cognitive	Behavioral/ intentional	Relationship variables	Individual variables	Contextual variables
Corporate image. Justice.	Stereotyping. Complaint intention. Word of mouth. Repurchase intention. Complaint to third party.		Gender.	Provider gender.
	Complaint intention.	Relationship duration.	Information control.	
Justice (distributive, procedural, interactional).				Industry.
	Loyalty.	Relationship age.		
Justice.	Repurchase. Word of mouth. Third-party action.			
	Revenge. Avoidance.	Relationship strength.		
Fairness.	Repurchase intention. Word of mouth. Complaint intention.		Attitude toward com- plaining.	
	Exit. Revenge. Word of mouth.			

Table 6.1   (continued)

Studies	Characteristics of failures	Recovery strategies	Post-recovery
			Affective
Rio-Lanza et al. (2009)			Emotions. Satisfaction.

Note: Studies were identified by a computerized bibliographic search; we searched for the terms "service failure" and "service recovery" in keywords and abstracts and then narrowed our search by including only empirical studies published in nine premier journal outlets for service marketing research during the period 1990–2009. In alphabetical order, these journals are *European Journal of Marketing, International Journal of Research in Marketing, Journal of Business Research, Journal of Marketing, Journal of Marketing Research, Journal of Retailing, Journal of Service Marketing, Journal of Service Research*, and *Journal of the Academy of Marketing Science.* We regret that worthwhile research published in other publications was omitted from this table owing to space considerations.

behavior in the enactment of procedures and delivery of outcomes). The three dimensions of justice – distributive, interactional, and procedural – are a function of both the severity of service failure (Ostrom and Iacobucci 1995) and subsequent recovery efforts (A.K. Smith et al. 1999). By extending the justice theory, more recent research has also incorporated the fairness theory and related constructs of equity and fairness into our understandings of consumers' emotional reactions to service failure and recovery. For instance, McColl-Kennedy and Sparks (2003) introduced the accountability of the failure (i.e., whom to blame) and counterfactual thinking aroused by the failure and recovery (i.e., what *could* have occurred, what *should* have occurred, and how it *would* have felt had alternative recovery action been taken) as two additional factors that influence customers' evaluation of service failure and recovery and subsequent emotions experienced.

Consumer perceptions of a recovery encounter are influenced by a number of factors. Early research demonstrated the importance of explanation, apology, customer voice, and compensation in recovery encounters (Bitner 1990; Goodwin and Ross 1992; Blodgett et al. 1993). Research highlights the important role that frontline employees play in recognizing and responding to failures in the appropriate manner; responsiveness, initiation of the recovery, effort (McColl-Kennedy and Sparks 2003), speed (e.g., A.K. Smith et al. 1999), demonstrated effort (e.g., McColl-Kennedy and Sparks 2003), empathy (e.g., A.K. Smith and Bolton 2002), courtesy (e.g., McCollough et al. 2000), and customer involvement in the recovery

	(failure) outcomes		Moderators	
Cognitive	Behavioral/ intentional	Relationship variables	Individual variables	Contextual variables
Justice.				

via co-creation (e.g., Dong et al. 2008) are all key variables which have the potential to influence consumer reactions to the recovery effort.

Post-Recovery Outcomes

Goodwin and Ross (1989) were the first to posit the relationship between service recovery perceptions and post-recovery satisfaction. Satisfaction with the recovery, or transaction-specific satisfaction, has been defined as "the degree to which a customer is satisfied with a service firm's transaction-specific service recovery effort following a service failure" (Boshoff 1999: 237). Service failure and recovery research consistently illustrates that satisfaction with the recovery serves as an important mediator linking perceptions of fairness to a number of post-complaint behaviors and attitudes (Huppertz et al. 1978; Mohr and Bitner 1995; Tax et al. 1998).

For example, the literature has established the relationship between (dis)satisfaction and word of mouth behavior, and the resulting communications about a product or service in which none of the participants are marketing sources (Richins 1983). In the case of a dissatisfactory experience, research consistently indicates that dissatisfied consumers actively report their negative experience to others, making negative word of mouth a potentially noteworthy outcome of a failed service failure and recovery encounter. Another widely studied behavioral outcome of service failure and recovery is repurchase intentions and repatronage, or the consumer's reported likelihood of future purchase behavior with or patronage of the service provider. While various marketing activities focus completely on attracting new customers, firms aim to encourage repeat purchasing by current customers through a reduction in customer defection.

Research indicates that justice is the key driver of emotions in the service failure and recovery encounter (Chebat and Slusarczyk 2005; Schoefer and Ennew 2005; Schoefer and Diamantopoulos 2008), and that consumers' affective reactions to service failure and recovery encounters influence how

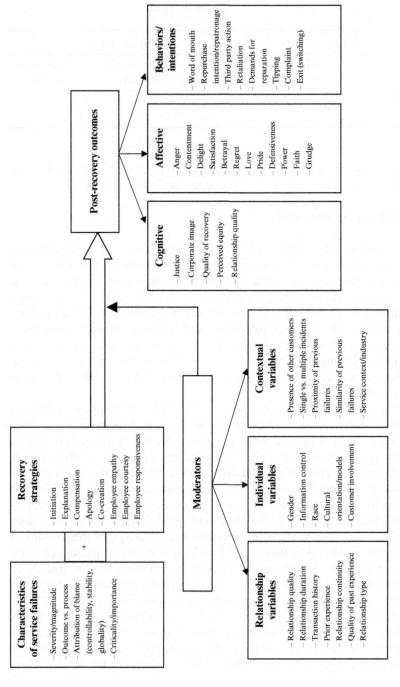

Figure 6.1   Model of the service failure and recovery process

they evaluate an organization's recovery efforts as well as post-recovery satisfaction (e.g., A.K. Smith and Bolton 2002; Schoefer and Ennew 2005; Menon and Dubé 2007). As illustrated in Figure 6.1, research has identified a number of affective outcomes of the service failure and recovery experience, with particular emphasis on anger. Anger and related negative states lie along a continuum from mild (e.g., annoyance) to strong (e.g., rage). Research finds that the more negative the emotions felt throughout a service encounter, the more negative the consumer's resulting perceptions, attitudes, and behaviors (Dubé and Morgan 1996; Kalamas et al. 2008). In the context of service failures, research indicates that angry customers have higher perceptions of injustice (McColl-Kennedy and Sparks 2003), are less satisfied (Rio-Lanza et al. 2009), report lower service evaluations and corporate image (Kalamas et al. 2008), are more likely to engage in exit, switching, and complaining behavior (Bougie et al. 2003; Chebat et al. 2005), and are more likely to engage in third party action (Bougie et al. 2003) or even aggressive behaviors (McColl-Kennedy et al. 2009). To the other extreme of emotions experienced by customers, delight was found to occur when customers' expectations from service recovery were exceeded to a surprising degree (Rust and Oliver 2000).

Moderators

In more recent years, researchers have focused on a number of variables operating outside and independent of the failure and recovery that moderate consumer perceptions of and reactions to the failure and recovery encounter. Researchers have long called for the need to examine more individual-level variables in affecting the relationship outcomes companies strive to achieve (Bendapudi and Berry 1997; Odekerken-Schröder et al. 2003). This is consistent with research from Reynolds and Beatty (1999), which found that personal characteristics motivate consumers to maintain relationships, and from Gwinner et al. (1998), which posits that the success of relationship marketing activities depends, in part, upon individual consumer traits and preferences. Accordingly, service failure and recovery research has begun to examine the role of moderating variables, including individual consumer characteristics (e.g., gender, race, cultural orientation), the nature of the consumer's relationship with the organization, and a range of contextual variables which moderate consumer perceptions, attitudes, and behaviors.

Individual variables
Research examining the role of gender in failure and recovery indicates male and female customers place different emphasis on elements of the

service recovery process (e.g., Kalamas et al. 2008). For instance, unlike men, women want their views to be heard during service recovery attempts (McColl-Kennedy et al. 2003). In international service settings, researchers have examined how one's cultural orientation shapes evaluations of service failure and recovery contexts, finding important differences across groups (e.g., Mattila and Patterson 2004; Poon et al. 2004; Wong 2004). Similarly, Ringberg et al. (2007) examine the influence of culture on service recovery expectations, identifying three distinct cultural models (relational, oppositional, and utilitarian) that consumers apply to goods or service failures. Combined with previous work (e.g., Winsted 1997; Mattila and Patterson 2004), these studies highlight the need to incorporate cultural factors into service failure and recovery research. In their review of cross-cultural studies in the service marketing literature, Zhang et al. (2008) have advocated for more studies on the cultural roles in the service failure and recovery process.

Relationship variables
Substantial research has focused on the ways in which the nature of the customer's relationship with the organization, the length and extent of that relationship, and the customer's perceptions of the firm (e.g., firm reputation) affect that customer's responses to a service failure and recovery encounter. Previous research has examined the quality and/or quantity of customers' prior experiences with the organization in a variety of ways. Several empirical studies have conceptualized this as the perceived quality of past service performance (Kelley and Davis 1994; Tax et al. 1998; Hess et al. 2003), the quality of the firm–customer relationship (Holloway et al. 2009), satisfaction with past service encounters (Kelley and Davis 1994; Forrester and Maute 2001), personal rapport with a specific service employee (DeWitt and Brady 2003), or involvement between the customer and firm (Goodman et al. 1995). While there is agreement with respect to the benefit of establishing high quality relationships with customers, there is not consistent or conclusive evidence as to whether these high quality relationships actually buffer or magnify the negative impact of encounters involving service failures on subsequent attitudes and behaviors (Hess et al. 2003, 2007).

Some researchers have argued that strong relationships can provide a sort of protection, as consumers who are engaged in relational exchanges are more likely to forgive a poor product or service experience – the forgiveness hypothesis (Anderson and Sullivan 1993; Tax et al. 1998; Singh and Sirdeshmukh 2000). For example, several studies find that a high quality relationship serves to buffer service organizations when failures occur because of the perceived relational benefits and/or the build-up of goodwill (Hennig-Thurau and Klee 1997; Tax et al. 1998; Forrester and Maute 2001; Mattila 2001; DeWitt and Brady 2003; Hess et al. 2003, 2007; Priluck 2003). This is consistent with the relationship marketing premise that customers are generally less likely to leave a service provider when they perceive relational benefits, including social and psychological benefits (Gwinner et al. 1998) and interpersonal bonds (Gremler and Brown 1998). However, other researchers also have posited that high quality relationships may in fact exaggerate customer responses following a service failure incident as a result of potentially greater disconfirmation experienced, i.e., the betrayal hypothesis (Kelley and Davis 1994; Goodman et al. 1995; Singh and Sirdeshmukh 2000; Grégoire et al. 2009; Holloway et al. 2009). In particular, research indicates that the raised expectations associated with strong relationships can lead to greater negative disconfirmation when a failure occurs (Oliver 1980). This service quality "gap" may be further exacerbated when the firm's subsequent attempt to recover is perceived to be inadequate or "incommensurate" to the problem experienced (A.K. Smith et al. 1999). For instance, Grégoire et al. (2009) found that firms' stronger-relationship customers have the longest unfavorable reactions and the revenge of these customers decreases more slowly and their avoidance increases more rapidly than that of weaker-relationship customers.

Contextual variables
Given the nature of inseparability of service production and its consumption, service contexts often demonstrate significant moderating effects in the service failure and recovery process. For instance, whether the encounter is B2C versus B2B (Homburg and Furst 2005), online versus offline (Harris et al. 2006), the presence (or lack thereof) of other customers (Baker et al. 2008), the service employee gender (Kalamas et al. 2008), and the service context or industry (A.K. Smith and Bolton 2002; Park et al. 2008) may all potentially moderate attitudinal and behavioral reactions to service failure and recovery experiences. For example, Homburg and Furst (2005) examined both mechanistic (based on established guidelines) and organic (based on creating a favorable internal environment) approaches to service recovery and found that the beneficial effects of mechanistic approaches are stronger in B2C settings than in B2B ones, and stronger for service firms than for manufacturing firms. The online/offline delivery of services, including self-service technology (SST), has also been shown to influence consumer recovery expectations, satisfaction, and post-recovery loyalty to service recovery strategies (Holloway and Beatty 2003; Harris et al. 2006). With regard to industry differences, A.K. Smith and Bolton (2002) found that customers in a hotel setting responded to the same

service failure encounters with more emotions and were more systematic in their evaluations of an organization's recovery performance. Similarly, Park et al. (2008) reported noticeable industrial differences in registered service failure complaints; the airline sector showed a higher percentage of complaints related to distributive justice, the cruise industry indicated a higher percentage of problems related to interactional justice, and e-travel and travel agents more frequently received complaints related to procedural justice. The presence of other customers represents another uncertain yet important component of customer experience (Baker et al. 2008), and provider gender has been shown to influence consumers' emotional and judgmental reactions to a service failure as well (Kalamas et al. 2008).

The Role of Technology in Service Failure and Recovery

Given the extraordinary growth in self-service technologies and online service providers, the literature has begun to address service recovery management in this context (e.g., Bitner et al. 2000; Holloway and Beatty 2003). The inherent features of online service delivery, such as the lack of physical presence of products and human interaction, have introduced new forms of service failure and created the need for new approaches to service recovery efforts. Thus, in place of employee interaction, other issues, such as privacy, on-time delivery, and ease of navigation, have surfaced as critical elements of the online service experience (Holloway and Beatty 2003; Wolfinbarger and Gilly 2003). Research indicates that the influence of technology in the service encounter has a meaningful impact on consumer attitudes and behaviors (e.g., Meuter et al. 2000; Parasuraman and Grewal 2000; Shankar et al. 2003). For example, consumers enter the world of online retailing with a wide range of experience with and knowledge about the Internet, and research indicates that the extent of consumers' cumulative online purchasing experience influences their perceptions of online encounters, including service failure and recovery experiences (Holloway et al. 2005). Similarly, research has focused on service quality issues unique to the online setting, as well as drivers of service failures in this context. For instance, Parasuraman et al. (2005) assess service quality offered by websites on which customers shop online, providing a four-dimensional scale for service quality (E-S-QUAL), including efficiency, fulfillment, privacy, and system availability, and a scale for measuring the quality of e-recovery service (E-R-QUAL), composed of responsiveness, compensation, and contact. Research from Holloway and Beatty (2008) uses the critical incident technique to examine the factors driving consumer dissatisfaction in the online service environment, identifying the top drivers of dissatisfactory encounters (i.e., which may result in service failures) in this context as fulfillment/reliability, website design/interaction, customer service, and security/privacy.

Research clearly demonstrates that the technology available today allows for vastly improved communications capabilities, as well as measurement and monitoring of customer perceptions of service and recovery quality. Research illustrates how service encounters can be enhanced through the effective use of technology, allowing customization, improved recoveries, and spontaneous delight (Bitner et al. 2000). However, research likewise highlights the potential negative outcomes associated with the incorporation of technology (e.g., Mick and Fournier 1998). There remain opportunities to consider the optimum "mix" of technology vis-à-vis interpersonal interactions in the service experience, including the service recovery process, in generating optimal customer reactions.

Building on the concept of value co-creation (Bendapudi and Leone 2003; Vargo and Lusch 2004), whereby customers are contributing to the process of marketing, consumption, and delivery of products or services, research has begun to examine service failure and recovery from this perspective as well. Conceptualizing a new construct, "customer participation in service recovery," Dong et al. (2008) find that, when customers actively participate in the service recovery process, they are more likely to report a number of favorable outcomes, including higher levels of role clarity, satisfaction with the service recovery, and intentions to co-create value in the future.

FUTURE RESEARCH DIRECTIONS

Despite the tremendous gains achieved in our understanding of service failure and recovery, there remain opportunities for further research on a range of topics. First, there are a number of methodological concerns that could be improved in future research. A majority of current empirical research relies on experiment designs with student samples or surveys asking respondents to retrospect on what happened to them before. There is a strong need for researchers to examine actual service failure and recovery encounters involving real companies and to utilize more viable methods to triangulate what we have learned from experiments and surveys. Similarly, with the noteworthy exception of Maxham and Netemeyer (2002), there remains the need for further longitudinal research on the topic to examine such issues as how fairness perceptions, trust, and commitment evolve over time when customers experience multiple failures with an ongoing service provider. Such research would allow an examination of the financial costs and benefits of specific service recovery programs in a live organizational environment. Conducting a financial assessment (e.g., cost of recovery, profit analysis, return on investment per customer, etc.) of a firm's recovery strategies over time would provide greater understanding of the value of service recovery management. Such an approach also would allow consideration of an optimal mix of investments into reliable service delivery versus superior service recoveries when failures occur.

Similarly, further examination of actual customer behavioral data (e.g., spending) would be a substantial improvement over dependency on self-report behaviors and behavioral intentions (e.g., repurchase and word of mouth intentions). In addition, a substantial percentage of research employs the critical incident technique (CIT) and other retrospective techniques that require respondents to recount previous service encounters and their reactions. It remains unclear, however, whether such approaches are accurate or biased, suggesting a need to ascertain a certain time threshold within which customers may accurately recall their specific perceptions (Maxham and Netemeyer 2002).

A continuing controversy in the service failure and recovery literature involves the service recovery paradox, the phenomenon by which highly effective recovery strategies result in post-recovery satisfaction levels that are higher than pre-failure levels (McCollough and Bharadwaj 1992; McCollough 2009). Evidence for the paradox remains mixed; while some studies find support for the service recovery paradox (e.g., A.K. Smith and Bolton 1998; Hocutt et al. 2006), others report contrary results, finding satisfaction is not restored despite strong, effective recoveries (e.g., McCollough et al. 2000; Maxham 2001). A meta-analytic review (see Matos et al. 2007) concludes that the service recovery paradox effect is more likely to occur for satisfaction than for repurchase intentions, word of mouth, or corporate image, suggesting the lack of an effect on these variables. While the authors report support for the service recovery paradox effect, they suggest the need to investigate whether cognitive or affective mechanisms are the drivers. Further, research (Kau and Loh 2006) fails to support the service recovery paradox effect on trust, finding that customers who were initially satisfied with the service expressed greater trust when compared to the satisfied complainants, thereby suggesting that service failures may be particularly detrimental to trust. The authors conclude by acknowledging the need for further research to understand the conditions under which the paradox may or may not occur.

As previously discussed, the service failure and recovery literature has begun to examine the individual consumer differences that may moderate perceptions of and reactions to a service failure and recovery encounter. Further opportunities remain to identify and test relevant individual variables, such as the consumer's level of technology readiness (Parasuraman 2000) in the case of online service encounters, or the consumer's level of receptivity to recovery communications and other relationship marketing efforts over time (Fournier et al. 1998; Noble and Phillips 2004). Similarly, research that further accounts for the multiple individual differences and responses to service recovery efforts may help firms to design a range of service recovery options to best meet the needs and wants of their individual customers. This is in line with the research of Ringberg et al. (2007), who suggest providers create an "adaptive service recovery approach," whereby recoveries are adapted dynamically to the personalities, needs, and presuppositions of their individual clients.

While the vast majority of service failure and recovery research is conducted in a B2C context, the topic remains highly relevant for B2B service providers, presenting a strong need to extend research to this context (Wang and Huff 2007). For instance, given the ongoing nature of business relationships, one would expect that the relationship variables would play an even more influential role in moderating the service failure and recovery experience, though this remains to be examined. On a related matter, the service design and operations management literatures examine service quality issues integral to service failure and recovery (e.g., Miller et al. 2000; Goldstein et al. 2002). However, there remains a need for further integration of these two streams of literature (i.e., consumer research and internal operations management) to provide a more systematic understanding of these issues.

Because the vast majority of customers choose not to complain to a firm following a dissatisfactory experience (Chebat et al. 2005; Voorhees et al. 2006), companies continue to be challenged to find effective ways to solicit complaints from dissatisfied customers. The result of unreported dissatisfactory experiences is angry customers, increased defections, negative word of mouth, and the lost potential for valuable organizational learning and quality improvements. Recent research has provided a strong foundation for understanding important differences between those who engage in complaint behavior and noncomplainers (Bodey and Grace 2006; Voorhees et al. 2006). However, there remains the need to identify innovative, effective strategies to increase propensity to complain, among both complainers and noncomplainers, and to transform such information into quality improvements.

Similarly, there remains a need to develop improved firm–customer communications during the service failure and recovery process. For instance, research indicates that, as interpersonal interactions between a firm's frontline employees and its customers increase, the likelihood of customers voicing a complaint also increases (Voorhees and Brady

2005). Similarly, research highlights the importance of "recovery voice," whereby the service provider solicits feedback from the customer in creating a satisfactory solution to a failure experienced (Karande et al. 2007). Furthermore, research emphasizes that the social aspects of service encounters (e.g., personalization, friendliness, self-disclosure) are critical to customer satisfaction and loyalty (e.g., Goodwin and Gremler 1996). And, given the potential ramifications of anger and other negative emotions, researchers should further investigate how frontline employees may identify and control affective reactions during the service recovery process (Kalamas et al. 2008). Similarly, research indicates that firms should effectively communicate to the customer what circumstances led to the failure, and inform the customer of failure prevention efforts it has in place (Choi and Mattila 2008). Research could build from these findings by identifying specific strategies by which customer-contact employees might not only identify service failures but also sustain enhanced customer communication throughout the service recovery process to maximize satisfaction.

Similarly, research has begun to examine strategies that include customer voice in co-creating the recovery effort. For instance, research on recovery voice indicates that customers perceive greater procedural justice and higher overall post-failure satisfaction when given the opportunity to contribute to the recovery effort (Karande et al. 2007). Research could build from this and other (Dong et al. 2008) research by further examining effective processes companies can use to involve the customer in the creation and delivery of recoveries. Similarly, there remains a need to identify the antecedents (individual and situational variables) that influence a customer's willingness to participate in the co-creation of a service recovery.

In conclusion, we hope this chapter highlights the critical role of service failure and recovery in every organization's relationship marketing strategies. Service providers must use recovery management as an effective means to identify service quality problems, to reduce customer defections, and to strengthen relationships with their customers over time. While we have achieved substantial understanding of service failure and recovery, given the importance of the topic there is a need for continued research.

REFERENCES

Anderson, Eugene W. and Mary W. Sullivan (1993), "The Antecedents and Consequences of Customer Satisfaction for Firms," *Marketing Science*, 12(2), 125–43.
Baker, Thomas L., Tracy Meyer and James D. Johnson (2008), "Individual Differences in Perceptions of Service Failure and Recovery: The Role of Race and Discriminatory Bias," *Journal of the Academy of Marketing Science*, 36, 552–64.

Bendapudi, N. and Leonard L. Berry (1997), "Customers' Motivations for Maintaining Relationships with Service Providers," *Journal of Retailing*, 73(1), 15–37.

Bendapudi, N. and R.P. Leone (2003), "Psychological Implications of Customer Participation on Co-Production," *Journal of Marketing*, 67(1), 14–28.

Bitner, Mary Jo (1990), "Evaluating Service Encounters: The Effects of Physical Surroundings and Employee Responses," *Journal of Marketing*, 54, 69–82.

Bitner, M., B. Booms and M. Tetreault (1990), "The Service Encounter: Diagnosing Favorable and Unfavorable Incidents," *Journal of Marketing*, 54(1), 71–84.

Bitner, M.J., Stephen W. Brown and M.L. Meuter (2000), "Technology Infusion in Service Encounters," *Journal of the Academy of Marketing Science*, 28(1), 138–49.

Blodgett, J.G. and R.D. Anderson (2000), "A Bayesian Network Model of the Consumer Complaint Process," *Journal of Service Research*, 2(4), 321–38.

Blodgett, Jeffrey G., Donald H. Granbois and Rockney G. Walters (1993), "The Effects of Perceived Justice on Complainants' Negative Word-of-Mouth Behavior and Repatronage Intentions," *Journal of Retailing*, 69(4), 399–428.

Bodey, K. and D. Grace (2006), "Segmenting Service "Complainers" and "Non-Complainers" on the Basis of Consumer Characteristics," *Journal of Services Marketing*, 20(3), 178–87.

Bonifield, Carolyn and Catherine A. Cole (2008), "Better Him than Me: Social Comparison Theory and Service Recovery," *Journal of the Academy of Marketing Science*, 36, 565–77.

Boshoff, C. (1999), "RECOVSAT: An Instrument to Measure Satisfaction with Transaction-Specific Service Recovery," *Journal of Service Research*, 1(3), 236–49.

Bougie, Roger, Rik Pieters and Marcel Zeelenberg (2003), "Angry Customers Don't Come Back, They Get Back: The Experience and Behavioral Implications of Anger and Dissatisfaction in Services," *Journal of the Academy of Marketing Science*, 31(4), 377–93.

Bunker, Matthew P. and Dwayne Ball (2008), "Causes and Consequences of Grudge-Holding in Service Relationships," *Journal of Services Marketing*, 22(1), 37–47.

Chebat, Jean-Charles and W. Slusarczyk (2005), "How Emotions Mediate the Effects of Perceived Justice on Loyalty in Service Recovery Situations: An Empirical Study," *Journal of Business Research*, 58(5), 664–73.

Chebat, Jean-Charles, Moshe Davidow and Isabelle Codjovi (2005), "Silent Voices: Why Some Dissatisfied Consumers Fail to Complain," *Journal of Service Research*, 7(4), 328–42.

Choi, Sunmee and Anna S. Mattila (2008), "Perceived Controllability and Service Expectations: Influences on Customer Relations Following Service Failure," *Journal of Business Research*, 61, 24–30.

Colgate, Mark, Vicky Thuy-Uyen Tong, Christina Kwai-Choi Lee and John U. Farley (2007), "Back from the Brink: Why Customers Stay," *Journal of Service Research*, 9(3), 211–28.

Dallimore, Karen S., Beverley A. Sparks and Ken Butcher (2007), "The Influence of Angry Customer Outbursts on Service Providers' Facial Displays and Affective States," *Journal of Services Marketing*, 10(1), 78–92.

DeWitt, Tom and Michael K. Brady (2003), "Rethink Service Recovery Strategies," *Journal of Services Marketing*, 6(2), 193–207.

DeWitt, Tom, Doan T. Nguyen and Roger Marshall (2008), "Exploring Customer Loyalty Following Service Recovery," *Journal of Service Research*, 10(3), 269–81.

Dong, Beibei, Kenneth R. Evans and Shaoming Zou (2008), "The Effects of Customer Participation in Co-Created Service Recovery," *Journal of Business Research*, 36, 123–37.

Dubé, Laurette and M. Morgan (1996), "Trend Effects and Gender Differences in Retrospective Judgments of Consumption Emotions," *Journal of Consumer Research*, 23, 156–62.

Forbes, Lukas P. (2008), "When Something Goes Wrong and No One Is Around: Non-Internet Self-Service Technology Failure and Recovery," *Journal of Services Marketing*, 22(4), 316–27.

Forbes, Lukas P., Scott W. Kelly and K. Douglas Hoffman (2005), "Typologies of

E-Commerce Retail Failures and Recovery Strategies," *Journal of Services Marketing*, 19(5), 280–92.

Forrester, W.R. and M.F. Maute (2001), "The Impact of Relationship Satisfaction on Attributions, Emotions, and Behaviors Following Service Failure," *Journal of Applied Business Research*, 17(1), 1–14.

Fournier, Susan, Susan Dobscha and David Glen Mick (1998), "Preventing the Premature Death of Relationship Marketing," *Harvard Business Review*, 76 (January–February), 42–51.

Goldstein, S.M., R. Johnston, J. Duffy and J. Rao (2002), "The Service Concept: The Missing Link in Service Design Research?," *Journal of Operations Management*, 20, 121–34.

Goodman, P.S., M. Fichman, F.J. Lerch and P.R. Snyder (1995), "Customer–Firm Relationships, Involvement, and Customer Satisfaction," *Academy of Management Journal*, 38(5), 1310–24.

Goodwin, Cathy and Dwayne D. Gremler (1996), "Friendship over the Counter," in Stephen W. Brown, David Bowen and Teresa Swartz (eds.), *Advances in Services Marketing and Management*, Vol. V, Greenwich, CT: JAI Press.

Goodwin, Cathy and Ivan Ross (1989), "Salient Dimensions of Perceived Fairness in Resolution of Service Complaints," *Journal of Satisfaction, Dissatisfaction, and Complaining Behavior*, 2, 87–92.

Goodwin, C. and Ivan Ross (1992), "Consumer Responses to Service Failures: Influence of Procedural and Interactional Fairness Perceptions," *Journal of Business Research*, 25, 149–63.

Grégoire, Yany and Robert J. Fisher (2008), "Customer Betrayal and Retaliation: When Your Best Customers Become Your Worst Enemies," *Journal of the Academy of Marketing Science*, 36, 247–61.

Grégoire, Yany, Thomas M. Tripp and Renaud Legoux (2009), "When Customer Love Turns into Lasting Hate: The Effects of Relationship Strength and Time on Customer Revenge and Avoidance," *Journal of Marketing*, 73(6), 18.

Gremler, Dwayne D. and Stephen W. Brown (1998), "Service Loyalty: Antecedents, Components, and Outcomes," in D. Grewal and C. Pechmann (eds.), *1998 AMA Winter Educators' Conference: Marketing Theory and Applications*, Chicago: American Marketing Association, pp. 165–6.

Grewal, Dhruv, Anne L. Roggeveen and Michael Tsiros (2008), "The Effect of Compensation on Repurchase Intentions in Service Recovery," *Journal of Retailing*, 4, 424–34.

Grönroos, C. (1988), "Service Quality: The Six Criteria for Goods Perceived Service Quality," *Review of Business*, 9(3), 10–23.

Gwinner, Kevin, Dwayne D. Gremler and Mary Jo Bitner (1998), "Relational Benefits in Services Industries: The Customer's Perspective," *Journal of the Academy of Marketing Science*, 26 (Spring), 101–14.

Harris, K.E., L.A. Mohr and K.L. Bernhardt (2006), "Online Service Failure, Consumer Attributions and Expectations," *Journal of Services Marketing*, 20(7), 453–8.

Hart, Christopher W.L., James L. Heskett and W. Earl Sasser, Jr. (1990), "The Profitable Art of Service Recovery," *Harvard Business Review*, 68 (July–August), 148–56.

Hedrick, Natalie, Michael Beverland and Stella Minahan (2007), "An Exploration of Relational Customers' Response to Service Failure," *Journal of Services Marketing*, 21(1), 64–72.

Hennig-Thurau, T. and A. Klee (1997), "The Impact of Customer Satisfaction and Relationship Quality on Customer Retention: A Critical Reassessment and Model Development," *Psychology and Marketing*, 14(8), 737–64.

Hess, Ronald L., Jr. (2008), "The Impact of Firm Reputation and Failure Severity on Customers' Responses to Service Failures," *Journal of Services Marketing*, 22(5), 385–98.

Hess, Ronald L., Jr., Shanker Ganesan and Noreen Klein (2003), "Service Failure and Recovery: The Impact of Relationship Factors on Customer Satisfaction," *Journal of the Academy of Marketing Science*, 31(2), 127–45.

Hess, Ronald L., Jr., Shanker Ganesan and Noreen Klein (2007), "Interactional Service

Failures in a Pseudorelationship: The Role of Organizational Attributions," *Journal of Retailing*, 83 (1), 79–95.

Hocutt, Mary Ann, Michael R. Bowers and D. Todd Donavan (2006), "The Art of Service Recovery: Fact or Fiction?," *Journal of Services Marketing*, 20(3), 199–207.

Hoffman, K. Douglas, Scott W. Kelley and H.M. Rotalsky (1995), "Tracking Service Failures and Employee Recovery Efforts," *Journal of Services Marketing*, 9(2), 49–61.

Hoffman, K. Douglas, Scott W. Kelley and Laure M. Soulage (1995), "Customer Defection Analysis: A Critical Incident Approach," in *Proceedings of the American Marketing Association Summer Educators' Conference*, Chicago: American Marketing Association, pp. 346–52.

Holloway, Betsy B. and Sharon E. Beatty (2003), "Service Failure in Online Retailing," *Journal of Services Marketing*, 6(1), 92–105.

Holloway, Betsy Bugg and Sharon E. Beatty (2008), "The Online Shopping Environment: An Examination of Satisfactory and Dissatisfactory Experiences," *Journal of Service Research*, 10(4), 347–64.

Holloway, Betsy Bugg, Sijun Wang and Janet T. Parish (2005), "The Role of Cumulative Online Purchasing Experience in Service Recovery Management," *Journal of Interactive Marketing*, 19(3), 54–66.

Holloway, Betsy Bugg, Sijun Wang and Sharon E. Beatty (2009), "Betrayal? Relationship Quality Implications in Service Recovery," *Journal of Services Marketing*, 23(6), 385–96.

Homburg, Christian and Andreas Furst (2005), "How Organizational Complaint Handling Drives Customer Loyalty: An Analysis of the Mechanistic and the Organic Approach," *Journal of Marketing*, 69, 95–114.

Huppertz, John W., Sidney J. Arenson and Richard H. Evans (1978), "An Application of Equity Theory to Buyer–Seller Exchange Relationships," *Journal of Marketing Research*, 15 (May), 250–60.

Kalamas, Maria, Michel Laroche and Lucy Makdessian (2008), "Reaching the Boiling Point: Consumers' Negative Affective Reactions to Firm-Attributed Service Failures," *Journal of Business Research*, 61, 813–24.

Karande, Kiran, Vincent P. Magnini and Leona Tam (2007), "Recovery Voice and Satisfaction after Service Failure," *Journal of Services Marketing*, 10(2), 187–203.

Kau, Ah-Keng and Elizabeth Wan-Yiun Loh (2006), "The Effects of Service Recovery on Consumer Satisfaction: A Comparison between Complainants and Non-Complainants," *Journal of Services Marketing*, 20(2), 101–11.

Kelley, Scott W. and M.A. Davis (1994), "Antecedents to Customer Expectations for Service Recovery," *Journal of the Academy of Marketing Science*, 22(1), 52–61.

Magnini, Vincent P., John B. Ford, Edward P. Markowski and Earl D. Honeycutt, Jr. (2007), "The Service Recovery Paradox: Justifiable Theory or Smoldering Myth?," *Journal of Services Marketing*, 21(3), 213–25.

Matos, Celso Augusto de, Jorge Luiz Henrique and Carlos Alberto Vargas Rossi (2007), "Service Recovery Paradox: A Meta-Analysis," *Journal of Service Research*, 10(1), 60–77.

Matos, Celso Augusto de, Carlos Alberto Vargas Rossi, Ricardo Teixeira Veiga and Valter Afonso Vieira (2009), "Customer Reaction to Service Failure and Recovery: The Moderating Role of Attitude toward Complaining," *Journal of Services Marketing*, 23(7), 462–75.

Mattila, Anna S. (2001), "The Impact of Relationship Type on Customer Loyalty in a Context of Service Failures," *Journal of Services Marketing*, 4(2), 91–101.

Mattila, Anna S. (2006), "The Power of Explanations in Mitigating the Ill-Effects of Service Failures," *Journal of Services Marketing*, 20(7), 422–8.

Mattila, Anna S. and Paul G. Patterson (2004), "The Impact of Culture on Consumers' Perceptions of Service Recovery Efforts," *Journal of Retailing*, 80, 196–206.

Maxham, James G., III (2001), "Service Recovery's Influence on Consumer Satisfaction, Positive Word-of-Mouth, and Purchase Intentions," *Journal of Business Research*, 54(1), 11–24.

Maxham, James G., III and Richard G. Netemeyer (2002), "A Longitudinal Study of

Complaining Customers' Evaluations of Multiple Service Failures and Recovery Efforts," *Journal of Marketing*, 66, 57–71.

McColl-Kennedy, Janet R. and Beverley A. Sparks (2003), "Application of Fairness Theory to Service Failures and Service Recovery," *Journal of Services Marketing*, 5(3), 251–66.

McColl-Kennedy, Janet R., Catherine S. Daus and Beverley A. Sparks (2003), "The Role of Gender in Reactions to Service Failure and Recovery," *Journal of Services Marketing*, 6(1), 66–82.

McColl-Kennedy, Janet R., Paul G. Patterson, Amy K. Smith and Michael K. Brady (2009), "Customer Rage Episodes: Emotions, Expressions and Behaviors," *Journal of Retailing*, 85, 222–37.

McCollough, Michael A. (2009), "The Recovery Paradox: The Effect of Recovery Performance and Service Failure Severity on Post-Recovery Customer Satisfaction," *Academy of Marketing Studies Journal*, 13(1), 89–104.

McCollough, Michael A. and S.G. Bharadwaj (1992), "The Recovery Paradox: An Examination of Consumer Satisfaction in Relation to Disconfirmation, Service Quality, and Attribution Based Theories," in C.T. Allen and T. Madden (eds.), *Marketing Theory and Applications*, Chicago: American Marketing Association.

McCollough, Michael A., Leonard L. Berry and Manjit S. Yadav (2000), "An Empirical Investigation of Customer Satisfaction after Service Failure and Recovery," *Journal of Services Research*, 3(2), 121–37.

Menon, Kalyani and Laurette Dubé (2007), "The Effect of Emotional Provider Support on Angry versus Anxious Consumers," *International Journal of Research in Marketing*, 24, 268–75.

Meuter, Matthew L., Amy L. Ostrom, Robert I. Roundtree and Mary Jo Bitner (2000), "Self-Service Technologies: Understanding Customer Satisfaction with Technology-Based Service Encounters," *Journal of Marketing*, 64, 50–64.

Mick, D.G. and S. Fournier (1998), "Paradoxes of Technology: Consumer Cognizance, Emotions and Coping Strategies," *Journal of Consumer Research*, 25(2), 123–47.

Miller, J.L., C.W. Craighead and K.R. Karwan (2000), "Service Recovery: A Framework and Empirical Investigation," *Journal of Operations Management*, 18, 387–400.

Mittal, Vikas, John W. Huppertz and Adwait Khare (2008), "Customer Complaining: The Role of Tie Strength and Information Control," *Journal of Retailing*, 82, 195–204.

Mohr, L.A. and M.J. Bitner (1995), "The Role of Employee Effort in Satisfaction with Service Transactions," *Journal of Business Research*, 32, 239–52.

Noble, S. and J. Phillips (2004), "Relationship Hindrance: Why Would Consumers Not Want a Relationship with a Retailer?," *Journal of Retailing*, 80(4), 289–303.

Odekerken-Schröder, G., K. De Wulf and P. Schumacher (2003), "Strengthening Outcomes of Retailer–Consumer Relationships: The Dual Impact of Relationship Marketing Tactics and Consumer Personality," *Journal of Business Research*, 56(3), 177–90.

Oliver, R. L. (1980), "A Cognitive Model of the Antecedents and Consequences of Satisfaction Decisions," *Journal of Marketing Research*, 17(4), 460–69.

Ostrom, Amy and Dawn Iacobucci (1995), "Consumer Trade-Offs and the Evaluation of Services," *Journal of Marketing*, 59 (January), 17–28.

Parasuraman, A. (2000), "Technology Readiness Index (Tri): A Multiple-Item Scale to Measure Readiness to Embrace New Technologies," *Journal of Service Research*, 2(4), 307–20.

Parasuraman, A. and Dhruv Grewal (2000), "The Impact of Technology on the Quality–Value–Loyalty Chain: A Research Agenda," *Journal of the Academy of Marketing Science*, 28(1), 168–74.

Parasuraman, A., Valarie A. Zeithaml and A. Malhotra (2005), "E-S-QUAL: A Multiple-Item Scale for Assessing Electronic Service Quality," *Journal of Service Research*, 7(3), 213–33.

Park, Oun-Foung, Xinran Lehto and Fung-Kun Park (2008), "Service Failures and Complaints in the Family Travel Market: A Justice Dimension Approach," *Journal of Services Marketing*, 22(7), 520–32.

Patterson, Paul G., Elizabeth Cowley and Kriengsin Prasongsukarn (2006), "Service Failure Recovery: The Moderating Impact of Individual-Level Cultural Value Orientation on Perceptions of Justice," *International Journal of Research in Marketing*, 23, 263–77.

Poon, Patrick S., Michael K. Hui and Kevin Au (2004), "Attributions on Dissatisfying Service Encounters: A Cross-Cultural Comparison between Canadian and PRC Consumers," *European Journal of Marketing*, 38 (11/12), 1527–40.

Priluck, R. (2003), "Relationship Marketing Can Mitigate Product and Service Failures," *Journal of Services Marketing*, 17(1), 37–52.

Raimondo, Maria Antonietta, Gaetano "Nino" Miceli and Michele Costabile (2008), "How Relationship Age Moderates Loyalty Formation: The Increasing Effect of Relational Equity on Customer Loyalty," *Journal of Service Research*, 11(2), 142–60.

Reynolds, K. and Sharon E. Beatty (1999), "Customer Benefits and Company Consequences of Customer–Salesperson Relationships in Retailing," *Journal of Retailing*, 75(1), 11–32.

Richins, M.L. (1983), "Negative Word-of-Mouth by Dissatisfied Customers: A Pilot Study," *Journal of Marketing*, 47, 68–78.

Ringberg, Torsten, Gaby Odekerken-Schröder and Glenn L. Christensen (2007), "A Cultural Models Approach to Service Recovery," *Journal of Marketing*, 71, 194–214.

Rio-Lanza, Ana Belen del, Rodolfo Vazquez-Casielles and Ana M. Diaz-Martin (2009), "Satisfaction with Service Recovery: Perceived Justice and Emotional Response," *Journal of Business Research*, 62, 775–81.

Roos, Inger (1999), "Switching Processes in Customer Relationships," *Journal of Service Research*, 2(1), 68–85.

Rust, R.T. and R.L. Oliver (2000), "Should We Delight the Customer?," *Journal of the Academy of Marketing Science*, 28(1), 86–94.

Schoefer, Klaus and Adamantios Diamantopoulos (2008), "The Role of Emotions in Translating Perception of (In)justice into Postcomplaint Behavioral Responses," *Journal of Service Research*, 11(1), 91–103.

Schoefer, Klaus and Christine Ennew (2005), "The Impact of Perceived Justice on Consumers' Emotional Responses to Service Complaint Experiences," *Journal of Services Marketing*, 19(5), 261–70.

Shankar, Venkatesh, Amy K. Smith and Arvind Rangaswamy (2003), "The Relationship between Customer Satisfaction and Loyalty in Online and Offline Environments," *International Journal of Research in Marketing*, 20(2), 153–75.

Singh, Jagdip and Deepak Sirdeshmukh (2000), "Agency and Trust Mechanisms in Relational Exchanges," *Journal of the Academy of Marketing Science*, 28 (Winter), 150–67.

Smith, Amy K. and Ruth N. Bolton (1998), "An Experimental Investigation of Customer Reactions to Service Failure and Recovery Encounter: Paradox or Peril?," *Journal of Service Research*, 1 (August), 65–81.

Smith, Amy K. and Ruth N. Bolton (2002), "The Effect of Customers' Emotional Responses to Service Failures on Their Recovery Effort Evaluations and Satisfaction Judgments," *Journal of the Academy of Marketing Science*, 30(1), 5–23.

Smith, Amy K., Ruth N. Bolton and Janet Wagner (1999), "A Model of Customer Satisfaction with Service Encounters Involving Failure and Recovery," *Journal of Marketing Research*, 36 (August), 356–72.

Smith, Jeffery S. and Kirk R. Karwan (2010), "Empirical Profiles of Service Recovery Systems: The Maturity Perspective," *Journal of Service Research*, 13(1), 111–25.

Smith, Jeffery S., Kirk R. Karwan and Robert E. Markland (2009), "An Empirical Examination of the Structural Dimensions of the Service Recovery System," *Decision Sciences*, 40(1), 165–86.

Tax, Stephen S., Stephen W. Brown and Murali Chandrashekaran (1998), "Customer Evaluations of Service Complaint Experiences: Implications for Relationship Marketing," *Journal of Marketing*, 62 (April), 60–76.

Vargo, Stephen L. and Robert F. Lusch (2004), "Evolving to a New Dominant Logic for Marketing," *Journal of Marketing*, 68 (January), 1–17.

Verma, Harsh V. (2003), "Customer Outrage and Delight," *Journal of Services Marketing*, 3(1), 119–33.
Voorhees, Clay M. and Michael K. Brady (2005), "A Service Perspective on the Drivers of Complaint Intentions," *Journal of Service Research*, 8(2), 192–205.
Voorhees, Clay M., Michael K. Brady and David M. Horowitz (2006), "The Silent Majority: A Comparative Analysis of Noncomplainers," *Journal of the Academy of Marketing Science*, 31(4), 514–27.
Wang, Sijun and Lenard C. Huff (2007), "Explaining Buyers' Responses to Sellers' Violation of Trust," *European Journal of Marketing*, 41(9/10), 1033–52.
Weun, Seungoon, Sharon E. Beatty and Michael A. Jones (2004), "The Impact of Service Failure Severity on Service Recovery Evaluations and Post-Recovery Relationship," *Journal of Services Marketing*, 18(2), 133–46.
Winsted, Kathryn Frazer (1997), "The Service Experience in Two Cultures: A Behavioral Perspective," *Journal of Retailing*, 73(3), 337–60.
Wolfinbarger, M. and M.C. Gilly (2003), "eTailQ: Dimensionalizing, Measuring and Predicting Etail Quality," *Journal of Retailing*, 79(3), 183–97.
Wong, Nancy Y. (2004), "The Role of Culture in the Perception of Service Recovery," *Journal of Business Research*, 57, 957–63.
Zeithaml, Valarie A., Leonard L. Berry and A. Parasuraman (1993), "The Nature and Determinants of Customer Expectations of Service," *Journal of the Academy of Marketing Science*, 21(1), 1–12.
Zhang, Jingyun, Sharon E. Beatty and Gianfranco Walsh (2008), "Review and Future Directions of Cross-Cultural Consumer Services Research," *Journal of Business Research*, 61, 211–24.

7. From theory to bedside and back: relationship marketing and medical care
Michael J. Howley, Jr.

INTRODUCTION

I am a latecomer to the field of relationship marketing. When Len Berry first used the "relationship marketing" term (Berry 1983), I was a medical provider (a physician assistant) on a surgical team caring for critically ill patients after trauma and major surgical procedures. While scholars pondered the nature of marketing relationships in the late 1980s and early 1990s, my career had changed gears and I was working in a rural family practice. I was preoccupied with treating earaches in toddlers and heart failure in their grandparents as researchers established the foundational principles of marketing relationships. I moved from direct patient care, to managing a surgical practice, and finally to academia, as marketing scholars pounded out the theoretical details of relationship marketing during the 1990s. Now, as a marketing academic, I reflect on the relationship marketing literature in light of my 20 years of managing medical relationships as a clinician, and I see many exciting opportunities for future research.

Experience and theory are different kinds of knowledge. It is important occasionally to examine how theory works in the real world, because "all purportedly theoretical constructions must be . . . capable of explaining and predicting real-world phenomena. The truth of the matter is that *if it is not all right in practice, it cannot be all right in theory!*" (Hunt 2002: 195, italics in original). This chapter is an exercise in theoretical arbitrage (Van de Ven and Johnson 2006). Comparing and contrasting theory and experience illuminate opportunities both to refine practice with fresh theoretical insights and to highlight research opportunities. In this chapter, I will focus on how the experience of clinical medical relationships can contribute to relationship marketing theory.

Research on medical relationships offers marketing scholars a unique opportunity to contribute to one of the most important social issues of our time. Most countries in the world are struggling with health care crises. The root cause of many of these crises is dysfunctional provider–patient relationships, leading to uneven demand, variations in quality, and overuse of health care resources. A recent study found that 67 percent of excessive U.S. health care spending originated within provider–patient relationships in the office setting. In comparison, hospital costs (6 percent), administrative expenses (14 percent), and pharmaceutical costs (15 percent) accounted for relatively little excessive spending (Farrell et al. 2008). Effective health care reform for any of the world's health systems will require considerable additional relationship marketing research.

More research is also needed at the level of individual provider–patient relationships. Considerable evidence suggests that these relationships are not working well. About 75 percent of patients do not follow prescribed therapies (Scott 2007). Almost 20 percent of patients have switched medical providers in the past two years, and an additional 41 percent are prone to switch in the future (Deloitte Consulting 2008a). Millions of patients across the world travel to receive medical care in other countries because they don't trust their provider at home (Deloitte Consulting 2008b). On the other side of the relationship, doctors are increasingly dissatisfied with medical practice, and there is now a nursing shortage because so many nurses have abandoned their practice out of frustration (Zugar 2004; AACN 2008). Restoring these relationships to a more functional level will require considerable future relationship marketing research.

Before proceeding, let me acknowledge that my observations are influenced by my clinical experiences. All of my 20 years of clinical practice were in the U.S. health care system. About 40 percent of my experience was in market-based care, about 40 percent was in single-payer systems (e.g., veterans' care, Medicare, Medicaid), and the rest was charity care. Although my medical experience is exclusively in the U.S. system, the underlying relational dynamics are relevant to any of the world's health systems (Coulter and Cleary 2001). Instead of using "doctor" or "physician," I use the more generic "provider" term. While patients today see a variety of doctors (allopaths, osteopaths, naturopaths, or chiropractors), physician assistants, nurses, nurse practitioners, and therapists, the relational dynamics are similar. When I refer to "medical relationships," I mean the patient–provider relationship. Medical relationship marketing is defined here as the coproduction activities designed to restore, preserve, or enhance patients' health (Berry 1995; Parvatiyar and Sheth 2000; Vargo and Lusch 2004). I use the more specific term "medical care," instead of the more generic "health care," because a lot of health care marketing research focuses on the pharmaceutical industry or on wellness care. While relationships are important in these settings, medical relationships when patients are sick or traumatized are qualitatively different.

AN AGENDA FOR RELATIONSHIP MARKETING RESEARCH IN A MEDICAL CARE CONTEXT

In this section, I draw on a review of the medical literature and my clinical experiences to describe ten current or future controversies related to medical relationships that also have the potential to advance relationship marketing theory. Medical relationships are obviously well suited to studying established relational constructs such as trust and commitment, but in this chapter I will focus more on issues and controversies that have not yet been adequately addressed. I do not intend to review the relationship marketing literature, since there are already excellent reviews available (e.g., R.N. Bolton and Tarasi 2006). I have tried to select issues that have the potential not only to contribute to marketing theory but also to address difficult medical problems that currently affect patient care. While this list is necessarily incomplete, it should serve to demonstrate that there are many relationship marketing research opportunities in the health care context.

1. Managing Relationship Intensity

Optimal health outcomes for patients occur at a *moderate* level of health care consumption. At the lower end of the continuum, providing basic medical services to people who have had inadequate care rapidly improves health. Beyond a moderate level of care, as shown in Figure 7.1, additional services do not improve outcomes (Fisher et al. 2003a, 2003b). Intensive consumption of medical services at the high end of the continuum can actually *decrease* medical outcomes, as patients have complications from unjustifiable examinations and side effects from unwarranted treatments (Fisher and Welch 1999). The challenge in medical relationships is to moderate consumption of services. Some of these relational interventions are quite simple. For example, when providers discuss with a terminal patient how he or she would like to die, costs are reduced by 30 percent and the quality of death improves (Zhang et al. 2009).

Many times, the relational issues involved are more complicated. Consider the case of Mrs. Thomasina, a patient who chronically feels poorly and enthusiastically searches the internet for new medical tests to diagnose her ailments. Mrs. Thomasina has decided she would like a total-body CAT scan to see what is wrong with her (Miksanek 2008). Her doctor, Tony Miksanek, refuses. There is no clinical reason to perform a total-body CAT scan. In addition, the test is expensive, is a waste of resources, and will not assuage her chronic anxiety. Perhaps more

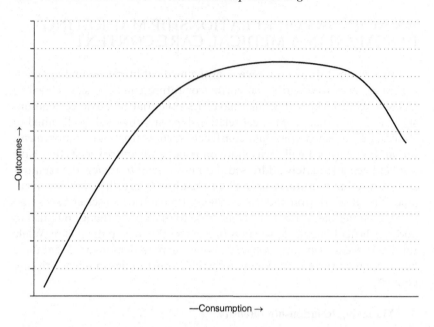

Figure 7.1   The relationship between patient health and the amount of medical care consumption and outcomes

importantly, Dr. Miksanek worries that the CAT scan will expose Mrs. Thomasina to high levels of radiation and potential complications from surgical procedures to diagnose incidental CAT scan findings. In other words, Dr. Miksanek is trying to protect Mrs. Thomasina from herself. Since they are in a relationship, though, Dr. Miksanek can't just reject every request Mrs. Thomasina makes, because she would defect and find a more compliant doctor. He has to keep her engaged, but "I don't know how much longer I can hold out . . . God knows I've told Mrs. Thomasina 'No' on many occasions . . . yet she has a way of wearing me down" (Miksanek 2008: 1425, quotes in original).

The case of Mrs. Thomasina illustrates how "soft" relationship factors can influence the decision to consume expensive resources, even in the face of "hard" medical guidelines. Some medical scientists have been working to erode these soft relational influences by establishing more explicit standards of care through evidence-based medicine. The hope is that these standards will persuade patients and providers to use health care resources only when there is good scientific evidence for doing so (Van de Ven and Schomaker 2002). But, despite the broad availability of these standards (e.g., see www.cochrane.org), there is still wide variation in adherence to these guidelines, as the soft relational factors continue to overwhelm the scientific evidence (Jacobson and Wolff 2009).

Relatively little marketing research has addressed these demarketing issues (exceptions are Kotler and Levy 1971; Kotler 1973). In the past, research has shown that demarketing efforts are generally ineffective and often counterproductive because the perceived unavailability of a resource increases its perceived desirability and value (Harvey and Roger 1977; Teel et al. 1979; Lynn 1992). For example, attempts to limit gasoline consumption during World War II through rationing and patriotic appeals only led to the creation of a black market (Alexander 1945). Most of this previous research has occurred at the population level, examining how mass appeals affect consumption (Pechmann et al. 2003). Further relationship marketing research is needed to explore not only methods of regulating relational intensity but also the theoretical mechanisms by which this relational regulation takes place. Additional research could explore the relational variables that are associated with patient willingness to forgo unnecessary care and the role of expert standards in the willingness to reduce consumption of services.

2.   Managing Patient Coproduction

Coproduction means that customers must participate in the creation of value in a relationship (Bendapudi and Leone 2003; Vargo and Lusch 2004). Coproduction is particularly important in medical care. Success in treating many diseases is dependent on the patient's ability to fulfill his or her coproduction roles. Adult-onset diabetes, for example, most commonly presents in overweight patients. The most important factor in controlling the diabetes and preventing complications is the patient's ability to lose weight rather than the effectiveness of any prescribed medicine. While research has demonstrated the importance of medical relationships in weight loss (e.g., Dellande et al. 2004; Sacks et al. 2009), there are still no effective weight loss regimens available to bring patients down to a normal weight. Even with the most effective diets,[1] patients only lost about 9 lb. on a two-year diet, with starting weights about 275 lb. to 300 lb. (i.e., 125 kg to 135 kg) (Sacks et al. 2009). Much more research is needed to focus on the specific relational characteristics that improve coproduction.

I have seen two general categories of coproduction issues present in the medical context. The first is ineffective coproduction. Patients must overcome many barriers to effective coproduction. They are often in pain or impaired by injury, metabolic conditions, or medications. Add to that the 15 percent of the population that is functionally illiterate or the 15 percent of the population that is diagnosable with mental illness and you begin to understand some of the typical coproduction challenges that medical providers confront every day. Figure 7.2 summarizes some of the ways that patients are ineffective coproducers over the course of a typical medical encounter. Much more research is needed on medical relationships to understand how patients can improve their coproduction efforts.

A second coproduction issue involves patients who refuse to accept their role. Do you remember the case of the "TB traveler" (Paddock 2007)? This American was diagnosed with tuberculosis (TB) just before a planned honeymoon. Despite warnings not to travel, he still went on his European honeymoon trip. When officials tracked him down and advised him that he had a particularly dangerous form of tuberculosis, he was afraid he might be prevented from re-entering the U.S. He evaded further contact with public health authorities and snuck back into the U.S., risking the health of all his unsuspecting fellow travelers. This man simply refused to accept his coproduction responsibilities. Coproduction refusal is also seen in other contexts. For example, about 15 percent of the U.S. population refuses to participate in mandatory health or automobile insurance programs (McQueen 2008; Steinbrook 2008).

Future relationship marketing research should explore these coproduction issues. In my clinical experience, coproduction problems are often related to the patient's self-concept or identity. Patients who do not see themselves as sick are often not motivated to take on coproduction roles or perform them effectively. While marketers have conducted considerable research on identity (L.E. Bolton and Reed 2004), the issue of how to induce appropriate identity changes in ways that enhance coproduction has not yet been addressed.

3.   Provider Balancing in Marketing Relationships

Over 15 years ago, Fournier et al. (1998) announced the premature death of relationship marketing secondary to marketing malpractice. In their critique, they noted that firms often seem more interested in making money than in having a relationship, give preference to one customer over another, and exploit customer vulnerabilities (Fournier et al. 1998). The common thread in their critique is that marketers do a poor job of "relationship balancing," in which providers must realize disparate or even contradictory goals within a relationship. Since the state of marketing relationships has not improved in the past decade (Broetzmann and Grainer 2005), I believe that relationship balancing is an important area of future scholarly research.

Medical relationships offer an interesting context for this research. Providers must often balance the needs of their patients against financial

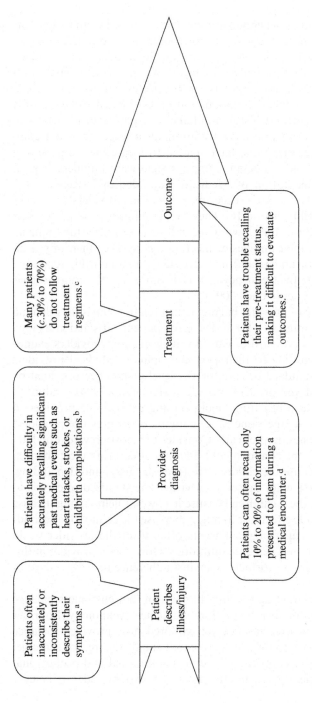

Notes:

a Boyer et al. (1995).
b Wincupp et al. (1998); Hopkins et al. (2007).
c DiMatteo (2004).
d McGuire (1996).
e Lingard et al. (2001).

Figure 7.2 Patient coproduction issues over the course of a typical medical encounter

incentives or pressures. Depending on the nature of the health system, the financial pressures might range from cost containment to financial incentives to order excessive tests and procedures. Some people are troubled by the idea that medical providers might be swayed by financial considerations. They see medical practice as a noble profession that is somehow excluded from the usual marketplace pressures. Uwe Reinhardt effectively dissects this argument in a historical analysis of physician responses to financial incentives. Doctors have traditionally insisted on being compensated on a piecework basis, have tended to locate their practices in lucrative areas, and did not begin caring for significant numbers of poor patients until the institution of Medicare and Medicaid (Relman and Reinhardt 1986). At the same time, most medical providers take their fiduciary responsibility seriously. They work diligently to place their patients' interests above their own while still trying to meet the financial goals of supporting their families or meeting the needs of their organization. We still do not understand how providers maintain this relational balancing act despite the frequency of this dilemma and the controversies surrounding these issues (Cohen 2008).

A second example of provider balancing in a relationship is the dilemma in which providers must weigh the desire for patient satisfaction against the need to follow a standard of care. In medical care, providers cannot simply practice according to their personal opinion. Medical providers must adhere to a standard of care, or the level of practice provided by a reasonably skilled and prudent provider (McConkey 1994). Failure to adhere to the standard of care is unethical and exposes the provider to malpractice claims. At the same time, patients often pressure providers to deviate from the standard of care. Consider the most prevalent malady in medicine today – the common cold. Parents often bring their children to pediatricians because the children are feverish, fussy, and demanding. They typically have a cold, caused by a virus. The standard of care is to avoid antibiotics in these children because it 1) won't help, 2) might cause a drug reaction or side effects, or 3) might increase the chance of a secondary infection with "super-bugs." Parents often want the provider to do something, however, and demand antibiotics. How does a provider in this situation balance parent satisfaction against adherence to the standard of care?

While previous marketing research has shown that customers balance multiple motivations in their interactions with a new technology (Fournier and Glen 1999), research has not yet explored how providers balance multiple contradictory goals. Future research could explore, for example, how providers resolve conflicts between organizational and professional identification. While I have briefly described two provider balancing dilemmas here, there are many others available to examine in the medical care context.

4. Managing Relationships across Multiple Customers

A typical family (general) practice provider cares for 2000 to 2500 patients at a time. When I was a family practice provider, I typically saw 25 to 30 patients per day. Consider what needed to be accomplished in a 15-minute office visit: review the chart, greet the patient, do some social bonding, interview the patient about his or her presenting problem, examine the patient, discuss my findings, call specialists, negotiate a treatment plan, educate the patient about the plan, write up requests for diagnostic tests, write all the prescriptions, and then document everything in a way that would withstand legal scrutiny. There simply isn't enough time to do everything, and "many necessary tasks must be omitted or given short shrift" (Zugar 2004: 74). Providers typically balance their time across multiple patients. When one patient needs additional time, the provider "borrows" the time from another patient. Patients are typically tolerant of these balancing processes, so long as they do not get shorted too often. I can recall three heuristics to successful balancing: keep a list of all the patients I shorted each day and find some way to pay back the time and attention I owed them, never short the same patient twice in a row, and never let the patient know you are shorting them to give more attention to another patient.

More research is needed on managing relationships across multiple patients. When rebalancing, must providers always rebalance in the same dimension, as suggested by resource exchange theory, or is it acceptable to rebalance in a different dimension? Can providers delegate rebalancing efforts to an assistant or another provider? Will electronic communication make up for lack of personal contact? I do not see queuing management as being a productive approach to these issues, because it relies on two false assumptions: 1) that somehow you can someday "catch up" with patient backlogs and 2) once you develop a queue it will remain stable, like a bank line. Patients in queues frequently get worse and sometimes get better, which requires constant rebalancing of the queue. One operational issue that should be a research priority, however, is how to build slack into service systems in ways that optimize productivity. Because services are not stored, most providers book themselves at full capacity, which leads to overload. All of these research issues are about to get more important in the U.S. Political momentum is building to bring an additional 47 million people into the health care system, which will increase demand for physician services by up to 20 percent.

5.   Customer Relationships across Multiple Providers: The Service Network

Complex services often require that multiple specialized providers collaborate in the service delivery process (Vargo and Lusch 2004). Little relationship marketing research has been devoted to the issue of how customers develop and maintain relationships across multiple providers, but initial research on service networks has shown that customer evaluations of a provider are affected by customer evaluations of other providers in the network (F. Morgan 2004). If a general practitioner refers a patient to a specialist, for example, the patient's evaluation of the general practitioner will be affected by the performance of the specialist.

Medical practice offers an interesting context in which to study service networks, because an effective relationship between multiple providers is critical to a patient's quality of care. At the same time, the state of provider–provider relationships is quite poor. Providers, especially doctors, have a reputation for being arrogant, abrasive, and disruptive (Stillman 2008; Tarkan 2008). As time pressure has increased, providers have found it increasingly difficult to coordinate patient care (Moore et al. 2007). Some providers have even called their patients to check on them only to find that they have died while under the care of a specialist (Stillman 2008).

One recent development in service networks is that the medical service network is extending across international boundaries. For example, a CAT scan performed in the middle of the night in a New York City hospital may be read by a radiologist in India (Wachter 2006; Miltein and Smith 2007). Some hospitals are now even considering monitoring critically ill patients using providers on the other side of the world. How will patient families accept a critically ill patient in New York City being monitored by a doctor in India? Would that patient or family prefer a sleepy New York City doctor or an awake Indian doctor monitoring the care?

Research on service networks has just begun, and there are many opportunities for future studies. For example, how will customers allocate blame across the service network after a service failure? Do the credentials of a specialist or the stronger relationships with the family doctor offer more protection after an adverse outcome? Once a patient is seeing multiple specialists, it becomes difficult for generalist providers to stay involved in the network. Can we maintain network stability as new providers are added? Hunter and Perreault (2007) found that technology can improve the effectiveness of sales forces, but can it improve coordination across a service network? Does an email elicit the same provider cooperation as a personal phone call? All of these issues have the potential to improve the quality of patient care and extend relationship marketing theory. This issue of using technology in relationships is large, so I address it further in the next section.

6. Technology Mediates Patient Relationships

Waves of technology are washing across the health care system, dramatically changing provider–patient relationships. Marketing research has shown that customer evaluations of service encounters involving technologies differ from evaluations of purely interpersonal service encounters (Meuter et al. 2000). Adoption of technology is based on customer motivation, abilities, and technology orientation (Meuter et al. 2005). This research has focused, however, on the initial adoption of a technology and how a technology affects evaluations of single encounters. Much more research is needed on the use of technology in managing long-term marketing relationships. I will discuss three examples of how technology has affected patient–provider relationships.

Some medical providers have begun to conduct patient visits across a video link. Pilot programs have focused on situations where the patient lives far away or is institutionalized (e.g., in prison, a psychiatric hospital, or a nursing home). Preliminary studies suggest that doctors and patients are very satisfied with these telemedicine visits (Dixon and Stahl 2008). But how far can you push this? Would patients still positively evaluate a long-term relationship if it was only conducted over a video link? Could a therapist still be equally effective speaking to a mentally ill patient on the telephone, in a chat room, or over a video link compared to in-person visits?

Cell phone and email greatly improve patient access to providers. This immediacy and access, however, can also break down relational norms and appropriate boundaries. Consider the example of a surgeon who performs breast biopsies after abnormal mammograms. How should the surgeon communicate the biopsy results, given that these results are benign (i.e., no cancer found) about 95 percent of the time? Scheduling every patient return to the office to discuss the results is inefficient and prolongs the anxious waiting for patients (Kahn and Luce 2003). Phoning the results to patients greatly expedites the process, but what happens when patients get the "You have breast cancer" call on their cell phone in the middle of a business meeting, walking down Main Street, or in the middle of a class? Patients in this situation may not be psychologically prepared for the cancer diagnosis, because they are distracted or may not have any social support available. Delivering results by cell phone or email greatly enhances communication between the patient and provider but also may be more traumatic.

A third example of the effects of technology on medical relationships relates to the tremendous availability of medical information on the internet. It is not clear, though, whether this access to more information has improved patient coproduction or the quality of care. Mrs. Thomasina, described earlier in the chapter, used the information on the internet to feed her anxiety. The majority of adults (77 percent) with internet access had searched for medical information on the web, and 80 percent of these people had looked online in the past month (Harris Interactive 2006). Interestingly, patients often do not discuss their internet information searches with their providers. One reason is concerns for turf issues, in which providers prefer to be the source of authoritative medical information. Other patient concerns included fears that they would be dismissed or ridiculed (Imes et al. 2008). There certainly seems to be a negative connotation for online health services. Harris Interactive (2006) refers to *anyone* who searches online for information as a "cyberchondriac," even though only 14 percent of these patients had searched online for medical information ten or more times in the previous month.

The recurrent theme in these three examples is that technology is increasingly mediating provider–patient relationships. Considerable future research is needed not only to document how technology changes these relationships over the long term, but also to explore the theoretical mechanisms at work.

In the previous sections, all of my comments have been focused at the dyadic level of a relationship. In the next two sections, I focus on the individual participants in relationships, first the provider and then the customer. The final two topics will address two impending changes in medical care on medical relationships.

7.   Healing Wounded Providers

All service providers are volunteers (Berry 2007). The amount of discretionary effort required for most services typically exceeds the relative compensation for delivering that service. Volunteerism is a particularly important issue in medical relationships. Patients present at all hours of the day and night and can be demanding or even abusive. A 2003 survey of U.K. doctors found that 50 percent of providers had experienced verbal abuse or physical violence from dissatisfied, intoxicated, or mentally ill patients and their families (Kmeitowicz 2003).

Many years ago, a doctor wrote a semi-autobiographical novel about his medical practice initiation and training (Shem 1978). His book, *The*

House of God, became a cult classic in the medical community in the spirit of *Catch-22*. The book details the psychological trauma experienced by new doctors from exposure to patient suffering, grinding responsibility, lack of sleep, cynical colleagues, an unsupportive hierarchy, and abusive patients. One of the laws of the House of God is "they can always hurt you more." While some aspects of the book are clearly farcical, the experiences described in the book have resonated to the point that some doctors have trouble reading passages 30 years later because the memories are still too painful (Katz 2008; Markel 2008).

David Hilfiker (1985) describes the provider who has incurred harm while providing medical care as the "wounded healer." Table 7.1 describes some of the issues in medical relationships that wound providers. Wounding does not occur just in highly consequential services. I have seen counter workers at McDonald's verbally abused over incorrect hamburger orders. Wounding seems an inevitable part of being a service provider. While it is tempting simply to assign blame to unsupportive management and let the issue rest, let me illustrate the depth and complexity of this issue by discussing two other parties who may have some responsibility for wounded providers – the patient and the provider him- or herself.

In a marketing relationship, what does the customer owe the service provider? In the medical context, does a patient have any responsibility to the provider beyond paying for the service? I see support for the notion that customers have obligations to providers in both the marketing and the medical literature. First, Bagozzi (1995) suggests that reciprocity is a fundamental principle of marketing relationships. Reciprocity implies that relationships are bidirectional, with each party having obligations to the other. As a result, principles of reciprocity would support the notion that customers do indeed have some obligation to providers.

The medical literature also supports the idea that patients bear some responsibility to providers. Ethicists have explored the limits of patient autonomy by examining the obligations of patients to consider the effects of their illness on other people with whom they are in relationships (Minow 1994; Herring 2008). For example, if a wife's illness has the potential to harm the husband, then the provider has some degree of responsibility to the husband. Should this same ethical principle also be extended to the provider? Ethicists considered these issues during the early stages of the AIDS epidemic, before there were any effective HIV treatments. The consensus was that no patient should ever be denied care because of provider anxiety of getting infected, but providers did have some rights to protect themselves from harm (Freedman 1988). In summary, if these are

Table 7.1   Sources of medical provider wounding

Emotional labor	Providers must manage their affective displays even when exposed to difficult or abusive patients, fatigued from staying up all night on call, or distracted by time pressures. This becomes increasingly difficult when patients make choices with which the provider disagrees.
Emotional trauma or grief	David Hilfiker describes an incident where he had to perform routine check-ups on patients within minutes after attempting to resuscitate a child he personally knew who died from drowning (Hilfiker 1985).
Time pressures	"Doctors' anguish seems to come from violating every day what they know they ought to be doing. The pain is from the degree to which they espouse values then can't live up to them" (Renee Fox, cited in Zugar 2004: 173).
Vigilance	Data on hundreds of patients are continually pouring into the typical medical practice. Overlooking a single number, even the decimals, can harm a patient and lead to a malpractice lawsuit.
Physical fatigue	Dr. Paul Austin describes what it meant to get called at 3 a.m.: "It didn't mean that I was getting the opportunity to help someone, or that I was getting a case I could learn from. It just meant that I was getting screwed out of the few hours of sleep I'd been hoping to steal" (Austin 2007: 47).
Mistakes	Here's how some providers reacted to finding out they had made a mistake: – "The room was shrinking around me fast. My eardrums felt as though they were about to implode from the pressure . . . I felt sick, cold, and damp, terrified" (Rowe 2004: 147). – "It was mind-shattering, ego-shattering" (Marjoribanks et al. 1996: 167).
Interruptions	I once shared call with a family practice doctor who received 25 to 40 calls per hour when on call. This was an average of one call every 1.5 to 2 minutes – which continued around the clock.
Difficult patients	Many patients in a medical practice have personality disorders or mental health issues.
Synergistic effects	"Eventually the pain became too much . . . the conflicting pressures, which often seem to defy solution, and of the responses . . . [providers] come up with, which often become problems in their own right. It is by now one of the world's most poorly kept secrets that anxiety, depression, loneliness, and burnout are major factors in the lives of many [providers]" (Hilfiker 1985: 11).

truly provider–patient *relationships*, there must be some degree of responsibility of the patient to the provider.

Providers also have some responsibility to heal themselves. In the sales literature, a key mediating variable with salesperson effectiveness is experienced meaningfulness, or the degree to which the work gives a sense of accomplishment (Thakor and Joshi 2005). Victor Frankl has argued that people can tolerate mistreatment far beyond what a service provider might experience as long as they can find meaning in the experience (Frankl [1959] 1992). Thus, the provider might have some responsibility to exert effort to find meaning in his or her work, thus buffering the negative effects of service experiences.

Research on the wounded provider is in a primordial state. Considerable future research is needed to further describe the phenomenon, classify the types of wounding, and explore the mechanisms of wounding and healing, and the effects of wounding on provider performance and customer evaluations.

8.   Customers in Negative Relationships

Some marketing relationships can also be negative experiences for customers. While the marketing literature has described negative services (I. Morgan and Rao 2003; Miller et al. 2009), considerable research is still needed. Once again, medical relationships offer an excellent context in which to study negative services. Medical relationships are often negative because patients must deal with unpleasant issues that they would rather avoid (Berry and Bendapudi 2007). Table 7.2 lists some of the negative aspects of service relationships.

One consequence of the lack of research in this area is seen in how medical satisfaction surveys are conducted. I have found that many patients are surveyed just at the time that they *should be dissatisfied* because they are coping with a negative medical service. For example, patients who survive massive multiple trauma often go through a period of grief and dysphoria as they start to realize all the losses that have resulted from their injuries. It is a normal and important phase of the service process. If these patients are given a satisfaction survey during this time, however, the scores will likely be quite low and the providers will be subject to management interventions.

Recent studies have begun to explore the issue of negative services (Miller et al. 2009), but much more research is needed in this area. Possible topics include the types of services classified as negative and how relationships function in a negative service over time. One idea that is relevant to negative services is customer coping. Coping refers to the

Table 7.2   Potential sources of service negativity in medical relationships

Potential threat of harm	One previously researched area in negative services is the issue of false-positive mammograms. The vast majority of women who have abnormal mammograms do not have breast cancer. About 95 percent of surgical biopsies after an abnormal mammogram are benign, or show no evidence of cancer. Despite the good news, these false-positive mammograms increase anxiety, decrease future adherence to mammography recommendations, and unnecessarily increase utilization of other health services.
Identity threats	All physical exams typically start with the words "well-developed, well-nourished." It is universal boilerplate phrasing to mean "This person is not dangerously malnourished." I had a patient who became very angry with me when he read his medical record of a physical I had performed: "You think I'm fat!"
Therapeutic effects – patients are supposed to be threatened or dissatisfied	It may be somewhat antithetical to marketers, but in medical care it is sometimes the proper outcome that patients *should* be dissatisfied. Dr. Friedman gives the example of a patient in counseling who was dissatisfied with her care and constantly demanded to change providers. While changing providers would be expedient, it was not in the patient's best interest. Her dissatisfaction and negative emotional reactions were a sign the treatment was working (Friedman 2006).
Frustration	Many medical encounters offer no hope of feeling better. These typically happen with chronic disease management such as heart failure, depression, or arthritis. Frustration is an unpleasant inner condition that will result when patients do not receive a reward for their coproduction efforts (Stauss et al. 2005).

complex set of cognitive and behavioral customer processes aimed at restoring a desirable emotional state (Duhachek 2005). More research is needed to illuminate the theoretical processes by which customers cope with negative service experiences and investigate how providers can assist coping. Extended medical encounters offer opportunities to study these issues.

All of the research questions discussed up to this point involve current issues in medical care. In the next two sections, I will discuss two upcoming controversies that will have important implications for relationship marketers. It is difficult to offer specific research topics on these issues at this time, but both of these controversies will be rich sources of insights for relationship marketing scholars prepared to study these issues as they unfold.

9.   The Dawn of the Genetics Revolution

It may sound trite, but we used to treat sick people when I started my medical training in the 1970s. All patient care was focused on resolving an illness, alleviating pain, or relieving troublesome symptoms. While medical care was a service high in credence properties, there was at least an outcome on which to base evaluations of the quality of the service. Patients usually got better as a result of their medical care.

Preventive medicine became popular in the 1980s. Patient care changed from treating sick people to detecting illness before it presented. For example, providers began to spend more time treating high cholesterol instead of caring for heart attacks. This focus on prevention has affected medical relationships in two ways. First, with preventive care, the patient's story is less important. Since there are no symptoms, the provider does not need a history of the illness. The patient's story is replaced by a test. There are no symptoms with high cholesterol – the test tells you everything you need to know. With preventive care, the patient and provider can drift apart. The patient can have a blood test at the lab and be notified of the results by mail.

The preventive medicine phase of medical care also made it more difficult to quantify relational benefits. Instead of relief from pain and suffering, the patient's test number improved. The patients still have to pay in terms of time, money, inconvenience, and discomfort (think colonoscopy here), but the best possible outcome is that they feel the same. The result is that costs increase relative to perceived benefits, decreasing perceived value, which may decrease patient coproduction.

Preventive medicine is also much less gratifying for providers. Most providers entered the profession to be healers. Instead, they end up as computer workers managing test numbers. The real work of medical care increasingly takes place on a computer desktop away from the patient, and "the patient in the bed has become a mere icon for the *real* patient in the computer" (Verghese 2007: 9).

We now stand at the cusp of the genetics revolution and the era of personalized medicine. Rapid advances in decoding the human genome and the ability to diagnose some conditions have raised the possibility that medical providers will soon be able to diagnose and treat genetic abnormalities before they become manifest in a screening test or disease. But this vision of our genetic medical future is not yet a reality. While scientists are now able to decode genes, understanding how the code translates into disease has turned out to be frustratingly difficult.

This delay in the start of the era of personalized medicine allows time for relationship marketing scholars to prepare themselves for future research opportunities. While the goal of preventive medicine is to intervene just as a disease is presenting, the purpose of personalized genetic medicine will be to intercede before there is even any manifestation based on a genetic aberration. Much of the work of medical care will move to counseling patients on genetic risk. Patients already have a difficult time and are prone to bias in evaluating perceived risk. For example, many women believe that the greatest risk to their health comes from breast cancer. In reality, breast cancer is not the leading cause of death, or even of cancer deaths, in women. Lung cancer is the most common cancer in women, and heart disease and stroke are much greater risks to the health of women than either of these cancers. Despite these facts, however, breast cancer *seems* to be a greater threat. A cardiologist recently told me that she asked 30 consecutive female patients, "What is the greatest risk to your health?" All 30 women responded "Breast cancer," even though all of these women had recently survived a heart attack! Despite the immediate cardiac health threat, these women still thought breast cancer was a greater threat. In a similar way, genetic testing results may potentially distort perceived health risks. Strong and functional provider–patient relationships will be necessary in order to provide the proper balance in evaluating these risks. The era of genetic medicine will also change medical relationships in ways that are difficult to predict now, but there will no doubt be many interesting relationship marketing research opportunities.

10.   An Impending Power Struggle: The Electronic Medical Record

The upcoming electronic medical record (EMR) will have significant consequences for medical relationships. EMR refers to a computerized record-keeping system that stores all health care information. The benefits of EMR include completeness and accessibility. Everything relevant to a patient's health is retained in the EMR, so providers can access this information from any location. Even if a patient presents unconscious to an emergency room in another part of the world, providers should be able to access important medical information about the patient and deliver appropriate treatment.

Aside from the obvious security issues and the technical problems involved with integrating thousands of legacy medical record-keeping systems, I see two potential adverse relational consequences of the EMR.

First, the EMR reduces patient–provider communication during the initial visit. The provider's focus turns away from the patient to entering the data into the correct field. "The electronic medical record . . . means your doctor is half-turned away from you at your visit, busy typing, and so misses the consternation on your face, misses your body language of annoyance, because the courtesies you expect even of your third grader ('Look at me when I talk to you') are not in evidence" (Verghese 2007: 10, quotes and parentheses in original). In other words, the EMR risks depersonalizing medical care.

A second relational consequence of the EMR is that patients lose control over their story. *Everything* goes into the EMR – not just embarrassing episodes resolved long ago and now irrelevant, but also miscommunications and misdiagnoses, which remain forever with no way for a patient to remove them. "All of us are conditioned to respect the printed word, particularly when it appears repeatedly on a hospital computer screen, and once a misdiagnosis enters into the electronic medical record, it is rapidly and virally propagated" (Groopman and Hartzband 2009: A15). None of the current EMR proposals permit a patient to remove incorrect or irrelevant diagnoses from his or her record. So how does a patient who is misdiagnosed with anxiety, but really has asthma, get the incorrect and stigmatizing diagnosis removed from the record?

As a result, widespread introduction of the EMR will likely have important consequences for provider–patient relationships. Relationship marketing researchers will be well positioned to explore these issues as they unfold.

SUMMARY AND CONCLUSION

Although considerable research effort has been expended developing the principles of relationship marketing, the evidence suggests that there is much more work to be done to improve the quality of care delivered through medical relationships. In this chapter, I have tried to describe the experience of medical relationships in a way that illuminates research opportunities to extend marketing theory and improve the quality of health care for patients. These research topics, summarized in Table 7.3, are only a brief introduction to potential relationship marketing research opportunities in medical care.

Table 7.3   A summary of relationship marketing research topics

1. Managing relationship intensity	How can marketers regulate or moderate the consumption of services to an optimal level?
2. Managing patient coproduction	How can customer coproduction abilities be enhanced or managed?
3. Provider balancing in marketing relationships	How do providers balance multiple or conflicting goals in a relationship?
4. Managing relationships across multiple customers	How can providers manage multiple simultaneous relationships?
5. Customer relationships across multiple providers: the service network	How can multiple providers manage a relationship with a single customer?
6. Technology mediates patient relationships	What are the long-term effects of using technology to mediate relationships?
7. Healing wounded providers	What are the different ways providers become wounded and how can they be healed?
8. Customers in negative relationships	What are the different types of negative relationships and how can providers enhance customer coping?

Future controversies:
9. The dawn of the genetics revolution
10. An impending power struggle: the electronic medical record

NOTE

1. Surgical procedures are somewhat more effective, with an average 16 percent of weight loss over ten years. The average starting weight was 264 lb., or 120 kg (Sjostrom et al. 2004).

REFERENCES

AACN (American Association of Colleges of Nursing) (2008), "Nursing Shortage Fact Sheet."
Alexander, R.S. (1945), "Wartime Adventures in Equitable Distribution Short of Rationing: Voluntary Allocation Systems," *Journal of Marketing*, 10 (July), 1–13.
Austin, Paul (2007), "Mrs. Kelly," *Creative Nonfiction*, 33, 40–56.
Bagozzi, Richard. P. (1995), "Reflections on Relationship Marketing in Consumer Markets," *Journal of the Academy of Marketing Science*, 23(4), 272–7.
Bendapudi, Neeli and Robert P. Leone (2003), "Psychological Implications of Customer Participation in Coproduction," *Journal of Marketing*, 67(1), 14–28.

Berry, Leonard L. (1983), "Relationship Marketing," in L.L. Berry, G.L. Shostak and G.D. Upah (eds.), *Emerging Perspectives on Services Marketing*, Chicago: American Marketing Association.

Berry, Leonard (1995), "Relationship Marketing of Services – Growing Interest, Emerging Perspectives," *Journal of the Academy of Marketing Science*, 23(4), 236–45.

Berry, Leonard L. (2007), "The Best Companies are Generous Companies," *Business Horizons*, 50, 263–9.

Berry, Leonard L. and Neeli Bendapudi (2007), "Health Care: A Fertile Field for Service Research," *Journal of Service Research*, 10(2), 111–23.

Bolton, Lisa E. and Americus Reed (2004), "Sticky Priors: The Perseverance of Identity Effects on Judgment," *Journal of Marketing Research*, 41(4), 397–410.

Bolton, Ruth N. and Crina O. Tarasi (2006), "Managing Customer Relationships," in Naresh K. Malhotra (ed.), *Review of Marketing Research*, Vol. 3, Armonk, NY: M.E. Sharpe, pp. 3–38.

Boyer, G.S., D.W. Templin, W.P. Goring, J.C. Cornoni-Huntley, D.F. Everett, R.C. Lawrence, S.P. Heyse and A. Bowler (1995), "Discrepancies between Patient Recall and the Medical Record," *Archives of Internal Medicine*, 155(17), 1868–72.

Broetzmann, Scott M. and Marc M. Grainer (2005), "First Results from the 2005 Customer Rage Study," Compete through Service Symposium, Arizona State University, Tempe, http://www.ccareall.org/read.html.

Cohen, Elizabeth (2008), "Don't Become a Victim of Medical Marketing," http://www.cnn.com/2008/HEALTH/0821/ep.conflicts/index.html?iref=mpstoryview (accessed August 21, 2008).

Coulter, Angela and Paul D. Cleary (2001), "Patient's Experiences with Hospital Care in Five Countries," *Health Affairs*, 20(3), 244–65.

Dellande, Stephanie, Mary C. Gilly and John Graham (2004), "Gaining Compliance and Losing Weight: The Role of the Service Provider in Health Care Services," *Journal of Marketing*, 68(3), 78–91.

Deloitte Consulting, Center for Health Solutions (2008a), "Health Care Consumerism," http://www.deloitte.com/view/en_US/us/Industries/Health-Plans-Healthcare-Health-Care/Center-for-Health-Solutions-Health-Plans/index.htm.

Deloitte Consulting, Center for Health Solutions (2008b), "Medical Tourism: Consumers in Search of Value," http://www.deloitte.com/view/en_US/us/Industries/Health-Plans-Healthcare-Health-Care/Center-for-Health-Solutions-Health-Plans/index.htm.

DiMatteo, M. Robin (2004), "Variations in Patients' Adherence to Medical Recommendations," *Medical Care*, 42(3), 200–209.

Dixon, Ronald F. and James E. Stahl (2008), "Virtual Visits in a General Medicine Practice: A Pilot Study," *Telemedicine and Health*, 14(6), 525–30.

Duhachek, Adam (2005), "Coping: A Multidimensional, Hierarchical Framework of Responses to Stressful Consumption Episodes," *Journal of Consumer Research*, 32(1), 41–53.

Farrell, Diana, Eric Jensen, Bob Kocher, Nick Lovegrove, Fareed Melhem, Lenny Mendonca and Beth Parish (2008), "Accounting for the Cost of US Health Care: A New Look at Why Americans Spend More," McKinsey Global Institute, http://www.mckinsey.com/mgi/publications/US_healthcare/.

Fisher, Elliot S. and H. Gilbert Welch (1999), "Avoiding the Unintended Consequences of Growth in Medical Care: How Might More Be Worse?," *Journal of the American Medical Association*, 281(5), 446–53.

Fisher, Elliot S., David E. Wennberg, Therese A. Stukel, Daniel J. Gottlieb, F.L. Lucas and Etoile L. Pinder (2003a), "The Implications of Regional Variations in Medicare Spending, Part 1: The Content, Quality, and Accessibility of Care," *Annals of Internal Medicine*, 138(4), 273–87.

Fisher, Elliot S., David E. Wennberg, Therese A. Stukel, Daniel J. Gottlieb, F.L. Lucas and Etoile L. Pinder (2003b), "The Implications of Regional Variations in Medicare Spending,

Part 2: Health Outcomes and Satisfaction with Care," *Annals of Internal Medicine*, 138(4), 288–98.

Fournier, Susan and David Glen Mick (1999), "Rediscovering Satisfaction," *Journal of Marketing*, 63(3), 5–23.

Fournier, Susan, Susan Dobscha and David Glen Mick (1998), "Preventing the Premature Death of Relationship Marketing," *Harvard Business Review*, January–February, 42–51.

Frankl, Victor ([1959] 1992), *Man's Search for Meaning*, Boston, MA: Beacon Press.

Freedman, Benjamin (1988), "Health Professions, Codes, and the Right to Refuse to Treat HIV-Infected Patients," *Hastings Center Report*, April/May, 20–25.

Friedman, Richard (2006), "Well-Served as Patients, Dissatisfied as Customers," *New York Times*, January 3, http://www.nytimes.com/2006/01/03 /health/03essa.html (accessed February 10, 2009).

Groopman, Jerome and Pamela Hartzband (2009), "Obama's $80 Billion Exaggeration," *Wall Street Journal*, March 12.

Harris Interactive (2006), "Number of 'Cyberchondriacs' – Adults Who Have Ever Gone Online for Health Information – Increases to an Estimated 136 Million Nationwide," *Harris Poll* No. 59.

Harvey, Michael and Kerin Roger (1977), "Perspectives on Demarketing during the Energy Crisis," *Journal of the Academy of Marketing Science*, 5(4), 327–38.

Herring, Jonathan (2008), "Caregivers in Medical Law and Ethics," *Journal of Contemporary Health Law and Policy*, 25(1), 1–37.

Hilfiker, David (1985), *Healing the Wounds: A Provider Looks at His Work*, New York: Pantheon Books.

Hopkins, Linda M., Aaron B. Caughey, Jeanette S. Brown, Christina L. Wassel Fyr, Jennifer M. Creasman, Eric Bittinghoff, Stephen K. Van Den Eeden and David H. Thom (2007), "Concordance of Chart Abstraction and Patient Recall of Intrapartum Variables up to 53 Years Later," *American Journal of Obstetrics and Gynecology*, 196(3), 233e1–233e6.

Hunt, Shelby D. (2002), *Foundations of Marketing Theory: Toward a General Theory of Marketing*, Armonk, NY: M.E. Sharpe.

Hunter, Gary K. and William D. Perreault, Jr. (2007), "Making Sales Technology Effective," *Journal of Marketing*, 71(1), 16–34.

Imes, Rebecca S., Carma L. Bylund, Christina M. Sabee, Tracy R. Routsong and Amy A. Sanford (2008), "Patients' Reasons for Refraining from Discussing Internet Health Information with Their Healthcare Providers," *Health Communication*, 23, 538–47.

Jacobson, Joseph O. and Antonio C. Wolff (2009), "Evidence-Based Medicine: Do Clinical Practice Guidelines Contribute to Better Patient Care?," http://www.medscape.com/view-article/589088 (accessed March 18, 2009).

Kahn, Barbara E. and Mary Frances Luce (2003), "Understanding High Stakes Consumer Decisions: Mammography Adherence Following False-Alarm Test Results," *Marketing Science*, 22(3), 393–410.

Katz, Alan R. (2008), "Looking Back on the House of God," *Journal of the American Medical Association*, 299(20), 2390.

Kmeitowicz, Zosia (2003), "Half of Doctors Experience Violence or Abuse from Patients," *British Medical Journal*, 327, 889.

Kotler, Philip (1973), "The Major Tasks of Marketing Management," *Journal of Marketing*, 37(3), 42–9.

Kotler, Philip and Sidney J. Levy (1971), "Demarketing, Yes Demarketing," *Harvard Business Review*, November–December, 74–80.

Lingard, Elizabeth A., Elizabeth A. Wright and Clement B. Sledge (2001), "Pitfalls of Using Patient Recall to Derive Preoperative Status in Outcome Studies of Total Knee Arthroplasty," *Journal of Bone and Joint Surgery*, 83-A(8), 1149–56.

Lynn, Michael (1992), "The Psychology of Unavailability," *Basic and Applied Social Psychology*, 13(1), 3–7.

Marjoribanks, Timothy, Mary-Jo Delvecchio Good, Ann G. Lawthers and Lynn M. Peterson

(1996), "Physicians' Discourses on Malpractice and the Meaning of Medical Practice," *Journal of Health and Social Behavior*, 37 (June), 163–78.

Markel, Howard (2008), "The House of God: Thirty Years Later," *Journal of the American Medical Association*, 299(2), 227–9.

McConkey, Sam A. (1994), "Simplifying the Law in Medical Malpractice: The Use of Practice Guidelines as the Standard of Care in Medical Malpractice Litigation," *West Virginia Law Review*, 97, 491.

McGuire, Lisa C. (1996), "Remembering What the Doctor Said: Organization and Adults' Memory for Medical Information," *Experimental Aging Research*, 23, 403–28.

McQueen, M.P. (2008), "Road Risks Rise as More Drivers Drop Insurance," *Wall Street Journal*, December 17.

Meuter, Matthew L., Amy L. Ostrom, Robert I. Roundtree and Mary Jo Bitner (2000), "Self-Service Technologies: Understanding Customer Satisfaction with Technology-Based Service Encounters," *Journal of Marketing*, 64 (July), 50–64.

Meuter, Matthew L., Mary Jo Bitner, Amy L. Ostrom and Stephen W. Brown (2005), "Choosing among Alternative Service Delivery Modes: An Investigation of Customer Trial of Self-Service Technologies," *Journal of Marketing*, 69 (April), 61–83.

Miksanek, Tony (2008), "On Caring for 'Difficult' Patients," *Health Affairs*, 27(5), 1422–8.

Miller, Elizabeth Gelfand, Mary Frances Luce, Barbara E. Kahn and Emily F. Conant (2009), "Understanding Emotional Reactions for Negative Services: The Impact of Efficacy Beliefs and Stage in Process," *Journal of Service Research*, 12(1), 87–99.

Miltein, Arnold and Mark Smith (2007), "Will the Surgical World Become Flat?," *Health Affairs*, 26(1), 137–41.

Minow, Martha (1994), "Who's the Patient?," *Maryland Law Review*, 53, 1173–92.

Moore, Carlton, Thomas McGinn and Ethan Halm (2007), "Tying Up Loose Ends," *Archives of Internal Medicine*, 167, 1305–11.

Morgan, Felicia (2004), "Brand Image Formation and Updating across Multiple-Episode Experiences within Service Networks," doctoral dissertation, Department of Marketing, Arizona State University, Tempe.

Morgan, Ivor and Jay Rao (2003), "Growing Negative Services," *MIT Sloan Management Review*, Spring, 69–74.

Paddock, Catharine (2007), "TB Traveller Discharged," *Medical News Today*, July 27.

Parvatiyar, Atul and Jagdish Sheth (2000), "The Domain and Conceptual Foundations of Relationship Marketing," in Jagdish Sheth and Atul Parvatiyar (eds.), *Handbook of Relationship Marketing*, Thousand Oaks, CA: Sage, pp. 3–38.

Pechmann, Cornelia, Guangzhi Zhao, Marvin E. Goldberg and Ellen Thomas Reibling (2003), "What to Convey in Antismoking Advertisements for Adolescents: The Use of Protection Motivation Theory to Identify Effective Message Themes," *Journal of Marketing*, 67 (April), 1–18.

Relman, Arnold S. and Uwe E. Reinhardt (1986), "Debating For-Profit Health Care and the Ethics of Physicians," *Health Affairs*, Summer, 5–31.

Rowe, Michael (2004), "Doctors' Responses to Medical Error," *Critical Reviews in Oncology Hematology*, 52, 147–63.

Sacks, Frank M., George A. Bray, Vincent J. Carey, Steven R. Smith and Donna Ryan (2009), "Comparison of Weight-Loss Diets with Different Compositions of Fat, Protein, and Carbohydrates," *New England Journal of Medicine*, 360(9), 859–73.

Scott, Doug (2007), "Negotiating Compliance with Patients the Best Approach," *American Academy of Physician Assistant News*, June 30, 13.

Shem, Samuel (1978), *The House of God*, New York: Dell.

Sjostrom, Lars, Anna-Karin Lindroos, Markku Pelton, Jarl Torgerson and Claude Bouchard (2004), "Lifestyle, Diabetes, and Cardiovascular Risk Factors 10 Years after Bariatric Surgery," *New England Journal of Medicine*, 351(26), 2683–93.

Stauss, Bernd, Maxie Schmidt and Andreas Schoeler (2005), "Customer Frustration in Loyalty Programs," *International Journal of Service Industry Management*, 16(3/4), 229–52.

Steinbrook, Robert (2008), "Health Care Reform in Massachusetts – Expanding Coverage, Escalating Costs," *New England Journal of Medicine*, 359(26), 2757–9.

Stillman, Michael D. (2008), "Physicians Behaving Badly," *Journal of the American Medical Association*, 300(1), 21–2.

Tarkan, Laurie (2008), "Arrogant, Abusive and Disruptive – and a Doctor," *New York Times*, December 2, http://nytimes.com/2008/12/02/health/02rage.html (accessed December 2, 2008).

Teel, Sandra J., Jesse E. Teel and William O. Bearden (1979), "Lessons Learned from the Broadcast Cigarette Advertising Ban," *Journal of Marketing*, 43(1), 45–50.

Thakor, Mrugank V. and Ashwin W. Joshi (2005), "Motivating Salesperson Customer Orientation: Insights from the Job Characteristics Model," *Journal of Business Research*, 58, 584–92.

Van de Ven, Andrew H. and Paul E. Johnson (2006), "Knowledge for Theory and Practice," *Academy of Management Review*, 31(4), 802–21.

Van de Ven, Andrew H. and Margaret S. Schomaker (2002), "Commentary: The Rhetoric of Evidence-Based Medicine," *Health Care Management Review*, 27(3), 89–91.

Vargo, Stephen L. and Robert F. Lusch (2004), "Evolving to a New Dominant Logic for Marketing," *Journal of Marketing*, 68(1), 1–17.

Verghese, Abraham (2007), "Introduction," in L. Gutkind (ed.), *Creative Nonfiction: Silence Kills: Speaking Out and Saving Lives*, Pittsburgh, PA: Whitston Publishing.

Wachter, Robert M. (2006), "The "Dis-Location" of U.S. Medicine – the Implications of Medical Outsourcing," *New England Journal of Medicine*, 354(7), 661–5.

Wincupp, P.H., A.G. Shaper, L.T. Lennon and A.G. Thompson (1998), "Validation of Patient Recall of Doctor-Diagnosed Heart Attack and Stroke," *American Journal of Epidemiology*, 148, 355–61.

Zhang, Baohui, Alexi A. Wright, Haiden A. Huskamp, Matthew E. Nilsson, Paul K. Maceijewski and Holly G. Prigerson (2009), "Health Care Costs in the Last Week of Life," *Archives of Internal Medicine*, 169(5), 480–88.

Zugar, Abigail (2004), "Dissatisfaction with Medical Practice," *New England Journal of Medicine*, 350(1), 69–75.

8. Self-service technologies: building relationships with Indian consumers
Rajan Saxena, Mona Sinha and Hufrish Majra

INTRODUCTION

India's journey to a leadership position in the world began with the unleashing of its economy in 1991. In the years before liberalization India typically posted 2.5 percent growth rates and the economy was constrained by a vicious cycle of low investments and a punishing regulatory regime. Post-liberalization, India's growth rate increased from 5.9 percent in 1994 to about 9 percent in 2008 (Tata Services 2009). At a time when major developed economies registered negative growth, India was expected to grow at about 6.2 percent in 2009–10 (Warrier 2009).

By the 1980s, India had gradually transformed from an agrarian to a manufacturing economy. In the 1990s, however, it rapidly turned into a services economy. This was accompanied by three major changes: liberalization of the Indian economy, adoption of technology by firms and consumers, and changing consumer demographics.

For India, as an emerging economy, the banking industry played an important role in propelling the economy forward. It was also instrumental in meeting national goals for poverty reduction and thus was being urged to expand coverage, drive financial inclusion, and bridge the rural–urban divide. Many opportunities for growth in banking remained untapped given that just 44.9 percent of Indian earners had bank accounts (62 percent in urban areas and 38 percent in villages) (Naik 2008). Though income levels continued to rise and 81 percent of households saved, about 36 percent kept their savings at home as cash (*Marketing Whitebook 2009–2010*).

Technology offered a speedier and more cost effective route to expansion as compared to setting up physical branches, and accordingly Indian banks moved technology from a back-end focus to a customer relationship building focus, introducing many self-service technologies (SSTs). SSTs are "technological interfaces that enable customers to produce a service independent of direct service employee involvement" (Meuter et al. 2000: 50), for example self-checkout at retail stores or hotels, automated teller machines (ATMs), telephone or Internet banking, and websites with online purchase options.

On the one hand, SSTs build customer equity (Rust and Kannan 2003) by providing customer benefits such as customization, flexibility, improved service recovery, and spontaneous delight (Bitner et al. 2000). On the other hand, these benefits may be negated when these technologies fail, are poorly designed, or there is no service recovery such as apologies or compensation after a service failure (Bitner 2001). Further, consumers varied in their degree of comfort with technology, which Parasuraman (2000) examined as consumers' "technology readiness." Indeed, ever since Davis et al. (1989) proposed their "technology acceptance model" (TAM), consumer acceptance of technology has been actively researched both by academics and by firms, though mostly in developed countries.

Indian banks aggressively adopted SSTs to extend reach, as well as improve service quality. This was in line with emergent thought in services marketing of increasing profitability by leveraging technology for improving customer satisfaction, rather than for reducing costs (Rust and Kannan 2003). However, interacting with technology rather than service personnel can impact consumers' perception of service quality, value, and loyalty (Parasuraman and Grewal 2000). Apart from technological challenges, Indian banks also faced many socio-economic and psychological challenges to the adoption of technology.

Relatively little was known thus far about technology adoption in emerging markets, particularly India, which faced a paucity of research in the public domain. Research in some markets outside the United States indicated that culture and values could impact consumers' propensity to adopt technology (Lee et al. 2007; Elliott and Meng 2009). In India, technology was a recent introduction, and the drivers and impediments to technology adoption were not yet well understood. For the Indian banking industry aiming for rapid expansion, actively pushing for adoption of SSTs such as ATMs and online banking was important for reaching out to those Indians who were young, educated, and tech-savvy, as well as those who lived in areas that were either not served or underserved. In this context understanding how Indian consumers adopt technology in general and banking SSTs in particular was critical.

In this chapter, we first set the context with a brief description of India and Indian consumers. We then provide insights into technology adoption by Indian consumers, before delving specifically into adoption of banking SSTs and its impact on customer relationships. We draw attention to global research on SST adoption and juxtapose it with some initial research in India and a few other emerging economies, which suggests that consumers of emerging economies, and in particular India, may differ from consumers from developed countries.

THE CHANGING PROFILE OF INDIAN CONSUMERS: CHALLENGE FOR BANKERS

In 1991, the Indian government, faced with a balance of payments problem, liberalized the Indian economy and allowed market forces to operate with fewer restrictions than in the past. Competition intensified as domestic players rose to the challenge posed by new multinational entrants. A population of more than a billion, with an expanding middle class, appeared at first glance to be very attractive, but defied logic, as many multinationals found to their peril. India was large in size but small in terms of per capita income. It had strong domestic brands, a culture of entrepreneurship that had been fostered despite bureaucratic and government impediments, and tremendous consumer diversity. "Mass" marketers with "value-for-money" propositions (e.g., Nokia and Honda) had so far performed far better in India than "class" marketers (e.g., Nike and Mercedes), which struggled to fit in with strongly rooted traditions (Bijapurkar 2007; *Marketing Whitebook 2007–2008*).

As the Indian marketplace evolved, key demographic changes also emerged. India had turned into a predominantly young market, with almost 60 percent of the total population in the range 15–59 years of age, and it was expected to remain young until at least 2050. Growing literacy rates, from 52.2 percent in 1997 to 64.8 percent in 2009, led to a 100 percent increase in enrollments in institutes of higher education, including profes-sional programs (Tata Services 2009). From 1995 to 2005, the shape of the income distribution changed from the poor country pyramid shape to a diamond, with fewer people at the bottom and the top but a lot more in the middle. Over the next two decades India's middle class was expected to grow from 5 percent of the population to more than 40 percent, creating what many expected to be the fifth largest consumer market, where middle class was defined as an annual disposable income of $4380 to $21 890 in real 2000 terms ($23 530 to $117 650 on a purchasing-power-parity basis) (Beinhocker et al. 2007).

India had tremendous consumer diversity, for example in terms of geography, religion, literacy, income, age, and occupation. The vastly different consumption values, beliefs, and traditions challenged mar-keters' creativity in their relationship building strategies. For example, young post-liberalization Indians with free-market, capitalist inclinations viewed debt as a sign of confidence in future earnings, and vied for debt for financing consumption and assets. Yet, unlike their counterparts in other BRIC countries, they were not "wannabe westerns," but exhib-ited both an ethnic and an international outlook. In contrast, the older, pre-liberalization Indians held on to their "Gandhian" values of simple living and socialism, and still associated borrowing with social stigma (Bijapurkar 2007).

THE PROLIFERATION OF TECHNOLOGY IN THE INDIAN MARKET

Post-1991 and especially after 2000, technology proliferated rapidly, drawing consumers from all social classes into the consumption fold, transforming the average Indian consumer's life. Innovative solutions aimed at boosting consumption by expanding the middle- and bottom-of-the-pyramid markets brought once-premium products to Indian consumers at affordable prices. From satellite television in the early 1990s, to cell phones in the early 2000s, and more recently the Internet, technology provided new modes of reaching out to consumers and building relationships.

For example, Internet connectivity surged from 5 million users in 2000 to 81 million users by 2008. Yet with just 7.1 percent penetration there was considerable scope for growth (Internet World Statistics 2009). Research on Internet usage showed that 73 percent of Internet users were young (42 percent in the range 15–24 years and 31 percent in the range 25–34 years). Internet usage for e-commerce was only 6.5 percent, but this was growing. Major transformation, however, brought about the rapid penetration of cell phones. The availability of base model cell phones at $25 and entry level pre-paid airtime at $2 made it easier to acquire a cell phone than a land line (Saxena 2009). Not surprisingly this led to 375 million cell phones, constituting 91 percent of the total phone lines in the country (Behl 2009). Technologies, such as cell phones, became the great leveler, drawing in consumers irrespective of income and education, and deftly reaching into rural interiors.

Technology drove economic and social development by enabling the creation of innovative, high quality goods and services at low prices that worked even in areas suffering infrastructural constraints such as lack of roads and electricity. As a result, India witnessed a technological revolution, leap-frogging the technological curve in several product categories. For example, while it took more than 30 years for television to reach 1 million Indian consumers (Rogers and Singhal 2001), the Internet introduced in 1993 achieved this milestone in five years, while cell phones introduced in 1995 took less than three years (Saxena 2009). Increasingly, Indian companies leveraged information technology and telecommunications to expand in domestic markets as well as enter global markets.

STRUCTURE OF THE INDIAN BANKING INDUSTRY

Indian banks were classified as public sector (i.e., government owned) banks, old generation private sector banks, new generation private sector banks, and multinational banks. Of these, the latter two were a product of liberalization. In their initial years, new generation private sector banks and multinational banks had to adopt the SST route to expansion, owing to government restrictions on setting up branches. As regulatory restrictions eased and competition intensity increased, the market share of branches and bank deposits changed as follows: 27 public sector banks with 85.8 percent of the branches and 77 percent of deposits; 21 private sector banks with 13.7 percent of the branches and 18 percent of deposits; and 30 multinational banks with 0.5 percent of branches and 5.2 percent of deposits (see Table 8.1 for key statistics of Indian banks).

TECHNOLOGY ADOPTION BY INDIAN BANKS

The banking sector had undergone significant changes since the early 1990s to meet changing consumer needs, led chiefly by new generation private Indian banks such as ICICI Bank and HDFC Bank, and multinational banks such as Citibank and HSBC. The combination of demographic

Table 8.1   Indian banks: key statistics (2008–09)

Parameters	Public sector banks	Private sector banks	Global banks	Total
Number of banks	27	21	30	78
Number of employees	734661	174073	30304	939038
Number of branches	55438	8877	293	64608
Business per employee (in USD millions)	42.10	26.65	83.09	151.84
Profit per employee (in USD millions)	0.254	0.220	2.350	2.824
Deposits (in USD millions)	622550	145363	42815	810728

Note: $1 = Rs50.

Source: Adapted from "A Profile of Banks," in www.rbi.org.in (accessed November 1, 2009).

dynamics and rapid economic growth was potentially a double edged sword, boosting retail lending in the short term but resulting in higher defaults in the long term (India Knowledge @ Wharton 2008). Driven primarily by the aggressive private and multinational banks, low interest rates, monthly payment plans, and a host of other offerings common in the developed world but new to the Indian market now became available. The banks' flexibility came not only from the post-liberalization easing of banking norms but also their move away from back-end to consumer-facing technologies, which ushered in a service-oriented culture.

The automation of Indian public sector banks had begun in a phased manner in 1985 and gained momentum in the early 1990s with techno-logical as well as regulatory advances. The focus on back-end operations resulted in 35 percent partial and 28 percent full computerization of the bank branches by 2003 (Sharma 2009). However, major use of technol-ogy began only with the advent of private and multinational banks, which leveraged technologies such as ATM and online banking to reach out to areas where they lacked branches or direct marketing affiliates, with resultant improvements in product and service quality levels (Dutta and Dutta 2009).

The use of technology also facilitated the expansion of banks in semi-urban and rural areas. Until recently only public sector banks had operated in unprofitable rural areas, and that too was due to government mandate. Not surprisingly there were only about 30 570 rural bank branches in 2006 (Naik 2008). Increasing competitive intensity in urban markets and growing prosperity in rural markets resulted in private banks scrambling to make inroads in rural areas. With cell phone connectivity in rural areas expected to increase to 200 million by 2012, there was scope for further growth in smaller towns where current cell phone density was only about 10 percent (Sindhu 2008). Thus, banks were "banking" on expansion, not only by increasing the coverage of existing SSTs such as ATMs and online banking, but also by introducing new SSTs such as mobile banking.

SSTs also helped banks prune costs. For example, D.K. Gupta and Gupta (2008) estimated that it cost a bank Rs50 ($1) per branch transac-tion and Rs15 (30 cents) if conducted at an ATM, while an online trans-action cost Rs4 (8 cents). For banks entering rural markets, reduced cost was an added incentive to promote SSTs in rural areas, where transactions were typically high volume but very low value, and so keeping costs low was a major challenge to expansion (Naik 2008).

Thus, technology adoption marked the next major phase of growth for banks. However, public sector banks lagged behind private and multina-tional banks in this endeavor, owing to resistance to change and highly political unions. Consequently, public sector banks were left with older consumers (50 years and above), who were mostly averse to adopting new technology, while private and multinational banks' clientele was mostly urban and young (20–40 years), and had higher exposure to technology (De and Padmanabhan 2002).

Technology resulted in consumers becoming consumers of the bank rather than of a branch (Mohan 2004). The bank's central servers became the data repository rather than branches. The relationship managers at the branches became part of the central or regional customer relationship management team at the bank and helped the bank connect with its customers. Additionally, banks began using 24/7 help-lines to facilitate customer transactions. Even public sector banks attempted to regain market share by making organizational changes, including extensive branch renovations. New open-office designs enabled customers to transact with a banker across the table rather than by standing behind the counter – a sea-change from the way Indian consumers were accustomed to being served.

Accordingly, the banking habits of consumers also underwent a marked change, and SST adoption grew. In a survey of 6365 Internet users in 2005–06 across India, preferred modes of banking were identified as ATMs (53 percent), Internet (23 percent), branch (18 percent), phone (4 percent) and cell phone (2 percent) (IAMAI 2006). We briefly review the two key SSTs used by Indian banking consumers.

Automated Teller Machines in India

Though the first ATM was introduced by Barclays Bank in London in 1967, it was only in 1987 that HSBC set up the first ATM in India (Banknet India 2007). Between 2004 and 2008 there was a 32.2 percent increase in the usage of ATMs in India (Tata Services 2009), with banks increasingly setting up ATMs at locations other than branches. ATMs as a percentage of branches were highest for multinational banks and lowest for public sector banks (see Table 8.2 for ATMs and branches of Indian banks). On April 1, 2009 the Reserve Bank of India waived the fees charged for using ATM cards of one bank at another bank's machine. This was likely to increase ATM penetration within as well as outside of urban areas.

ATMs helped banks expand their coverage and offered conveniences such as 24/7 service, shorter waiting times, and at times avoidance of discourteous or apathetic bank staff. Further, in the quest for rural expansion, many innovative ATMs were designed to overcome usage and availability constraints. For example, ATMs that offered local languages were voice-enabled (Union Bank of India 2010), used biometrics instead of PIN codes (*Outlook* 2009), came at a quarter the cost and one-twentieth

Table 8.2   Indian banks: ATMs and branches

Parameters	Public sector banks	Private sector banks		Global banks	Total
		Old	New		
Number of branches	55438	4673	4204	293	64608
Number of ATMs	27277	2674	12646	1054	43651
ATMs as percentage of branches	50%	57%	300%	359%	68%

Source: Adapted from "Operations and Performance of Commercial Banks," in www.rbi. org.in (accessed November 1, 2009).

the power consumption of regular ATMs, and could run on solar power (Rao 2009). It was no longer unusual to see ATM machines loaded on a van, winding through dusty village roads covering a number of villages on its daily route (S.D. Gupta 2006). ATMs that doubled up as kiosks that offered railway ticket bookings, cell phone recharge cards, news, sports, movie, and weather information, and agribusiness prices were also being introduced (Banknet India 2007).

Internet Banking in India

The first online banking website in India was set up by ICICI bank in 1996. However, usage increased only after 1999 following lowering of prices and increased penetration of personal computers. Relatively new in the Indian markets, banking websites ranged from those with minimum functionality that offered only access to deposit account data to highly sophisticated websites enabling integrated sales of add-on products and access to other financial services such as investment and insurance.

In the IAMAI (2006) survey discussed earlier, 35 percent of the respondents used online banking, of whom 83 percent were male, 43 percent were 26–35 years, 25 percent were 18–25 years, 19 percent were 36–45 years, and 12 percent were above 46 years. In general, online banking was used by young, educated, and largely urban consumers, for convenience (51 percent), saving time (44 percent), and greater control over finances (22 percent), augmenting the bank's core service offering. As Berry (2002) noted, such value additions contributed to the firm–consumer relationship.

However, the online environment also raised new service quality issues such as efficiency, fulfillment, system availability, and privacy (Parasuraman et al. 2005). A study evaluating service quality in India found that consumers did not find Internet banking to be user-friendly, though they were satisfied with the reliability of services provided. Concerns about security and order fulfillment also lowered service quality perceptions (Khan et al. 2009). In response to customer preferences and technology innovations, banks offered enhanced new-to-the-market services such as improved navigation, integrating multiple services into single systems, viewing of returned checks, onsite purchase of retail goods, and seamless integration with e-commerce retail sites. Such initiatives were aimed at building customer loyalty, cross-selling, and encouraging repeat business.

ADOPTION OF SELF-SERVICE BANKING TECHNOLOGIES: APPLYING GLOBAL LESSONS TO THE INDIAN CONTEXT

Banks, like other services, were able to use the growth of Internet connectivity and cellular phones to offer SSTs that consumers could use without any intermediary and support from the service provider (Barnes et al. 2000). However, the success of any technology-enabled service depended largely on the diffusion of technology and the maturity and inclination of consumers to adopt the technology (Rogers 1995). Without knowledge of how Indian consumers were adopting the SSTs offered by banks, future customer acquisition and retention goals based on SSTs rather than physical branches remained unclear.

The world over, SSTs had transformed service delivery by altering, reducing, or even completely removing humans from consumer–firm interactions, offering many consumer conveniences such as saving time and providing 24/7 access. In a study of 800 critical incidents Meuter et al. (2000) found that 63 percent of the outcomes in the incidents studied were attributed to technology, of which 29 percent were satisfying while 34 percent were dissatisfying. Interestingly, of those who had a satisfactory outcome, 68 percent rated the technological interaction better than an interpersonal one, but the authors noted that, unlike an interpersonal interaction, a technological interaction did not offer opportunity for a service recovery.

At times technology-enabled service delivery could malfunction or consumers did not have the skills to manage technology. This could impede customer access, intimidating users, depersonalizing the service encounter, and causing frustration or hostility (Walker and Craig-Lees 2000). Walker et al. (2002) suggest that in high risk situations consumers may exhibit technologically induced hostility because contact personnel may be perceived as inseparable from the service organization, customers may desire a high degree of personal attention, and consumers may lack the ability to use technology or may not perceive any advantage to using the technology. Managing every negative SST experience was important from a relationship perspective for two reasons. First, consumers of SSTs tended to use multiple technology-enabled channels in a complementary way based on how that particular technology contributed to satisfaction in the overall service offering (Patricio et al. 2003). Second, heavy SST users relied on their attitudes towards specific SSTs, whereas light SST users relied more on their global attitude towards SSTs (Curran et al. 2003).

Extant research suggested that technology adoption depended on factors such as usefulness of the technology, convenience, ease of use, need or avoidance of service employee, and social influence (Davis et al. 1989; Meuter et al. 2000; Szymanski and Hise 2000; Dabholkar and Bagozzi 2002). The extent to which consumers changed their habits and adopted SSTs, by engaging in co-production (Bendapudi and Leone 2003), also depended on their attitudes (Curran et al. 2003) and emotions (Mick and Fournier 1998), which contributed to their "readiness" to adopt technology (Parasuraman 2000).

Technology readiness has been defined by Parasuraman (2000) as an individual's propensity to embrace and use new technologies for accomplishing goals at home or at work. The Technology Readiness Index (TRI) has been a useful tool for understanding consumers' inclination to adopt technologies and was based on two contributors and two inhibitors of technology adoption: *optimism* (a positive view of technology and a belief that it offers people increased control, flexibility, and efficiency in their lives); *innovativeness* (a tendency to be a technology pioneer and thought leader); *discomfort* (a perceived lack of control over technology and a feeling of being overwhelmed by it); and *insecurity* (a distrust of technology and skepticism about its ability to work properly) (2000: 311).

Based on people's beliefs, the TRI segmented five types of technology customers (Parasuraman and Colby 2001): *explorers* (16 percent of the U.S. population; most optimistic, most innovative, greater discomfort, more insecure); *pioneers* (27 percent of the U.S. population; more optimistic, more innovative, greater discomfort, more insecure); *skeptics* (21 percent of the U.S. population; less optimistic, less innovative, less discomfort, less insecure); *paranoid* (20 percent of the U.S. population; more optimistic, less innovative, greatest discomfort, most insecure); and *laggards* (14 percent of the U.S. population; less optimistic, less innovative, greatest discomfort, most insecure).

Recent research indicates that speed and manner of adoption of SSTs in some countries differed from that of the U.S. (Rogers 1995; Lee et al.

2007). A study of Chinese consumers' use of SSTs in retailing indicated that culture and values influenced desire to use technology and anxiety towards technology (Elliott and Meng 2009). The authors identified three clusters based on the TRI: *unconvinced consumers* (50 percent of the sample; did not believe that technology can be beneficial and were concerned about reliability and accuracy); *receptive consumers* (29 percent of the sample; early adopters, very optimistic about the benefits of technology, had low risk perceptions, and moderate concern about breakdowns); *adventurous consumers* (21 percent of the sample; optimistic and innovative, used new technology even if lacking confidence to do so).

Adhikari and Rao (2006) argued that, in the case of emerging economies like India where the availability of technology was recent and computer penetration was low, consumers' adoption of technology depended not only on their readiness, but also on their inclination to fulfill life's needs with technology-enabled methods rather than traditional methods. In their study, with 407 respondents in 12 Indian cities, they identified four segments on the basis of technology inclination: *techno-resist*, who did not see any benefits of technology and preferred traditional processes (23 percent of the sample; mostly women older than 44, low education); *techno-inclined*, who perceived the benefits of technology but were mostly inclined to traditional methods (36 percent of the sample; mostly men 35–45 years, graduates); *techno-prone*, who found technology convenient and highly beneficial but were concerned about security (25 percent of the sample; men and women 35 years and above, undergraduates and graduates); *techno-savvy*, who perceived high benefits of using technology and used it without any security concerns (16 percent of the sample; men 18–30 years, many of whom were graduates).

Although the categorization differed across the three studies described above, overall it appeared that about 41 percent of the respondents in the U.S. (skeptics and paranoids), 50 percent of those in China (unconvinced), and 59 percent of those in India (techno-resist and techno-inclined) were less likely than others to adopt technology. Further, though Parasuraman and Colby (2001) found age, education, and income to be significant factors affecting technology readiness, Adhikari and Rao (2006) found that, in India, age and education significantly affected technology inclination but income did not. They surmised that this might be because in India only middle to upper income groups had access to technology.

Another model traditionally applied to test adoption propensity is the technology adoption model (TAM) based on perceived usefulness of the technology and perceived ease of use (Davis et al. 1989). TAM has been tested in some countries other than the United States. For example Amin (2009) found that Malaysian consumers' intention to adopt online banking was based on TAM factors (perceived usefulness and perceived ease of use) as well as on perceived credibility of the provider in protecting security and privacy, and social norms that associate technology adoption as an important vehicle for displaying personal and social identity.

One study employed the TAM to study the effect of culture on information technology adoption in India. It was found that consumers' expectation about the technology's performance was the most important factor in adopting technology. This was especially so for older male users with lower income. Other significant factors were consumers' expectations about the effort they would have to invest and social influence. The authors suggested that the TAM did not successfully test outside of the U.S. because of non-inclusion of cultural variables (Bandhopadhyay and Fraccastoro 2007).

Thus, cross-cultural research provided some initial evidence that the technology adoption by non-U.S. consumers, especially those of emerging markets, would likely be different than that of consumers in other parts of the world.

THE ROAD AHEAD

The banking industry plays a critical role in the socio-economic development of India, and financial inclusion at low cost can happen only by leveraging technology (Indian Express 2008). Global research indicates that technology based services should provide the same high level of service as a human interaction (Bitner 2001). However, in emerging markets, it may be necessary for technology to go beyond providing the same level of service. Local insights may indicate intermediate solutions, such as a telephone inside an ATM booth to call for help if the consumer is unable to operate the ATM or training sessions to educate users about usage and benefits. To avoid technology-induced hostility such training would first have to educate users about banking services and then train them on technology.

Developing hybrid models for banking SSTs that combine technology as well as human interaction may be a possible solution, but has strategic and financial implications for banks, and cannot be based only on global lessons from research in developed or other emerging markets. Further, along with consumers' readiness, their willingness to adopt technology must also be examined. This may be no average task given that India has largely been viewed as an amalgamation of many "little Indias" (Bijapurkar 2007). This will undoubtedly add several layers of complexity to the task of identifying the type and number of Indian consumers who are likely to change their traditional methods of doing business to adopt technological solutions. Thus, we emphasize a compelling need for more concerted research focus on Indian consumers' attitudes and beliefs about technology in general and SSTs in particular, to help bankers better decide what technologies (hybrid or otherwise) to offer to different target audiences in India and how technology can spur out-of-the-box thinking to extend banking services to areas and socio-economic classes with hitherto untargeted consumers.

As India prospers, the promise of technology in facilitating market expansion attracts domestic and international companies from a variety of industries. Yet, even amongst Asian economies, India has been known to show a certain distinctiveness. Thus, any study of Indian consumers must take into account the large diversity of the Indian population, and its historical and cultural roots and value systems. Further, this understanding must be viewed in the context of India's geographical expanse, infrastructural constraints, and socio-economic realities, for which perhaps ethnographic studies may be particularly useful. For businesses, addressing the financial, technological, and social challenges posed by India's diversity requires a concerted research agenda and innovative thought.

With this chapter, we hope to spark research interest in how the consumption behavior of Indian consumers compares to that of their counterparts in other markets. This would also address the issue of limited information and data availability on India, in the public domain, which is a key limitation of our work as well. Although in this chapter we focus on banking, our line of thought could well be applied to any industry competing in India which has technology as its core product (e.g., goods like computers, or services like software), the mode of distribution (e.g., website or ATM), an ancillary service (e.g., online help desk, call centers), or even a communication tool (e.g., emails).

We believe that studying consumers' attitude towards and usage of technology in India will yield valuable insights that likely will differ from those gleaned from other parts of the world. This will contribute to academic knowledge in the domain of adoption of technologies, especially SSTs, and consumer behavior, and will also strategically prepare businesses in building long-term, mutually beneficial relationships with Indian consumers.

REFERENCES

Adhikari, Atanu and A.K. Rao (2006), "Technology Inclination-Based Segments of Indian Customers," *Journal of Creative Communications*, 1(3), 219–32.

Amin, Hanudin (2009), "An Analysis of Online Banking Usage Intentions: An Extension of the Technology Acceptance Model," *International Journal of Business and Society*, 10(1), 27–40.

Bandhopadhyay, Kakoli and Katherine A. Fraccastoro (2007), "The Effect of Culture on User Acceptance of Information Technology," *Communications of the Association for Information Systems*, 19, 522–43.

Banknet India (2007), *Report on Indian ATM Industry*, May, Mumbai: Banknet Publications, pp. 10–11.

Barnes, G. James, Peter A. Dunne and William J. Glynn (2000), "Self Service and Technology: Unanticipated and Unintended Effects on Customer Relationships," in T.A. Swartz and D. Iacobucci (eds.), *Handbook of Services Marketing and Management*, Thousand Oaks, CA: Sage.

Behl, Tejeesh N.S. (2009), "Rural to the Rescue," *Business Today*, April 5, 46–66.

Beinhocker, Eric D., Diana Farrell and Adil S. Zainulbhai (2007), "Tracking the Growth of India's Middle Class," *McKinsey Quarterly*, August, 51–61.

Bendapudi, Neeli and Robert P. Leone (2003), "Psychological Implications of Customer Participation in Coproduction," *Journal of Marketing*, 67(1), 14–28.

Berry, Leonard L. (2002), "Relationship Marketing of Services – Perspectives from 1983 and 2000," *Journal of Relationship Marketing*, 1(1), 59–77.

Bijapurkar, Rama (2007), *We Are Like That Only: Understanding the Logic of Consumer India*, Noida, India: Penguin Books.

Bitner, Mary Jo (2001), "Self-Service Technologies – What Do Customers Expect?," *Marketing Management*, 10(1), 10–11.

Bitner, Mary Jo, Stephen W. Brown and Matthew L. Meuter (2000), "Technology Infusion in Service Encounters," *Journal of the Academy of Marketing Science*, 28(1), 138–49.

Curran, James M., Matthew L. Meuter and Carol F. Surprenant (2003), "Intention to Use Self-Service Technologies: A Confluence of Multiple Attitudes," *Journal of Service Research*, 5(3), 209–24.

Dabholkar, Pratibha A. and Richard P. Bagozzi (2002), "An Attitudinal Model of Technology-Based Self-Service: Moderating Effects of Consumer Traits and Situational Factors," *Journal of Academy of Marketing Science*, 30(3), 184–201.

Davis, Fred D., Richard P. Bagozzi and Paul R. Warshaw (1989), "User Acceptance of Computer Technology: A Comparison of Two Theoretical Models," *Management Science*, 35(8), 982–1003.

De, Rajneesh and Chitra Padmanabhan (2002), "Internet Opens New Vistas for Indian Banks," *Express Computer Weekly*, September 16.

Dutta, Kirti and Anil Dutta (2009), "Consumer Expectations and Perceptions across the Indian Banking Industry and the Resultant Financial Implications," *Journal of Services Research*, 9(1), 31–49.

Elliott, Kevin M. and Juan (Gloria) Meng (2009), "Assessing Chinese Consumers' Likelihood to Adopt Self-Service Technologies," *International Business and Economics Research Journal*, 8(2), 27–40.

Gupta, Dinesh Kumar and Pradeep Gupta (2008), "Mother Tongue Friendly E-Delivery Banking Channels in India – Ultimate Solution for its Popular Usage," www.ssrn.com (accessed October 31, 2009).

Gupta, Surjeet Das (2006), "How IT Is Changing Rural India," http://www.rediff.com/money/2006/apr/07spec.htm (accessed November 1, 2009).

IAMAI (2006), "IAMAI's Report – Online Banking 2006," Internet and Mobile Association of India, www.iamai.in (accessed June 13, 2009).

India Knowledge @ Wharton (2008), "Retail in India: Capturing the Opportunities of a Complex Consumer Class," http://knowledge.wharton.upenn.edu/india/article. cfm?articleid=4289 (accessed June 13, 2009).

Indian Express (2008), "Use Technology to Bring Banking to Billions in India," http://www. indianexpress.com/news/use-technology-to-bring-banking-to-billions/328022/ (accessed June 22, 2009).

Internet World Statistics (2009), http://www.internetworldstats.com/asia.htm#in (accessed July 9, 2009).

Khan, M.S., Siba Sankar Mahapatra and Sreekumar (2009), "Service Quality Evaluation in Internet Banking: An Empirical Study in India," *International Journal of Indian Culture and Business Management*, 2(1), 30–46.

Lee, Inseong, Boreum Choi, Jinwoo Kim and Se-Joon Hong (2007), "Culture–Technology Fit: Effects of Cultural Characteristics on the Post-Adoption Beliefs of Mobile Internet Users," *International Journal of Electronic Commerce*, 11(4), 11–51.

Marketing Whitebook 2007–2008, Kolkata: Business World.

Marketing Whitebook 2009–2010, Kolkata: Business World.

Meuter, Matthew L., Amy L. Ostrom, Robert I. Roundtree and Mary Jo Bitner (2000), "Self-Service Technologies: Understanding Customer Satisfaction with Technology-Based Service Encounters," *Journal of Marketing*, 64(3), 50–64.

Mick, David Glen and Susan Fournier (1998), "Paradoxes of Technology: Consumer, Cognizance, Emotions, and Coping Strategies," *Journal of Consumer Research*, 25(2), 123–43.

Mohan, Rakesh (2004), "Indian Banking and E-Security," http://www.rakeshmohan.com/ docs/RBIBulletinNov2004–1.pdf (accessed June 28, 2009).

Naik, S.D (2008), "From 'Class Banking' to 'Mass Banking,'" *Hindu Business Line*, http:// www.thehindubusinessline.com/2008/08/22/stories/2008082250160800.htm (accessed June 22, 2009).

Outlook (2009), "SBI to Introduce 150 Biometric ATMs in Gujarat," http://news.outlookin-dia.com/item.aspx?653536 (accessed October 31, 2009).

Parasuraman, A. (2000), "Technology Readiness Index (Tri): A Multiple-Item Scale to Measure Readiness to Embrace New Technologies," *Journal of Service Research*, 2(4), 307–20.

Parasuraman, A. and Charles L. Colby (2001), *Techno-Ready Marketing: How and Why Your Consumers Adopt Technology*, New York: Free Press.

Parasuraman, A. and Dhruv Grewal (2000), "The Impact of Technology on the Quality–Value–Loyalty Chain: A Research Agenda," *Academy of Marketing Science Journal*, 28(1), 168–74.

Parasuraman, A., Valarie A. Zeithaml and Naresh Malhotra (2005), "E-S-Qual: A Multiple Item Scale for Assessing Electronic Service Quality," *Journal of Service Research*, 7(3), 213–33.

Patricio, Lia, Raymond P. Fisk and Joao Falcao e Cunha (2003), "Improving Satisfaction with Bank Service Offerings: Measuring the Contribution of Each Delivery Channel," *Managing Service Quality*, 13(6), 471–82.

Rao, Srinivas (2009), "Cash Machines for Rural India," *Technology Review*, http://www. rediff.com/money/2006/apr/07spec.htm (accessed November 1, 2009).

Rogers, Everett M. (1995), *Diffusion of Innovations*, New York: Free Press.

Rogers, Everett M. and Arvind Singhal (2001), *India's Communication Revolution: From Bullock Carts to Cyber Marts*, New Delhi: Sage.

Rust, Ronald T. and P. Kannan (2003), "E-Service: A New Paradigm for Business in the Electronic Environment," *Communications of the ACM*, 46(6), 36–42.

Saxena, Rajan (2009), *Marketing Management*, New Delhi: Tata McGraw-Hill.

Sharma, Dhiraj (2009), "India's Leapfrogging Steps from Bricks-and-Mortar to Virtual Banking: Prospects and Perils," *ICFAI Journal of Management Research*, VIII(3), 45–61.

Sindhu, Seema (2008), "Rural Users Yet to Take a Call on Mobile Banking," http://www. business-standard.com/india/storypage.php?autono=336855 (accessed June 22, 2009).

Szymanski, David M. and Richard T. Hise (2000), "E-Satisfaction: An Initial Examination," *Journal of Retailing*, 76(3), 309–22.

Tata Services (2009), *Statistical Outline of India 2008–2009*, Mumbai: Tata Services.

Union Bank of India (2010), "Kisan ATM," http://www.unionbankofindia.co.in/personal_alternet_kisan.aspx (accessed December 10, 2010).

Walker, Rhett H. and M. Craig-Lees (2000), "Technology-Enabled Service Delivery: At Risk of Compromising the Customer–Service Provider Connection?," in S.T. Cavusgil and R.B. McNaughton (eds.), *Advances in International Marketing*, Greenwich, CT: JAI Press, pp. 305–22.

Walker, Rhett H., Margaret Craig-Lees, Robert Hecker and Heather Francis (2002), "Technology-Enabled Service Delivery: An Investigation of Reasons Affecting Customer Adoption and Rejection," *International Journal of Service Industry Management*, 13(1), 91–106.

Warrier, Krishna (2009), "Real GDP Estimate Revised Upwards for Second Consecutive Month," Centre for Monitoring Indian Economy, www.cmie.com (accessed November 13, 2009).

9. Taxonomy of hotel loyalty program members: examining differences in service quality perceptions
George Deitz and John D. Hansen

INTRODUCTION

Perhaps the most tangible evidence of marketing's paradigm shift toward relational exchange has been the widespread diffusion of corporate loyalty programs. Loyalty programs seek to bond customers to the firm by offering incentives that reward continued patronage, such as frequent flyer miles, customer loyalty bonuses, free gifts, and personalized coupons (Peterson 1995). A census of the US loyalty program industry found individual program memberships topped 1.3 billion, an increase of over 35 percent since 2000 (Ferguson and Hlavinka 2007). Moreover, the appeal of these programs spans a broad array of service industries, including credit card issuers (e.g., American Express), restaurants (e.g., Subway), hotels (e.g., Holiday Inn), rental car companies (e.g., Hertz), and entertainment firms (e.g., Disney).

In the race to expand membership rolls, however, it would seem many program managers have lost sight of the goal of producing long-term, mutually beneficial customer relationships. Shugan (2005: 186) suggested that many programs are no more than price promotions in sheep's clothing, stating "[T]hese so-called loyalty programs are shams in the sense that they produce liabilities rather than assets . . . Rather than demonstrating trust by committing to the customer, the firm asks the customer to trust that, in return for current revenue, the firm will provide future customer rewards." In effect, the cumulative effects of faulty program design and short-sighted managerial decision making have been: 1) to attract a relatively larger percentage of transactional customers; and 2) to condition customers who would otherwise have been open to establishing long-term relationships toward more transactional behaviors.

Customer relationship quality and behavioral loyalty cannot be inferred from nominal program membership; neither can it be assumed that all program participants will equally engage in firm-favored behaviors (Reinartz and Kumar 2002; Noble and Phillips 2004). Nonetheless, loyalty programs remain managed predominantly at the aggregate level with scant attention paid to individual member differences (Kumar and Shah 2004). It would be more logical to expect that there exist groups of customers within nearly every loyalty program who differ considerably with respect to the attitudes they hold and behaviors they exhibit toward the host organization. To date, however, little research has investigated segmentation approaches within loyalty programs, the drivers of potential differences among segments, or the most appropriate managerial responses to loyalty program segment differences (cf. Allaway et al. 2006).

Given the marginal returns many firms have received on their customer relationship management (CRM) investments, it appears to us that a need exists for greater conceptual work that isolates distinguishing characteristics of loyalty program customers. This study reports the results of an effort to identify distinct patronage segments in a services-based loyalty program context using data drawn from two global hotel chains. Using separately fit CFA mixture models, we find four distinct segments of customers in each sample. In addition, the inclusion of behavioral loyalty covariates in the mixture model enabled us concurrently to develop a predictive model of class membership through multinomial logistic regression. Following class identification, we test the validity of our classification using multigroup SEM in assessing the extent to which class members' service quality perceptions varied in a theoretically consistent manner. Based upon these results, we offer detailed profiles of our four customer types – transactionals, transitionals, devoteds, and dissatisfieds – and suggest general class-specific approaches for enhancing member loyalty.

The study contributes to the literature by bringing to the forefront the types of significant customer differences routinely found within loyalty programs. Given the proliferation of loyalty programs and ever-increasing competitive pressures, program populations have become exceedingly diverse. Our study builds upon earlier efforts (e.g., Allaway et al. 2006) that have highlighted the need for segmentation in loyalty program design and customized relationship management efforts. In addition, the study advances understanding of the ways through which loyalty programs may best be managed. Paradoxically, it has been suggested that the meteoric rise in the number of loyalty programs has resulted in their commoditization, limiting their effectiveness as a tool for building strong customer relationships (Dowling 2002). While we agree that the presence of a loyalty program is not a silver-bullet strategy for marketplace success, we believe that effective program management represents a rare and unique resource upon which sustainable advantages can be built (Morgan and Hunt 1994). The taxonomic framework depicted within this study provides managers a useful tool through which segments can be more effectively identified and resources more efficiently allocated.

CONCEPTUAL DEVELOPMENT

The first step in the development of an empirical taxonomy is the identification and justification of the variables used in identifying segments.
For this study, we focus on category involvement, which refers to the
degree of personal relevance, interest, or importance a given product or
service category holds for the customer (Zaichkowsky 1985; Higie and
Feick 1989; Coulter et al. 2003). The effects of involvement have primarily
been investigated with respect to customer search behavior, information
processing, and persuasion (Andrews et al. 1990). In terms of search,
prior work has shown higher levels of involvement lead to the use of more
complex decision processes and a greater ability to discern differences
between offerings on a wider variety of attributes (Mittal and Lee 1989).
With regard to information processing and persuasion, low-involvement
customers tend to depend on the most easily accessible inputs, whereas
high-involvement customers seek the most relevant inputs in carefully
making their appraisals (Petty et al. 1983; Celsi and Olson 1988).

For low-involvement customers, loyalty programs represent an easily
accessible peripheral cue, often no further away than their billfold. The
availability of price-based discounts and promotions obscures differences between offerings on non-price attributes, reinforcing the limited
search strategies and simplified decision-making processes they favor.
Conversely, for highly involved customers, cue accessibility is not as
important as relevance. This is not to say that cognitive resources con-
servation is unimportant to more highly involved customers, only that
they will not sacrifice accuracy in the process. For this reason, research
has noted that high-involvement customers are more likely to participate
and derive value from marketing relationships (Gordon et al. 1998; Varki
and Wong 2003). This is particularly true in the context of high-contact,
customized services (De Wulf et al. 2001). Little consensus exists regarding the relationship between involvement and customer loyalty (Broderick
2007). Early research suggested highly involved individuals would be more
inclined to establish strong brand preferences (Beatty et al. 1988). More
recent research has questioned this assumption, proposing that there are
instances in which customer loyalty may be high even when involvement
is low (Coulter et al. 2003). In an empirical examination, Warrington and
Shim (2000) found that groups of equally high-involvement customers
exhibited varying levels of loyalty. Martin (1996) suggested that the intangible nature of services leads many customers to "sample" services in an
effort to determine the desirability of a relationship with the provider. This
would seem a plausible explanation for the lack of "monogamy" exhibited
by many loyalty program members (Ehrenberg 1988).

We believe a more fundamental source for these contrary findings lies in the unobserved heterogeneity that exists within program populations. Exploring this, we included a set of behavioral covariates in the analysis to assist in fleshing out class differences. Morgan (1999) categorizes relational outcomes into economic, strategic, and social content benefits. We examined share-of-customer and propensity to remain as economic outcome variables, positive word-of-mouth communications and customer feedback as strategic outcome variables, and active voice as a social outcome variable.

TAXONOMIC PROCEDURE

Segments were derived using a CFA mixture model with covariates. Mixture modeling refers to modeling with latent variables that represent subpopulations where membership is not known *a priori*, but is inferred from the data (Muthén and Muthén 2006). Within marketing, various types of mixture (i.e., latent class) models have been utilized in segmentation studies (Kamakura and Russell 1989; Wedel and DeSarbo 2002) as well as research examining market phenomena at the customer (Bowman et al. 2004; Park and Fader 2004; Telang et al. 2004) and firm level (DeSarbo et al. 2006). This technique offers several advantages in identifying unobserved population heterogeneity. In contrast to k-means cluster analysis, which utilizes an arbitrarily chosen criterion for minimizing within-cluster variability, the mixture approach is model-based, allowing for more rigorous statistical tests in comparing alternative cluster solutions (Vermunt and Magidson 2002). Further, as mixture models are latent variable models, the technique allows for the decomposition of observed scores into a score on an underlying latent variable and a residual containing measurement error. Finally, mixture models offer greater flexibility, making it possible for researchers to analyze continuous and categorical latent variables as well as include covariate effects within a single level of analysis.

In all cases, the question of mixtures may be regarded as a question about parameter invariance (Gagné 2006). When population membership is known in advance, there are widely recognized procedures for addressing such issues. For example, in ANOVA, available information about population membership is used to estimate a mean for each population represented in the sample for the purpose of statistically testing the invariance of population means. However, when membership is not known *a priori*, mixture models can be employed to address similar statistical questions. More specifically, confirmatory factor mixture modeling tests for the presence of multiple populations that differ on one or more parameters of a factor model in a sample lacking *a priori* information about population membership.

Data Acquisition

A marketing consulting firm specializing in loyalty program management sponsored the study and provided access to customer contact information through the loyalty program database of a global hotel chain. The chain is a full-service provider which primarily targets frequent business travelers. Though the chain operates and franchises more than 410 hotels and resorts across 63 countries, the sample was limited to American customers. Managers were offered a summary report and customized data analysis in return for their participation.

Data were gathered through an online survey. A total of 2000 sample members were randomly drawn from the company loyalty program database. These individuals were contacted via email and asked to complete the survey in reference to their relationship with the hotel. The email contained information as to the nature of the survey and directed sample members to the website hosting it. A total of 791 responses were received for a response rate of 39.6 percent. Seven respondents were later removed from the sample because of missing data concerns, leaving a usable sample of 784 respondents. Respondents reported a mean age of 46, three-quarters were married, and the annual income for approximately two-thirds of the sample was between $50 000 and $150 000.

The likelihood of non-response bias was assessed for each sample by comparing the responses of early and late respondents across all constructs (Armstrong and Overton 1977). The analysis was conducted through means of a MANOVA, with all study constructs serving as the dependent variables and response time (early versus late) as the independent factor. Based on the lack of statistical significance for any construct ($p < 0.05$), non-response was not considered a serious concern.

Measurement

Scale items utilized in the study are provided in the Appendix at the end of the chapter. All items were drawn from previous research and adapted for use in the hotel environment. Involvement, share-of-customer, propensity to remain, customer feedback, and active voice were utilized as mixture model variables. Involvement was measured via the three-item measure of De Wulf et al. (2001), propensity to remain via the three-item measure of Bluedorn (1982), positive word-of-mouth communications via the three-item measure of Gremler and Gwinner (2000), customer feed-back via the four-item measure of Lacey et al. (2007), and active voice via the three-item measure of Crutchfield (1998). A single item was used to measure share-of-customer.

Service quality and satisfaction were utilized (in addition to propensity to remain) as post hoc constructs. Service quality was assessed via 21 items adapted from the SERVQUAL scale of Parasuraman et al. (1988), while a three-item measure of satisfaction was adapted from Ruekert and Walker (1987). The share-of-customer item was measured on a ten-point scale (1 = 0–10%/10 = 90–100%), while all others were measured on seven-point scales (1 = strongly disagree/7 = strongly agree).

To first establish face validity for the items, marketing managers from the hotel were asked to assess the suitability of item wording and content accuracy. Based on their feedback, one of the empathy items contained in the original SERVQUAL scale ("[Hotel X] has operating hours con-venient to all its customers") was deemed irrelevant in the hotel context and discarded. The managers also suggested that the performance-based approach (e.g., Cronin and Taylor 1992) to measuring SERVQUAL be used over one which examines the gap between expectations and percep-tions. As research has tended to support the superiority of this approach (cf. Brady et al. 2002), this suggestion was adhered to.

The reliability and validity of the variables utilized in the mixture modeling process were assessed through confirmatory factor analysis. In specifying the measurement model, a reliability of 0.90 was assumed for the share-of-customer item, with the factor loading set equal α^2 and the error variance equal $1 - \alpha$ (Hayduk 1987). Results from this analysis are provided in Table 9.1. Model results revealed a good fit between the model and data: $\alpha^2_{(90)} = 376.85$, non-normed fit index (NNFI) = 0.98, compara-tive fit index (CFI) = 0.98, incremental fit index (IFI) = 0.98, RMSEA = 0.064 and SRMR = 0.040. In support of convergent validity, all item loadings were statistically significant at the 0.01 level. Reliability was assessed for each construct by computing composite reliability (Fornell and Larcker 1981) and average variance extracted (Anderson and Gerbing 1988). For a construct to possess good reliability, composite reliability should be greater than 0.60 and the average variance extracted should exceed 0.50 (Bagozzi and Yi 1988). All measures surpassed these stand-ards. In order to test for discriminant validity, we examined whether the average variance extracted for each construct was greater than its highest shared variance with any other latent construct (i.e., greater than the largest squared intercorrelation for the construct) (Fornell and Larcker 1981). In all cases, this standard was met.

Table 9.1   Mixture model confirmatory factor analysis

Item	Loading	t-value	Composite reliability	Average variance extracted	Highest shared variance
Involvement:					
INV1	0.91		0.94	0.84	0.08
INV2	0.92	41.88			
INV3	0.92	41.90			
Share-of-customer:					
SOC	1.00				0.29
Propensity to remain:					
PRE1	0.90		0.96	0.89	0.46
PRE2	1.00	56.49			
PRE3	0.92	43.80			
Positive word-of-mouth:					
WOM1	0.94		0.95	0.87	0.46
WOM2	0.91	45.47			
WOM3	0.95	52.79			
Customer feedback:					
CFE1	0.76		0.88	0.71	0.25
CFE2	0.93	25.80			
CFE3	0.83	24.17			
Active voice:					
ACV1	0.85		0.88	0.71	0.25
ACV2	0.85	27.03			
ACV3	0.83	26.57			
$\chi^2_{(90)}$	376.85				
SRMR	0.040				
RMSEA	0.064				
NNFI	0.98				
CFI	0.98				
IFI	0.98				

CFA Mixture Model with Covariates

We conducted the CFA mixture model analysis utilizing MPlus 5.2 software. The covariance matrix and means of the observed indicators for involvement were structured in terms of the common factor model, such that measurement error was taken into account. In order to improve parameter estimation and recovery, composite indicators were constructed for all multi-item covariates. The mean and variance of involvement was freed to differ across classes. In addition, the latent variable representing

involvement and the categorical latent variable representing class membership were regressed onto the behavioral loyalty covariates (i.e., share-of-
customer, propensity to remain, positive word-of-mouth communications,
customer feedback, and active voice), enabling an assessment of the extent
to which customer behavioral intentions were predictive of involvement
level and class membership, respectively.

Identifying the optimal solution for the factor mixture model involved
an iterative process by which models with progressively more classes were
specified and parameters freed until the best-fitting model was found.
Results from the analysis indicated that the best-fitting model was a four-
class model in which the means were freed to vary across all four classes,
with the variances constrained equal across only the last two classes. Of the
784 total sample members, 210 were categorized to class 1 (26.8 percent),
220 (28.1 percent) were categorized to class 2, 178 (22.7 percent) were
categorized to class 3, and 176 (22.4 percent) were categorized to class 4.

Class Interpretation

In order to better interpret the classes, the data were subjected to a series
of ANOVAs in which the mixture model variables were positioned as
dependent variables and class was positioned as a fixed factor. The results
of these tests are provided in Table 9.2. The table presents the F-values
associated with each fixed factor, overall R^2 statistics, construct means by
class, and the results from Scheffe post hoc tests which were conducted to
better understand differences across particular classes.

As can be seen, class had a significant effect on each of the dependent
variables ($p < 0.01$). The means reported by class and Scheffe post hoc test
results reveal that class 1 members (low-involvement) were significantly
less involved than class 2 members (medium-involvement) and that class
2 members were significantly less involved than class 3 or class 4 members
(high-involvement). There was no statistically significant difference in
mean involvement level between class 3 and class 4 members ($p = 0.83$).
Class 3 respondents were significantly higher than class 2 respondents
across all behavioral outcome variables ($p < 0.01$), while class 2 respondents were significantly higher than class 1 respondents across all variables
($p < 0.01$). There was no difference between class 1 respondents and class 4
respondents in terms of share-of-customer ($p = 1.00$) and active voice ($p =
0.24$); however, class 1 respondents were significantly higher than class 4
respondents across all other variables ($p \leq 0.05$). Thus, it would appear
as though all high-involvement loyalty program members are not created
the same; they can differ quite drastically in terms of the behaviors they
exhibit.

Table 9.2   Mixture model mean differences by class

	INV	SOC	PRE	WOM	CFE	ACV
F-values	414.84	162.15	217.99	486.38	73.44	30.23
R^2 values	0.62	0.38	0.46	0.65	0.22	0.10
Class means:						
Class 1	4.21	17.79	4.63	3.47	4.50	5.15
Class 2	5.28	48.45	6.02	5.19	5.17	5.58
Class 3	6.61	57.46	6.66	5.99	6.26	6.15
Class 4	6.48	16.72	4.35	2.84	5.11	5.38
Scheffe post hoc tests:						
1–2	0.00	0.00	0.00	0.00	0.00	0.00
1–3	0.00	0.00	0.00	0.00	0.00	0.00
1–4	0.00	1.00	0.05	0.00	0.00	0.24
2–3	0.00	0.00	0.00	0.00	0.00	0.00
2–4	0.00	0.00	0.00	0.00	1.00	0.35
3–4	0.83	0.00	0.00	0.00	0.00	0.00

Note: INV = involvement, SOC = share-of-customer, PRE = propensity to remain, WOM = positive word-of-mouth, CFE = customer feedback, ACV = active voice.

Post Hoc Analysis

In order to establish the validity of the identified segments, a post hoc analysis was performed to examine whether theoretically consistent differences existed across segments in terms of: 1) their service quality perceptions; and 2) the extent to which customer satisfaction and behavioral loyalty were driven by different service quality components. In this post hoc analysis, we focus on the concept of service quality. While some debate exists regarding its proper conceptualization and measurement, academicians and practitioners generally agree that service quality is a critical determinant of business performance as well as firms' long-term viability (Bolton and Drew 1991; Gale 1994). Research generally suggests that higher levels of service quality lead to customer satisfaction, which in turn has a positive impact on customer word-of-mouth, attitudinal loyalty, and purchase intentions (e.g., Bolton and Drew 1991; Cronin and Taylor 1992; Zeithaml et al. 1996; Cronin et al. 2000). It is therefore important managers understand how different segments of customers may differ in terms of their service quality perceptions.

As a first step in performing the post hoc analysis, we assessed the reliability and validity of the post hoc variables (service quality, satisfaction, and propensity to remain) through confirmatory factor analysis. Service quality was initially conceptualized in terms of five dimensions: reliability, responsiveness, assurance, tangibles, and empathy. Results from this analysis first revealed that one of the items intended to reflect the tangible environment ("[Hotel X]'s employees are neat-appearing") had a low standardized loading (0.51), and it was subsequently dropped from the analysis. Model fit results were still poor with this item discarded, and discriminant validity was not achieved across the SERVQUAL dimensions. Based on these results and managers' suggestions, the decision was made to model service quality in terms of employee service quality and tangible service quality. Eight items were utilized to reflect the employee service quality construct, while three were used for tangible service quality (see Appendix).

As highlighted in Table 9.3, results from the subsequent CFA revealed a good fit between the measurement model and data: $\chi^2_{(113)}$ = 446.23, NNFI = 0.99, CFI = 0.99, IFI = 0.99, RMSEA = 0.061 and SRMR = 0.026. All item loadings were statistically significant ($p < 0.01$). Using the metrics described in the discussion of the mixture model measures, ample evidence was found in support of reliability and discriminant validity.

Differences in path estimates across the four classes were analyzed through multi-group structural equation modeling. We were specifically interested in path differences from employee and tangible service quality to satisfaction, and from satisfaction to propensity to remain. Prior to investigating path differences across classes, tests were performed to ensure measurement invariance across the classes (i.e., to ensure that the latent constructs held the same meaning across classes). As can be seen in the upper portion of Table 9.4, partial metric invariance was attained across all pairwise comparisons (class 1 versus class 2, class 2 versus class 3, class 3 versus class 4). Table 9.4 notes the equality constraints that were relaxed in order to attain partial invariance across each of the analyses.

In order to assess perceptual differences, a series of ANOVAs was performed in order to determine whether respondents differed in terms of how they perceived the hotel on service quality and satisfaction. Results from this test are provided in Table 9.5. As can be seen, significant differences indeed existed across the classes. In general, class 3 respondents held more favorable perceptions than did class 2 respondents, who in turn held more favorable perceptions than class 1 respondents. Class 4 respondents scored significantly lower than all other classes on tangible service quality and satisfaction. In terms of employee service quality, class 1 and class 4 respondents did not differ significantly ($p = 0.44$). Thus, we note systematic differences existed across classes in terms of perceptions of service quality and customer satisfaction.

Results from the tests for path differences across classes are provided

Table 9.3   Post hoc confirmatory factor analysis

Item	Loading	t-value	Composite reliability	Average variance extracted	Highest shared variance
Employee service quality			0.97	0.80	0.61
ESQ1	0.89				
ESQ2	0.91	40.80			
ESQ3	0.95	45.76			
ESQ4	0.82	32.22			
ESQ5	0.88	37.50			
ESQ6	0.94	43.92			
ESQ7	0.91	40.09			
ESQ8	0.84	33.75			
Tangible service quality			0.93	0.82	0.49
TSQ1	0.89				
TSQ2	0.94	41.18			
TSQ3	0.89	37.01			
Satisfaction			0.96	0.90	0.61
SAT1	0.93				
SAT2	0.97	55.08			
SAT3	0.94	49.36			
Propensity to remain			0.96	0.89	0.40
PRE1	0.90				
PRE2	1.00	56.39			
PRE3	0.92	43.70			

Goodness of fit: $\chi^2_{(113)} = 446.2, p < 0.01$; SRMR $= 0.026$; RMSEA $= 0.06$; CFI $= 0.99$; TLI $= 0.99$

in the lower portion of Table 9.4. In comparing class 1 (low-involvement/ low-loyalty) and class 2 (medium-involvement/medium-loyalty) respondents, the standardized path estimate between satisfaction and propensity to remain was significantly stronger ($\Delta\chi^2_{(1)} = 14.24, p < 0.01$) in class 1 ($\beta = 0.45$) than it was in class 2 ($\beta = 0.11$). No significant differences emerged across class 2 and class 3. Lastly, the effects of satisfaction upon propensity to remain were significantly less pronounced ($\Delta\chi^2_{(1)} = 18.54, p < 0.01$) in class 3 ($\beta = 0.11$) relative to class 4 ($\beta = 0.49$).

Table 9.4 Post hoc invariance tests

	df	χ^2	RMSEA	NNFI	CFI	IFI	Δdf	$\Delta\chi^2$	p	ΔCFI
Measurement invariance tests:										
Class 1–class 2										
Configural invariance	226	479.47	0.070	0.98	0.98	0.98				
Metric invariance	239	554.39	0.077	0.97	0.98	0.98	13	74.92	0.00	0.00
Partial metric invariance[1]	234	494.94	0.070	0.98	0.98	0.98	8	15.47	0.05	0.00
Class 2–class 3										
Configural invariance	226	470.65	0.072	0.97	0.98	0.98				
Metric invariance	239	510.91	0.073	0.97	0.98	0.98	13	40.26	0.00	0.00
Partial metric invariance[2]	238	480.97	0.069	0.98	0.98	0.98	12	10.32	0.59	0.00
Class 3–class 4										
Configural invariance	226	410.50	0.063	0.98	0.98	0.98				
Metric invariance	239	455.25	0.067	0.98	0.98	0.98				
Partial metric invariance[3]	237	428.96	0.062	0.98	0.98	0.98	11	18.46	0.07	0.00
Structural invariance tests:										
	Class 1	Class 2	$\Delta\chi^2$	p						
ESQ → SAT	0.54	0.41	3.00	0.08						
TSQ → SAT	0.49	0.39	1.69	0.19						
SAT → PRE	0.45	0.11	14.24	0.00						
	Class 2	Class 3	$\Delta\chi^2$	p						
ESQ → SAT	0.50	0.47	0.14	0.71						
TSQ → SAT	0.44	0.34	1.38	0.24						
SAT → PRE	0.17	0.12	0.39	0.53						

Class 3–class 4	Class 3	Class 4	$\Delta\chi^2$	p
ESQ → SAT	0.45	0.51	0.57	0.45
TSQ → SAT	0.30	0.43	2.25	0.13
SAT → PRE	0.11	0.49	18.54	0.00

Notes:
ESQ = employee service quality, TSQ = tangible service quality, SAT = satisfaction, PRE = propensity to remain.
1 Equality constraint on PRE2, SAT3, REL3, REL2, and PRE3 relaxed.
2 Equality constraint on PRE3 relaxed.
3 Equality constraint on TAN3 and RES1 relaxed.

Table 9.5   Post hoc mean differences by class

	ESQ	TSQ	SAT
F-values	145.39	62.39	216.27
R^2 values	0.36	0.19	0.45
Class means:			
Class 1	4.18	4.39	4.33
Class 2	5.20	5.14	5.44
Class 3	5.88	5.50	6.00
Class 4	3.99	4.08	3.63
Scheffe post hoc tests:			
1–2	0.00	0.00	0.00
1–3	0.00	0.00	0.00
1–4	0.44	0.05	0.00
2–3	0.00	0.01	0.00
2–4	0.00	0.00	0.00
3–4	0.00	0.00	0.00

Note: ESQ = employee service quality, TSQ = tangible service quality,
SAT = satisfaction.

DISCUSSION

The results of our mixture model indicated substantial population heterogeneity existed within the examined loyalty programs. Our findings confirm
that not all customers, even those within the same loyalty program, equally
desire relational exchanges. While segments differed slightly across hotels
in terms of the distribution of customers across classes and the comparative mean levels, it is noteworthy that the nature of the classes remained
constant. We found low-involvement/low-loyalty, medium-involvement/
medium-loyalty, high-involvement/high-loyalty, and high-involvement/
low-loyalty classes in each population.

Implications

Study findings provide insight into the role involvement plays in the
relationship-building process. Our results suggest the relationship between
category involvement and customer loyalty is non-linear (Warrington
and Shim 2000); that is, loyalty programs are composed of mixtures of
variously involved customers, each with distinct relationship-maintenance
motivations. While the favorability of customer attitudes and behaviors
does increase with involvement levels in some cases, we also isolated

a class of high-involvement customers whose behaviors more closely resembled those of their low-involvement counterparts. This countervailing class provides substantial insight into the mixed results of prior work that has examined the link between involvement and loyalty. It could be that the contrasting results found in prior research may have been driven more by the heterogeneity of the samples investigated and less by the true relationship between the variables in question (Shugan 2006). Through mixture modeling we were able to identify and account for sources of unobserved heterogeneity within the samples that differentially affected this relationship.

We found customers' behavioral intentions were predictive of involvement levels with the hotel category and, by inference, the level of involvement they have with the loyalty program. For managers, this suggests customer types can be identified with a reasonable level of confidence based upon recordable customer actions. Incorporating such information into CRM systems can assist managers in identifying segments and developing customized marketing programs aimed at increasing customer satisfaction and profitability for loyalty program members. Further research aimed at the identification of drivers explaining different loyalty patterns can be an important subject of study for both academicians and managers.

Findings from the post hoc analysis examining the effects of service quality and satisfaction across classes have significant managerial and theoretical implications associated with them. Results from this analysis revealed that, while the relationships between the two service quality components (i.e., employee and tangible service quality) and satisfaction were relatively stable across the four classes identified, the relationship between satisfaction and customers' propensity to remain was not. Specifically, the relationship was significantly stronger for class 1 and class 4 respondents, relative to those from class 2 and class 3.

Taking this into account along with the finding that the mean satisfaction scores were lowest across classes 1 and 4 indicates that *dissatisfaction* has a stronger effect on propensity to remain than does *satisfaction*. This would indicate that satisfaction is viewed as a "minimal bar" as opposed to a differentiator, as something that customers expect yet do not reward the company for. Theoretically, this may be attributable to the fundamental tenet underlying prospect theory (Kahneman and Tversky 1979) – that individuals focus on and weigh potential losses more heavily than they do potential gains. Previous research supports this possibility. Results from the meta-analysis conducted by Szymanski and Henard (2001) revealed that customer satisfaction explains less than 25 percent of the variance in customers' future purchase intentions. Reichheld (1996) similarly found that 65–85 percent of all customers who ultimately defected from a firm reported that they were either satisfied or very satisfied with the firm.

This finding carries significant managerial implications. Specifically, across different classes of customers, the strategy regarding satisfaction may well be different. For those in class 1 and class 4, it appears more appropriate for the firm to focus on means through which the potential causes of dissatisfaction can be eliminated. Conversely, for those respondents in class 2 and class 3, strategies designed to enhance the level of satisfaction provided the customer are in order. This type of approach should also be emphasized in communications sent from the firm to customers across the varying classes.

Study Limitations and Future Research Directions

A limitation common to empirical taxonomies is that the results obtained may not be generalizable beyond the sample used in deriving them. While our results were replicated across two hotel chain loyalty programs, it is possible that samples from alternative hotels or loyalty program contexts might have resulted in an optimal model with different customer types. However, the point of this research was not to set forth a grand theory specifying member types that exist universally across all settings. Instead, the study offers a general process through which researchers can investigate the heterogeneity that likely exists within many loyalty programs and use it to identify theory-driven differences in relationships. In addition, this study would have benefited from the availability of behavioral data to match our measured behavioral intentions. However, given the importance of attitudes and behaviors in evaluating loyalty, our design augments prior work on segmenting loyalty program members which has relied exclusively on behavioral data sources (e.g., Allaway et al. 2006).

Future research should continue to explore unobserved heterogeneity within other loyalty program samples, using both survey and behavioral data, in order to discern the extent to which the classes we identified are recurring as well as potentially to uncover additional customer types. In so doing, researchers can more closely scrutinize the role of competitive factors and individual program design characteristics (e.g., frequent flyer reward structures) that contribute in determining the makeup of customer types within loyalty programs as well as their distribution across the identified classes. Further, as exchange relationships are evolutionary in nature, future research should examine the migratory patterns of loyalty program customers and non-program customers over time. Gaining knowledge of the mechanisms that favorably influence the likelihood of customers remaining within, or transitioning into, more favorable classes and programs would be of considerable interest to researchers and managers.

CONCLUSION

Classification allows the researcher to form theories about marketing phenomena without resorting to grand theories that assert relevance to all individuals or companies, providing the basis for midrange theorizing about customer–firm interactions (Moore et al. 1980). Thus, this research contributes to the literature by demonstrating how population hetero-geneity within loyalty programs confounds the efforts of managers and scholars in explaining and enhancing customer loyalty. Our results suggest the need for greater segmentation efforts in the execution of program design and communication strategies.

REFERENCES

Allaway, A.W., R.M. Gooner, D. Berkowitz and L. Davis (2006), "Deriving and Exploring Behavior Segments within a Retail Loyalty Card Program," *European Journal of Marketing*, 40(11/12), 1317–39.

Anderson, James C. and David W. Gerbing (1988), "Structural Equation Modeling in Practice: A Review and Recommended Two-Step Approach," *Psychological Bulletin*, 103(3), 411–23.

Armstrong, J. Scott and Terry S. Overton (1977), "Estimating Nonresponse Bias in Mail Surveys," *Journal of Marketing Research*, 14(3), 396–402.

Bagozzi, R.P. and Y. Yi (1988), "On the Evaluation of Structural Equation Models," *Journal of the Academy of Marketing Science*, 16(2), 74–94.

Beatty, S.E., P. Homer and L.R. Kahle (1988), "The Involvement–Commitment Model: Theory and Implications," *Journal of Business Research*, 16(2), 149–67.

Bluedorn, A.C. (1982), "The Theories of Mover: Causes, Effects, and Meaning," in S.B. Bacharach (ed.), *Perspectives in Organizational Sociology: Theory and Research*, Vol. 1. Greenwich, CT: JAI Press.

Bolton, Ruth N. and James H. Drew (1991), "A Multistage Model of Customers' Assessments of Service Quality and Value," *Journal of Consumer Research*, 17(4), 375–84.

Bowman, D., C.M. Heilman and P.B. Seetharaman (2004), "Determinants of Product-Use Compliance Behavior," *Journal of Marketing Research*, 41(3), 324–38.

Brady, Michael K., J. Joseph Cronin, Jr. and Richard R. Brand (2002), "Performance-Only Measurement of Service Quality: A Replication and Extension," *Journal of Business Research*, 55(1), 17–31.

Broderick, A.J. (2007), "A Cross-National Study of the Individual and National-Cultural Nomological Network of Consumer Involvement," *Psychology and Marketing*, 24(4), 343–74.

Celsi, R.L. and J.C. Olson (1988), "The Role of Involvement in Attention and Comprehension Processes," *Journal of Consumer Research*, 15(2), 210–24.

Coulter, R.A., L.L. Price and L. Feick (2003), "Rethinking the Origins of Involvement and Brand Commitment: Insights from Postsocialist Central Europe," *Journal of Consumer Research*, 30(2), 151–69.

Cronin, J. Joseph, Jr. and Steven A. Taylor (1992), "Measuring Service Quality: A Reexamination and Extension," *Journal of Marketing*, 56(3), 55–68.
Cronin, J. Joseph, Jr., Michael K. Brady and G. Tomas M. Hult (2000), "Assessing the Effects of Quality, Value, and Customer Satisfaction on Consumer Behavioral Intentions in Service Environments," *Journal of Retailing*, 76(2), 193–216.
Crutchfield, Tammy N. (1998), "Customer Retention in Consumer Services: A Multiple Sources–Multiple Commitments Model of Marketing Relationships," doctoral dissertation, University of Alabama.
DeSarbo, W.S., C.A. Di Benedetto, K. Jedidi and M. Song (2006), "Identifying Sources of Heterogeneity for Empirically Deriving Strategic Types: A Constrained Finite-Mixture Structural-Equation Methodology," *Management Science*, 52(6), 909–24.
De Wulf, K., G. Odekerken-Schröder and D. Iacobucci (2001), "Investments in Consumer Relationships: A Cross-Country and Cross-Industry Exploration," *Journal of Marketing*, 65(4), 33–50.
Dowling, G.R. (2002), "Customer Relationship Management: In B2C Markets, Often Less Is More," *California Management Review*, 44(2), 87–104.
Ehrenberg, A.S.C. (1988), *Repeat-Buying: Facts, Theory, and Applications*, 2nd edn., London: Charles Griffin.
Ferguson, R. and K. Hlavinka (2007), "The COLLOQUY Loyalty Marketing Census: Sizing Up the U.S. Loyalty Marketing Industry," *Journal of Consumer Marketing*, 24(5), 313–21.
Fornell, C. and D.F. Larcker (1981), "Evaluating Structural Equation Models with Unobservable Variables and Measurement Error," *Journal of Marketing Research*, 18(3), 39–50.
Gagné, P. (2006), "Introduction to Mean and Covariance Structure Mixture Models," in G.R. Hancock and R.O. Mueller (eds.), *Structural Equation Modeling: A Second Course*, Greenwich, CT: Information Age Publishing.
Gordon, M.E., K. McKeage and M.A. Fox (1998), "Relationship Marketing Effectiveness: The Role of Involvement," *Psychology and Marketing*, 15(5), 443–59.
Gremler, D.D. and K.P. Gwinner (2000), "Customer–Employee Rapport in Service Relationships," *Journal of Service Research*, 3(1), 82–104.
Hayduk, Leslie A. (1987), *Structural Equation Modeling with Lisrel: Essentials and Advances*, Baltimore, MD: Johns Hopkins University Press.
Higie, R.A. and L.F. Feick (1989), "Enduring Involvement: Conceptual and Measurement Issues," in T.K. Srull (ed.), *Advances in Consumer Research*, Vol. 16, Provo, UT: Association for Consumer Research.
Kahneman, Daniel and Amos Tversky (1979), "Prospect Theory: An Analysis of Decision under Risk," *Econometrica*, 47(2), 263–91.
Kamakura, W.A. and G.J. Russell (1989), "A Probabilistic Choice Model for Market Segmentation and Elasticity Structure," *Journal of Marketing Research*, 26(4), 379–90.
Kumar, V. and D. Shah (2004), "Building and Sustaining Profitable Customer Loyalty for the 21st Century," *Journal of Retailing*, 80(4), 317–30.
Lacey, R., J. Suh and R.M. Morgan (2007), "Differential Effects of Preferential Treatment Levels on Relational Outcomes," *Journal of Service Research*, 9(3), 241–56.
Martin, C.L. (1996), *Owning and Operating a Service Business*, Menlo Park, CA: Crisp Publications.
Mittal, B. and M.-S. Lee (1989), "A Causal Model of Consumer Involvement," *Journal of Economic Psychology*, 10(3), 363–89.
Moore, L.F., G. Johns and C.C. Pinder (1980), "Toward Middle Range Theory," in C.C. Pinder and L.F. Moore (eds.), *Middle Range Theory and the Study of Organizations*, Hingham, MS: Martinus Nijhoff.
Morgan, R.M. (1999), "Relationship Based Competitive Advantage: The Role of Relationship Marketing in Marketing Strategy," *Journal of Business Research*, 46(3), 281–90.
Morgan, R.M. and S.D. Hunt (1994), "The Commitment-Trust Theory of Relationship Marketing," *Journal of Marketing*, 58(3), 20–38.

Muthén, L.K. and B.O. Muthén (2006), *MPlus: Statistical Analysis with Latent Variables: User's Guide*, 4th edn., Los Angeles: Muthén & Muthén.

Noble, S.M. and J. Phillips (2004), "Relationship Hindrance: Why Would Consumers Not Want a Relationship with a Retailer?," *Journal of Retailing*, 80(4), 289–303.

Parasuraman, A., Valarie A. Zeithaml and Leonard L. Berry (1988), "SERVQUAL: A Multiple-Item Scale for Measuring Consumer Perceptions of Service Quality," *Journal of Retailing*, 64(1), 12–40.

Park, Y.-H. and P.S. Fader (2004), "Modeling Browsing Behavior at Multiple Websites," *Marketing Science*, 23(3), 280–303.

Peterson, R.A. (1995), "Relationship Marketing and the Consumer," *Journal of the Academy of Marketing Science*, 23(4), 278–81.

Petty, R.E., J.T. Cacioppo and D. Schumann (1983), "Central and Peripheral Routes to Advertising Effectiveness: The Moderating Role of Involvement," *Journal of Consumer Research*, 10(2), 135–46.

Reichheld, Frederick F. (1996), *The Loyalty Effect*, Boston, MA: Harvard Business School Press.

Reinartz, W.J. and V. Kumar (2002), "The Mismanagement of Customer Loyalty," *Harvard Business Review*, 80(7), 86–94.

Ruekert, Robert W. and Orville C. Walker, Jr. (1987), "Marketing's Interaction with Other Functional Units: A Conceptual Framework and Empirical Evidence," *Journal of Marketing*, 51(1), 1–19.

Shugan, S.M. (2005), "Brand Loyalty Programs – Are They Shams?," *Marketing Science*, 24(2), 185–93.

Shugan, S.M. (2006), "Errors in the Variables, Unobserved Heterogeneity, and Other Ways of Hiding Statistical Error," *Marketing Science*, 25(3), 203–16.

Szymanski, David M. and David H. Henard (2001), "Customer Satisfaction: A Meta-Analysis of the Empirical Evidence," *Journal of the Academy of Marketing Science*, 29(1), 16–35.

Telang, R., P. Boatwright and T. Mukhopadhyay (2004), "A Mixture Model for Internet Search-Engine Visits," *Journal of Marketing Research*, 41(2), 206–14.

Varki, S. and S. Wong (2003), "Consumer Involvement in Relationship Marketing of Services," *Journal of Service Research*, 6(1), 83–91.

Vermunt, J.K. and J. Magidson (2002), "Latent Class Cluster Analysis," in J.A. Hagenaars and A.L. McCutcheon (eds.), *Applied Latent Class Analysis*, Cambridge: Cambridge University Press.

Warrington, P. and S. Shim (2000), "An Empirical Investigation of the Relationship between Product Involvement and Brand Commitment," *Psychology and Marketing*, 17(9), 761–82.

Wedel, M. and W.S. DeSarbo (2002), "Market Segment Derivation and Profiling via a Finite Mixture Model Framework," *Marketing Letters*, 13(1), 17–25.

Zaichkowsky, J.L. (1985), "Measuring the Involvement Construct," *Journal of Consumer Research*, 12(3), 341–52.

APPENDIX

Survey Items

Involvement
Generally, I am someone:
INV1 . . . who finds it important which hotel I stay at.
INV2 . . . who is interested in the hotel I stay at.
INV3 . . . for whom it means a lot which hotel I stay at.

Share-of-customer
(1 = 0–10%/10 = 90–100%)
SOC1 As a percentage, how often do you stay at [Hotel X] compared to other hotels?

Propensity to remain
What is the likelihood you will remain:
PRE1 . . . in the relationship with [Hotel X] over the next six months?
PRE2 . . . in the relationship with [Hotel X] over the next year?
PRE3 . . . in the relationship with [Hotel X] over the next two years?

Positive word-of-mouth
I am willing to:
WOM1 . . . encourage friends and relatives to do business with [Hotel X].
WOM2 . . . recommend [Hotel X] whenever anyone seeks my advice.
WOM3 . . . go out of my way to recommend [Hotel X].

Customer feedback
How willing are you to cooperate with [Hotel X] regarding the following activities?
CFE1 Share my feelings about unmet needs.
CFE2 Provide feedback about new services [Hotel X] is considering offering.
CFE3 Discuss my views about [Hotel X]'s service quality.

Active voice
In the event I have a problem with [Hotel X]:
ACV1 . . . I am comfortable talking with them about my complaint.
ACV2 . . . I am not afraid to discuss my complaint with them.
ACV3 . . . I discuss my complaint with them.

Employee service quality

ESQ1 When [Hotel X]'s employees promise to do something by a certain time, they do it.

ESQ2 When I have a problem, [Hotel X]'s employees show a sincere interest in solving it.

ESQ3 [Hotel X]'s employees perform the service right the first time.

ESQ4 [Hotel X]'s employees insist on error-free records.

ESQ5 [Hotel X]'s employees tell me exactly when services will be performed.

ESQ6 [Hotel X]'s employees give me prompt service.

ESQ7 [Hotel X]'s employees are always willing to help me.

ESQ8 [Hotel X]'s employees are never too busy to respond to my requests.

Tangible service quality

TSQ1 [Hotel X] has modern looking facilities.

TSQ2 [Hotel X]'s physical facilities are visually appealing.

TSQ3 [Hotel X]'s materials (e.g., advertisements, statements, etc.) are visually appealing.

Satisfaction

SAT1 I am satisfied with my relationship with [Hotel X].

SAT2 I am pleased with my relationship with [Hotel X].

SAT3 My relationship with [Hotel X] has more than fulfilled my expectations.

Note:
* Item removed during measurement purification process.

10. NASCAR: driving relationship equity through the sponsorship supply chain
Susan Cadwallader, Tom Boyd and Aaron Thomas*

A DAY AT THE RACES

Watching dozens of drivers fight through a pack of multimillion-dollar machines at speeds well over any highway legal limit is breathtaking, and coupled with the thunderous rumble as the cars race past the grandstands onlookers can't help but have goose bumps. Unlike with most sports, these spectators don't just watch an event; NASCAR fans *feel* the rush, *live* the sport and *experience* a race.

Over 100 000 fans roar with excitement from the stands, and millions more watch from home, mesmerized as billions of dollars scream around oval tracks. Each week high-speed, heart-pounding, adrenaline-pumping excitement entices millions of fans to watch NASCAR on television, attend races and even make weekend trips just to follow a driver. From humble beginnings as a regional interest in the southern United States in the 1940s, the National Association for Stock Car Racing (NASCAR) is responsible for generating increasing nationwide demand for NASCAR tickets, gear, television shows and, most importantly, marketing sponsorships.

According to the MRI+ database, in the fall of 2008 over 50 million people watched NASCAR on television and over 17 million attended races throughout the season. Of these, nearly 29 million fans watched events more than once a month, and over 2 million attended more than one race per month. Additionally, when compared with previous years, the number of fans attending and watching NASCAR events more than once a month increased 15 percent and 17 percent respectively.

Because of these staggering statistics, hundreds of companies have adopted the 200 mile per hour billboard by choosing to sponsor NASCAR race cars and races, making it difficult to think about NASCAR without simultaneously thinking about a myriad of NASCAR-affiliated brands. Companies plaster their name, products and logo anyplace they can, on cars, drivers and booths throughout the NASCAR pits, hoping that fans' affinity for NASCAR will rub off on the sponsoring brands. Rather than spoil the sport, however, this blatant targeting of NASCAR fans has enhanced the overall fan experience.

Days before an actual race takes place, NASCAR tracks open their venues to fans, allowing onlookers to get personally acquainted with drivers, their teams, cars and sponsors. Attendees spend hours and walk miles to experience all a NASCAR event has to offer; from games to autograph sessions to race simulators, the excitement of NASCAR boils in all fans' hearts from the second they step through the gates. On race day, fans are likely to spend more time listening to live music, seeing live animals, sampling products, and playing games than sitting watching the race. This complete "NASCAR experience" is the result of careful cooperation between its creators – everyone from drivers to track employees to sponsors.

Although sponsorship marketing is not unique to NASCAR, it is of central importance to sports marketing in general and can be viewed in broader terms as a conceptual link to aspects of general marketing (Farrelly and Quester 2003; Sam et al. 2005) and strategic planning (Amis et al. 1997). Sponsorship has always been one of the primary revenue sources for sports, yet sponsorships can also help to drive loyalty programs, develop affinity and build a sense of community, each of which increases relationship equity, a key component of the customer equity model (Rust et al. 2000, 2004).

The customer equity model (Rust et al. 2000, 2004) was one of the first models to link corporate marketing actions with customer spending actions. Its authors propose that value equity, brand equity and relationship equity drive customer equity, which is defined as the total of the discounted lifetime values summed over all an organization's current and potential customers. The model is viewed as the basis for a new framework from which to build and measure the success of customer-centric marketing programs (Vogel et al. 2008) like the sponsorship programs used by NASCAR and NASCAR sponsors.

This chapter uses the customer equity model (Rust et al. 2004) as a framework to introduce fan equity, presenting relationship equity as the key driving force in its development. NASCAR's unique approach to increasing relationship equity is then discussed, with specific focus placed on the NASCAR supply chain, composed of an array of sponsor, team, driver and fan relationships, featuring the sponsor as both a consumer and a producer of fan equity. The chapter concludes by suggesting how NASCAR's approach to creating relationship equity to drive fan equity may be applied outside a sports marketing context to increase customer equity.

FAN EQUITY MODEL

A sports fan has noticeably different characteristics than a stereotypical customer. While standard purchasing involves specific (often standardized) goods and services, a sports fan obtains a customized, singular experience. This experience is created and delivered through the coordination of multiple parties attempting to maximize value for their partners and customers. Therefore, an extension of the customer equity model must be developed whereby relationship marketing, primarily through sponsorship marketing efforts, is proposed to be the driver which has the greatest impact on NASCAR customer equity – what we call *fan equity*.

Concepts such as fan loyalty (Depken 2000) and team identification (Wann and Branscombe 1993; Madrigal 2001) have been provided as intangible, psychological measures of outcomes from sports marketing efforts. The result of building fan loyalty or team identification can serve as a precursor of financial success; for example, fans with high levels of team identification are more likely to purchase licensed team merchandise (Wann and Branscombe 1993; Fisher and Wakefield 1998) and attend games (Fisher and Wakefield 1998) or events. However, these concepts take a narrow view of the team–fan relationship, as they minimize the impact other entities (e.g., sponsors, team members, governing sports bodies) may have relative to leveraging the relationship to maximize value and profits.

The customer equity model identifies different drivers – value, brand and relationship equity – that increase customer equity. Value equity is the customer's objective assessment of the utility of a brand based on perceptions of what is given up for what is received. Brand equity is the assessment of a brand beyond its objectively perceived value. Relationship equity expresses a customer's tendency to stay committed to the brand beyond objective and subjective assessments. This model relates an organization's marketing strategy and affiliated investments to the customer actions which generate revenue. Although it provides a useful framework to measure sports marketing success metrics, it must be modified to best capture the nuance of the critical sponsor–fan relationship in NASCAR. This extension 1) substitutes a new concept, fan equity, for customer equity and 2) considers relationship equity, primarily driven by sponsorship marketing efforts, to be the driver with the greatest impact on fan equity.

Fan Equity

Fan equity is a sports-marketing-specific interpretation of customer equity. The concept of fan equity is new to marketing; however, two definitions have been mentioned in the finance literature tied to the concept of loyalty. A definition of "fan equity" derived from the investment bank Salomon Brothers (1997) acknowledges fan loyalty's accumulated value as a capital asset which decreases the volatility of earnings when the team experiences failure. It is described as a predictable capital resource which investors may exploit by buying into guaranteed loyalty, but whose capital realization is denied to fans (Free and Hudson 2006). From a financial perspective, fan equity represents a value for investors (sponsors) which acts as a safety net in case a team or sport does not perform well.

One limitation to the customer equity model is it assumes that there is one brand or product in the firm and does not explicitly consider cross-selling between a single firm's (Rust et al. 2004), or a myriad of firms', brands or products. Fan equity to a large extent is driven by relationship building efforts, which tend to veer from more traditional promotional activities to more experiential co-marketing or branding efforts involving multiple sponsors to create a deep connection between a fan and these firms. Hence, a definition of fan equity must consider this conscious and subconscious relationship between a sport and a fan. *Fan equity* can therefore be better defined as the net present value of current and potential revenues, driven by a fan's relationship with a particular sport.

Relationship Equity

Relationship equity expresses the tendency of customers to stay in a relationship with the brand, beyond objective and subjective assessments of the brand (Rust et al. 2004). Sports sponsors pay for access to fans with the understanding that association with the sport establishes a connection with the sponsor over the long term. Fan equity can therefore be maximized to the sponsor's benefit by the sponsor working with the sport to strengthen the connection between a fan and a sport by building relationship equity.

NASCAR SPONSORSHIP STRUCTURE

Over the last 20 years, the U.S. sports consumer has been introduced to an increasing number of sporting-event options. Aside from the "big four" sports (football, baseball, basketball and hockey) the growth of alternative sports such as Arena League football, NASCAR, and extreme sports has produced a heightened level of competition for consumers' sports dollar. In such a competitive environment, the ability to manage fan perception of a team brand effectively is placed at a premium (Boyle and Magnesson

2007). In recent years, and as shown in Figure 10.1, NASCAR growth in event attendance and television ratings has outperformed that of most other professional sports. To date, NASCAR's model and resulting performance gains have not been successfully imitated by other organizations.

NASCAR's success is due largely to its unique approach to sponsorship, which emphasizes value creation both for its fans and for its sponsors. Started in 1948 by Bill France, Sr., NASCAR legitimized the sport of stock car racing. Today NASCAR is considered to be a national, even global, sport, owing largely to the efforts of Bill France, Sr.'s son, Bill Jr., who aggressively pursued sponsors, negotiated national television rights, and expanded races into the Midwest and West during the 1970s. In the late 1990s, Bill's son, Brian, negotiated a package deal which consolidated television rights with three major networks, Fox, NBC and TNT, yielding a $2.4 billion deal under the NASCAR umbrella (O'Keefe 2005).

Sponsorship and Fan Equity

The idea of sponsors paying for access to fans, who become more valuable as the result of increased fan equity, serves as justification for making the marketing investment. Naturally, higher fan equity equates to more sponsorship value, which in turn demands a higher price. The NASCAR governing body drives fan loyalty by leveraging sponsorships and integrating sponsors into events with more than stereotypical signage and advertising. Sports events cannot rely strictly on the entertainment of a sporting event, but must create a memorable experience for fans. Because maximizing fan equity is at the center of the NASCAR–sponsor relationship, sponsors willingly focus efforts on improving the overall fan experience. Therefore, the sponsor not only pays for access to NASCAR fans but actually helps to increase fan equity, making the sponsor *both* a customer and supplier.

While on the surface it may appear that NASCAR is simply catering to its fans (consumers) and providing entertainment, there is actually a collaborative effort by all supply chain members to create relationship equity, which then drives fan equity. This fan equity is then sold back to a different type of customer – the NASCAR sponsors. The fan experience therefore is a byproduct, which provides supplemental income to the NASCAR supply chain, while fan equity acts as a primary product. NASCAR's competition tends to reverse this view, seeing sponsorship as a subsidy for event operations.

For example, a sponsor's presence in the NASCAR pits allows fans to see the link between the sponsor and NASCAR close up and *experience*, not just attend, a race. It is common knowledge that sports fans pay to watch an event, and thus the natural inclination is that a sports

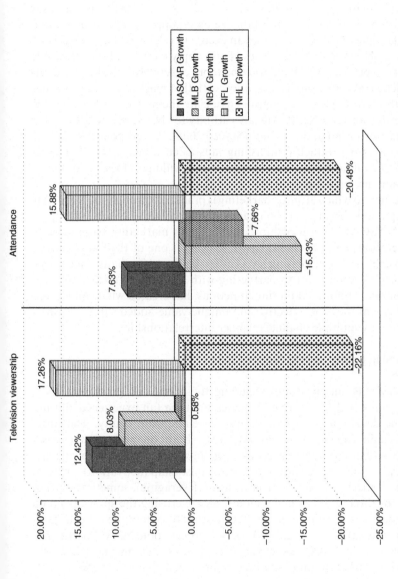

Source: Television viewership data from Nielsen Media Research, 2007, as referenced in internal NASCAR reports. Attendance data compiled from **MRI+** database, 2008.

Figure 10.1   Percentage growth in viewership and event attendance (more than once a month), 2002–07

organization's goal is to provide this service to fans. The most significant difference between NASCAR and its competition is that, rather than simply providing a sporting event and activities associated with it, NASCAR manages a complex set of track, team, driver and sponsor relationships – which we conceptualize as a supply chain – to create a "lifestyle," where the race becomes an excuse to celebrate that lifestyle and the role of NASCAR in fans' lives. This supply chain enables NASCAR sponsors to practice affinity marketing more effectively – the act of targeting a niche market through association with that market's preferred activity. In the NASCAR case, sponsors associate themselves with NASCAR in order to transfer a NASCAR fan's affinity for NASCAR to affinity for the sponsor's brand and products (Stanco 2008). At this point, NASCAR is refining its byproduct, establishing fans as customers. The sponsor is expected to intensify the fan experience and willingly does so to inspire loyalty and increase fan equity.

The extent to which affinity marketing is practiced throughout NASCAR is only possible because of the relationships within the NASCAR supply chain. NASCAR's sponsorship design is both marketing (sponsorship) and operations (supply chain) based, making it one of the few organizations to deliver ever increasing levels of fan equity to its channel members. NASCAR's commitment to partnering with sponsors to create value for both fans and sponsors, and similar actions, has created what can be considered one of the most effective and unique value-added supply chains – one driven by multiple channel member interrelationships.

Relationship Equity and the Supply Chain

The NASCAR supply chain, including the NASCAR governing body, tracks, teams and team drivers, creates the base fan experience and initiates the development of fan equity via relationship equity. The entire supply chain (including sponsors) works both on and off the track through activated and leveraged sponsorships. Rather than simply paying NASCAR, sponsors will advertise their sponsorship (activation), promoting their association with a driver or team (leveraging), sometimes spending two or three times as much money on advertising the sponsorship on top of the amount paid to NASCAR in order to obtain the official sponsorship designation (Giangola 2007). Sometimes sponsors will participate in delivering the NASCAR experience at races, maximizing the effects of affinity marketing, intensifying the fan experience and increasing fan equity through relationship equity building marketing efforts.

Similar to the case in manufacturing, an ordinary NASCAR fan is exposed to a series of value-added processes which establish a rela-

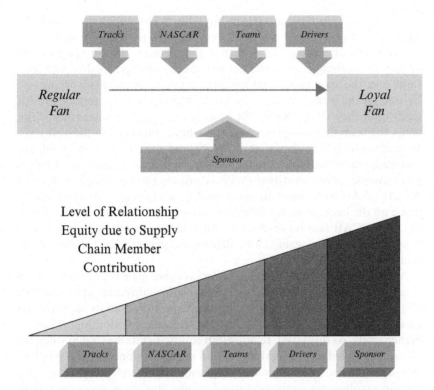

Figure 10.2   Relationship equity due to sponsorship supply chain members

tionship with the sport (and thus with every member of the supply chain). Figure 10.2 illustrates the level of relationship equity due to each NASCAR supply chain member's contribution in building it.

As depicted in Figure 10.2, the value added by each supply chain member intensifies the relationship with the fan, and increases the fan's loyalty, thus building relationship equity and increasing fan equity. The triangular shape of the figure implies that fan equity is greatest when all members of the supply chain work together cooperatively to create the most valuable fan experience.

The running theme throughout the following explanation is that all members are working toward the same goal, recognizing that the value of fan equity is directly proportional to the value added by each member in creating relationship equity. So, while race tracks are necessary for hosting NASCAR races, they provide the least amount of value to the process, because a fan's relationship with or loyalty to a track tends not to be intense. The NASCAR brand is stationed second because, although fans are more likely to have a relationship with NASCAR than a particular track, this relationship is distant at best. In third position are race teams, because fans may often feel a part of the team by cheering them on to victory or listening in on a headset as the crew chief barks driver instructions over the team radio, and wishing they were in the pits working side by side on the team car. Fans are more likely to be loyal to a NASCAR team than they are to NASCAR as a whole or a particular track; thus, when the team factor is present, relationship equity rises to the next level. In many sports, the driver or "player" and "team" sections might be reversed, particularly because the big four sports are heavily team based. For example, although Albert Pujols is a driving force of the Los Angeles Angels of Anaheim baseball team, and fans may wear jerseys with his name on the back, a fan is labeled an "Angels fan," not an "Albert Pujols fan." NASCAR fans however are often described as fans of a driver, who is associated with a team. Thus, drivers are placed above teams on the figure.

At this point in the value-added process other sports governing bodies consider their supply chain complete and relationship equity at a maximum value. NASCAR however incorporates its sponsors into its supply chain to intensify the fan experience further and take relationship equity to higher levels. As displayed, relationship equity is at its maximum when the sponsor is added into the value creation process. Sponsors peak relationship equity because they create the highest level of fan loyalty. By extending fan involvement from spectatorship into fans' lives, sponsors add to the fan experience, maximizing relationship and fan equity. Examples range from having sponsored drivers make personal appearances at a sponsor's retail stores to providing NASCAR simulators at races so that fans can experience driving a race car. Direct benefits can be seen through the purchasing habits of the most loyal fans, who will buy a sponsor's products simply because the sponsor supports a particular driver or team. It is this loyalty that encompasses the concept of relationship equity and drives the NASCAR supply chain. The entire focus of this value-added process is to develop and sustain strong fan relationships, which in turn provide the highest level of fan equity to the final purchaser: the sponsor.

Although Figure 10.2 depicts each supply chain member's contribution in creating relationship equity as a quasi-building block, in order to maximize the level of relationship equity no one member can perform their task without the cooperation of the rest of the supply chain. If any member were to be removed from the process the subsequent levels could not exist. Thus, one must conclude that it is the *collaboration* and *interorganizational relationships* that allow relationship equity to peak.

It must be noted that, in other businesses, and in particular other sports, there are often constraints that make it much more difficult to implement this approach. For example, in the NBA the players are unionized; thus demanding their participation in promotional events is limited to their contractual obligations, whereas NASCAR requires its drivers to attend classes on how to interact with fans and sponsors. Since NASCAR is run by a single entity, it more effectively organizes its sponsors, holding events to allow them to interact and generate business opportunities with one another. In other sports, team sponsors are not well connected to sponsors of other teams.

For non-sport businesses, the challenges are often even greater. Perhaps the only other supply chain with a leader as dominant as NASCAR is Wal-Mart. In Wal-Mart's case, a path of dominance has been taken to reduce cost and have a highly cooperative supply chain focused on logistical efficiency and cost reduction. However, the NASCAR supply chain offers Wal-Mart and other firms an exemplar on how better to organize their partners with each other. For example, Wal-Mart might consider meeting with multiple suppliers to integrate logistical functions with each other and not just with Wal-Mart. This could result in reduced warehousing costs, higher profits for all parties and, for Wal-Mart's suppliers, the belief that Wal-Mart helps them create new profitable relationships, thus increasing supplier loyalty. This kind of cooperative practice could enhance the efficiency of Wal-Mart's logistics even further; however this would only be possible if all supply chain members worked towards the same goal and built strong relationships.

SPONSORSHIP MARKETING ACTIVITIES

NASCAR's unique supply chain integration is notably quite complicated. NASCAR integrates its customer into its production team and in so doing creates a more valuable product. However, NASCAR's method of integrating its customer revolves around effectively integrating marketing activities into its supply chain to maximize coordination and add value. These activities hinge largely on relationship management and value maximization rather than mere product creation. To maximize value, the parties must develop relationships that improve the fan experience. The unique driving force for NASCAR is the simultaneous cooperation of several entities constituting an *interorganizational sponsorship structure* that recognizes the benefits of the long term relationship.

This sponsorship structure can be visualized using four theoretical supply chain perspectives (Palmatier et al. 2007), each focusing on different factors influencing performance, as a framework to present examples of successful NASCAR sponsorship activities. Each perspective provides a different means to view the uniqueness of the NASCAR supply chain; however, all center on the concept that effective relationship marketing leads to successful supply chain performance.

Transaction Cost Economics

The transaction cost economics (Williamson 1975) perspective argues that transaction-specific investments and opportunism influence exchange partners' relationship decisions and affect interorganizational performance (Heide and John 1990; Noordewier et al. 1990). Essentially, when supply chain members make relationship-specific investments to build relationship equity, they will be less likely to engage in opportunistic behaviors, thus increasing cooperation among members. This can be illustrated by the huge investment NASCAR sponsors make to sponsor a team or car. Similarly, NASCAR makes major investments to hire support staff for sponsors, thus facilitating their ability to leverage their sponsorships.

Relational Norms Perspective

The relational norms perspective (Macneil 1980; Kaufmann and Dant 1992) takes the view that the strength of relational behavioral norms drives long term relationships. Research suggests that these relational norms lead to improved exchange performance (Lusch and Brown 1996; Cannon et al. 2000). In contrast to sports that see sponsors as a way to subsidize operational expenses, NASCAR sees sponsors as partners in delivering the customer experiences and thus brings the sponsor into the NASCAR culture. In Major League Baseball (MLB) sponsors will pay for giveaways like "bobbleheads" in exchange for name billing at the game. Alternatively, a NASCAR sponsor is part of the team and as such works through NASCAR and team personnel to provide fan experiences on and off (e.g., at community events, in grocery stores or through product tie-ins) the track.

Relational norms are also reflected in the extent to which NASCAR is willing to make adjustments to, or even set aside, contractual agreements to work through difficult situations. One example of this occurred when Sprint became the title sponsor of NASCAR. Both Cingular and Alltel were car sponsors at the time, and NASCAR negotiated with all parties to keep those sponsors with their cars by grandfathering them in, though this defied sport industry practice. This required flexibility from both Sprint and NASCAR and reflects NASCAR's commitment to its sponsors. Similarly, when Kevin Harvick showed up in his sponsor's fire-suit

(Pennsoil/Shell) at a race sponsored by Sonoco (a Pennsoil/Shell rival), NASCAR intervened to ensure that the race sponsorship was not spoiled by the team sponsor and worked to have the fire-suit removed (Giangola 2007). NASCAR's relational norm is thus to ensure sponsors receive promised value from sponsorships while resolving conflict between rival sponsors on a per-case basis.

Commitment and Trust

This perspective (Morgan and Hunt 1994) hypothesizes that commitment and trust are better predictors of performance than dependence or power. This can be illustrated by the dependence asymmetry of the NASCAR/track dyad. Although highly asymmetric, with power residing on the NASCAR side, the high level of commitment and trust both parties hold toward each other has helped enrich both partners. When Brian France persuaded tracks to sign over their broadcast rights to the NASCAR organization they were showing high levels of trust. Their faith was rewarded with a contract that resulted in total revenues for all events increasing from a few million for each event to a package contract of $2.4 billion with the NBC, Fox and TNT networks (O'Keefe 2005).

High levels of commitment and trust are also evidenced by NASCAR's financial commitment to its sponsors. NASCAR continually makes large investments of both human and financial resources to help sponsors maximize the value of their sponsorships. The NASCAR sponsor support staff, otherwise known as the "Partnership Marketing Staff," includes six account executives, two directors and one vice president. They also have a business solutions group designed specifically to help sponsors figure out how to best activate their sponsorships (Giangola 2007).

Dependence

This perspective (Bucklin and Sengupta 1993; Hibbard et al. 2001) posits that dependence asymmetry and interdependence will predict relationship performance, because greater interdependence motivates parties to behave cooperatively. The NASCAR sponsorship structure illustrates both of these perspectives. Strong dependence asymmetry exists between drivers or teams and the NASCAR organization. In the early 1960s Bill France, Sr. faced off against drivers who were attempting to unionize and won, demonstrating that the drivers needed NASCAR much more than NASCAR needed the drivers (Pierce 2001). In this case, the asymmetry has proved to be helpful in allowing a centralized decision-making body to act in the best interests of a diverse community of tracks, teams and drivers. Similarly supply chains like Wal-Mart's rely heavily on dependence asymmetry.

On the other hand, NASCAR has a highly interdependent relationship with its sponsors. Though commitment and trust are certainly prominent factors, dependence also plays a role in the NASCAR–sponsor relationship. Andrew Giangola, Director of Business Communications for NASCAR, described NASCAR's dependence when he claimed that "The sport could not operate without sponsors" (Giangola 2007). A primary, non-funding-related example of NASCAR's dependence on sponsors is the exposure the 50th anniversary of the Daytona 500 received as a result of sponsors' leveraging activities. As a result of the sponsors' leveraging activities involving grocery store promotions of various kinds, the event was promoted in 25 000 grocery stores around the country (Giangola 2007). At the same time, given the high degree of loyalty and purchase rates of fans, NASCAR sponsorship is not substitutable. Thus, NASCAR needs sponsors, and sponsors have only inferior substitutes for NASCAR sponsorships, creating an interdependent relationship. The effect of this is recognition from both parties that a mutually dependent relationship ultimately results in the greatest fan equity.

NASCAR's integration of sponsorship marketing techniques, specifically value creation for partners and relationship management, has led to maximized fan equity. It is not only the monetary investment but the investment of time, resources, knowledge and capabilities that provides the basis for robust supply chain relationships. It is the unifying effort of NASCAR supply chain members and relationship management which builds relationship equity, thus maximizing fan equity.

APPLICATION BEYOND SPORTS MARKETING

Once the NASCAR sponsorship supply chain is understood and analyzed it can be applied to the corporate environment in four important ways:

1. Create long term, committed relationships incorporating financial and non-monetary investments with partners to improve product offerings and maximize value. Just as NASCAR maximizes its fan equity (final product) by creating strong, long term relationships with its partners and supply chain members, businesses can improve their products or services by creating firm foundational relationships among supply chain members. For services, this can be as simple as partnering with reputable companies and leveraging the relationship. Above all, it is clear that a strong bond between the entities (or indi-

viduals) maximizes value for the end consumer and all supply chain members.

2. Include customers in the development of a product as much as possible to increase the value of both the good or service and the relationship. Preliminary customer involvement can be seen in trends like mass customization, where the consumer is partially involved in the development, design or even creation of the product. Retailers have also taken steps towards integrating customers by including self-checkout lines, which engage the customer in obtaining the final good; this extends the product offering to create a better customer experience (albeit a limited one). By engaging the customer, however, the company inspires loyalty and strengthens the customer relationship. This kind of engagement (integration) is crucial to applying NASCAR techniques.

3. Integrate marketing techniques and relationship management into supply chain processes to increase cooperation and add value for all members. In the manufacturing sector, powerful relationships can also play a significant role in value creation. It has been commonly understood that higher quality can be achieved by increased cooperation and collaboration among supply chain members, but rarely will a supply chain attempt to include its end user in the creation of value or quality. Similarly, rather than focus on providing value for end users only, supply chain members should emphasize value for their partners, encouraging support and long term relationships. Just as services can improve by strengthening the relationships between service providers (e.g., Amazon.com and FedEx), manufacturing can increase product value by improving relationships and integrating marketing concepts into its supply chain management (e.g., Apple and AT&T).

4. Redefine the traditional customer and partner roles. Recognize that customer loyalty can serve as an asset to supply chain members and that viewing partners as consumers and producers of customer loyalty can strengthen relationships. Examples in industry are common, but the perspective for understanding the reason for their success is not. When manufacturers use ingredient branding such as "Intel inside" they are demonstrating recognition that the end users are also in effect a product that they offer to Intel for brand building. Through adoption of NASCAR's perspective on sponsorship partnering, this practice could be expanded to allow a greater presence for Intel at the retail level, giving it opportunities to show customers directly how it is interested in contributing to an enhanced computing experience. Traditional thinking stops it at ingredient branding, but more

opportunities exist for Intel to partner with products that use Intel processors.

Ultimately, the NASCAR example should lead to the understanding that supply chains require more than traditional operational characteristics. To be truly effective, supply chains must incorporate more creative approaches to how they view value creation, including thinking about who is a customer and who is a partner in less restrictive ways. The first step in this development is forming long term, mutually dependent and beneficial relationships; this is most easily accomplished when both parties recognize that the value of the product mirrors the value of the relationship. In the NASCAR supply chain, *the relationship creates the value of the product*. As Figure 10.2 illustrates, it is only when all members work together to increase relationship equity that fan equity, the end product, is maximized. Organizations must understand that it is the combination of all NASCAR practices that has led to maximum fan equity, just as it is the incorporation of all these practices that leads to higher value. Thus, to experience similar success, organizations must attempt to create the necessary relationships, integrate all supply chain members and incorporate more open definitions of "customer" and "partner" into their supply chain to build relationship equity and increase customer equity.

NOTE

* The authors acknowledge California State University, Fullerton and the Office of the Dean of the Steven G. Mihaylo College of Business for their support in funding the project. The authors sincerely thank executives within the California Motor Speedway and NASCAR for their guidance and for providing access to employees.

REFERENCES

Amis, J., N. Pant and T. Slack (1997), "Achieving a Sustainable Competitive Advantage: A Resource-Based View of Sport Sponsorship," *Journal of Sport Management*, 11, 80–96.
Boyle, B.A. and P. Magnesson (2007), "Social Identity and Brand Equity Formation: A Comparative Study of Collegiate Sports Fans," *Journal of Sport Management*, 21, 497–520.
Bucklin, L.P. and S. Sengupta (1993), "Organizing Successful Co-Marketing Alliances," *Journal of Marketing*, 57 (April), 32–46.
Cannon, J.P., R.S. Achrol and G.T. Gundlach (2000), "Contracts, Norms, and Plural Form Governance," *Journal of the Academy of Marketing Science*, 28 (Spring), 180–94.
Depken, C.A. (2000), "Fan Loyalty and Stadium Funding in Professional Baseball," *Journal of Sports Economics*, 1(2), 124–38.

Farrelly, F. and P.G. Quester (2003), "What Drives Renewal of Sponsorship Principal/Agent Relationships," *Journal of Advertising Research*, 43 (December), 353–60.
Fisher, R.J. and K. Wakefield (1998), "Factors Leading to Group Identification: A Field Study of Winners and Losers," *Psychology and Marketing*, 15, 23–40.
Free, M. and J. Hudson (2006), "Common Culture, Commodity Fetishism and Cultural Contradictions of Sport," *International Journal of Cultural Studies*, 9(1), 83–104.
Giangola, Andrew (2007), Interview with the Director of Business Communications for NASCAR, June.
Heide, J.B. and G. John (1990), "Alliances in Industrial Purchasing: The Determinants of Joint Action in Buyer–Supplier Relationships," *Journal of Marketing Research*, 27 (February), 24–36.
Hibbard, J.D., N. Kumar and L.W. Stern (2001), "Examining the Impact of Destructive Acts in Marketing Channel Relationships," *Journal of Marketing Research*, 38 (February), 45–61.
Kaufmann, P.J. and R.P. Dant (1992), "The Dimensions of Commercial Exchange," *Marketing Letters*, 3(2), 171–85.
Lusch, R.F. and James R. Brown (1996), "Interdependency, Contracting, and Relational Behavior in Marketing Channels," *Journal of Marketing*, 60 (October), 19–38.
Macneil, I. (1980), *The New Social Contract: An Inquiry into Modern Contractual Relations*, New Haven, CT: Yale University Press.
Madrigal, R. (2001), "Social Identity Effects in a Belief–Attitude–Intentions Hierarchy: Implications for Corporate Sponsorship," *Psychology and Marketing*, 18, 145–65.
Morgan, R.M. and S.D. Hunt (1994), "The Commitment-Trust Theory of Relationship Marketing," *Journal of Marketing*, 58 (July), 20–38.
Noordewier, T., G. John and J.R. Nevin (1990), "Performance Outcomes of Purchasing Arrangements in Industrial Buyer–Vendor Relationships," *Journal of Marketing*, 54 (October), 80–93.
O'Keefe, B. (2005), "America's Fastest Growing Sport," *Fortune*, 152(5), 48–64.
Palmatier, R.W., R.P. Dant and D. Grewal (2007), "A Comparative Longitudinal Analysis of Theoretical Perspectives of Interorganizational Relationship Performance," *Journal of Marketing*, 71 (October), 172–94.
Pierce, D. (2001), "The Most Southern Sport on Earth: NASCAR and the Unions," *Southern Cultures*, 7, 8–33.
Rust, R.T., V.A. Zeithaml and K.N. Lemon (2000), *Driving Customer Equity Home*, New York: Free Press.
Rust, R.T., K. N. Lemon and V.A. Zeithaml (2004), "Return on Marketing: Using Customer Equity to Focus Marketing Strategy," *Journal of Marketing*, 68 (January), 109–27.
Salomon Brothers (1997), "UK Football Clubs: Valuable Assets," *Global Equity Research: Leisure*, London: Salomon Brothers, pp. 9–10.
Sam, M.P., R. Beatty and R.G.K. Dean (2005), "A Transaction Cost Approach to Sport Sponsorship," *Sport Management Review*, 8, 1–17.
Stanco, P. (2008), "Effective Affinity Marketing Programs," *Businessweek.com*, http://www.businessweek.com/smallbiz/tips/archives/2007/10/effective_affin.htm.
Vogel, V., H. Evanschitzky and B. Ramaseshan (2008), "Customer Equity Drivers and Future Sales," *Journal of Marketing*, 72 (November), 98–108.
Wann, D.L. and N.R. Branscombe (1993), "Sports Fans: Measuring Degree of Identification with Their Team," *Journal of Sport Psychology*, 24, 1–17.
Williamson, O.E. (1975), *Markets and Hierarchies: Analysis and Antitrust Implications*, New York: Free Press.

11. Aligning service dominant logic and the relationship marketing view of the customer
Thomas W. Gruen

INTRODUCTION

It has now been ten years since the publication of the seminal article that introduced the concept of "service dominant logic," as a shift in perspective, as the organizing approach to marketing. In that article, Vargo and Lusch (2004) proposed that marketing is evolving to a "new dominant logic" that subsumes what they identified as seven developing separate lines of thought towards marketing as a social and economic process. These lines of thought have developed around various themes such as market orientation, services marketing, relationship marketing (RM), quality management, network analysis, and so on, and these occurred where academic researchers found the goods dominant (G-D) perspective of marketing lacking in its ability to explain the phenomena that were being investigated. Service dominant logic (SDL) has clearly emerged as a major contribution to marketing, having generated an unprecedented number of conceptual articles resulting from the framework. The 2004 article has been the highest-cited article published in the *Journal of Marketing* since 2000 (AMA 2011; Ehrenthal 2013).

While "relationship marketing" was only one of seven lines of thought used in the development of the SDL view, the concept of the relationship is critical to its understanding. SDL proposes that, "marketing has moved from a goods dominant view, in which tangible output and discrete transactions were central, to a service dominant view, in which intangibility, exchange processes, and *relationships* are central" (Vargo and Lusch 2004: 2, italics added). Thus, the SDL perspective relies on relationship marketing for some of its fundamental ideas or propositions (FPs), particularly where the firm–customer relationship is considered. Indeed, one of the most noted, FP6, "the customer is always a co-creator of value," requires relationship thinking. SDL views value as being co-created by the reciprocal application of operant resources (knowledge and skills) by resource integrators (actors) and their networks (e.g., a firm and its suppliers) to the benefit of the receiving entity (e.g., a customer). SDL sees value creation as continuous through the relational interaction in networks of actors (Chandler and Vargo 2011; Grönroos 2011).

While Vargo and Lusch (2004, 2008) demonstrate the SDL paradigm in a relational perspective, in more recent work on SDL Vargo (2009) examines practices and concepts that have been derived from relationship marketing, such as customer lifetime value (CLV) and customer relationship management (CRM), and sees these – through their focus on repeat patronage – as primarily being anchored in the G-D logic. From this basis, he questions first the degree to which relationship marketing can evolve into the SDL view, and second if there is a higher-order relationship conceptualization that can transcend its traditional understanding that is rooted in the G-D logic (Vargo 2009: 373).

This chapter addresses these two questions by focusing on the relationship marketing view of the customer. First, it examines the degree to which the premises of relationship marketing are consistent with SDL. Second, it examines the practices of relationship marketing that appear to be anchored in the G-D logic, particularly CRM and CLV, and examines the degree to which these could be prerequisites for co-production and co-created value, and thereby contribute to Vargo's (2009) quest for "a higher-order, S-D logic-compatible relationship conceptualization."

Some of what follows is perspectives that I shared in a previous article I wrote based on a talk I gave to the Relationship Marketing Conference in Berlin in 2008 (see Gruen and Hofstetter 2010). This chapter takes those basic arguments and augments them with both development of the SDL paradigm, and subsequent research integrating SDL into manufacturer–retailer relationships (Ehrenthal et al. 2014).

THE GOODS DOMINANT AND SERVICE DOMINANT LOGIC PERSPECTIVES OF THE CUSTOMER

To understand the SDL view of the customer, it is best to contrast it with the G-D view. In the goods-centered approach to marketing, customers are acted on (marketers segment them, distribute to them, promote to them, satisfy them). From a perspective of value, the value of a good is contained in the good itself, and the key focus is on the exchange, i.e., value for value: the good in exchange for money (assuming a monetary and not a barter economy). At the point of exchange, the good is handed off to the customer, who then consumes it, thus consuming or destroying the value inherent in the good. Whether or not the customer purchases the good in a single transaction, or repurchases many times, the focus remains on the exchange of value for value at a specific point in time (or multiple points of time). Through market research, the firm seeks to improve the value of the good by enhancing customer satisfaction through product improvements, price improvements, place improvements, or information and communication improvements. It is important to note that the good does not have to be a physical item, but can be services such as car repairs, manicures, or tax returns. In summary, in the G-D approach, the customer is "acted upon." Another particular limitation of the G-D approach to the customer is that it assumes that the dyadic nature of the relationship is self-contained, i.e., party 1 acts upon, or interacts with, party 2. This view does not consider the networks of actors surrounding the firm and the customer that affect and are affected by the relationship (Chandler and Vargo 2011).

SDL takes a very different approach to the customer. Vargo (2009: 374) notes that "the central tenet of SDL is that service is the fundamental basis for exchange." It is important to clarify the term "service," which is the application that is rendered from the offering, and to contrast that with the category of offers that are called "services" generally, owing to their intangible nature (like the car repairs or manicures mentioned previously). The service that is rendered is seen as a collection of resources available to the customer, who then adds and blends the resources provided by the seller, which in combination provide a benefit or a service to the customer and the seller. This collection of resources brought together by the seller and the customer includes an entire network of resources that have already been working to produce value, and, in their joining together, they become transformed to create new value in the form of service to both the seller and the customer. In the SDL view of Vargo and Lusch (2004), the customer functions as an active participant in the creation of value, and in doing so becomes a co-creator of the service that is also being consumed. This point is crucial because, as Vargo (2009: 374) states, "in S-D logic, the firm cannot create value, but only offer value propositions (FP7) and then collaboratively create value with the beneficiary (FP6)" (note that the terms "FP6" and "FP7" will be described below). In the SD view, value is customer determined, and this is consistent with the dominant view of value in marketing, which is defined as a calculation by the customer of benefits proportional relative to costs (Kotler 2003).

From a relationship perspective of the firm and the customer, in SDL "the customer is primarily an operant resource. Customers are active participants in relational exchanges and co-production" (Vargo and Lusch 2004: 7). They continue: "The service-centered view of marketing perceives marketing as a continuous learning process that involves . . . cultivating relationships that involve the customers in developing customized, competitively compelling value propositions to meet specific needs" (2004: 5). Vargo (2009: 375) summarizes: "It is through these joint, interactive, collaborative unfolding and reciprocal roles in value creation that S-D logic conceptualizes relationship."

SDL is captured in ten foundational premises, or FPs (Vargo and Lusch 2004, 2008). While the notion of the customer relationship is embedded in all of the ten FPs, three of the ten FPs of the S-D logic directly address the customer relationship and need to be stated in order to compare the RM view of the customer with the S-D view of the customer. These include (quoted from Vargo and Lusch 2004: 10–12, but updated using the terminology that evolved in Vargo and Lusch 2008):

> FP6: The customer is always a cocreator of value
> – The customer is always involved in the creation of value.
> – In using the product, the customer is continuing the marketing, consumption, and value-creation and delivery processes.
> – The customer becomes primarily an operant resource (cocreator) rather than an operand resource (target) and can be involved in the entire value and chain.
> FP7: The enterprise cannot deliver value, but only offer value propositions
> – Instead of being embedded in goods, value emerges for customers through use and is perceived by customers. The firm cannot create value alone.
> FP8: A service-centered view is inherently customer oriented and relational
> – Even if the firm or the customer does not desire multiple transactions, neither are freed from the relationship.

The above propositions summarize and provide the basic view of SDL and the customer. To compare this view of relationship with the view of RM, a complex array of definitions of RM needs to be examined.

THE RELATIONSHIP MARKETING VIEW OF THE CUSTOMER

The RM view of the customer has been confusing because of the multitude of definitions of relationship marketing. Here are a few that represent typical but various perspectives. Each of these contribute to some degree to Vargo's (2009) question regarding the ability of an RM conceptualization to be S-D logic compatible:

- Relationship marketing refers to all marketing activities *directed toward* establishing, developing, and maintaining successful relational exchanges (Morgan and Hunt 1994). In this view, the customer is being acted upon by a set of marketing activities focused on multiple, repetitive exchanges.

- Relationship marketing is attracting, maintaining, and enhancing customer relationships (Berry 1983). This definition emphasizes the quality and duration of the relationship with the customer, yet neglects the creation or distribution of value.
- Relationship marketing is part of the developing "network paradigm" that recognizes that global competition occurs increasingly between networks of firms (Thorelli 1986). This view emphasizes the role of the relational actors in value chains to cooperate to produce value for the customer. The customer may interact with a combined set of supply chain actors, rather than with a single contact.
- It is the creation and retention of profitable customers through ongoing collaborative business and partnering activities between a supplier and a customer on a one-to-one basis for the purpose of creating better customer value at reduced cost (Sheth and Parvatiyar 1995). While this view emphasizes the value co-creating nature of the relationship, it focuses on the dyadic nature of a firm and a customer.

Based on this sampling of definitions of relationship marketing – from individual customer relationships (Berry) to global networks (Thorelli) – one can draw the conclusion, similar to Vargo's (2009), that RM is rooted in a G-D perspective, while, based on the co-producing nature, RM has elements of the SDL FPs outlined in the previous section.

Such confusion in discussion surrounding RM is nothing new. It was at the center of an exchange between Gruen (1997) and Petrof (1997). In opposing articles, Petrof argued that RM was a mere restatement of the marketing concept, while Gruen argued that RM was distinct from the marketing concept in both theory and practice. Placed in the context of the SDL today, this argument would be stated differently in current terms. Petrof's arguments would mirror Vargo's (2009) concerns that RM is anchored in the G-D view, and thus is not different from the established marketing concept (Webster 1992). Gruen's views would suggest that the fundamental aspects of RM theory and practice are distinct and clearly fit within SDL.

Similar to Vargo and Lusch (2004) distinguishing G-D from SDL, Gruen (1997) distinguished transaction marketing from relationship marketing both by the way value is created and by the type of relationship. He argues that, in the transaction approach, competition and self-interest are drivers of value creation, and that marketing efficiency is gained through an arm's-length relationship, even while the customer is considered the nucleus of business decision making, a key principle of the marketing concept. In practice, improved manipulation of the marketing mix would lead to sustainable competitive advantage through enhanced customer satisfaction. Alternatively, the relationship orientation developed as the assumptions of the transaction approach were being challenged. Gruen (1997: 33) states:

> the axiom that held competition and self-interest as the drivers of value creation was being challenged by the notion of interdependence and cooperation as more efficient and effective at creating value. Founded on this notion of interdependence and cooperation, relationship marketing developed as a business strategy paradigm that focuses on the systematic development of ongoing, collaborative business relationships as a key source of sustainable competitive advantage.

He continues (1997: 34):

> Relationship marketers consider value creation a fundamental concept upon which strategic competitive advantage is built. Previously, value was considered to be created by the supplier and then determined in the exchange with the buyer. Under the marketing concept, the job of marketing is to satisfy a customer through the value obtained in the exchange (transaction). In relationship marketing, however, supplier and customer organizations recognize that though interdependent, collaborative relationships, they are able to create greater value than they can through independent arm's-length exchanges. Procter & Gamble and Wal-Mart, for example, have joined hands to clash the overall costs of production, distribution, and inventory. Such value is passed along to the consumer who rewards the companies with loyal patronage.

In summary, there are three general clusters of the view of the customer in RM. The first is clearly G-D anchored, as it focuses on increased profit to the firm by focusing on maintaining and enhancing relationships with existing customers. The second is somewhat mixed between a G-D anchoring and SDL, as it focuses on providing improved value to the customer through better understanding of customer needs, but the customer is involved to some degree in this process. Examples of this cluster are customer-specific co-developed products, such as those produced by Bosch for Mercedes-Benz, and aligned business processes, such as the Procter & Gamble/Wal-Mart ones described above. The third cluster is anchored in SDL, and it involves the co-creation of customer value through the involvement with the selling firm and their combined networks of actors.

THE PARADOX OF RM AND THE S-D VIEW OF THE CUSTOMER

As the above discussion shows, there is clearly good reason for Vargo (2009) to question the ability of RM to find its place as the marketing evolves to the SDL. As Vargo (2009) states, RM has gravitated towards a prescriptive imperative with a focus on long-term relationships with repetitive transactions, which is anchored in G-D logic. The focus of RM is often on maximizing repeat patronage, as customers consolidate and become more scarce, and the cost of serving existing customers is viewed as being clearly lower than the cost of acquiring new customers. This is seen as a unidirectional, firm-centric approach where measures include share of wallet, retention rates, and customer lifetime value. In practice, this view of RM is manifested in customer relationship management, which will be described in more detail later. Thus, Vargo (2009) argues that RM has become an extension of the customer orientation, maintaining firm–customer bonds (Dwyer et al. 1987), and governed by relational norms (Morgan and Hunt 1994), which is a G-D approach. Moreover, Vargo (2009) sees RM as focusing on the dyad of the seller and the customer, whereas the S-D view sees relationships as being nested in networks and occurring between networks of relationships. He concludes (2009: 374): "As RM has developed, it has increasingly gravitated toward a prescriptive imperative – to foster long term associations resulting in repetitive transactions." To evolve into SDL, RM needs a higher-order SDL-compatible conceptualization.

RELATIONSHIP MARKETING AND CO-CREATION OF VALUE

The notion of viewing customers as value co-creators has long been a well-established foundation of RM thought, although the field has typically used the G-D anchored term "co-producer" (Gummesson 1987). In RM practice, involving the customer in increasingly greater co-production roles has been a strategy that many successful firms have followed, lowering costs through joint planning and shared tasks. In doing so, they have given up traditional activities provided for the customer, and required the customer to absorb these roles. A customer that learns the processes of the supplier firm not only lessens the need for the supplier to be involved with the customer's activities, but may also assist other customers learning the processes through networking, both online (communities) and offline (user meetings) (Gruen et al. 2006). As such, the value equation (benefits less costs) would seem to indicate that some costs of the customer would increase, thus decreasing value. One would think that customers would not appreciate having extra work to obtain what they need, but that has not been the case. Apparently the benefits of joint production, control, and customized outputs appear to outweigh the extra costs of learning and involvement, increasing the value to the customer. This reconfiguration of roles along the value chain allows for the various economic actors to work together to co-produce value (Normann and Ramirez 1993).

As an example of this reconfiguration of roles, in the airline industry, loyalty of frequent flyers remains crucial. These customers are generally more time sensitive than price sensitive, providing major airlines higher profits. The primary rewards offered to these customers in exchange for their loyalty (assuming the basic service level has been met, such as safety, schedules, destinations, and general on-time performance) are convenience benefits and preferential treatment benefits (Gwinner et al. 1998). The top customer groups for airline, normally referred to as "elite" level frequent fliers, are offered preferential treatment as the primary reward in exchange for their loyalty. For the elite group, airlines offer the advantages of going to the front of the line, preferred seating in the roomy exit rows and near the front of the aircraft, and the opportunity of an upgrade to first class. However, these elite customers also must do more work for themselves to realize this value. These customers can book a reservation directly on the airline's web site, check in, and print their boarding pass before leaving for the airport. The first airline employee they need to interact with is at the gate when they are ready to get on board, and some airlines now even provide automated self-check-in at the gate. The airline has effectively shifted multiple work tasks previously performed by an airline employee onto the customer, who expends more personal effort while being involved with the airline's web site, and subsuming other processes that were previously handled by airline personnel. However, rather than receiving less value (assuming the extra work is viewed as an increased cost), the customer is now an active participant in the service's value creation and, with the added responsibility and sense of control, obtains more value through co-creation than when being "acted upon" by a customer service agent.

The concept of partnering with customers has grown out of relationship marketing. Rackham et al. (1996) present a three-component model of partnering based on their research. These components are impact, intimacy, and vision. Each of these is considered to be bilateral and jointly shared. Impact involves specific value that will be formed when the partnership is established, intimacy involves the sharing of information, and vision needs to be jointly created and understood as the initiator and long-term driver of the partnership. In the partnership view, interdependence and cooperation replace arm's-length antagonism, enabling joint, trust-based collaboration to drive new value. For example, Eaton, a supplier of gas valves, and Whirlpool partnered to develop a new gas stove (Rackham et al. 1996). In a traditional approach, Whirlpool would ask Eaton and other suppliers to submit a bid for the job and then select the best supplier based on criteria established for the bidding process. Eaton focused its marketing activities to build a relationship with Whirlpool so that it could become a partner through all the design and production processes of the new stove. Through the reshaping of organizational boundaries and the coordinating of the design teams of both companies to work together, the new stove came to market several months faster that if Whirlpool had relied on its own design capacity. Moreover, a long and expensive search for a supplier was eliminated. While Whirlpool gave up the ability to guarantee lowest price, it gained the ability to slash costs and time to market through the partnership with Eaton. This example shows how the concept of the partnership and value co-creation derived in RM fits the SDL paradigm.

This reconfiguration of roles provides new ways for value to be created. In the language of S-D logic FP7, this provides new ways that the enterprise can offer "value propositions that strive to be better or more compelling than those of competitors" (Vargo and Lusch 2004: 11). From the basic understanding that value is a calculation by the customer of benefits less costs, the new value propositions that can be offered provide new means of increasing benefits or lowering costs. Another example here is furniture retailer IKEA, which has shifted traditional tasks of furniture manufacturers and retailers to the shoppers to provide a different set of value propositions from those of its competitors. As Normann and Ramirez (1993: 67) state, "IKEA wants its customers to understand that their role is not to *consume* value, but to *create* it . . . IKEA invents value by enabling customers' own value-creating activities" (italics in original). As the above examples and discussion show, the RM view of value creation is consistent with SDL FP6, with the customer viewed as a co-creator.

RELATIONSHIP MARKETING AND ORGANIZATIONAL STRUCTURE OF MARKETING

In order to implement the S-D logic approach where the customer is viewed always as a co-creator of value, the way that firms organize for marketing must support this approach. The organization of marketing in the firm that has been developed in the RM view supports the SDL by distributing the role of marketing throughout the organization. Gummesson (1996) espoused the idea that, in the RM view, everyone in the organization should be considered a "part-time marketer." And, indeed, there have been huge changes in firms to implement a customer-focused perspective that pervades the entire organization. Consistent with SDL FP7, the dissemination of the role of marketing throughout the organization provides the ability of the firm to make an increased number of value propositions, owing to increased points of contact with the customer. However, to evolve fully into SDL, these points of contact need to be viewed as increased opportunities for value co-creation.

The marketing concept sanctioned a strong marketing function in the firm in order to inform the other business functions of customer needs (Webster 1992). RM distributes the role of marketing throughout the firm, thus shrinking the size of the function while the role of marketing expands throughout the firm. Grönroos (2004) goes so far as to suggest that a strong marketing department can actually be counterproductive to the development of a market orientation. The distribution of marketing across organizational functions provides the opportunity for an increased number of touch points to make an increased number of value propositions (FP7) with the customer. It also brings a greater number of network nodes into play, which further increases the potential number and mix of resources that can be employed in co-production.

As an example, the fast-moving consumer goods industry has seen the establishment of customer business development (CBD) teams, multifunctional teams that have been organized around a customer to work with the customer to produce joint solutions to problems and joint value for both organizations. Some of these teams are even located near the customer premises. These can include members from sales, merchandising, logistics, manufacturing, finance, accounting, and human resources. Recognizing that within key accounts there are often separate buyers, payers, and users (Sheth and Mittal 2004), the selling organization needs to match its sales reps with the buyers, its finance and accounting with the payers, and its customer service with the users. The opportunity for value co-creation with the customer is distributed across the entire group that maintains the relationship with the customer. The CBD team interfaces with multiple entities at the customer, which is also multi-functional (in the Sheth and Mittal context, the buyers, payers, and users). When these two groups interface, their intermingling goes well beyond a series of presentations of proposals from the CBD team and rather focuses on joint value creation. The CBD team and the customer counterparts jointly team-develop plans that deliver improved offerings to their common customer, the shopper or consumer in the store. By jointly developing plans, they are able to gain great efficiencies in terms of speed and cost, and deliver these savings to the consumer.

The digital world provides more opportunities for this practice as customers function as "part-time marketers." Customer-provided reviews have become a major source of information for prospective consumers, and online know-how exchange by users has become a crucial retention activity (Gruen et al. 2006). With the advent of crowdsourcing, customers become active in the role of co-creating new products, suggesting features and benefits that extend the focal firm's capabilities well beyond traditional capacity (O'Hern and Rindfleisch 2010).

This view of value co-creation as central to the relationship with the customer is expressed in Figure 11.1 (Vargo 2008; Ehrenthal 2013). This view of customer relationships shows where RM fits the S-D logic, and it also addresses the concern that Vargo (2009) expresses about the focus of RM on the dyad. Here the dyad is shown in context with its greater network. Whether the context is value co-creation through the supply chain collaboration activities, CBD team activities, customer participation in online reviews, or new product development through crowdsourcing, the key concept in relationship marketing of the customer as the "part-time marketer" involves value co-creation. Admittedly, relationship marketing has been slow to adopt SDL language (as indeed SDL also recognized in Vargo and Lusch 2008, where several of the FPs were updated as a result of their G-D language), and must reduce reliance on terms such as "part-time marketer" and "crowdsourcing" that also depend on G-D language. Consistent with Figure 11.1, suggestions might include "network knowledge integrator" and "customer value co-creator."

In the views provided above, RM reorients the positions of suppliers and customers through a business strategy of bringing them together in cooperative, trusting, and mutually beneficial relationships. These in turn are able to provide increased value propositions to their joint customers. The domain of RM seeks to provide the means and direction for organizations to create and manage an environment dedicated to mutual value creation.

RM PRACTICES: CRM AND CLV

The two previous sections have shown where the RM provides consistency with the S-D view through co-production of value with the customer (FP6) and organizing structures to allow new forms of value propositions (FP7). To a degree, it also incorporates FP9, "All social and economic actors are resource integrators" (Vargo and Lusch 2008).

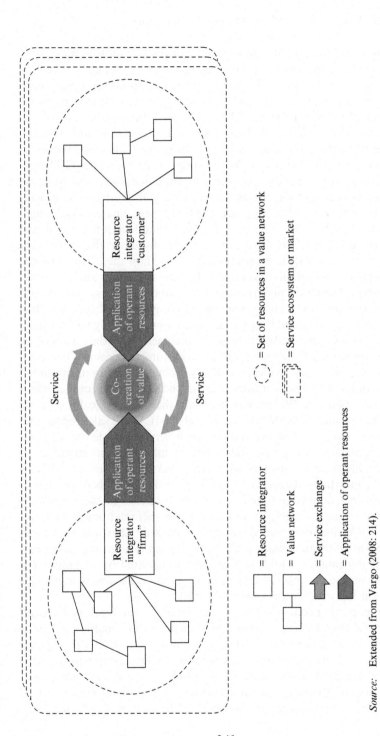

Source: Extended from Vargo (2008: 214).

Figure 11.1 Integration of firm and customer network resources

However, as Vargo (2009) shows, some of the key tools and measurements that have grown out of the relationship marketing perspective, notably customer lifetime value and customer relationship management systems, are anchored in the G-D view and have yet to transcend (or fit into) the SDL view. CRM and CLV are two of the dominant themes in the practice of RM. Other RM practices and measures include share of customer (or share of wallet) and the treatment of the customer as an asset, and these practices are, as Vargo suggests, rooted in the G-D view. Perhaps, however, depending on the way these measures and practices are deployed, there are some consistencies with SDL. Perhaps, by viewing them in light of SDL FP1, "Service is the fundamental basis of exchange" (Vargo and Lusch 2008), a way to reconcile relationship marketing and SDL may be found. This examination begins by describing CRM and CLV, and then examines a perspective that shows how these can transcend their traditional definitions and approaches and move into an SDL view.

Customer relationship management grew out of relationship marketing as an industry practice. There were two driving forces of this. The first was that firms had learned that existing customers generally had a greater ability to be more profitable than new customers, and thus a focus on customer retention of the more profitable customers became a company objective. Second, when working with key accounts, the organization has multiple contacts in the organization to match the multiple contact points of a single customer. Within key accounts there are typically separate buyers, payers, and users (Sheth and Mittal 2004). While sales representatives, finance and accounting, and customer service people are all likely to be in contact with the customer, few organizations are structured so that internally these groups talk with each other. From these two driving forces, organizations recognized that they needed to embed systems to share customer information across multiple functions in their organization. The systems that emerged were called customer relationship management, or CRM, and they were developed on basic database platforms that could hold all of the information about a customer in a central depository. Customer information could be accessed and updated by all individuals involved with the customer, which in total enhanced the ability to manage the relationship with the customer effectively.

Direct marketing companies, and other retailers that developed a direct channel, also found that the collection of customer information provided them with a very efficient and extremely effective way to boost response rates of direct marketing initiatives. While the relationship with the customer was kept at arm's length, and overtures were one-way promotions (as opposed to two-way communications), CRM databases provided the mechanism to manage this important information. Customers were viewed as an asset not only by direct marketing firms, but by all firms (Gupta et al. 2004).

These applications have continued to develop and become central to the organization's strategy. Many of these have been extended to operate remotely beyond the organization's walls through internet access, and some are shared with customers, allowing customer access. However, the objectives of CRM systems remain unchanged: maintain all information about a customer so that customers can be served according to their level of profitability, and allow all individuals in the organization who have contact with a customer to have access to complete customer information. This view of CRM is clearly anchored in G-D logic, as customers are treated as operand resources, owned and operated by the firm.

Using the same fundamental assumption as in CRM that customers are assets of the firm, customer lifetime value is also similarly approached from a G-D perspective in that it creates a valuation of the customer to the firm. Typical CLV calculations take a rudimentary approach to calculating the value to the firm, and do not begin to examine value provided to or by the customer. It is one-way, and focuses on the dyad of the customer and the firm. At its most basic level, CLV generally requires three variables for its calculation. The first is the retention rate, or the expected time a customer will be making economic exchanges with the firm. This estimate is based on history, and is typically presented as a percentage rate likelihood out of 100 percent that the customer will defect during the next time period. The second variable is the economic contribution of the customer's exchanges with the firm. This is also estimated based on historical data, and typically represents the gross margin the customer will produce over the same time period used for the retention rate, less estimated marketing expenditures specifically spent towards retaining the customer. The third variable is the cost of capital, recognizing that calculating future value must be discounted to its current value. This is typically estimated on historical cost of capital, and the time period is the same as for the other two variables. These variables are placed in a relatively simple algebraic formula to calculate the expected CLV. If the cost of acquisition of a customer is known, then this is typically subtracted from the CLV amount.

CLV does not take into account a multitude of other potential value enhancers or detractors. A prominent omitted factor is word of mouth from the customer, which can add considerably to the customer's value, or seriously decrease it if the customer is dissatisfied or cannot make a strong recommendation. Since other customers are greatly impacted by current customers, this is a major limitation of CLV calculations. CLV also only examines the dyadic relationship, and does not consider the impact of the networks that surround the firms. For example, if the customer represents a strong identity, then anyone affected by this identity (supporters and detractors) can also have an impact on the firm. Finally, CLV doesn't consider non-monetary costs and benefits, such as the resource commitment to manage the relationship or the knowledge and learning potential from the customer, customer inputs into process design, or joint cost reduction activities.

CRM AND CLV: GOODS DOMINANT OR SERVICE DOMINANT LOGIC?

While the above discussion validates Vargo's (2009) argument that RM practices are rooted in the G-D view, they can be viewed – at least to some degree – as SDL when considered in an appropriate context that considers how the key FPs of SDL would be incorporated. The following is provided to show how these RM practices could transcend to the SDL approach:

1. The focus on CRM is actually a prerequisite for the ability of the firm to engage in collaborative value-creation practices with customers. When a business understands that it may cost six to ten times more to acquire a customer than to retain a customer, the anonymous faceless customer base begins to become a well-defined and well-understood set of distinct attributes, with which relationships can be built and joint value can be created. At this point the firm can maintain a G-D approach, and use this information database to act on the customer as an operand resource. Alternatively, the firm can use this information to approach the customer from an SDL perspective, operating from a view that service is the fundamental basis of exchange (FP1), and collaborating with the customer to provide additional value propositions for the customer (FP7).
2. CLV forms the rudimentary basis for valuation and determination of ongoing collaborative relationships. While CLV typically only considers an estimated retention rate, an estimated customer economic contribution, and the discount rate (time value of money), this can also serve as the starting point of more sophisticated key performance indicator (KPI) analysis of the firm to the customer. While initially one-way (seller to customer), this can evolve into a joint evaluation of the firm to the customer and the customer back to the selling firm. When this information is shared between both parties, it becomes the place where sources of joint value creation can be identified. For example, the consumer packaged goods industry has developed a joint scorecard where suppliers and retailers can score each other on a

number of shared KPIs and then view the score from their respective partners. Moreover, because these data get aggregated at an industry level, industry benchmarks can be provided to see how scores rank relative to industry averages (www.globalscorecard.net). The overall aggregated results of the data are regularly shared at an industry conference where the manufacturers and retailers can learn about best practices in collaboration. This broader view recognizes that, in addition to the dyad, the relationship is part of a greater network, where there are a number of interdependencies.

3. Using CRM and CLV to focus on profitable customers and to design partnering strategies to leverage customer resources, the efficiency and effectiveness of marketing efforts can be enhanced. When relationships are properly formed and managed, productivity is increased not only through lower search and transactions costs, but also through the new value that is created from integrating supplier and customer functions. Such relationships and joint value creation do not spontaneously appear. They grow over time and have to be actively managed by both parties in the relationship. Taking a view of service as the fundamental basis of exchange (FP1), Ehrenthal et al. (2014) demonstrated an astonishing number of ways that relationship value can be destroyed by simply not having items available for customers. Using the resource integration approach of SDL, they demonstrated the extreme effects of disturbing the resource integration networks of both the supplier and the customer. Such an SDL approach can be applied to other marketing situations to show the potential for value creation and loss.

4. CRM and CLV also provide the place for a firm to know in which customers it should not invest time and resources, i.e., where co-produced value is likely to be minimal. SDL FP10 states that "Value is always uniquely and phenomenologically determined by the beneficiary" (Vargo and Lusch 2008), and this suggests that some customers will simply not see the value or may distort the value. Partnering with a customer to develop joint value can take considerable resources. Since resources of co-creation of value are finite to both the firm networks and the customer networks, knowing which relationships to dissolve or at best treat as arm's-length transactions is beneficial. Even a rudimentary CLV calculation can help point the firm in the direction of customers where joint value creation may be more likely to be realized.

5. In RM, a fundamental transformation in approach from traditional marketing occurs. The relationships shift from adversarial to cooperative, and the goals shift from market share to share of customers.

The view of "share of customer," or "share of wallet," can be a G-D approach, where the firm is seen as having and keeping its hands in the customer's pocket as long as possible. However, RM sees the key to attaining a higher share of each customer's lifetime business as the systematic development and management of cooperative and collaborative partnerships. Cooperation and collaboration have to be managed and governed in some manner. RM views trust-based relational governance to be superior to contractual governance for cooperation and collaboration, and ultimately increased opportunities for co-created value. Such an approach to relational governance is rooted in an SDL view.

6. The RM concept of the treatment of the customer as an asset to be managed is traditionally approached in the G-D view, where the firm acts upon and manages the customer asset. As long as the focus is on the asset side of the balance sheet, then the G-D view would appear to prevail. However, an asset must be offset with either liabilities or equity on the balance sheet. In consumer goods, this is termed "brand equity," and in B2B this is termed "relationship equity." Equity, by its nature, is valued by the market, not by the firm. This is consistent with the SDL, where value is defined by the customer (FP10). When RM takes the perspective that the equity represents the composite of the total consumer loyalty towards the brand, then in essence the value does not rest with the brand itself, but rather with the relationship that the consumer has with the brand. This latter view is in line with SDL.

Even though some practices and tools of RM have been rooted in the transaction-based G-D logic, the goal of these is to provide the ability for firms to manage in an ever more complex and information-rich environment. RM practices such as CRM and CLV can be practiced in a dyadic fashion, from a G-D logic approach, and, in many situations (probably most), that is the case. But the practice can also transcend the dyad and the view that the customer is to be acted upon. Practices such as CRM and measures such as CLV can provide a necessary basis for firms to select, deselect, and manage their resources towards joint value creation with the customer, rather than simply marketing an offering to the customer. Such an approach clearly provides the basis for transcending into SDL thinking.

CONCLUSION

This chapter has shown that relationship marketing offers two views of the customer, one that is anchored in service dominant logic and the other that is anchored in the goods dominant paradigm. Studying the history of relationship marketing shows that these represent dual paths in the development of research and practice in relationship marketing. Understanding these dual paths helps sort through the issues posed by Vargo (2009) as to the extent that RM is compatible with the SDL view. The answer proposed in this chapter is that for one path, where the customer is seen as co-creator of value, the answer is yes, they are compatible. For the other path, it appears anchored in the G-D view. However, seen in the light of being facilitators of larger processes, tools and measures such as CRM, CLV, share of wallet, and the asset view of the customer of RM can be viewed in a larger context that transcends its traditional understanding and is part of a new-order SDL conceptualization.

REFERENCES

AMA (2011), "Journal of Marketing: Most-Cited Articles," http://www.marketingpower. com/AboutAMA/Pages/AMA\%20Publications/AMA\%20Journals/Journal\%20of\%20 Marketing/JMmostcitedarticles.aspx (accessed July 4, 2012).

Berry, Len (1983), "Relationship Marketing," in L.L. Berry, G.L. Shostak and G.D. Upah (eds.), *Emerging Perspectives on Services Marketing*, Chicago: American Marketing Association, pp.25–6.

Chandler, Jennifer D. and Steven L. Vargo (2011), "Contextualization and Value-in-Context: How Context Frames Exchange," *Marketing Theory*, 11(1), 35–49.

Dwyer, Robert F., Paul Schurr and S. Oh (1987), "Developing Buyer–Seller Relationships," *Journal of Marketing*, 51 (April), 11–27.

Ehrenthal, Joachim C.F. (2013), "A Review of Service Dominant Logic 2004–2012," unpublished dissertation, University of St. Gallen, Switzerland.

Ehrenthal, Joachim, Thomas Gruen and Joerg Hofstetter (2014), "Value Attenuation and Retail Out-of-Stocks: A Service-Dominant Logic Perspective," *International Journal of Physical Distribution and Logistics Management*, 44(1/2), 39–57.

Grönroos, Christian (2004), "The Relationship Marketing Process: Communication, Interaction, Dialogue, Value," *Journal of Business and Industrial Marketing*, 19(2), 99–113.

Grönroos, Christian (2011), "Value Co-Creation in Service Logic: A Critical Analysis," *Marketing Theory*, 11(3), 279–301.

Gruen, Thomas W. (1997), "Relationship Marketing: The Route to Marketing Efficiency and Effectiveness," *Business Horizons*, November–December, 32–8.

Gruen, Thomas W. and Joerg S. Hofstetter (2010), "The Relationship Marketing View of the Customer and the Service Dominant Logic Perspective," *Journal of Business Market Management*, 2010(4), 231–45.

Gruen, Thomas W., Talai Osmonbekov and Andrew Czaplewski (2006), "eWOM: The Impact of Customer-to-Customer Online Know-How Exchange on Customer Value and Loyalty," *Journal of Business Research*, 59(4), 449–56.

Gummesson, Evert (1987), "The New Marketing – Developing Long-Term Interactive Relationships," *Long Range Planning*, 20(4), 10–20.

Gummesson, Evert (1996), "Relationship Marketing: The Emperor's New Clothes or Paradigm Shift?," in U. Schöneberg (ed.), *Research Methodologies for "The New Marketing," ESOMAR/EMAC Symposium, Latimer, UK, November 1996*, Amsterdam: ESOMAR/EMAC, pp. 3–19.

Gupta, Sunil, Donald Lehmann and Jennifer A. Stuart (2004), "Valuing Customers," *Journal of Marketing Research*, 41(1), 7–18.

Gwinner, Kevin, Dwayne Gremler and Mary Jo Bitner (1998), "Relational Benefits in Services Industries: The Customer's Perspective," *Journal of the Academy of Marketing Science*, 26(2), 101–14.

Kotler, Philip (2003), *A Framework for Marketing Management*, Upper Saddle River, NJ: Pearson Education.

Morgan, Robert and Shelby Hunt (1994), "The Commitment-Trust Theory of Relationship Marketing," *Journal of Marketing*, July, 20–38.

Normann, Richard and Rafael Ramirez (1993), "From Value Chain to Value Constellation: Designing Interactive Strategy," *Harvard Business Review*, July–August, 65–77.

O'Hern, Matthew S. and Aric Rindfleisch (2010), "Customer Co-Creation: A Typology and Research Agenda," in Naresh K. Malhotra (ed.), *Review of Marketing Research*, Vol. 6, Armonk, NY: M.E. Sharpe, pp. 84–106.

Petrof, John (1997), "Relationship Marketing: The Wheel Reinvented?," *Business Horizons*, November–December, 25–31.

Rackham, Neil, Lawrence Friedman and Richard Ruff (1996), *Getting Partnering Right*, Columbus, OH: McGraw-Hill.

Sheth, Jagdish and Banwari Mittal (2004), *Consumer Behavior: A Managerial Perspective*, Mason, OH: Thomson South-Western Press.

Sheth, Jagdish and Atul Parvatiyar (1995), "The Evolution of Relationship Marketing," *International Business Review*, 4(4), 397–418.

Thorelli, Hans B. (1986), "Networks: Between Markets and Hierarchies," *Strategic Management Journal*, 7(1), 37–51.

Vargo, Stephen L. (2008), "Customer Integration and Value Creation – Paradigmatic Traps and Perspectives," *Journal of Service Research*, 11(2), 211–15.

Vargo, Stephen L. (2009), "Toward a Transcending Conceptualization of Relationship: A Service-Dominant Logic Perspective," *Journal of Business and Industrial Marketing*, 24(5/6), 373–9.

Vargo, Stephen L. and Robert F. Lusch (2004), "Evolving to a New Dominant Logic for Marketing," *Journal of Marketing*, 68 (January), 1–17.

Vargo, Stephen L. and Robert F. Lusch (2008), "Service Dominant Logic: Continuing the Evolutions," *Journal of the Academy of Marketing Science*, 36 (Spring), 1–10.

Webster, Frederick E., Jr. (1992), "The Changing Role of Marketing in the Corporation," *Journal of Marketing*, October, 1–17.

12. Gratitude in relationship marketing
Randle D. Raggio, Anna Green Walz, Mousumi Bose and Judith Anne Garretson Folse

For centuries, gratitude has been portrayed by theologians, moral philoso-
phers, and writers as an indispensable manifestation of virtue – an excellence of character. For example, gratitude is not only a highly prized human
disposition in Jewish, Christian, Muslim, Buddhist, and Hindu thought, but
deemed an unrivaled quality in these traditions, essential for living life well.
The consensus among the world's religious and ethical writers is that people
are morally obligated to feel and express gratitude in response to received benefits. For example, Adam Smith, the legendary economist and philosopher,
proposed [in *The Theory of Moral Sentiments*] that gratitude is a vital civic
virtue, absolutely essential for the healthy functioning of societies. (Emmons
2004: 3, internal citations removed)

In 1759 (250 years ago at this writing), Adam Smith ([1759] 2000: 94)
wrote in *The Theory of Moral Sentiments*: "The sentiment which most
immediately and directly prompts us to reward, is gratitude . . . To reward,
is to recompense, to remunerate, to return good for good received." The
concept of "reward" may seem inappropriate in the realm of economic
exchanges that are governed by formal and informal governance structures designed to force compliance and ensure performance. Indeed,
actions prompted by structures established to mitigate opportunism and
hold parties to their respective obligations hardly seem consistent with the
notion of a "reward." Yet relationship marketing occurs in the context
of economic exchanges and seeks to meet the objectives of all parties "by
a mutual giving and fulfillment of promises" (Grönroos 1997: 407) and
to "create or enhance mutual economic value" (Sheth and Parvatiyar
2000: 9). We suggest such actions can be seen as returning good for good
received; thus, they are consistent with Smith's ([1759] 2000) definition of
reward and have the potential to produce gratitude in participants in economic exchanges. Given this insight, we consider gratitude a foundational
concept that should be given serious consideration by those studying
relationship marketing.

An example is instructive. The first author's battery died – really died –
when his son accidentally left the car door open overnight. The car would
start with a jump from his wife's Honda Odyssey, but died again when
the lights were turned on. It took three jumps to get the car out of the

driveway; even driving it for several miles did not recharge the battery. So it was no surprise that the car was dead when he tried to restart it after working out at the gym.

The plan was simple: since they lived close to campus, his wife, who was at home with their children, would drive to school to jump his car; both would drive home; she would bring him to campus; she would call the American Automobile Association (AAA), which has a battery-replacement service they had used for the same car in a different AAA region six years before; the car would be fixed; she would pick him up from work that evening when she picked up their children from gymnastics practice on campus. Unlike most of his plans, this one worked brilliantly. Not only did the AAA service specialist arrive within 30 minutes with a new battery and a copy of the warranty on the old one, but, upon seeing that a connector cable was corroded, he drove to the local auto parts store, purchased a new cable with his own money, and replaced it as well. The author's wife paid the invoice and reimbursed the service specialist for the cable. Immediately upon entering the house, she changed her Facebook status to ". . . is thankful for AAA battery service!!!" One other piece of information is important: the service specialist had performed the same battery service for a friend whose battery had died the month before (thankfully, not the author's son that time; his friend forgot to close the back door when he removed his luggage). The friend had AAA, but was not aware of the battery service until the author related his positive prior experience.

The story is instructive because we can identify a "reward" given by both buyer and seller in what was more than a single, discrete, or transactional economic exchange for both parties. The buyer had used, and greatly appreciated, various AAA services over the years. The seller (in this case the technician) had received two service calls from the buyer's house and had met the buyer the month before. The seller provided a reward of additional service (purchase of the cable), and the buyer provided the reward of positive word of mouth, first on Facebook (several friends inquired about the service after seeing the status) and now in this volume. Like Smith ([1759] 2000), we suggest that gratitude is the sentiment which, even in the economic context of a contractually governed service encounter, prompted both parties to reward. (Having been one of the parties, the first author makes this suggestion with some authority.)

In fact, researchers find that buyers reward sellers through their actions. For example, Lynn and McCall (2000: 211, emphasis added) conducted a meta-analysis of 13 studies covering 2547 dining parties at 20 different restaurants and conclude: "Consumers use tips to *reward* waiters and waitresses for services rendered." Morales (2005) finds that, even when a firm's effort has no impact on perceptions of product quality, it does have a significant impact on gratitude toward the high-effort firm. "Consumers recognize that effort is a controllable behavior and as a result, feel gratitude toward firms that uphold their moral responsibility to work hard, even when they are working to market their products. This gratitude then motivates consumers to *reward* firms" through higher willingness to pay, store choice, and more positive overall ratings (Morales 2005: 811, emphasis added).

Furthermore, the story highlights the fact that gratitude can be experienced by either party to an exchange; either party can be a benefactor or beneficiary of benefits. Psychologists studying gratitude have identified three prosocial or moral functions of gratitude (McCullough et al. 2001). Gratitude works as a *moral barometer* when it lets us know that we have been the intentional recipient of benefits. It functions as a *moral motive* when the feeling of gratitude causes us to seek ways to benefit our benefactor and not do him/her harm; the experience of gratitude also causes us to act more prosocially toward others beyond the original benefactor. Finally, gratitude is a *moral reinforcer* when the receipt of a sincere expression of gratitude causes us to act more prosocially toward the expresser and others. Recognize that the first two functions (barometer and motive) relate to the impact of feelings of gratitude on the beneficiary, while the third (reinforcer) relates to the impact of expressions of gratitude from the beneficiary to the original benefactor. Thus, gratitude has implications for either party to an exchange, a feature that makes it instrumental in the development and maintenance of relationships.

In a review paper on the role of gratitude in the relational exchange paradigm (Raggio et al. 2009), we suggest that the experience and expression of gratitude by buyers and sellers can help transform transactional exchanges into relational ones through the process of a "gratitude cycle" (i.e., benefit–gratitude–expression–acknowledgment). This transformation occurs because gratitude helps maintain a dynamic equilibrium between donor and receiver (Heilbrunn 1972), builds stronger bonds of friendship with long-term benefits (Fredrickson 2004), encourages beneficial reciprocal behavior (Emmons and McCullough 2004; Algoe 2006), and encourages the development of long-term relationships (Bartlett and DeSteno 2006), all of which are important in both social and economic relationships, especially if parties are to desire future exchanges, a key characteristic of relational exchanges (as opposed to transactional ones) as described by Dwyer et al. (1987).

Next we formally define gratitude, and then add to the theoretical foundation of gratitude by reviewing consumer-related studies of gratitude, emphasizing its role in relationship development and maintenance, and positioning it alongside commitment and trust as an important relational mediator, and offer future research topics and directions. We conclude with a call for marketing scholars to pursue the implications of gratitude for relationship marketing.

GRATITUDE

Fredrickson (2004: 150) defines gratitude as the emotion that arises "when an individual (beneficiary) perceives that another person (benefactor) or source (e.g., God, luck, fate) has intentionally acted to improve the beneficiary's well being." This definition emphasizes the perceived intent of the benefactor, is consistent with Smith's ([1759] 2000) notion of returning good for good, and works equally well for both interpersonal and commercial exchanges (Raggio et al. 2009). Expressions of gratitude build stronger bonds of friendship, as well as skills in support of loving and showing appreciation, which can have lasting rewards far beyond the benefit–gratitude exchange (Fredrickson 2004). Komter (2004: 211) notes gratitude's relevance for trust, one of the most widely studied relational exchange constructs, by writing: "Without the ties created by gratitude, there would be no mutual trust, no moral basis on which to act, and no grounds for maintaining the bonds of community."

It may be tempting to suggest that reciprocity, not gratitude, is at work in the examples cited above and in commercial exchanges (cf. Bagozzi 1975; Houston and Gassenheimer 1987). But this view misses the point that gratitude (in its moral barometer and motive roles) alerts us to the existence of a benefit and then prompts us to act on this information. While relational norms such as reciprocity are important, gratitude acts as the emotional core of reciprocity (Becker 1986), prompting appropriate action. The fact that certain behavior is expected in relationships neither addresses the motivation for compliance with such norms nor precludes feelings of gratitude from resulting from an exchange partner's actions. Consistent with this view, Palmatier et al. (2009) suggest that gratitude generates psychological pressure to return a favor. Indeed, researchers find that reciprocating can generate pleasure, while failure to reciprocate can lead to guilt (Becker 1986; Buck 2004; Dahl et al. 2005). Interestingly, Watkins and colleagues (2006: 217) state that "the debt of gratitude is internally generated, and is not analogous to an economic form of indebtedness." In their studies, feelings of gratitude decrease as expectations about a return benefit increase. As a result, in certain situations, the norm of reciprocity may actually diminish feelings of gratitude, further evidence that gratitude acts as a motivator of action.

Gratitude may result any time a person perceives that another has intended that he or she receive a benefit, but "Good consequences devoid of good intentions do not create a debt of gratitude" (Seneca, quoted in Harpham 2004: 23). Similarly, Bahya Ibn Pakuda, the tenth-century Jewish writer, argues that, "When a favor is done for us unintentionally, we have no obligation of gratitude to anybody" (quoted in Schimmel 2004: 46). However, because intentionality must be determined subjectively, neither good intentions on the part of the benefactor nor an actual benefit necessarily is required for a person to feel gratitude (Roberts 2004); rather, simply the perception of good intentions may be sufficient. This statement suggests that the benefactor does not need either to engage in true effort or to ensure a positive outcome, as long as the beneficiary attributes the benefactor's actions to benevolence.

What Is Necessary for Gratitude to Exist?

Gratitude encompasses cognitive, affective, and behavioral components, such that the beneficiary recognizes a benefit bestowed by a benefactor (cognition), appreciates that benefit (emotion), and acknowledges the benefit (behavior). As David Steindl-Rast (2004: 283) recognizes:

> The more I allow my gratitude to take hold of me, the more I come to under-stand the gift. The more I understand the gift, the more also the volitional aspect grows: I want to acknowledge my appreciation by giving recognition for the gratuitousness of the gift. All three components of gratitude resonate together in the French expression *Je suis reconnaissant* [I am grateful] – I recog-nize (intellectually), I acknowledge (willingly), I appreciate (emotionally). Only when all three come together is gratitude complete.

However, we suggest that only recognition and appreciation are nec-essary for gratitude to exist. Without recognition, a person does not see him- or herself as a beneficiary. Thus, the cognitive component makes gratitude possible and becomes a necessary but not sufficient precursor to gratitude. Without appreciation, a person may recognize that he or she has received a benefit, but the emotion of gratitude may not exist if the beneficiary believes the benefit is deserved (i.e., due to his or her own efforts), the benefit is less than expected (i.e., the effort expended pro-duces an insufficient outcome), or the benefactor's intent is perceived to be something other than his or her benefit (e.g., intended harm, but good occurred). Consistent with this view, Steindl-Rast (2004) categorizes his third component (appreciation) as emotional rather than behavioral.

In summary, for gratitude to exist, it must contain both a cognitive and an affective component. Although experiencing the emotion of gratitude may encourage its expression, a behavioral response is not necessary for gratitude to exist. However, as we have demonstrated elsewhere (Raggio et al. 2009), "closing the loop" and acknowledging a benefit (or even a "thank you") is instrumental in the development and encouragement of buyer–seller relationships.

Transactional and Relational Exchanges versus Zero-Sum and Positive-Sum Gratitude

Adam Smith is most well known as the author of *The Wealth of Nations*, but Harpham (2004: 31) suggests that Smith's focus on self-interest in *The Wealth of Nations* ([1776] 2003) is only understood within the context of his earlier work, *The Theory of Moral Sentiments* ([1759] 2000), in which he lays the moral foundations for the society in which self-interest functions:

> Smith's analysis of merit and demerit [in Part II of *The Theory of Moral Sentiments*] moves our understanding of gratitude forward along a number of different dimensions. First, it explains clearly where gratitude fits into our social world and why self-interest is not enough to tie people together or bring about the many benefits of social interaction. *The Wealth of Nations* was predicated on the assumption that self-interest is a more reliable foundation than beneficence and gratitude for securing the basic economic needs of a society. But it did not eliminate the need for either benevolent acts or responses of gratitude. As Smith showed in *The Theory of Moral Sentiments*, gratitude plays a vital role in making the world we live in a better place.

As Harpham (2004: 32) recognizes, Smith identifies self-interest "as a factor that can warp and even pervert proper feelings of gratitude in a human being." If a seller's view is so clouded by self-interest that he believes that customers owe him their business, nothing his customers do is likely to produce feelings of gratitude. Thus, what is at play in economic life should be characterized as "bounded self-interest" (see Ireland 1990; Jolls et al. 1998), leaving open the possibility for gratitude to play a part in our economic lives.

Unfortunately, as psychologists and sociologists have defined and operationalized gratitude, they have developed a false dichotomy between the interpersonal and economic domains. For example, Buck (2004) distinguishes between *gratitude of exchange* and *gratitude of caring*, such that the former is a zero-sum game in which a less powerful beneficiary expresses gratitude for a benefit given by a more powerful benefactor, involving "issues of equity, reciprocity and obligation" (Buck 2004: 101). In contrast, gratitude of caring is a positive-sum game in which both benefactor and beneficiary gain from the giving of benefits and expressions of gratitude, so "judgments of exchange, equity, reciprocity, and obligation are not relevant" (Buck 2004: 101). We note that Buck was not the creator of, nor alone in perpetuating, this dichotomy. For example, the Roman Stoic philosopher Seneca also differentiates between debts of gratitude and debts in the marketplace (see Harpham 2004).

However, when we consider definitions of relationship marketing, we see that the focus is not on one-sided or zero-sum gains. Rather, researchers and managers consider the "objectives of all parties," and "mutual giving and fulfillment of promises" (Grönroos 1997), and "cooperation," "collaboration," and "mutual economic value" (Sheth and Parvatiyar 2000). These concerns do not fit with Buck's zero-sum gratitude of exchange.

Instead of contrasting interpersonal and economic exchanges, we offer a more important dichotomy: that between transactional and relational exchanges. A *transactional exchange* occurs between two parties when there is no intention of a future exchange. A *relational exchange* occurs when multiple, interrelated exchanges occur between two parties and future exchanges are expected or desired (Dwyer et al. 1987). When we consider economic exchanges, it is clear that our goal is to develop relational ones, not simply transactional ones. The seller benefits from implementing relational exchange include increased sales and profits (e.g., Palmatier et al. 2006, 2007), higher levels of cooperation (e.g., Morgan and Hunt 1994), reduced conflict (e.g., Palmatier et al. 2007), higher share of purchases (Reynolds and Beatty 1999), and lower costs (e.g., Cannon and Homburg 2001). Although the buyer benefits do not appear as often in studies, relational exchanges provide benefits such as socialization, customization, and financial rewards (e.g., Gwinner et al. 1998).

If we consider the definition of relationship marketing offered by Dwyer et al. (1987), we see the desire to continue in a relationship, which is impossible in a scenario where only one party wins. Thus the important dichotomy is between transactional and relational exchanges, deemphasizing the differences between economic and interpersonal exchanges, and making the issue of gratitude a relevant and important consideration in the study of buyer–seller relationships generally, and relationship marketing specifically.

For the remainder of this chapter, unless explicitly noted, we refer to the positive-sum gratitude, as described by Buck's (2004) "gratitude of caring," when we mention gratitude, even though he did not consider it appropriate for economic exchanges. This emphasis is consistent with Fredrickson's (2004) definition that we have adopted, which emphasizes the benefactor's intent to improve the beneficiary's well-being, is the focus of relational exchange, and has been demonstrated in the economic context.

Consumer-Related Studies of Gratitude

In addition to those mentioned above, we recognize that other scholars have considered gratitude in their consumer-related research and now provide a brief review. Carey et al. (1976) directly manipulate an expression of gratitude by either thanking customers for their recent purchases or thanking and also notifying the customers of an upcoming sale. They conclude that thanking customers reduces the number of delinquent credit accounts and that thanking customers for their business alone has a larger effect on sales than thanking and also mentioning the upcoming sale. Though gratitude was not directly measured, Holbrook (1993: 277) finds that "a residue of student sentiment will remain [after other factors are considered] and will express itself as a component of MBA attitudes [that impact the *Business Week* rankings] ranging from strong appreciation to strong ungratefulness." Soscia (2007) finds that gratitude, but not happiness, predicts repurchase intention and positive word of mouth. In a preview of a subsequent section, we note that this finding, along with the AAA battery story related earlier, raises the question of the relationship between gratitude and other constructs such as satisfaction and happiness, which we address in our section on future research topics and directions.

In research addressing the last component of the gratitude cycle (acknowledgment), Bone and colleagues (2008) explore the impacts of a company's acknowledgment of (or failure to acknowledge) a customer's "thank you" and find that acknowledgment has a positive impact on loyalty – what they call the "you're welcome effect." For instance, one recent study found that the perceived sincerity of an expression of gratitude from the State of Louisiana in the aftermath of Hurricane Katrina had a positive impact on people's attitudes toward the state, its people, products, services, and travel, willingness to spread positive word of mouth about the state, and willingness to pay for products, services, and travel from or to Louisiana (Raggio and Folse 2007). Interestingly, the results held both for those who actually gave to or participated in relief or rebuilding activities and those who did not participate and were not in any way associated with the state, indicating that expressions of gratitude may have positive impacts beyond the intended recipient.

Countless studies aim to identify the drivers and facilitating conditions that lead to relational benefits in an effort to assist managers in formulating appropriate marketing strategies (e.g., Palmatier et al. 2006, 2007). Most studies rely on the precedent set by previous researchers who pioneered the relational exchange paradigm by borrowing constructs from other disciplines to understand social relationships such as friendships, partnerships, and marriage (Macneil 1980; Levitt 1983; Dwyer et al. 1987). Examples of these borrowed constructs include commitment (e.g., Morgan and Hunt 1994), trust (e.g., Ganesan 1994), satisfaction (e.g., Garbarino and Johnson 1999), communication and cooperation (e.g., Anderson and Narus 1990), loyalty (Oliver 1999), interdependence (Price and Arnould 1999), and functional conflict (Anderson and Narus 1990).

Absent from this list is gratitude. This oversight by relationship marketing researchers seems surprising, especially because the disciplines from which they typically borrow – sociology and psychology – consider gratitude essential for building and preserving social relationships (Bartlett and DeSteno 2006) and are foundational to the development and maintenance of trust (Komter 2004; Young 2006). The research stream by Palmatier stands in contrast to this trend. Palmatier et al. (2006) conducted a meta-analysis of more than 38 000 relationships and conclude that commitment and trust alone do not fully explain the impact of relationship marketing investments on seller performance. Palmatier et al.'s (2007) longitudinal study of interorganizational relationship performance provided evidence that researchers should consider additional relational mediators such as gratitude alongside commitment and trust. They suggested that gratitude may help build relational exchanges because it represents an intermediate step between exchanges and motivates future transactions. In his 2008 MSI monograph, Palmatier positioned gratitude alongside commitment and trust in a model of interpersonal relationship marketing that proposes to explain both short- and long-term seller performance outcomes. Finally, Palmatier et al. (2009) provided empirical support for including gratitude in relationship marketing models. Their results indicated an average 23 percent greater impact of gratitude on seller outcomes (customer repurchase intentions, share of wallet, sales revenue, and sales growth) than that found for commitment. Gratitude also, indirectly, impacts seller outcomes through a positive impact on customer trust in the seller, which positively impacts commitment, which then directly impacts seller outcomes. Palmatier et al. (2009) concluded that "[M]arketing research that neglects gratitude and focuses exclusively on trust and commitment may fail to capture the full effects of relationship marketing and systematically underestimate the true return on investment of relationship marketing activities."

We expect this is only the first study in a long line that will show positive impacts of gratitude in relationship marketing and, recognizing the fact that either buyer or seller can be a benefactor, encourage researchers to expand this investigation to consider positive impacts of *seller* gratitude (as could be generated through loyal customers willing to share positive word of mouth or act as "ambassadors") to determine impacts on customer outcomes. With thoughts of future research in mind, we now turn to the development of future research topics and directions for those considering including gratitude in their research.

FUTURE RESEARCH TOPICS AND DIRECTIONS

The Effects of Gratitude apart from the Gratitude Cycle

As with other emotions, gratitude has two aspects that can be dissociated: the experiential and the expressive (Buck 2004).[1] Both of these aspects can enhance the development of a relational exchange between parties. But an important question is whether unexpressed feelings of gratitude still have a positive impact on subsequent transactions, since the benefactor does not get an opportunity to understand the beneficiary's true feelings. Prior research suggests that the experience of the positive emotion of gratitude will make future transactions more likely whether a gratitude cycle occurs or not (e.g., Buck 2004; Fredrickson 2004; Morales 2005; Soscia 2007). The experience of gratitude represents an internal acknowledgment that the benefactor has acted to the advantage of the focal beneficiary; in turn, such recognition leads to a greater trust in the benefactor on the part of the beneficiary (Buck 2004). While it would seem that a complete gratitude cycle may produce more relationship benefits than unexpressed gratitude, there is clear evidence that even unexpressed feelings of gratitude may positively affect the relationship (Fredrickson 2004). An interesting area for further inquiry is what factors facilitate expressions of gratitude. Certainly advances in technology, including social networking and online feedback, help, but more work needs to be done to determine if these are sufficient to maximize the positive benefits of feelings and expressions of gratitude.

Similarities between Gratitude and Other Relational Constructs

Before exploring the relationships among gratitude and other frequently studied relational mediators, we first note similarities between gratitude and other relational constructs. While the list of constructs studied in the literature concerning commercial relationships is quite substantial, for brevity we will compare gratitude to three of the most frequently studied constructs: satisfaction, trust, and loyalty.

Satisfaction is similar to gratitude in the sense that both constructs are emotional reactions to a cognitive appraisal. Satisfaction is considered the emotional state that occurs in response to a product or service experience (Garbarino and Johnson 1999). Models of satisfaction development have been debated over the years. However, as in the case of gratitude, most include a cognitive component (i.e., an evaluation of the discrepancy between perceived performance and expectations or desires) that results in an affective component (i.e., satisfaction) (Oliver 1980).

Trust represents belief in a partner's integrity and reliability; it is Party A's belief that Party B has Party A's interest at heart (Ganesan 1994; Morgan and Hunt 1994). This belief develops and increases over time, based on the interactions between the two parties. It is a cumulative assessment of the past (e.g., Doney and Cannon 1997). Gratitude is similar to trust, in that it is also an assessment of the past and is based on perceived intent.

Loyalty has been conceptualized in many different ways, including repeat purchase frequency or emotional attachment (see Jacoby and Chestnut 1978 for a review). Oliver (1999: 34) defines loyalty as "a deeply held commitment to rebuy or repatronize a preferred product/service consistently in the future ... despite situational influences and marketing efforts having the potential to cause switching behavior." Loyalty development can be described in the following stages: 1) cognitive loyalty; 2) affective loyalty; 3) conative loyalty; and 4) action loyalty. Cognitive loyalty is recognition of preferable attributes in a product, affective loyalty is a liking that has developed toward the product, conative loyalty is an intention to rebuy the brand, while action loyalty is where these intentions are converted to actual purchase. The development of loyalty and the development of gratitude are alike in the sense that gratitude's components occur in a similar order (i.e., cognitive, affective, behavioral).

In sum, gratitude is similar to each of these constructs in that it includes a cognitive component (i.e., the perception that a benefactor has intended benefit to the beneficiary) that results in an affective component (i.e., feelings of gratitude), with the potential (as in the cases of satisfaction and loyalty) for a behavioral response. We also note that customers can have or develop satisfaction, trust, and loyalty with or toward the firm, its products, or its sales representatives (e.g., Dick and Basu 1994; Doney and Cannon 1997), but their relationships with "key contacts" within firms can be more pronounced (Czepiel 1990; Gwinner et al. 1998; Bendapudi and Leone 2002). Based on the similarities of the underlying structure of gratitude relative to these other relational constructs, consumers can also experience gratitude towards different representatives of the firm based on the different roles that each plays. Structural commonalities between gratitude and other common relational mediators abound, but an important question is whether similar outcomes can be expected. Palmatier et al. (2009) provided the first empirical evidence supporting such effects. But additional research should seek to identify the unique contributions of gratitude apart from those of other relational mediators, and the best approaches for implementing these in the buyer–seller context.

Relationship among Gratitude, Happiness, Satisfaction, and Delight

Satisfaction, delight, and gratitude all involve the appraisal of performance and its resulting benefits. However, gratitude does not require an evaluation in comparison with prior expectations and may not require an actual benefit but rather only a strong and appreciated effort (Buck 2004). Researchers distinguish between satisfaction with process and satisfaction with outcome (e.g., Bendapudi and Leone 2003). We note that happiness, gratitude, satisfaction, and delight may result from appraisals of either processes or outcomes.

Previous scholars have directly linked satisfaction to happiness (Westbrook and Oliver 1991; Oliver and Westbrook 1993; Soscia 2007). According to Weiner and Graham (1989), happiness is a generic response to pleasant circumstances, and Soscia (2007) equates satisfaction with mild and short-term forms of happiness. Her results show significant correlations (0.98) between happiness and satisfaction.

Gratitude is not the same as gladness or happiness (Westbrook and Oliver 1991; Oliver and Westbrook 1993; Soscia 2007); thus the exact relationship of gratitude to satisfaction and delight remains an open question. In this subsection, we review three appraisal theory (Roseman 1991) categories, goal congruence, causation, and intent, along with the cognitive and/or emotional activation required to address this relationship and propose that, in the same way that satisfaction relates to happiness, gratitude relates to delight.

Goal congruence

In appraisal theory, goal congruence "refers to the extent to which a transaction is consistent or inconsistent with what the person wants – that is, it either thwarts or facilitates personal goals" (Lazarus 1991: 150). According to appraisal theory, the desirability of outcomes provides an important appraisal category for a consumption experience (Soscia 2007). When consumers reach a personal goal, they experience positive emotions (Weiner 1985; Ortony et al. 1998). Similarly, happiness, gratitude, satisfaction, and delight all may occur when the results or effort is congruent with a person's goals, such that the person gets something he or she wants (outcome) or appreciates the effort expended on his or her behalf (process). We restrict our discussion to scenarios that produce goal-congruent outcomes, because goal-incongruent outcomes can only produce negative emotions such as sadness, guilt, anger, and dissatisfaction (Soscia 2007).

Perceived causation

A second important category of appraisals relates to the perceived causation of events or attribution of agency (Scherer 1985). Soscia (2007) addresses outcomes caused by another party, oneself, and general circumstances. Because an external benefactor must exist to induce gratitude, only those scenarios in which causation indicates a responsible party (individual, corporation, organization) other than him- or herself can produce gratitude. For example, an investor who makes his or her own trading decisions may be happy, satisfied, or delighted with the returns from a broad index stock fund but should (in an ethical scenario) attribute the results to an upturn in the economy, not a benefactor with the ability to engineer returns, so the potential for gratitude should not exist.[2]

Personal intent

Gratitude results from a cognitive appraisal of whether a party has acted with the intent to benefit a particular beneficiary. Therefore, a perception of personal intent is required to induce gratitude, but it is not required to induce happiness, satisfaction, or delight. Soscia (2007) finds that happiness may result whenever goal-congruent outcomes occur, whereas gratitude only occurs when buyers perceive that the goal-congruent outcomes were produced by sellers. The above-mentioned investor could feel gratitude toward a friend who shared a profitable stock tip, but would not feel gratitude toward officials whose job it is to improve the economy and who should have no intent toward any particular investor. Rust and Oliver (2000) suggest that delight may result from either a sense of personal intent (e.g., delight that the maid has done a great job) or generalized intent (e.g., fate, randomness, serendipity). Therefore, intent is a critical indicator of gratitude, but not of delight.

Emotional or cognitive activation

Moving beyond appraisal theory, we note that post-consumption affect research defines satisfaction as affect that arises when expectations generally are met (i.e., the outcome is "about as expected"; Churchill and Surprenant 1982; Oliver 1980, 1993) or in the absence of dissatisfaction (Selnes 1998). Delight results when performance exceeds expectations, especially significantly or by a surprising amount (Oliver et al. 1997; Rust and Oliver 2000). A key distinction between satisfaction and delight is the amount of emotion activated by each appraisal. Less emotional activation tends to occur with the experience of satisfaction, whereas delight is associated with higher levels of emotional activation (Westbrook and Oliver 1991; Oliver and Westbrook 1993; Ngobo 1999). For example, Rust and Oliver (2000: 86) describe delight as a "profoundly positive emotional state generally resulting from having one's expectations exceeded to a surprising degree." According to Oliver et al. (1997: 317), delight requires "backward processing" (Kahneman and Miller 1986), the retrieval of expectations and the likely probability of an outcome's occurrence, and then a realization of how positively surprisingly unusual the event is.

Happiness relates to an "aimless activation" that resembles "generic urges to do nothing in particular or engage in non-directed explorations or expressions of affect" (Soscia 2007: 881). This description is consistent with notions of satisfaction that define the term simply as the "absence of dissatisfaction" (Selnes 1998). That is, there is no emotional trigger to alert the person to a situation that requires attention, whether negative or extremely positive. According to the affect infusion model (Forgas 1995), affect links directly to cognition, because it informs cognition and judgment by facilitating access to related cognitive categories during heuristic or substantive processing. Cognitive resources, beyond those required by mere satisfaction, may be necessary to evaluate a situation and conclude that the actual outcome has (far) surpassed expectations (i.e., backward processing). The higher emotional activation caused by surprisingly positive expectations may facilitate this cognitive process. Similarly, gratitude requires an appraisal of a situation's favorability, an attribution of causality, and a perception of the intent to benefit, all of which require cognitive resources similar to those required by delight.

Happiness and satisfaction, gratitude and delight
As a result of the preceding analysis, we suggest that gratitude relates more closely to delight, whereas happiness coincides with satisfaction. We summarize these propositions in Table 12.1 (adapted from Soscia 2007), which demonstrates that gratitude is possible only when the scenario includes an intentional agent's intent to benefit a particular person and high emotional and/or cognitive activation results (P1h). Happiness, satisfaction, and delight are possible in many more scenarios, including those in which gratitude is possible, but delight is restricted to scenarios with high emotional and/or cognitive activation positions. Thus, the constructs of gratitude and delight appear much closer in conceptual space than does gratitude to either satisfaction or happiness. Our propositions are consistent with Soscia's (2007) equation of happiness and satisfaction and offer intriguing opportunities for future study.

*Table 12.1   Propositions related to the relationships among gratitude,
satisfaction, happiness, and delight*

Intent	Emotional/cognitive activation	Causation		
		Self	Other1	Circumstances
General	High activation	P1a Happiness Delight	P1b Happiness Delight	P1c Happiness Delight
	Low activation	P1d Happiness Satisfaction	P1e Happiness Satisfaction	P1f Happiness Satisfaction
Personal	High activation	P1g Happiness Delight	P1h Happiness Delight Gratitude	P1i Happiness Delight
	Low activation	P1j Happiness Satisfaction	P1k Happiness Satisfaction	P1l Happiness Satisfaction

Notes:
1   P1m: Gratitude may be induced in any of the "other"-caused conditions, but only in the personal intent with high activation condition does it resemble the positive-sum gratitude of caring described by Buck (2004), which forms the basis of our analysis.
P5n: The gratitude induced in the other "other"-caused cells would more likely be induced by a desire to conform to societal norms, consistent with Buck's (2004) zero-sum gratitude of exchange.

Source: Adapted from Soscia (2007).

These propositions offer much to researchers studying satisfaction and delight, for, if as we propose gratitude is closely associated with delight, researchers studying delight could borrow concepts and measures related to gratitude from the psychology literature and perhaps assess delight more accurately. If gratitude and delight co-occur in other-caused scenarios with personal intent, measures of gratitude also may help distinguish delight more clearly from satisfaction. This link offers specific direction for research into delight. It may be that gratitude is an emotional marker distinguishing satisfaction from delight and possibly providing an answer to the question of whether the actual outcome has sufficiently surpassed expectations to indicate that delight (rather than satisfaction) is the emotion being experienced. As a result, it may be possible to take definitions and tools from the psychological study of gratitude to help us better understand and diagnose delight.

CONCLUSION

Cicero called gratitude the parent of all the other virtues (quoted in McCullough and Tsang 2004). It is apparent that we benefit in our personal lives from its experience and expression. But we also are beginning to understand that gratitude plays an important role in our economic relationships as well. What is not fully understood is what behaviors have the potential to generate gratitude in the economic context, how appropriately to express such feelings, and the impact of feelings and expressions on buyer and seller outcomes. Putting up a billboard or running a print advertisement that says "thank you" may be appropriate to acknowledge those who assisted after a national disaster, but it is doubtful that such expressions from a company engaged in everyday business will have the same positive effects. We call on scholars to explore further the concept of gratitude and its implications for relationship marketing.

NOTES

1. It is possible for one to feel grateful without showing it or to convey gratitude when it is not felt (Buck 2004). While these offer viable areas for future research, we focus exclusively on actual feelings of gratitude, as characterized by the "gratitude of caring" (Buck 2004), and sincere expression.
2. Of course, the investor may attribute the improvement in the economy to various financial, business, or political leaders, in which case gratitude may exist, but the example works in its basic form and is particularly instructive in the next appraisal theory category of intent.

REFERENCES

Algoe, Sarah B. (2006), "A Relational Account of Gratitude: A Positive Emotion that Strengthens Interpersonal Connections," *Dissertation Abstracts International: Section B: The Sciences and Engineering*, 66(9-B), 5137.
Anderson, James C. and James A. Narus (1990), "A Model of Distribution Firm and Manufacturer Firm Working Partnerships," *Journal of Marketing*, 54 (January), 42–58.
Bagozzi, R.P. (1975), "Marketing as Exchange," *Journal of Marketing*, 39 (October), 32–9.
Bartlett, Monica Y. and David DeSteno (2006), "Gratitude and Prosocial Behavior," *Psychological Science*, 17 (April), 319–25.
Becker, Lawrence C. (1986), *Reciprocity*, New York: Routledge & Kegan Paul.
Bendapudi, Neeli and Robert P. Leone (2002), "Managing Business-to-Business Customer Relationships Following Key Contact Employee Turnover in a Vendor Firm," *Journal of Marketing*, 66 (April), 83–101.
Bendapudi, Neeli and Robert P. Leone (2003), "Psychological Implications of Customer Participation in Co-Production," *Journal of Marketing*, 67 (January), 14–28.
Bone, Sterling A., Katherine N. Lemon, Katie Liljenquist and R. Bruce Money (2007),

"The Power of a 'Thank You': The Influence of Customer Complimenting Behavior on Customer Loyalty," working paper, Brigham Young University, Provo, UT.

Buck, Ross (2004), "The Gratitude of Exchange and the Gratitude of Caring: A Developmental-Interactionist Perspective of Moral Emotion," in Robert A. Emmons and Michael E. McCullough (eds.), *The Psychology of Gratitude*, New York: Oxford University Press, pp. 100–122.

Cannon, Joseph P. and Christian Homburg (2001), "Buyer–Supplier Relationships and Customer Firm Costs," *Journal of Marketing*, 65 (January), 29–43.

Carey, J. Ronald, Stephen H. Clicque, Barbara A. Leighton and Frank Milton (1976), "A Test of Positive Reinforcement of Customers," *Journal of Marketing*, 40 (October), 98–100.

Churchill, Gilbert A., Jr. and Carol Surprenant (1982), "An Investigation into the Determinants of Customer Satisfaction," *Journal of Marketing Research*, 19 (November), 491–504.

Czepiel, John A. (1990), "Service Encounters and Service Relationships: Implications for Research," *Journal of Business Research*, 20 (January), 13–21.

Dahl, Darren W., Heather Honea and Rajesh V. Manchanda (2005), "Three Rs of Interpersonal Consumer Guilt: Relationship, Reciprocity, Reparation," *Journal of Consumer Psychology*, 15, 307–15.

Dick, Alan S. and Kunal Basu (1994), "Customer Loyalty: Toward an Integrated Conceptual Framework," *Journal of the Academy of Marketing Science*, 22 (Spring), 99–113.

Doney, Patricia M. and Joseph P. Cannon (1997), "An Examination of the Nature of Trust in Buyer–Seller Relationships," *Journal of Marketing*, 61 (April), 35–51.

Dwyer, F. Robert, Paul H. Schurr and Sejo Oh (1987), "Developing Buyer–Seller Relationships," *Journal of Marketing*, 51 (April), 11–27.

Emmons, Robert A. (2004), "The Psychology of Gratitude: An Introduction," in Robert A. Emmons and Michael E. McCullough (eds.), *The Psychology of Gratitude*, New York: Oxford University Press, pp. 3–16.

Emmons, Robert A. and Michael E. McCullough (eds.) (2004), *The Psychology of Gratitude*, New York: Oxford University Press.

Forgas, Joseph P. (1995), "Mood and Judgment: The Affect Infusion Model (AIM)," *Psychological Bulletin*, 117 (January), 39–57.

Fredrickson, Barbara L. (2004), "Gratitude, Like Other Positive Emotions, Broadens and Builds," in Robert A. Emmons and Michael E. McCullough (eds.), *The Psychology of Gratitude*, New York: Oxford University Press, pp. 145–66.

Ganesan, Shankar (1994), "Determinants of Long-Term Orientation in Buyer–Seller Relationships," *Journal of Marketing*, 58 (April), 1–19.

Garbarino, Ellen and Mark S. Johnson (1999), "The Different Roles of Satisfaction, Trust, and Commitment in Customer Relationships," *Journal of Marketing*, 63 (April), 70–87.

Grönroos, Christian (1997), "Value-Driven Relational Marketing: From Products to Resources and Competencies," *Journal of Marketing Management*, 13 (July), 407–19.

Gwinner, Kevin P., Dwayne D. Gremler and Mary Jo Bitner (1998), "Relational Benefits in Services Industries: The Customer's Perspective," *Journal of the Academy of Marketing Science*, 26 (Spring), 101–14.

Harpham, Edward J. (2004), "Gratitude in the History of Ideas," in Robert A. Emmons and Michael E. McCullough (eds.), *The Psychology of Gratitude*, New York: Oxford University Press, pp. 19–36.

Heilbrunn, Gert (1972), "Thank You," *Journal of the American Psychoanalytic Association*, 20 (July), 512–16.

Holbrook, Morris B. (1993), "Gratitudes and Latitudes in M.B.A. Attitudes: Customer Orientation and the *Business Week* Poll," *Marketing Letters*, 4(3), 267–78.

Houston, Franklin S. and Julie B. Gassenheimer (1987), "Marketing and Exchange," *Journal of Marketing*, 51 (October), 3–18.

Ireland, Thomas R. (1990), "The Formation of Organizations, Networks and Markets," *Journal of Behavioral Economics*, 19 (Spring), 103–24.

Jacoby, Jacob and Robert W. Chestnut (1978), *Brand Loyalty: Measurement and Management*, New York: Wiley.
Jolls, C., C.R. Sunstein and R. Thaler (1998), "A Behavioral Approach to Law and Economics," *Stanford Law Review*, 50, 1471–1550.
Kahneman, Daniel and Dale T. Miller (1986), "Norm Theory: Comparing Reality to Its Alternatives," *Psychological Review*, 93 (April), 136–53.
Komter, Aafke Elisabeth (2004), "Gratitude and Gift Exchange," in Robert A. Emmons and Michael E. McCullough (eds.), *The Psychology of Gratitude*, New York: Oxford University Press, pp. 195–212.
Lazarus, R.S. (1991), *Emotions and Adaptation*, New York: Oxford University Press.
Levitt, Theodore (1983), "After the Sale Is Over ...," *Harvard Business Review*, 61 (September–October), 87–93.
Lynn, Michael and Michael McCall (2000), "Gratitude and Gratuity: A Meta-Analysis of Research on the Service–Tipping Relationship," *Journal of Socio-Economics*, 29(2), 203–14.
Macneil, Ian (1980), *The New Social Contract: An Inquiry into Modern Contractual Relations*, New Haven, CT: Yale University Press.
McCullough, Michael E. and Jo-Ann Tsang (2004), "Parent of the Virtues? The Prosocial Contours of Gratitude," in Robert A. Emmons and Michael E. McCullough (eds.), *The Psychology of Gratitude*, New York: Oxford University Press, pp. 123–40.
McCullough, Michael E., Shelley D. Kilpatrick, Robert A. Emmons and David B. Larson (2001), "Is Gratitude a Moral Affect?," *Psychological Bulletin*, 127(2), 249–66.
Morales, Andrea C. (2005), "Giving Firms an 'E' for Effort: Consumer Responses to High-Effort Firms," *Journal of Consumer Research*, 31 (March), 806–12.
Morgan, Robert M. and Shelby D. Hunt (1994), "The Commitment-Trust Theory of Relationship Marketing," *Journal of Marketing*, 58 (July), 20–38.
Ngobo, Paul-Valentin (1999), "Decreasing Returns in Customer Loyalty: Does It Really Matter to Delight the Customers?," *Advances in Consumer Research*, 26(1), 469–76.
Oliver, Richard L. (1980), "A Cognitive Model of the Antecedents and Consequences of Satisfaction Decisions," *Journal of Marketing Research*, 17 (November), 460–69.
Oliver, Richard L. (1993), "Cognitive, Affective, and Attribute Bases of the Satisfaction Response," *Journal of Consumer Research*, 20 (December), 418–30.
Oliver, Richard L. (1999), "Whence Customer Loyalty?," *Journal of Marketing*, 63 (Special Issue), 33–44.
Oliver, Richard L. and Robert A. Westbrook (1993), "Profiles of Consumer Emotions and Satisfaction in Ownership and Usage," *Journal of Consumer Satisfaction, Dissatisfaction and Complaining Behavior*, 6, 12–27.
Oliver, Richard L., Roland T. Rust and Sajeev Varki (1997), "Customer Delight: Foundations, Findings, and Managerial Insight," *Journal of Retailing*, 73(3), 311–36.
Ortony, A., G.L. Clore and A. Collins (1988), *The Cognitive Structure of Emotions*, Cambridge: Cambridge University Press.
Palmatier, Robert W. (2008), *Relationship Marketing*, Cambridge, MA: Marketing Science Institute (MSI).
Palmatier, Robert W., Rajiv P. Dant, Dhruv Grewal and Kenneth R. Evans (2006), "Factors Influencing the Effectiveness of Relationship Marketing: A Meta-Analysis," *Journal of Marketing*, 70 (October), 136–53.
Palmatier, Robert W., Rajiv P. Dant and Dhruv Grewal (2007), "A Comparative Longitudinal Analysis of Theoretical Perspectives of Interorganizational Relationship Performance," *Journal of Marketing*, 71 (October), 172–94.
Palmatier, Robert W., Cheryl Burke Jarvis, Jennifer R. Bechkoff and Frank R. Kardes (2009), "The Role of Customer Gratitude in Relationship Marketing," *Journal of Marketing*, 73(5), 1–18.
Price, Linda L. and Eric J. Arnould (1999), "Commercial Friendships: Service Provider–Client Relationships in Context," *Journal of Marketing*, 63 (October), 38–56.
Raggio, Randle D. and Judith Anne Garretson Folse (2007), "Gratitude Works: An

Investigation of Moderators and the Mediating Role of Affective Commitment in Driving Positive Outcomes," working paper, Louisiana State University.

Raggio, Randle D., Anna Green Walz, Mousumi Bose and Judith Anne Garretson Folse (2009), "Gratitude in the Relational Exchange Paradigm," working paper, Louisiana State University.

Reynolds, Kristy E. and Sharon E. Beatty (1999), "Customer Benefits and Company Consequences of Customer–Salesperson Relationships in Retailing," *Journal of Retailing*, 75(1), 11–32.

Roberts, Robert C. (2004), "The Blessings of Gratitude: A Conceptual Analysis," in Robert A. Emmons and Michael E. McCullough (eds.), *The Psychology of Gratitude*, New York: Oxford University Press, pp. 58–80.

Roseman, I.J. (1991), "Appraisal Determinants of Discrete Emotions," *Cognition and Emotion*, 5, 161–200.

Rust, Roland T. and Richard L. Oliver (2000), "Should We Delight the Customer?," *Journal of the Academy of Marketing Science*, 28 (Winter), 86–94.

Scherer, K.R. (1985), "Criteria for Emotion-Antecedent Appraisal: A Review," in V. Hamilton, G.H. Bower and N.H. Frijda (eds.), *Cognitive Perspectives on Emotion and Motivation*, Dordrecht: Kluwer, pp. 89–126.

Schimmel, Solomon (2004), "Gratitude in Judaism," in Robert A. Emmons and Michael E. McCullough (eds.), *The Psychology of Gratitude*, New York: Oxford University Press, pp. 37–57.

Selnes, Fred (1998), "Antecedents and Consequences of Trust and Satisfaction in Buyer–Seller Relationships," *European Journal of Marketing*, 32(3), 305–22.

Sheth, Jagdish N. and Atul Parvatiyar (2000), *Handbook of Relationship Marketing*, Thousand Oaks, CA: Sage.

Smith, Adam ([1759] 2000), *The Theory of Moral Sentiments*, Amherst, NY: Prometheus.

Smith, Adam ([1776] 2003), *The Wealth of Nations*, New York: Bantam Dell.

Soscia, Isabella (2007), "Gratitude, Delight, or Guilt: The Role of Consumers' Emotions in Predicting Postconsumption Behaviors," *Psychology and Marketing*, 24 (October), 871–94.

Steindl-Rast, David (2004), "Gratitude as Thankfulness and as Gratefulness," in Robert A. Emmons and Michael E. McCullough (eds.), *The Psychology of Gratitude*, New York: Oxford University Press, pp. 282–90.

Watkins, Philip C. (2004), "Gratitude and Subjective Well-Being," in Robert A. Emmons and Michael E. McCullough (eds.), *The Psychology of Gratitude*, New York: Oxford University Press, pp. 167–94.

Watkins, Philip C., Jason Scheer, Melinda Ovnicek and Russell Kolts (2006), "The Debt of Gratitude: Dissociating Gratitude and Indebtedness," *Cognition and Emotion*, 20(2), 217–41.

Weiner, B. (1985), "An Attributional Theory of Achievement Motivation and Emotion," *Psychological Review*, 92, 548–73.

Weiner, B. and S. Graham (1989), "Understanding the Motivational Role of Affect: Lifespan Research from an Attributional Perspective," *Cognition and Emotion*, 3, 401–19.

Westbrook, Robert A. and Richard L. Oliver (1991), "The Dimensionality of Consumption Emotion Patterns and Consumer Satisfaction," *Journal of Consumer Research*, 18 (June), 84–91.

Young, Louise (2006), "Trust: Looking Forward and Back," *Journal of Business and Industrial Marketing*, 21(7), 439–45.

13. Anti-relationship marketing: understanding relationship-destroying behaviors

Stephen A. Samaha and Robert W. Palmatier

INTRODUCTION

Prior research in marketing highlights the important role that relationship marketing (RM) plays in building long-term, successful customer relationships. Relationship marketing generates positive word of mouth and enhances the customer's value to the firm by increasing the length, breadth, and depth of the buying relationship (Bolton et al. 2003; Verhoef 2003; Palmatier 2008). Furthermore, RM enhances both customer trust and commitment, leading to superior seller performance (Moorman et al. 1992; Morgan and Hunt 1994; Sirdeshmukh et al. 2002). Given these benefits, it is not surprising that most RM research emphasizes positive, long-term, and mutually beneficial relationships that enhance value.

Yet relationship research outside of marketing increasingly suggests that negative behaviors may affect close relationships more than do positive behaviors (Baumeister et al. 2001). For example, research into impression formation repeatedly has confirmed a positive–negative asymmetry effect (e.g. N.H. Anderson 1965; Skowronski and Carlston 1989), which suggests that negative information receives more processing attention and contributes more strongly to lasting impressions than does positive information. Research into successful marriages also finds that the absence of negative behaviors more strongly relates to relationship quality than does the presence of positive behaviors (Gottman 1979, 1994). Palmatier et al.'s (2006) meta-analysis from the marketing tradition supports this proposition; of all the antecedents studied, conflict has the largest absolute impact on relationship trust and commitment. The negative effects of conflict tend to overshadow the positive benefits associated with all other RM efforts. Taken together, these results imply that the long-term success of a relationship may depend more on not doing bad things than on doing good things.

If so, it becomes critical not only to emphasize and encourage positive RM behaviors but also to understand the important role of negative behaviors in terms of undermining marketing relationships, that is, anti-relationship marketing. Much prior research emphasizes growing marketing relationships; this chapter takes an opposite tack and studies the behaviors that can undermine relationship marketing. Specifically, we focus on three anti-relationship marketing or relationship-destroying behaviors: opportunism, conflict, and unfairness. Managing and suppressing these detriments can support long-term exchange relationships and their key outcomes, including performance, profitability, and satisfaction. Figure 13.1 presents an overview of the antecedents of these three relationship-destroying behaviors as well as the key exchange relationship outcomes influenced by them.

RELATIONSHIP-DESTROYING BEHAVIORS

Managing Opportunism

Understanding and managing opportunism are crucial for several reasons. To begin with, opportunism can damage the relational norms that enable long-lasting marketing relationships (Gundlach et al. 1995). Opportunism makes firms and business partners less likely to behave in flexible or compromising manners, which can have strong negative effects on performance (Samaha et al. 2009). Opportunism also decreases satisfaction (Rawwas et al. 1997) and may be perceived as an act of betrayal. A sense of betrayal likely prompts retaliatory behaviors, which destroy the relationship even further (Bacharach and Lawler 1980, 1981; Kumar 1996). Although opportunism may initially increase outcomes for the opportunistic party, it ultimately can restrict value creation, increase costs (especially transaction costs), and decrease revenues for both parties in an exchange relationship (Wathne and Heide 2000). For example, a firm faced with opportunism by its partner may be forced to invest in additional monitoring or surveillance technologies to curb that behavior. Finally, not only does opportunism tend to lead to lower levels of trust and commitment, which hinder RM efforts (Ting et al. 2007), but also it hampers the development of reciprocity. Thus, it is critical to identify and manage issues involving opportunism.

Managing Conflict

Conflict represents another, widely occurring, relationship-destroying behavior that has far-reaching implications across multiple dimensions. As a major source of dissatisfaction in dyadic relationships (Frazier et al. 1989; J.C. Anderson and Narus 1990), conflict can consume up to

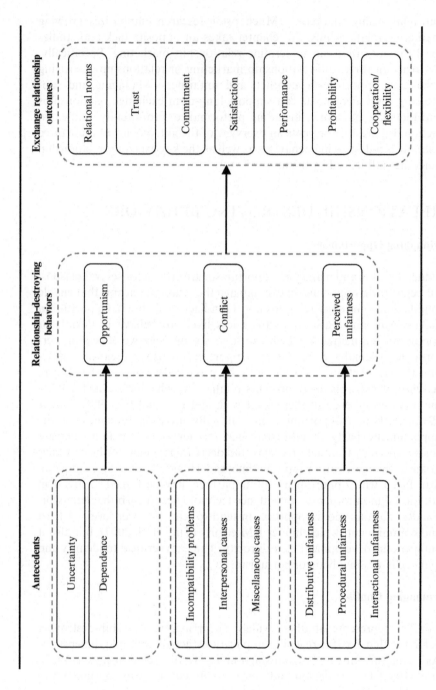

Figure 13.1   Antecedents and outcomes of relationship-destroying behaviors

20 percent of a relationship partner's time, which decreases the resources available to accomplish other tasks (Song et al. 2006). In addition, conflict may increase retaliatory behaviors and reduce productivity and profitability (Souder 1987; Cadogan et al. 2005), along with flexibility. Persistent, ongoing, disruptive conflicts over time prevent partners from making the necessary allowances for change, so the flexibility they might have used to achieve superior performance in dynamic environments disappears. Conflict may also make individual representatives more anxious, inhibit their cognitive functioning, and make them less receptive to the ideas of others (Jehn 1995; Jehn and Mannix 2001). In turn, the sharing of ideas and innovativeness needed to enhance performance may not occur (Matsuo 2005). Conflict even directly decreases performance in a variety of settings (e.g., Gaski 1984; Jehn 1994; Rose and Shoham 2004). By inhibiting communication, knowledge dissemination, and market orientation, conflict restricts the firm's ability to satisfy its customers' needs and expectations (Ruekert and Walker 1987; Jaworski and Kohli 1993). Finally, conflict may reduce commitment (E. Anderson and Weitz 1992). This vast range of negative behaviors and consequences makes it critical to suppress conflict, one of the negative behaviors we investigate.

Managing Unfairness

As with opportunism and conflict, perceptions of unfairness influence key exchange outcomes, including turnover, satisfaction, performance, productivity, commitment, and more. However, perceptions of unfairness may be even more salient, because the related issues tend to be highly emotionally laden: Unfairness increases feelings of anger, rage, hate, frustration, resentment, indignation, and so on (Sprecher 1986; Mikula 1987). Furthermore, though some degree of conflict and opportunism should be expected in exchange relationships, parties may perceive unfairness as more deliberate and intentional, which increases their tendency to assign blame, as well as their feelings of anger and aggression (Blount 1995). We also posit that perceptions of unfairness play a greater role in undermining relationships than has been acknowledged, particularly because reciprocity theory and equity theory suggest that people go out of their way to punish unfair behaviors, even at a cost to themselves (Kahneman et al. 1986; Offerman 2002). Thus, unfair acts could incite even greater negative retaliation and backlash than that provoked by other negative behaviors, owing to people's need to punish. Unfairness clearly is a critical negative behavior that must be managed and suppressed to build successful, long-term exchange relationships.

We provide a more in-depth overview of opportunism, conflict, and unfairness, as well as their antecedents and approaches for managing or suppressing them, in the following sections.

OPPORTUNISM

Williamson (1975: 6) defines opportunism as "self-interest seeking with guile" and provides examples such as withholding or distorting information, shirking or failing to fulfill promises or obligations, and exploiting a partner's assets or resources. Transaction cost economics suggests opportunism arises whenever it is feasible and profitable. People engage in such opportunistic behavior to influence value creation and wealth distribution (Ghosh and John 1999).

Wathne and Heide (2000) differentiate passive from active opportunism. Passive opportunism includes behaviors that are reactive in nature, such as refusing to adapt to changing circumstances, showing inflexibility, misrepresenting one's own abilities, failing to comply with requests, and evading obligations. Active opportunism instead features proactive acts that have been explicitly prohibited, like stealing joint assets, exploiting a partner firm's key personnel or know-how without provision or remedy, and cheating. It is important to note that opportunism does not include other forms of self-interest seeking, such as hard bargaining, intense negotiating, or frequent disagreements. What sets it apart from these self-interest-seeking behaviors is the notion of guile, that is, "lying, stealing, cheating and calculated efforts to mislead, distort, disguise, obfuscate or otherwise confuse" (Williamson 1985: 47). The fundamental essence of opportunism is the element of deceit involved (Macneil 1982).

Drivers of Opportunism

Table 13.1 provides a summary of antecedents of opportunism. We discuss two of them that reflect common situations in which opportunism arises: uncertainty and dependence.

Uncertainty
All other things being equal, when a firm has difficulty assessing or monitoring its partner's actions – that is, suffers substantial uncertainty in its exchange relationship – the likelihood of opportunism increases, because the other party recognizes its lower likelihood of getting caught and behaves opportunistically. Uncertainty generally is classified into two categories: behavioral and environmental.

Behavioral uncertainty (Williamson 1985) pertains to problems

Table 13.1   Antecedents of opportunism

Reference	Context	Implications
Williamson (1975)	Study of the economics of internal organizations	If transaction-specific assets make an exchange partner difficult to replace as a result of high switching costs, requests for adaptation may be opportunistically exploited.
John (1984)	Study of franchised dealers in an oil corporation	Franchisee opportunism is positively related to the franchisor's use of coercive power or perceptions of a bureaucratic mode of governance.
E. Anderson (1988)	Study of sales managers in electronic components industry	Higher levels of asset specificity and behavioral uncertainty are positively related to salesperson opportunism.
Dahlstrom and Boyle (1994)	Uses cognitive evaluation theory to assess interorganizational relationships in buyer–supplier relationships	The use of control or threats positively affects opportunism, which in turn affects a buyer's intrinsic motivation to purchase.
Heide (1994)	Study of interorganizational governance in marketing channels	Unilateral dependence or commitment may increase the likelihood of the other party behaving opportunistically.
Lee (1998)	Develops and tests a model of the determinants of exporters' intentions to form strategic alliances with their foreign exchange partners	Degree of decision-making uncertainty held by exporters, exporters' cultural distance, and exporters' economic ethnocentrism all have positive effects on opportunism.
Joshi and Stump (1999)	Integrates transaction cost analysis and relational exchange theory to identify antecedents of opportunism for purchasing managers in manufacturing industries	Uncertainty leads to reduced commitment and increased opportunism.
Gruen and Shah (2000)	Studies the determinants, outcomes, plan objectivity, and implementation in category management relationships	Supplier–retailer conflict increases opportunism.

Table 13.1   (continued)

Reference	Context	Implications
Li (2002)	Examines sales force opportunism in emerging markets	Opportunism is traced to behavioral and environmental uncertainty.
Crosno and Dahlstrom (2008)	Meta-analytic review of opportunism in exchange relationships	Environmental uncertainty is positively associated with partner opportunism.
Hawkins et al. (2008)	Research synthesis and new frontiers for opportunism	A review of antecedents and consequences of opportunism and a summary of past empirical research.

associated with monitoring an exchange partner's performance. These problems generally entail the challenges of assessing a partner's performance, actions, and compliance in an exchange relationship (Rindfleisch and Heide 1997). Environmental uncertainty instead refers to unanticipated changes in the circumstances or conditions associated with the exchange (Noordewier et al. 1990). It reflects the unpredictability of the environment and the inability to predict or plan for changes because of this uncertainty (Joshi and Stump 1999).

Dependence
Another important antecedent of opportunism, dependence exists when the rewards sought and received by a particular party in the relationship are not available outside of that relationship (Thibaut and Kelley 1959; Lambe et al. 2001). Dependence often results from the existence of transaction-specific assets (TSA), which can be thought of as nontransferable investments whose utility is unique to the specific relationship. These TSAs can be problematic, in that they cannot be redeployed easily in other relationships should the focal relationship fail. As a result, TSAs effectively create a lock-in situation for the party that has invested more resources in the relationship. When one party is substantially more invested than the other, it suffers the risk of opportunism, because the less invested party has less to lose.

Suppressors of Opportunism

Contract use
The notion of using contracts and governance mechanisms has attracted considerable attention in recent years, and scholars of marketing have

been particularly interested in the design of contracts or governance mechanisms that can limit the negative effects of opportunism. Not surprisingly, contracts historically have been viewed as important mechanisms for curbing opportunistic behaviors (Williamson 1979), because detailed contracts can protect against partner opportunism through the threat of legal enforcement (Joskow 1987). Prior research also has shown that contracts are effective for inhibiting opportunism in the context of joint ventures and alliances (Killing 1983; Schaan 1983).

Monitoring

Monitoring involves the explicit steps taken by a member to observe the actions of its exchange partners. Marketing literature distinguishes two types: output and behavior monitoring. Output monitoring involves measuring the visible consequences of a partner's actions, such as the supplier's delivery time, order accuracy, and product quality. In contrast, behavior monitoring focuses on scrutinizing and evaluating the processes that should produce the desired outcomes. For example, a buyer may insist on onsite inspections of its suppliers' manufacturing facilities to ensure they employ appropriate processes that will result in its desired final products. Conceptually, monitoring offers control by reducing the information asymmetry between exchange partners (Eisenhardt 1985; Balakrishnan and Koza 1993). Because deviations from established terms can result in penalties or termination of the relationship, parties are motivated to fulfill their responsibilities.

Bilateral idiosyncratic investments

Bilateral idiosyncratic investments occur when both parties make idiosyncratic investments in the relationship, whether tangible or intangible. These investments play an important role in stabilizing the relationships of exchange partners, because they represent a credible sign of each party's commitment to the relationship and signal their honorable intentions (E. Anderson and Weitz 1992; Brown et al. 2000). Moreover, such investments produce expectations of continued exchanges into the future, because the termination of the relationship would substantially reduce the value of these assets, which cannot be redeployed easily elsewhere.

Formalization

Formalization refers to the extent to which rules and explicit procedures govern the relationship between the interorganizational partners (Van de Ven 1976; John and Reve 1982). Defined as "the emphasis placed on following specific rules and procedures" (John and Martin 1984: 172), formalization offers a process control mechanism that seeks to set explicit standards and rules so that exchange partners do not deviate from their expected duties. In a meta-analytic review of opportunism in exchange relationships, Crosno and Dahlstrom (2008) conclude that formalization relates negatively to exchange partner opportunism.

Consequences of Opportunism

The failure to manage opportunism can result in a multitude of negative consequences for exchange relationships. In particular, opportunism may provoke retaliatory behaviors and cause parties to withdraw or limit their commitments over time (Bacharach and Lawler 1980, 1981), which would erode the long-term gains that accrue to both parties. In retailer–supplier relationships, opportunism reduces dyadic performance in the realms of product quality, delivery, and goal attainment (Lonsdale 2001). Opportunistic behaviors can also lower trust (Bell and Anderson 2000), diminish commitment to a relationship (Rousseau 2001), and reduce franchise system performance (Gassenheimer et al. 1996). Parkhe (1993) even demonstrates that perceptions of opportunistic behavior have significant and negative effects on alliance performance. Although opportunism may initially increase outcomes for the opportunistic party, this behavior ultimately restricts value creation, increases costs, and decreases revenues for both parties in the relationship (Wathne and Heide 2000).

When opportunism occurs, relational sentiments become undermined, so partners should be less willing to behave in a cooperative or flexible manner. If a firm perceives opportunism from another party, it may conclude that it has been too lenient and needs to be more restrictive to curb its opportunism. Such increased restrictiveness or rigidity likely diminishes interparty flexibility. Furthermore, firms that perceive the threat of opportunism sense a greater need to screen, negotiate, and monitor their partner firm's behavior, which increases their information costs (Hennart 1988; Nooteboom et al. 1997). As firms begin to spend more time monitoring and become less willing to trust or rely on their partners, coordination in terms of resource sharing and activity integration becomes more difficult and unstable. Interparty collaboration and cooperation also likely suffer. As Williamson and Ouchi (1981: 351) put it, "It is costly to sort out those who are opportunistic from those who are not." The increased uncertainty and monitoring costs that result from opportunism between exchange partners may ultimately result in reduced performance and interparty relationship failures.

CONFLICT

Many researchers likely agree that conflict is an inescapable component of close exchange relationships, pervading virtually all interorganizational activities (K. Lewin 1947; Thomas 1976). Issues involving conflict appear more critical than ever before, though, owing to greater workforce diversity and cultural issues, an increasing reliance on teams, and the frequent restructuring of many business organizations (Rahim et al. 2000; Jehn and Mannix 2001). Conflict tends to occur when one party perceives that the other is interfering with the attainment of its goals (Rosenbloom 1999; Stern and El-Ansary 1992). Rahim (2002: 207) defines conflict as "an interactive process manifested in incompatibility, disagreement or dissonance within or between social entities (i.e., individual, group organization, etc.)." Any definition therefore must include some degree of incompatibility between parties, as an antecedent of conflict.

At least three different types of conflict appear in prior organizational literature: relationship, task, and process conflict. The first form involves disagreements based on personal and social issues that are not related to work. Task conflict instead describes disagreements about work being done in groups. Finally, process conflict centers on work but in the context of the task strategy and delegation of duties and resources (Jehn 1995, 1997; Jehn et al. 1999).

Drivers of Conflict

We summarize, in Table 13.2, some antecedents of conflict.

Incompatibility problems
Rahim (2002) provides an excellent and detailed overview of the types of incompatibility that likely cause conflict. His research generally suggests that conflict arises from activities, preferences, or behaviors by one party that are incongruent or incompatible with the needs of the other party.

Interpersonal causes
Communications-based misunderstandings also provide a source of conflict. Minimal communication, for example, produces only low knowledge of others, which may cause coordination difficulties that can lead to conflict (Pondy 1967). Yet excessive communication also can be a source of misunderstanding and conflict (Putnam and Poole 1987). Words, facial expressions, body language, and speech all can lead to attributions of intent, which can cause conflict (Thomas and Pondy 1977).

Table 13.2 Antecedents of conflict

Reference	Context	Implications
Horwitz (1956)	Investigation of psychological needs as a function of social environments	Aggressive conflicts emerge when people perceive that their legitimate level of power within a given social environment has been reduced.
Pondy (1967)	Overview of organizational conflict	Conflict is treated as a series of stages, consisting of latency, feeling, perception, manifestation, and aftermath.
Walton et al. (1969)	Attempts to identify contextual factors that could account for interdepartmental conflict	Interdepartmental conflict is associated with the degree to which the operational objectives differ between two departments, as well as barriers to communication.
Roloff (1987)	Examination of communication and conflict	Conflict tends to occur when parties engage in activities that are incompatible with those of other exchange members.
Alter (1990)	An exploratory study of conflict in interorganizational systems	Higher levels of differentiation and complexity in interorganizational systems are associated with higher levels of conflict.
Stern and El-Ansary (1992)	Study of marketing channels	Conflict tends to occur when one party perceives another as interfering with the attainment of its goals.
J.A. Wall and Callister (1995)	Provides an overview of conflict, its core processes, and its effects	Causes of conflict are grouped broadly into three main categories: individual characteristics, interpersonal factors, and issues.
Jehn (1997)	Presents a multifaceted qualitative investigation of everyday conflict using organizational work teams	The presence is suggested of four dimensions of intragroup conflict: negative emotionality, importance, acceptability, and resolution potential.
Rahim (2002)	Examination of organizational conflict management	Six general scenarios in which conflict may occur and develop are outlined.
Hinds and Bailey (2003)	Identifies antecedents of conflict in geographically distributed teams	Overreliance on technology and geographical dispersion can increase conflict.

Table 13.2 (continued)

Reference	Context	Implications
Barki and Hartwick (2004)	Conceptualizes the construct of interpersonal conflict	Three properties generally associated with conflict situations are identified: disagreement, negative emotions, and interference.

Miscellaneous causes
A reduction of power due to the actions of another generally causes conflict to develop (Horwitz 1956), such as when one party tries to control the other, which causes eventual backlash or resistance to that control (Phillips and Cheston 1978). Conflict also is likely when one party's gains come at the expense of the other's (Walton et al. 1969), including situations that produce the perception that another party's intentions run counter to one's own payoffs (Pruitt and Rubin 1986; Winter 1987). In addition, when the other party's intentions appear to violate norms of fairness and equity or are perceived as deliberately harmful to the party, conflict probably results (Aram and Salipante 1981; V.D. Wall and Nolan 1987). Finally, conflict is more likely to develop in response to issues that are highly complex and involved.

Suppressors of Conflict

Miscellaneous approaches
Research on conflict resolution and management is somewhat disjointed and varied, with many different approaches advocated by many different scholars. Rahim (2002: 206) realizes: "There is no clear set of guidelines to suggest how conflict can be reduced, ignored or enhanced to increase organizational learning and effectiveness." Deutsch (1990) recommends that parties face the conflict directly and listen attentively to deal with their issues, but Hocker and Wilmot (1991) recommend that disputants should try to change the other party's behaviors, the conditions that cause the conflict, or their own behaviors. Baron (1984) also suggests improving the mood and/or expressing disagreements in a manner that is more agreeable, while Kottler (1994) recommends disputants take greater responsibility for their actions and avoid blaming others. Tjosvold (1985) offers an open-minded approach; Tjosvold et al. (1992) recommend establishing cooperative goals and engaging in open discussions about opposing views. According to Osgood (1962), trust can defuse conflict, though Eiseman

(1978) and Gray (1985) advocate an integrative thinking approach, whereby the disputing parties try to imagine the conflict from the other party's point of view. J.A. Wall and Callister (1995) summarize some of these approaches, as well as others used to manage conflict.

Use of third parties

Another frequently mentioned approach pertains to the use of third parties (e.g., arbitrators, mediators) as a means to defuse and resolve conflicts. These third parties get called in to help resolve issues when the disputants themselves are unable or unwilling to do so. The main advantage of third parties is they do not have an incentive to behave unfairly toward either disputing partner, which makes them seem unbiased and trustworthy (Conlon and Sullivan 1999). Third parties also can offer a rich set of unique tools for managing conflict. For example, J.A. Wall and Lynn (1993) assert that conflict mediators typically have 100 different types of conflict-management techniques at their disposal. Overall, third parties help improve communications between the disputing parties (Shaw 1985, 1986) and lower the amount of stress involved (Zarski et al. 1985).

Five styles of handling conflict

Some researchers advocate a set of five conflict-handling styles (Blake and Mouton 1964; Thomas 1976; Rahim 1983), which Rahim (1983) classifies into categories: 1) integrating, 2) obliging, 3) dominating, 4) avoiding, and 5) compromising. These five styles of conflict management can be distinguished along two dimensions: concern for self and concern for others. Rahim (1983) provides further detailed information.

Consequences of Conflict

Understanding the effects of conflict is important not only because it is common in interorganizational relationships but also because its negative effects are pervasive and have consequences for many different aspects of marketing (J.C. Anderson and Narus 1990). The negative consequences of conflict have been well documented, including dysfunctional outcomes such as reduced productivity and relationship deterioration (Souder 1987), reduced market performance (e.g., Menon et al. 1996), diminished profit performance (Cadogan et al. 2005), decreased individual and group performance (Jehn 1995; Jehn et al. 1999), lower innovativeness (Matsuo 2005), decreased satisfaction (Frazier et al. 1989; J.C. Anderson and Narus 1990), poor cooperation (Skinner et al. 1992), and lower relational norms (Koza and Dant 2007). One of the most frequent consequences of conflict is upset parties (Bergman and Volkema 1989), which can be manifested as anger, feelings of hostility (Thomas 1976), emotional separation (Retzinger 1991), tension (Thomas 1976), anxiety (Ephross and Vassil 1993), and stress. These negative emotions in turn lead to personal frustrations (Thomas 1976; Chesler et al. 1978), poor job satisfaction (Derr 1978; Filley 1978), and ultimately reduced motivation and performance (Bergman and Volkema 1989). Moreover, the quality and the volume of communication might change as a result of conflict. Communication likely becomes more hostile, with more insults, distortions, and misunderstandings, even as the amount of communication increases or decreases (Thomas 1976; Pruitt and Rubin 1986; Sternberg and Dobson 1987; Bergman and Volkema 1989). That is, conflict might cause some partners to voice additional issues (Robbins 1974) but make others clam up and avoid their opponent altogether (Bergman and Volkema 1989). Other negative effects of conflict include avoidance (Bergman and Volkema 1989), confrontation (Morrill and Thomas 1992), threats and uses of physical force (Sternberg and Soriano 1984; Sternberg and Dobson 1987; van de Vliert 1990), harm to others (Thomas 1976), and coercion, disorder, and protest (Schelling 1960). Long-term conflict then likely leads to decreased commitment (Derr 1978; Filley 1978), greater absenteeism, and reduced productivity (Pondy 1967; D. Lewin 1987; Tjosvold 1991).

UNFAIRNESS

Popular media reports create the perception that unfairness in business is widespread; stories detailing unfair business practices span a wide variety of industries. Web sites such as www.planetfeedback.com, which allows consumers to voice their dissatisfaction with unfair business practices, are becoming the norm rather than an exception. The pervasiveness of unfairness perceptions in the modern business environment makes it particularly important to study perceived unfairness as an important negative driver of interfirm relationships. Finkel (2001: 47) defines fairness as right dealing and reciprocity in institutionalized relationships, which further suggests that it is critical to RM, owing to its overlap with reciprocity. This connection between fairness and reciprocity was highlighted in a *New York Times Magazine* article (Walker 2009), which states that "Perceived unfairness can throw reciprocity instincts into reverse: instead of being disproportionately grateful, you might feel disproportionately spiteful – and take your business, and your loyalty, elsewhere." Most fairness research is based on equity theory, which suggests that people should receive benefits or rewards that are in proportion to their own relative efforts or inputs (Adams 1963, 1965). According to equity theory, people compare the ratios of their own perceived work outcomes (i.e., rewards) to their own perceived work inputs (i.e., contributions) against the corresponding ratios of a comparison other (e.g., coworker, partner). If the ratios are unequal, the party with the lower ratio is inequitably underrewarded and consequently likely to experience anger and tension. To resolve these feelings, the party may adjust its own inputs or contributions to shift the unpleasant state to a more pleasant, equitable one.

Social exchange theory also characterizes the relationship between partners as a reciprocal exchange of resources (Homans 1961; Cropanzano and Mitchell 2005). However, reciprocity norms and equity theory dictate that, if an exchange partner receives fewer resources from the other party than it believes its contributions have warranted, perceived unfairness may result, which prompts that exchange partner to engage in behaviors designed to restore fairness. These behaviors might include harmful or punitive behaviors that punish the other party (Folger and Skarlicki 1998; Cropanzano and Mitchell 2005).

The notion of fairness plays an important role both within and across organizations. Organizational fairness has remained one of the most frequently researched subjects in industrial-organizational psychology and organizational behavior in recent years (Cropanzano and Greenberg 1997; Colquitt et al. 2001). Researchers also acknowledge the important role of fairness as a basic requirement for both the effective functioning of organizations and the satisfaction of their employees (Moore 1978). Unfairness (similarly to opportunism and conflict) results in a wide variety of negative consequences.

Drivers of Fairness or Unfairness

Perceptions of unfairness can stem from three main sources: 1) distributive, 2) procedural, and 3) interactional unfairness. Table 13.3 summarizes prior literature pertaining to each of these sources.

Distributive unfairness

Building on work by Adams (1963, 1965), we can define distributive fairness as the fairness in the outcomes that a party receives (Folger and Cropanzano 1998). When people make a distributive fairness decision, they are assessing whether the outcome or end result is fair (Folger and Cropanzano 1998). Generally, positive outcomes result from higher levels of perceived fairness. Furthermore, distributive fairness involves three major concepts (Cropanzano and Schminke 2001). First, it is the *perception* of a decision, *not* objective standards, that determines fairness. Second, the outcomes themselves are the focus of the decision. Third,

Table 13.3   Antecedents of unfairness

Reference	Context	Implications
Adams (1965)	Examines inequity in social exchange	Equity theory is advanced as a means for determining fairness: people compare their output/input ratios to those of others to determine what is fair or not fair.
Thibaut and Walker (1978)	Introduces the study of process-oriented fairness	Perceptions of fairness are related to the fairness of how decisions are made and how they are implemented.
Leventhal et al. (1980)	Examination of theories of fairness and allocation preferences	Six criteria are outlined that should be met if a procedure is to be judged as fair.
Bies and Moag (1986)	Introduces the study of interactional fairness	Perceptions of fairness depend on how people are treated, as well as the amount of information that they receive during the enactment of procedures.
Greenberg (1986)	Study of fairness in performance appraisals	Seven distinct determinants of fairness in performance evaluations are identified, and then factor-analyzed as two distinct factors: procedural and distributive determinants of fairness.
Sheppard and Lewicki (1987)	Describes incidents of fair and unfair treatments by supervisors and the principles that make these actions fair or unfair	Sixteen principles or guiding judgments about perceived managerial fairness are aggregated into six major clusters of fairness concerns.
Folger and Cropanzano (1998)	Examines the conditions of employment that lead people to believe that they are being treated fairly or unfairly	Distributive fairness involves evaluating the perceived fairness of the outcomes that a person receives.
Cohen-Charash and Spector (2001)	Meta-analysis of past organizational fairness research	An overview is provided of the three types of fairness constructs, and it is found that these constructs are distinct.
Cropanzano and Schminke (2001)	Examination of social fairness to build effective work groups	Distributive fairness decisions involve 1) subjective perceptions of fairness and not objective standards, 2) emphasis on

Table 13.3   (continued)

Reference	Context	Implications
		outcomes as a focal point for fairness, and 3) comparison to a referent standard to determine fairness or unfairness.
Nowakowski and Conlon (2005)	Provides a brief review of how the concept of fairness has evolved from a single construct (distributive) to one represented by distributive, procedural, interpersonal, and informational fairness	Fairness literature needs to focus more intently on indentifying key moderators of fairness outcome relationships.

decisions involving distributive fairness are relative and must be compared against a referent standard to determine fairness or unfairness.

Research with respect to distributive fairness generally is based on work by Adams (1965), who used equity theory to evaluate fairness. As we have already noted, equity theory holds that people compare the ratios of their perceived work outcomes (i.e., rewards) to their perceived work inputs (i.e., contributions) with the corresponding ratios of a comparison other. The party with the lower ratio feels poorly rewarded and angry (Greenberg 1990), so should adjust its inputs to pursue a more pleasant, equitable state (Greenberg 1984). Such altered contributions may be either behavioral (e.g., altering job performance) or psychological (e.g., altering perceptions of work outcomes) (Walster et al. 1978).

Procedural unfairness
Despite the potential insights derived from examining distributive fairness, researchers also began to identify fairness issues that were more process-oriented rather than outcome-oriented. Such theorization led to the development of the concept of procedural fairness, which involves the fairness of rules, policies, and procedures. Whereas distributive fairness focuses on the perceived fairness of the *outcomes*, procedural fairness focuses on the perceived fairness of the *policies and procedures* used to make decisions. Thibaut and Walker (1978) originally introduced process-oriented fairness, and Leventhal (1980) and Leventhal et al. (1980) extended its principles by developing six criteria that a procedure should meet to be perceived as fair: 1) it is applied consistently across people and across time; 2) it is

free from bias; 3) it ensures that accurate information is collected and used to make decisions; 4) it has some mechanism for correcting flawed or inaccurate decisions; 5) it conforms to personal or prevailing standards of ethics or morality; and 6) it ensures that the opinions of various groups affected by the decision have all been taken into account.

Interactional unfairness

Finally, the third dimension of fairness, as introduced by Bies and Moag (1986), refers to the interpersonal treatment that people receive during the enactment of procedures (Bies and Shapiro 1987). In other words, interactional fairness focuses on the interpersonal side of fairness, including the treatment and communications of one party toward another, such as from management to employees. Interactional fairness consists of two distinct aspects: interpersonal fairness and informational fairness. The first dimension pertains to the extent to which people receive treatment marked by politeness, dignity, and respect from authorities or third parties involved in executing the procedures or determining the outcomes. The second dimension is concerned with the explanations provided for why certain procedures have been used or certain outcomes were allocated in a particular manner.

Suppressing Perceived Unfairness

As with equity theory, several approaches may reduce perceptions of unfairness. We provide a summary of them, though Leventhal (1976) discusses them in greater detail.

Compensating the unfairly treated party

To mitigate unfairness perceptions, one option is to compensate the unfairly treated party. This compensation often takes the form of increasing the victim's outcomes (e.g., increasing pay, granting financial rewards), but it may also include reducing the party's inputs. For example, an overworked and underpaid employee might receive extra time off with pay or be told to work no more than eight hours per day.

Changing the distribution of rewards and inputs for other parties

Rather than compensating the victim directly, a manager may elect to change the ratios of outcomes to inputs achieved by other members of the group, who are perceived to receive greater equity. This shift might take the form of reducing other members' outcomes or forcing them to increase their inputs.

Engaging in secrecy
Another strategy to minimize perceptions of unfairness is to impose secrecy about the distribution of rewards. The efficacy of this strategy relies on the assumption that people who cannot compare themselves to one another also cannot make inferences about whether the outcomes they receive are fair or not. The effectiveness of this approach depends critically on the maintenance of anonymity and secrecy about outcomes and rewards, which may not be feasible in some situations.

Denial of responsibility for the unfair act
A reward allocator or supervisor may be able to reduce perceptions of unfairness by manipulating others' understanding of the causes of that unfairness (Blau 1963). Specifically, if a manager can convince an unfairly treated employee that the causes of the unfairness are beyond the manager's control, the employee likely perceives the inequitable outcomes as less unfair (Cohen 1982). By denying responsibility for the unfair outcome or convincing the victim that the unfairness is "accidental," the manager can reduce not only perceptions of unfairness but also the negative emotions that result from it.

Justifying the decision
Recall that fairness depends on the person's perceptions of a decision, not objective standards. If a manager can convince an unfairly treated party that an outcome actually is fair, justifiable, and "deserved," then the perceptions of unfairness may diminish. For example, providing the unfairly treated party with incontrovertible evidence that the lower attained outcomes were actually due to his or her poorer performance should mitigate that person's sense of unfairness.

Altering the time frame used to evaluate outcomes
Because unfairness is a perceptual concept, managers may be able to reduce perceptions of unfairness by altering the time frame that an unfairly treated party uses to determine outcomes. For example, in the long run, the unfairly treated party might earn rewards and outcomes that are similar to those of others with similar job responsibilities in the organization, even if the short-run rewards seem lesser. Another means of doing so might highlight that present rewards are actually much higher than they previously have been.

Encouraging the unfairly treated party to shift the basis of comparison
If perceptions of unfairness are not absolute but rather relative, they must depend on the perception that a referent other is receiving a relatively

greater outcome-to-input ratio. A manager therefore could reduce percep-tions of unfairness by convincing the unfairly treated party to alter the object of comparison to someone with a poorer outcome-to-input ratio, such that the apparent magnitude of the first party's equitability appears magnified. For example, a manager might provide information about comparable others whose rewards are actually lower or that makes others with higher rewards seem less comparable.

Consequences of (Un)fairness

Colquitt et al.'s (2001) meta-analysis of more than 25 years of organiza-tional justice research reveals the effects of the three fairness dimensions on several key outcome variables. Regarding distributive fairness, they find that it shares strong positive correlations with outcome satisfaction, job satisfaction, organizational commitment, trust, and agent-referenced evaluations of authority, but it exhibits negative correlations with with-drawal. Likewise, procedural fairness shares strong positive correlations with outcome satisfaction, job satisfaction, organizational commitment, trust, and agent-referenced evaluations of authority. Finally, with regard to the two components of interactional fairness, namely, interpersonal fairness and informational fairness, Colquitt et al. find that interpersonal fairness is strongly related to agent-referenced evaluations of authority, whereas informational fairness relates to trust, agent-referenced evalua-tions of authority, and system-referenced evaluations of authority. Thus, fairness plays an important role in increasing key positive outcomes, as well as reducing undesirable ones.

Many other studies highlight the central role of fairness for key outcomes of interest. For example, DeConinck and Bachmann (2005) find that higher levels of organizational fairness lead to lower levels of turnover among retail buyers, because they increase their satisfaction and commitment. Ramaswami and Singh (2003) reveal that interactional fairness enhances a salesperson's job satisfaction significantly and that interactional fairness and distributive fairness are significantly associ-ated with supervisor trust. Enhanced performance also has been linked to all aspects of fairness: distributive (Lind and Tyler 1988; Pfeffer and Langton 1993; Ball et al. 1994), procedural (Konovsky and Cropanzano 1991; Cohen-Charash and Spector 2001), and interactional (Cropanzano and Prehar 1999; Masterson et al. 2000). Studies also suggest that dis-tributive (Roberts and Coulson 1999; Cohen-Charash and Spector 2001) and procedural (Cohen-Charash and Spector 2001) fairness both relate negatively to turnover intentions. Kumar et al. (1995) show that both distributive and procedural fairness have a positive impact on relationship quality. Furthermore, prior studies demonstrate that procedural fairness helps determine an employee's organizational commitment (Folger and Konovsky 1989; Konovsky and Cropanzano 1991; Sweeney and McFarlin 1993). Channels researchers suggest that perceived unfairness in outcomes ultimately will result in unfavorable affective reactions and conflict within channel relationships (Frazier 1983; Frazier et al. 1988). Similarly, Kaufmann and Stern (1988) indicate that perceived unfairness in dispute resolution procedures results in higher levels of retained hostility. Along the same lines, Blodgett et al. (2001) find that a lack of perceived fairness can cause customers to engage in negative word-of-mouth behaviors and never repatronize an offending retailer.

INTEGRATING RELATIONSHIP-DESTROYING BEHAVIORS

In Figure 13.2, we summarize approaches used to deal with opportunism, conflict, and unfairness.

Prior research in marketing generally studies these negative behaviors in isolation – for example, Gundlach et al. (1995) and Wathne and Heide (2000) for opportunism, Gaski (1984) and Frazier and Rody (1991) for conflict, and Kumar et al. (1995) for unfairness – which leaves a gap with regard to their joint effects or influences on marketing relationships. Because these commonly occurring negative behaviors certainly can appear together, it is crucial to be able to model their effects collectively rather than in isolation, especially considering the potential negative synergies that may exist among relationship-destroying behaviors. For example, unfair acts can incite strong negative retaliation and backlash, owing to people's need to punish, but the extent to which such intensified backlash translates into greater use of opportunism or increased conflict is not clear. In addition, the emotions stirred up by perceptions of unfairness may cloud the exchange parties' judgments and alter their responses to opportunism and conflict. Samaha et al. (2009) support this proposition; they find that unfairness worsens the negative effects of opportunism and conflict on interfirm cooperation and flexibility. However, more research is needed to explicate the interactions among these and other relationship-destroying behaviors.

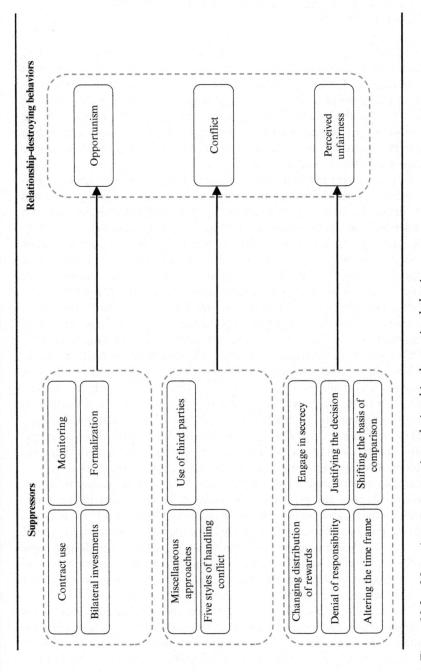

Figure 13.2 Managing or suppressing relationship-destroying behaviors

FURTHER RESEARCH DIRECTIONS AND CONCLUSIONS

The goal of this chapter has been to introduce three of the most common relationship-destroying behaviors in exchange relationships and present not only their causes or antecedents but also potential methods for managing them. We provide a summary of some of the negative consequences associated with these relationship-destroying behaviors and highlight the importance of integrating them into marketing theory. Our concluding remarks regarding opportunism, conflict, and unfairness thus lead us into areas for further research.

It is not surprising that opportunism is so prevalent in exchange relationships, given the competitive environment and increasing pressures for firms to deliver consistent advantages in multiple realms such as cost leadership, product differentiation, and service excellence (Porter 1980). One need not look very far to find examples of opportunism in modern business; the *Wall Street Journal* and other news media are fraught with reports of opportunistic behaviors and scandals in which organizations take advantage of their employees, shareholders, or partners. Dickerson (1998: 44) even goes so far as to contend that "organizations are fundamentally adversarial and act in ways that uniquely encourage opportunistic behavior . . . They are breeding grounds for opportunistic behavior."

Conflict, another widely occurring phenomenon, stems from many causes, which make its management nontrivial. Because conflict is such a complex and multidimensional construct, the goal of our discussion has not been to produce an all-encompassing list of solutions but rather to summarize some important elements and issues that are relevant for identifying and managing conflict. It is also worth noting that, though our discussion focuses on the negative aspects of conflict, other research suggests potential benefits associated with functional conflict in the workplace. For example, at moderate levels, functional conflict can positively influence group efficiency and productivity (Chesler et al. 1978; Derr 1978), stimulate creativity, and improve decision quality (Cosier and Dalton 1990). Through these effects, conflict can result in positive outcomes; interested readers should examine this research stream more fully. Yet, despite these potential benefits, we still emphasize the negative side, because most recommendations fall within the realm of reducing, resolving, or mitigating conflict whenever possible.

The past few decades have also provided an abundance of research on fairness, which outlines the many negative repercussions associated with unfair behaviors. This research underscores the importance of fairness in organizations and in marketing relationships. Not only does fairness build trust and commitment (Cohen-Charash and Spector 2001; Colquitt et al. 2001), but it also improves job performance (Colquitt et al. 2001; Rupp and Cropanzano 2002), fosters organizational citizenship behaviors (Cohen-Charash and Spector 2001), and enhances customer satisfaction and loyalty (Cropanzano et al. 2007). Despite these findings, many relationships and organizations remain plagued by various forms of unfairness, which can result in negative consequences across a multitude of dimensions. We therefore have included unfairness in our discussion to assist practitioners and researchers in identifying and managing unfairness perceptions.

Additional Research Directions

The final task of this chapter is to present a research agenda for ongoing analyses in the domain of relationship-destroying behaviors. Specifically, we consider it important for research to provide the following:

- *An enhanced understanding of how multiple negative behaviors that occur together can undermine relationships.* As we mentioned previously, current research has not investigated how the presence of multiple relationship-destroying behaviors (e.g., a simultaneous occurrence of opportunism, conflict, and unfairness) may work jointly to undermine relationships.
- *An understanding of how the efficacy of governance mechanisms may depend on multiple negative behaviors.* Although some prior studies advocate the use of governance mechanisms and contracts to control negative behaviors (Williamson 1979; Joskow 1987; Kumar 1996), little research has assessed how well these control mechanisms work in the presence of multiple relationship-destroying behaviors. Samaha et al. (2009) demonstrate that unfairness interacts negatively with contract use, such that contracts undermine relationships rather than protect them, but more research is needed to help determine how the expected effects of governance mechanisms may shift in the presence of multiple relationship-destroying behaviors.
- *A greater emphasis on environmental conditions to gain an understanding of how relationship-destroying behaviors act in different contexts.* Despite some studies that assess how relationship-destroying behaviors perform in different environmental contexts, we need further research in this area. Kumar et al. (1995) find that perceptions of distributive and procedural fairness enhance relationship quality, but these effects are moderated by environmental uncertainty; procedural fairness becomes even more important as environmental

uncertainty increases. It would be interesting to generalize such findings to encompass not only fairness and unfairness but also opportunism and conflict.

- *An improved understanding of how the selling context influences relationship-destroying behaviors.* Although prior studies investigate different industries and selling environments associated with relationship-destroying behaviors, there is still a lack of consensus about how different selling contexts (e.g., buyer–supplier relationships, retailer–customer relationships) may influence or moderate the effect of relationship-destroying behaviors on key outcome variables.
- *A greater emphasis on linking service recovery programs with the type of relationship-destroying behavior that originally caused the service failure.* Service recovery efforts could improve if the underlying causes of service failure were incorporated into the recovery process itself. Various service failures likely lead to different service recovery expectations (Ringberg et al. 2007), which raises the question: How might certain negative behaviors that cause a service failure create differing service recovery expectations, and how can firms modify their service recovery efforts to account for these different causes and expectations?
- *A greater awareness of how relationship-destroying behaviors affect the management of relationship marketing programs and efforts.* Past empirical evidence suggests that firms are often disappointed with the results of their RM activities (Kalwani and Narayandas 1995). In some cases, RM efforts even affect performance negatively (Dowling and Uncles 1997). To our knowledge, though, no extant studies have provided a comprehensive link between RM program failure and relationship-destroying behaviors or indicate how firms might adjust their RM programs in the presence of such negative behaviors.

REFERENCES

Adams, John S. (1963), "Toward an Understanding of Inequity," *Journal of Abnormal and Social Psychology*, 67, 422–36.
Adams, John S. (1965), "Inequity in Social Exchange," in L. Berkowitz (ed.), *Advances in Experimental Social Psychology*, Vol. 2, New York: Academic Press, pp. 267–99.
Alter, Catherine (1990), "An Exploratory Study of Conflict and Coordination in Interorganizational Service Delivery Systems," *Academy of Management Journal*, 33(3), 478–502.
Anderson, Erin (1988), "Transaction Costs as Determinants of Opportunism in Integrated and Independent Sales Forces," *Journal of Economic Behavior and Organization*, 9 (May), 247–64.

Anderson, Erin and Barton Weitz (1992), "The Use of Pledges to Build and Sustain Commitment in Distribution Channels," *Journal of Marketing Research*, 29(1), 18–34.

Anderson, James C. and James A. Narus (1990), "A Model of Distributor Firm and Manufacturer Firm Working Partnerships," *Journal of Marketing*, 54 (January), 42–58.

Anderson, Norman H. (1965), "Averaging versus Adding as a Stimulus-Combination Rule in Impression Formation," *Journal of Experimental Psychology*, 70(4), 394–400.

Aram, John D. and Paul F. Salipante (1981), "An Evaluation of Organizational Due Process in the Resolution of Employer/Employee Conflict," *Academy of Management Review*, 6(2), 197–204.

Bacharach, Samuel B. and Edward J. Lawler (1980), *Power and Politics in Organizations: The Social Psychology of Conflict, Coalitions and Bargaining*, San Francisco: Jossey-Bass.

Bacharach, Samuel B. and Edward J. Lawler (1981), *Bargaining: Power, Tactics and Outcomes*, San Francisco: Jossey-Bass.

Balakrishnan, Srinavasan and Mitchell P. Koza (1993), "Information Asymmetry, Adverse Selection and Joint Ventures," *Journal of Economic Behavior and Organization*, 20 (January), 99–117.

Ball, Gail A., Linda Klebe Trevino and Henry P. Sims, Jr. (1994), "Just and Unjust Punishment: Influences on Subordinate Performance and Citizenship," *Academy of Management Journal*, 37(2), 299–322.

Barki, Henri and Jon Hartwick (2004), "Conceptualizing the Construct of Interpersonal Conflict," *International Journal of Conflict Management*, 15(3), 216–44.

Baron, Robert A. (1984), "Reducing Organizational Conflict: An Incompatible Response Approach," *Journal of Applied Psychology*, 69(2), 272–9.

Baumeister, Roy F., Ellen Bratslavsky, Catrin Finkenauer and Kathleen D. Vohs (2001), "Bad Is Stronger than Good," *Review of General Psychology*, 5(4), 323–70.

Bell, G.G. and M. Anderson (2000), *Trust, Positional Security and Information Transfer in Four Network-Ideal Types: Exploring the Linkages between Forms of Social Capital*, Toronto: Academy of Management.

Bergman, Thomas J. and Roger J. Volkema (1989), "Understanding and Managing Interpersonal Conflict at Work: Its Issues, Interactive Processes and Consequences," in M. Afzalur Rahim (ed.), *Managing Conflict: An Interdisciplinary Approach*, New York: Praeger, pp. 7–19.

Bies, Robert J. and J.S. Moag (1986), "Interactional Justice: Communication Criteria of Fairness," in R.J. Lewicki, B.H. Sheppard and B.H. Bazerman (eds.), *Research on Negotiation in Organizations*, Vol. 1, Greenwich, CT: JAI Press, pp. 43–55.

Bies, Robert J. and Debra L. Shapiro (1987), "Interactional Fairness Judgments: The Influence of Causal Accounts," *Social Justice Research*, 1, 199–218.

Blake, Robert R. and Jane S. Mouton (1964), *The Managerial Grid*, Houston, TX: Gulf.

Blau, Peter M. (1963), *The Dynamics of Bureaucracy: A Study of Interpersonal Relations in Two Government Agencies*, Chicago: University of Chicago Press.

Blodgett, Jeffrey G., Donald H. Granbois and Rockney G. Walters (2001), "The Effect of Perceived Justice on Complainants' Negative Word-Of-Mouth Behavior and Repatronage Intentions," *Journal of Retailing*, 69(4), 399–428.

Blount, Sally (1995), "When Social Outcomes Aren't Fair: The Effect of Causal Attributions on Preferences," *Organizational Behavior and Human Decision Processes*, 63(2), 131–44.

Bolton, Ruth N., Amy K. Smith and Janet Wagner (2003), "Striking the Right Balance: Designing Service to Enhance Business-to-Business Relationships," *Journal of Service Research*, 5(4), 271–91.

Brown, James R., Chekitan S. Dev and Dong-Jin Lee (2000), "Managing Marketing Opportunism: The Efficacy of Alternative Governance Mechanisms," *Journal of Marketing*, 64 (April), 51–65.

Cadogan, John W., Sanna Sundqvist, Risto T. Salminen and Kaisu Puumalainen (2005), "Export Marketing, Interfunctional Interactions and Performance Consequences," *Journal of the Academy of Marketing Science*, 33(4), 520–35.

Chesler, Mark A., James E. Crowfoot and Bunyan I. Bryant (1978), "Power Training: An Alternative Path to Conflict Management," *California Management Review*, 21(2), 84–90.

Cohen, Ronald L. (1982), "Perceiving Justice: An Attributional Perspective," in Ronald L. Cohen and Jerold Greenberg (eds.), *Equity and Social Justice Behavior*, New York: Academic Press.

Cohen-Charash, Yochi and Paul E. Spector (2001), "The Role of Justice in Organizations: A Meta-Analysis," *Organizational Behavior and Human Decision Processes*, 86(2), 278–321.

Colquitt, Jason A., Donald E. Conlon, Michael J. Wesson, Christopher O.L.H. Porter and K. Yee Ng (2001), "Justice at the Millennium: A Meta-Analytic Review of 25 Years of Organizational Justice Research," *Journal of Applied Psychology*, 86(3), 425–45.

Conlon, Donald E. and Daniel P. Sullivan (1999), "Examining the Actions of Organizations in Conflict: Evidence from the Delaware Court of Chancery," *Academy of Management Journal*, 42(3), 319–29.

Cosier, Richard A. and Dan R. Dalton (1990), "Positive Effects of Conflict: A Field Assessment," *International Journal of Conflict Management*, 1(1), 81–92.

Cropanzano, Russell and Gerald Greenberg (1997), "Progress in Organizational Justice: Tunneling through the Maze," in C.L. Cooper and I.T. Robertson (eds.), *International Review of Industrial and Organizational Psychology*, Vol. 12, New York: Wiley, pp. 317–72.

Cropanzano, Russell and Marie S. Mitchell (2005), "Social Exchange Theory: An Interdisciplinary Review," *Journal of Management*, 31(6), 874–900.

Cropanzano, Russell and Cynthia A. Prehar (1999), "Using Social Exchange Theory to Distinguish Procedural from Interactional Justice," paper presented at the Annual Meeting of the Society for Industrial and Organizational Psychology, April, Atlanta, GA.

Cropanzano, Russell and M. Schminke (2001), "Using Social Justice to Build Effective Work Groups," in M.R. Turner (ed.), *Groups at Work: Theory and Research*, Mahwah, NJ: Erlbaum, pp. 143–72.

Cropanzano, Russell, David E. Bowen and Stephen W. Gilliland (2007), "The Management of Organizational Justice," *Academy of Management Perspectives*, 21(4), 34–48.

Crosno, Jody L. and Robert Dahlstrom (2008), "A Meta-Analytic Review of Opportunism in Exchange Relationships," *Journal of the Academy of Marketing Science*, 36, 191–201.

Dahlstrom, Robert and Brett A. Boyle (1994), "Behavioral Antecedents to Intrinsic Motivation in Capital Equipment Exchange Relationships," *Journal of Applied Business Research*, 10(2), 51–63.

DeConinck, James and Duane Bachmann (2005), "An Analysis of Turnover among Retail Buyers," *Journal of Business Research*, 58, 874–82.

Derr, Brooklyn C. (1978), "Managing Organizational Conflict," *California Management Review*, 21(2), 76–83.

Deutsch, Morton (1990), "Sixty Years of Conflict," *International Journal of Conflict Management*, 1(3), 237–63.

Dickerson, C.M. (1998), "Virtual Organizations: From Dominance to Opportunism," *New Zealand Journal of Industrial Relations*, 23(2), 35–46.

Dowling, Grahame R. and Mark Uncles (1997), "Do Customer Loyalty Programs Really Work?," *Sloan Management Review*, 38(4), 71–82.

Eiseman, Jeffrey W. (1978), "Reconciling 'Incompatible' Positions," *Journal of Applied Behavior Science*, 14(2), 133–50.

Eisenhardt, Kathleen M. (1985), "Control: Organizational and Economic Approaches," *Management Science*, 31(2), 134–49.

Ephross, Paul and Thomas V. Vassil (1993), "The Rediscovery of Real World Groups," in S. Wenocur, P.H. Ephross, T.V. Vassil and R.K. Vargese (eds.), *Social Work with Groups: Expanding Horizons*, Binghamton, NY: Haworth Press.

Filley, A.C. (1978), "Some Normative Issues in Conflict Management," *California Management Review*, 21(2), 61–6.

Finkel, Norman J. (2001), *Not Fair! The Typology of Commonsense Unfairness*, Washington, DC: American Psychological Association.

Folger, Robert G. and Russell Cropanzano (1998), *Organizational Justice and Human Resource Management*, Thousand Oaks, CA: Sage.

Folger, Robert G. and Mary A. Konovsky (1989), "Effects of Procedural and Distributive Justice on Reactions to Pay Raise Decisions," *Academy of Management Journal*, 32(1), 115–30.

Folger, Robert and Daniel P. Skarlicki (1998), "A Popcorn Metaphor for Employee Aggression," in Ricky W. Griffin, Anne O'Leary-Kelly and Judith M. Collins (eds.), *Dysfunctional Behavior in Organizations: Violent and Deviant Behavior*, London: JAI Press.

Frazier, Gary L. (1983), "Interorganizational Exchange Behavior in Marketing Channels: A Broadened Perspective," *Journal of Marketing*, 47 (Fall), 68–78.

Frazier, Gary L. and Raymond Rody (1991), "The Use of Influence Strategies in Interfirm Relationships in Industrial Product Channels," *Journal of Marketing*, 55 (January), 52–69.

Frazier, Gary L., Robert E. Spekman and Charles R. O'Neal (1988), "Just-in-Time Exchange Relationships in Industrial Markets," *Journal of Marketing*, 52 (October), 52–67.

Frazier, Gary L., James D. Gill and Sudhir H. Kale (1989), "Dealer Dependence Levels and Reciprocal Actions in a Channel of Distribution in a Developing Country," *Journal of Marketing*, 53(1), 50–69.

Gaski, John F. (1984), "The Theory of Power and Conflict in Channels of Distribution," *Journal of Marketing*, 48 (Summer), 9–29.

Gassenheimer, J.B., D.B. Baucus and M.S. Baucus (1996), "Cooperative Arrangements among Entrepreneurs: An Analysis of Opportunism and Communication in Franchise Structures," *Journal of Business Research*, 36(1), 67–79.

Ghosh, Mrinal and George John (1999), "Governance Value Analysis and Marketing Strategy," *Journal of Marketing*, 63(4) (Special Issue), 131–45.

Gottman, John Mordechai (1979), *Marital Interaction: Experimental Investigations*, New York: Academic Press.

Gottman, John Mordechai (1994), *Why Marriages Succeed or Fail*, New York: Simon & Schuster.

Gray, Barbara (1985), "Conditions Facilitating Interorganizational Collaboration," *Human Relations*, 38(10), 911–36.

Greenberg, Jerald (1984), "On the Apocryphal Nature of Inequity Distress," in R. Folger (ed.), *The Sense of Injustice: Social Psychological Perspectives*, New York: Plenum, pp. 167–86.

Greenberg, Jerald (1986), "Determinants of Perceived Fairness of Performance Evaluations," *Journal of Applied Psychology*, 71(2), 340–42.

Greenberg, Jerald (1990), "Organizational Justice: Yesterday, Today and Tomorrow," *Journal of Management*, 16(2), 399–432.

Gruen, Thomas W. and Reshma H. Shah (2000), "Determinants and Outcomes of Plan Objectivity and Implementation in Category Management Relationships," *Journal of Retailing*, 76(4), 483–510.

Gundlach, Gregory T., Ravi S. Achrol and John T. Mentzer (1995), "The Structure of Commitment in Exchange," *Journal of Marketing*, 59 (January), 78–92.

Hawkins, Timothy G., C. Michael Wittmann and Michael M. Beyerlein (2008), "Antecedents and Consequences of Opportunism in Buyer–Supplier Relations: Research Synthesis and New Frontiers," *Industrial Marketing Management*, 37, 895–909.

Heide, Jan B. (1994), "Interorganizational Governance in Marketing Channels," *Journal of Marketing*, 58(1), 71–85.

Hennart, J. (1988), "A Transaction Cost Theory of Equity Joint Ventures," *Strategic Management Journal*, 9, 361–74.

Hinds, Pamela J. and Diane E. Bailey (2003), "Out of Sight, Out of Sync: Understanding Conflict in Distributed Teams," *Organization Science*, 14(6), 615–32.

Hocker, Joyce L. and William W. Wilmot (1991), *Interpersonal Conflict*, Dubuque, IA: Wm. C. Brown.

Homans, George C. (1961), *Social Behavior: Its Elementary Forms*, New York: Harcourt, Brace & World.

Horwitz, M. (1956), "Psychological Needs as a Function of Social Environment," in L.D. White (ed.), *The State of Social Sciences*, Chicago: University of Chicago Press, pp. 162–83.

Jaworski, Bernard J. and Ajay K. Kohli (1993), "Market Orientation: Antecedents and Consequences," *Journal of Marketing*, 57 (July), 53–70.

Jehn, Karen A. (1994), "Enhancing Effectiveness: An Investigation of Advantages and Disadvantages of Value-Based Intragroup Conflict," *International Journal of Conflict Management*, 5(3), 223–38.

Jehn, Karen A. (1995), "A Multimethod Examination of the Benefits and Detriments of Intragroup Conflict," *Administrative Science Quarterly*, 40(2), 256–82.

Jehn, Karen A. (1997), "A Qualitative Analysis of Conflict Types and Dimensions in Organizational Groups," *Administrative Science Quarterly*, 42(3), 530–57.

Jehn, Karen A. and Elizabeth A. Mannix (2001), "The Dynamic Nature of Conflict: A Longitudinal Study of Intragroup Conflict and Group Performance," *Academy of Management Journal*, 44(2), 238–51.

Jehn, Karen A., Gregory B. Northcraft and Margaret A. Neale (1999), "Why Differences Make a Difference: A Field Study of Diversity, Conflict and Performance in Workgroups," *Administrative Science Quarterly*, 44(4), 741–63.

John, George (1984), "An Empirical Investigation of Some Antecedents of Opportunism in a Marketing Channel," *Journal of Marketing Research*, 21 (August), 278–89.

John, George and John Martin (1984), "Effects of Organizational Structure of Marketing Planning on Credibility and Utilization of Plan Output," *Journal of Marketing Research*, 21(2), 170–83.

John, George and Torger Reve (1982), "The Reliability and Validity of Key Informant Data from Dyadic Relationships in Marketing Channels," *Journal of Marketing Research*, 19(4), 517–24.

Joshi, Ashwin W. and Rodney L. Stump (1999), "Determinants of Commitment and Opportunism: Integrating and Extending Insights from Transaction Costs Analysis and Relational Exchange Theory," *Canadian Journal of Administrative Sciences*, 16(4), 334–52.

Joskow, Paul L. (1987), "Contract Duration and Relationship-Specific Investments: Empirical Evidence from Coal Markets," *American Economic Review*, 77(1), 168–85.

Kahneman, Daniel, Jack L. Knetsch and Richard Thaler (1986), "Fairness and the Assumptions of Economics," in Robin M. Hogarth and Melvin W. Reder (eds.), *Rational Choice: The Contrast between Economics and Psychology*, Chicago: University of Chicago Press.

Kalwani, Manohar U. and Narakesari Narayandas (1995), "Long-Term Manufacturer–Supplier Relationships: Do They Pay Off for Supplier Firms?," *Journal of Marketing*, 59 (January), 1–16.

Kaufmann, Patrick J. and Louis W. Stern (1988), "Relational Exchange Norms, Perceptions of Unfairness and Retained Hostility in Commercial Litigation," *Journal of Conflict Resolution*, 32 (September), 543–52.

Killing, J.P. (1983), *Strategies for Joint Venture Success*, New York: Praeger.

Konovsky, Mary A. and Russell Cropanzano (1991), "Perceived Fairness of Employee Drug Testing as a Predictor of Employee Attitudes and Job Performance," *Journal of Applied Psychology*, 76 (October), 698–707.

Kottler, Jeffrey A. (1994), *Beyond Blame: A New Way of Resolving Conflicts in Relationships*, San Francisco: Jossey-Bass.

Koza, Karen L. and Rajiv P. Dant (2007), "Effects of Relationship Climate, Control Mechanism and Communications on Conflict Resolution Behavior and Performance Outcomes," *Journal of Retailing*, 83(3), 279–96.

Kumar, Nirmalya (1996), "The Power of Trust in Manufacturer–Retailer Relationships," *Harvard Business Review*, 74(6), 92–106.

Kumar, Nirmalya, Lisa K. Scheer and Jan-Benedict E.M. Steenkamp (1995), "The Effects of Supplier Fairness on Vulnerable Resellers," *Journal of Marketing Research*, 32 (February), 54–65.

Lambe, C. Jay, C. Michael Wittmann and Robert E. Spekman (2001), "Social Exchange

Theory and Research on Business-to-Business Relational Exchange," *Journal of Business-to-Business Marketing*, 8(3), 1–36.

Lee, Dong-Jin (1998), "Developing International Strategic Alliances between Exporters and Importers: The Case of Australian Exporters," *International Journal of Research in Marketing*, 15(4), 335–48.

Leventhal, Gerald S. (1976), "The Distribution of Rewards in Groups," in Leonard Berkowitz and Elaine Walster (eds.), *Advances in Experimental Social Psychology*, Vol. 9, New York: Academic Press, pp. 91–131.

Leventhal, Gerald S. (1980), "What Should Be Done with Equity Theory?," in K.J. Gergent, M.S. Greenberg and R.H. Willis (eds.), *Social Exchange: Advances in Theory and Research*, New York: Plenum, pp. 27–55.

Leventhal, Gerald S., J. Karuza and W.R. Fry (1980), "Beyond Fairness: A Theory of Allocation Preferences," in G. Mikula (ed.), *Justice and Social Interaction*, New York: Springer-Verlag, pp. 167–218.

Lewin, David (1987), "Dispute Resolution in the Nonunion Firm," *Journal of Conflict Resolution*, 31(3), 465–502.

Lewin, Kurt (1947), "Frontiers in Group Dynamics," *Human Relations*, 1(1), 1–45.

Li, Lee (2002), "Research Note: Sales Force Opportunism in Emerging Markets: An Exploratory Investigation," *Thunderbird International Business Review*, 76(4), 483–510.

Lind, Edgar Allen and Tom R. Tyler (1988), *The Social Psychology of Procedural Justice*, New York: Plenum Press.

Lonsdale, C. (2001), "Locked-In to Supplier Dominance: On the Dangers of Asset Specificity for the Outsourcing Decision," *Journal of Supply Chain Management*, 37(2), 22–7.

Macneil, Ian R. (1982), Comments to the Workshop on Transaction Cost Analysis in Marketing, August, Evanston, IL.

Masterson, Suzanne S., Kyle Lewis, Barry M. Goldman and Susan M. Taylor (2000), "Integrating Justice and Social Exchange: The Differing Effects of Fair Procedures and Treatment on Work Relationships," *Academy of Management Journal*, 43(4), 738–48.

Matsuo, Makoto (2005), "Customer Orientation, Conflict and Innovativeness in Japanese Sales Departments," *Journal of Business Research*, 59, 242–50.

Menon, Anil, Sundar G., Bharadwaj and Roy Howell (1996), "The Quality and Effectiveness of Marketing Strategy: Effects of Functional and Dysfunctional Conflict in Intraorganizational Relationships," *Journal of the Academy of Marketing Science*, 24(4), 299–313.

Mikula, Gerold (1987), "Exploring the Experience of Injustice," in Gun R. Semin and Barbara Krahe (eds.), *Issues in Contemporary German Social Psychology*, London: Sage, pp. 74–96.

Moore, Barrington (1978), *Injustice: The Social Bases of Obedience and Revolt*, White Plains, NY: M.E. Sharpe.

Moorman, Christine, Gerald Zaltman and Rohit Deshpandé (1992), "Relationships between Providers and Users of Market Research: The Dynamics of Trust within and between Organizations," *Journal of Marketing Research*, 29 (August), 314–29.

Morgan, Robert M. and Shelby D. Hunt (1994), "The Commitment-Trust Theory of Relationship Marketing," *Journal of Marketing*, 58 (July), 20–38.

Morrill, Calvin and Cheryl King Thomas (1992), "Organizational Conflict Management as Disputing Process: The Problem of Social Escalation," *Human Communication Research*, 18(3), 400–428.

Noordewier, Thomas G., George John and John R. Nevin (1990), "Performance Outcomes of Purchasing Arrangements in Industrial Buyer–Vendor Relationships," *Journal of Marketing*, 54(4), 80–93.

Nooteboom, B., H. Berger and N.G. Noorderhaven (1997), "Effects of Trust and Governance on Relational Risk," *Academy of Management Journal*, 40, 308–38.

Nowakowski, Jaclyn M. and Donald E. Conlon (2005), "Organizational Justice: Looking Back, Looking Forward," *International Journal of Conflict Management*, 16(1), 4–29.

Offerman, Theo (2002), "Hurting Hurts More than Helping Helps," *European Economic Review*, 46(8), 1423–37.
Osgood, Charles Egerton (1962), *An Alternative to War or Surrender*, Urbana: University of Illinois Press.
Palmatier, Robert W. (2008), "Interfirm Relational Drivers of Customer Value," *Journal of Marketing*, 72 (July), 76–89.
Palmatier, Robert W., Rajiv Dant, Dhruv Grewal and Kenneth R. Evans (2006), "Factors Influencing the Effectiveness of Relationship Marketing: A Meta-Analysis," *Journal of Marketing*, 70 (October), 136–53.
Parkhe, Arvind (1993), "Strategic Alliance Structuring: A Game Theoretic and Transaction Cost Examination of Interfirm Cooperation," *Academy of Management Review*, 36(4), 794–829.
Pfeffer, Jeffrey and Nancy Langton (1993), "The Effect of Wage Dispersion on Satisfaction, Productivity and Working Collaboratively: Evidence from College and University Faculty," *Administrative Science Quarterly*, 38, 382–407.
Phillips, Eleanor and Ric Cheston (1978), "Conflict Resolution: What Works?," *California Management Review*, 21(4), 76–83.
Pondy, Louis R. (1967), "Organizational Conflict: Concepts and Models," *Administrative Science Quarterly*, 12(2), 296–320.
Porter, Michael E. (1980), *Competitive Advantage*, New York: Free Press.
Pruitt, Dean G. and Jeffrey Z. Rubin (1986), *Social Conflict: Escalation, Stalemate and Settlement*, New York: McGraw-Hill. Revised and updated as Pruitt, Dean G., Jeffrey Z. Rubin and Sung Hee Kim (1994), *Social Conflict: Escalation, Stalemate and Settlement*, 2nd edn., New York: McGraw-Hill.
Putnam, L.L. and M.S. Poole (1987), "Conflict and Negotiation," in F.M. Jablin, L.L. Putnam, K.H. Roberts and L.W. Porter (eds.), *Handbook of Organizational Communication: An Interdisciplinary Perspective*, Newbury Park, CA: Sage.
Rahim, M. Afzalur (1983), "A Measure of Styles of Handling Interpersonal Conflict," *Academy of Management Journal*, 26(2), 368–76.
Rahim, M. Afzalur (2002), "Toward a Theory of Managing Organizational Conflict," *International Journal of Conflict Management*, 13(3), 206–35.
Rahim, M. Afzalur, Nace R. Magner and Debra Shapiro (2000), "Do Justice Perceptions Influence Styles of Handling Conflicts with Supervisors?," *International Journal of Conflict Management*, 11(1), 9–31.
Ramaswami, Sridhar N. and Jagdip Singh (2003), "Antecedents and Consequences of Merit Pay Fairness for Industrial Salespeople," *Journal of Marketing*, 67 (October), 46–66.
Rawwas, Mohammed Y.A., Scott J. Vitell and James H. Barnes (1997), "Management of Conflict Using Individual Power Sources: A Retailers' Perspective," *Journal of Business Research*, 40, 49–64.
Retzinger, Suzanne M. (1991), "Shame, Anger and Conflict: Case Study of Emotional Violence," *Journal of Family Violence*, 6(1), 37–59.
Rindfleisch, Aric and Jan B. Heide (1997), "Transaction Cost Analysis: Past, Present and Future Applications," *Journal of Marketing*, 61(4), 30–54.
Ringberg, Torsten, Gaby Odekerken-Schröder and Glenn L. Christensen (2007), "A Cultural Models Approach to Service Recovery," *Journal of Marketing*, 71(3), 194–214.
Robbins, Stephen P. (1974), *Managing Organizational Conflict: A Non-Traditional Approach*, Englewood Cliffs, NJ: Prentice Hall.
Roberts, James A. and Kevin R. Coulson (1999), "Salesperson Perceptions of Equity and Justice and Their Impact on Organizational Commitment and Turnover," *Journal of Marketing Theory and Practice*, 7(1), 1–16.
Roloff, M.E. (1987), "Communication and Conflict," in C.R. Berger and S.H. Chaffee (eds.), *Handbook of Communication Science*, Newbury Park, CA: Sage, pp. 484–534.
Rose, Gregory M. and Aviv Shoham (2004), "Interorganizational Task and Emotional Conflict with International Channels of Distribution," *Journal of Business Research*, 57, 942–50.

Rosenbloom, Bert (1999), *Distribution Channels*, Fort Worth, TX: Dryden Press.

Rousseau, D.M. (2001), "Schema, Promise and Mutuality: The Building Blocks of the Psychological Contract," *Journal of Occupational and Organizational Psychology*, 74(4), 511–41.

Ruekert, Robert W. and Orville C. Walker, Jr. (1987), "Marketing's Interaction with Other Functional Units: A Conceptual Framework and Empirical Evidence," *Journal of Marketing*, 51 (January), 1–19.

Rupp, Deborah E. and Russell Cropanzano (2002), "The Mediating Effects of Social Exchange Relationships in Predicting Workplace Outcomes from Multifoci Organizational Justice," *Organizational Behavior and Human Decision Processes*, 89(1), 925–46.

Samaha, Stephen A., Robert W. Palmatier and Rajiv P. Dant (2009), "Perceived Unfairness: Relationship Poison," working paper, Foster School of Business, University of Washington.

Schaan, J.L. (1983), "Partner Control and Joint Venture Success: The Case of Mexico," Ph.D. dissertation, University of Western Ontario, London, Ontario.

Schelling, Thomas C. (1960), *The Strategy of Conflict*, Cambridge, MA: Harvard University Press.

Shaw, Margaret L. (1985), "Parent–Child Mediation: A Challenge and a Promise," *Mediation Quarterly*, 7, 23–33.

Shaw, Margaret L. (1986), "Family Mediation," *Review of Law and Social Change*, 14, 757–70.

Sheppard, Blair H. and Roy J. Lewicki (1987), "Toward General Principles of Managerial Fairness," *Social Justice Research*, 1(2), 161–76.

Sirdeshmukh, Deepak, Jagdip Singh and Barry Sabol (2002), "Consumer Trust, Value and Loyalty in Relational Exchanges," *Journal of Marketing*, 66 (January), 15–37.

Skinner, Steven J., Jule B. Gassenheimer and Scott W. Kelley (1992), "Cooperation in Supplier–Dealer Relations," *Journal of Retailing*, 68(2), 174–93.

Skowronski, John J. and Donal E. Carlston (1989), "Negativity and Extremity Biases in Impression Formation: A Review of Explanations," *Psychological Bulletin*, 105(1), 131–42.

Song, Michael, Barbara Dyer and R. Jeffrey Thieme (2006), "Conflict Management and Innovation Performance: An Integrated Contingency Perspective," *Journal of the Academy of Marketing Science*, 34(3), 341–56.

Souder, William (1987), *Managing New Product Innovation*, Lexington, MA: Lexington Books.

Sprecher, Susan (1986), "The Relation between Inequity and Emotions in Close Relationships," *Social Psychology Quarterly*, 49(4), 309–21.

Stern, Louis W. and Adel I. El-Ansary (1992), *Marketing Channels*, Englewood Cliffs, NJ: Prentice Hall.

Sternberg, Robert J. and Diane M. Dobson (1987), "Resolving Interpersonal Conflicts: An Analysis of Stylistic Consistency," *Journal of Personality and Social Psychology*, 52(4), 794–812.

Sternberg, Robert J. and Lawrence J. Soriano (1984), "Styles of Conflict Resolution," *Journal of Personality and Social Psychology*, 47(1), 115–26.

Sweeney, Paul D. and Dean B. McFarlin (1993), "Workers' Evaluations of the 'Ends' and the 'Means': An Examination of Four Models of Distributive and Procedural Justice," *Organizational Behavior and Human Decision Processes*, 55, 23–40.

Thibaut, John W. and Harold H. Kelley (1959), *The Social Psychology of Groups*, New York: Wiley.

Thibaut, John W. and Lauren S. Walker (1978), *Procedural Justice: A Psychological Analysis*, Hillsdale, NJ: Erlbaum.

Thomas, Kenneth W. (1976), "Conflict and Conflict Management," in Marvin D. Dunnette (ed.), *Handbook of Industrial and Organizational Psychology*, Chicago: Rand McNally, pp. 889–935.

Thomas, Kenneth W. and Louis R. Pondy (1977), "Toward an 'Intent' Model of Conflict Management among Principal Parties," *Human Relations*, 30(12), 1089–1102.

Ting, Shueh-Chin, Cheng-Nan Chen and Darrell E. Bartholomew (2007), "An Integrated Study of Entrepreneurs' Opportunism," *Journal of Business and Industrial Marketing*, 22(5), 322–35.

Tjosvold, Dean (1985), "Implications of Controversy Research for Management," *Journal of Management*, 11(3), 19–35.

Tjosvold, Dean (1991), *The Conflict Positive Organization: Stimulate Diversity and Create Unity*, Reading, MA: Addison-Wesley.

Tjosvold, Dean, Valerie Dann and Choy L. Wong (1992), "Managing Conflict between Departments to Serve Customers," *Human Relations*, 45(10), 1035–54.

Van de Ven, Andrew H. (1976), "On the Nature, Formation and Maintenance of Relations among Organizations," *Academy of Management Review*, 1 (October), 24–36.

van de Vliert, Evert (1990), "Sternberg's Styles of Handling Interpersonal Conflict: A Theory-Based Reanalysis," *International Journal of Conflict Management*, 1(1), 69 80.

Verhoef, Peter C. (2003), "Understanding the Effect of Customer Relationship Management Efforts on Customer Retention and Customer Share Development," *Journal of Marketing*, 67 (October), 30–45.

Walker, Rob (2009), "Favor Enhancement," *New York Times Magazine*, June 21, 19.

Wall, James A., Jr. and Ronda Roberts Callister (1995), "Conflict and Its Management," *Journal of Management*, 21(3), 515–58.

Wall, James A., Jr. and Ann Lynn (1993), "Mediation: A Current Review," *Journal of Conflict Resolution*, 37(1), 160–94.

Wall, Victor D. and Linda L. Nolan (1987), "Small Group Conflict: A Look at Equity, Satisfaction and Styles of Conflict Management," *Small Group Behavior*, 18(2), 188–211.

Walster, Elaine, G. William Walster and Ellen Berscheid (1978), *Equity: Theory and Research*, Boston, MA: Allyn & Bacon.

Walton, Richard E., John M. Dutton and Thomas P. Cafferty (1969), "Organizational Context and Interdepartmental Conflict," *Administrative Science Quarterly*, 14(4), 522–43.

Wathne, Kenneth H. and Jan B. Heide (2000), "Opportunism in Interfirm Relationships: Forms, Outcomes and Solutions," *Journal of Marketing*, 64 (October), 36–51.

Williamson, Oliver E. (1975), *Markets and Hierarchies: Analysis and Antitrust Implications*, New York: Free Press.

Williamson, Oliver E. (1979), "Transaction-Cost Economics: The Governance of Contractual Relations," *Journal of Law and Economics*, 22(2), 233–61.

Williamson, Oliver E. (1985), *The Economic Institutions of Capitalism*, New York: Free Press.

Williamson, Oliver E. and W.G. Ouchi (1981), "The Markets and Hierarchies Program of Research: Origins, Implications, Prospects," in A. Van de Ven and W.F. Joyce (eds.), *Perspectives on Organization Design and Behavior*, New York: Wiley, pp. 347–70.

Winter, David G. (1987), "Enhancement of an Enemy's Power Motivation as a Dynamic of Conflict Escalation," *Journal of Personality and Social Psychology*, 52(1), 41–6.

Zarski, Linda Pannell, Ruth Knight and John Joseph Zarski (1985), "Child Custody Disputes: A Review of Legal and Clinical Resolution Methods," *Contemporary Family Therapy*, 7(2), 96–106.

14. From relationship marketing to many-to-many marketing
Evert Gummesson

INTRODUCTION

Claiming that one can offer the true history of marketing is self-betrayal – and, worse: betrayal of the readers. History is a set of interpreted stories, mostly presented in chronological order. In marketing, history writing tries to make sense of the evolution of concepts, categories, models, theories, events, cases and statistical findings. Serious efforts to understand the history of relationship marketing and where it is heading are justified as long as they are understood as the author's interpretation based on subjectively chosen and incomplete data. In my case much of the evolution of relational approaches is self-lived and I have taken an active part in the developments. This is a personal synthesis of what I have learned during my journey in Marketingland. The input is research by me and others and knowledge acquired as business practitioner, professor, customer and citizen. There is explicit knowledge, but equally important is the tacit knowledge that cannot (yet) be readily communicated. I have become passionate about recognizing complexity, dispensing with the pseudo-logic of linearity and reductionism, and indulging in an effort to recognize the messiness and fuzziness of real-life marketing without hiding behind an illusion of objectivity. My interest and direction are grand theory, whereas most researchers in marketing focus on a substantive level and fragmented midrange theory (Gummesson forthcoming a). I hope it will inspire readers, who are of course free to add other knowledge and draw their own conclusions.

Allocating thoughts and events to years is hazardous and should not be taken as absolute and literal. There are parallel developments and overlaps, and there are wide differences between cultures, nations and markets. There are forerunners and laggards in scholarly research, textbooks and education as well as in practice.

The chapter will address the following aspects of the transition of dyadic relationship marketing into *many-to-many marketing* (Gummesson 2008, forthcoming b). In a rough chronology for initial guidance, they are as follows:

- 1950s–1970s: Marketing management and the marketing mix (famous from its 4Ps: product, price, promotion and place); the orientation of the firm moving from supplier centricity to customer centricity; focus on goods and no interest in services.
- 1970s–2000s: Focus on services and stressing differences between goods marketing and services marketing.
- 1980s–present: Relational approaches – relationship marketing, customer relationship management (CRM), one-to-one and specific models of these such as the 30 relationships (the 30Rs) – establish themselves in marketing; the orientation of the firm moves toward two-party (customer–supplier) centricity; and the 4Ps transform into an extended relational mix.
- 1990s–present: The Internet, social media, email and mobile communication offer a dramatically novel infrastructure for commercial and social relationships.
- 2000s–present: The evolution of three contributions to a grand marketing theory based on value and service: many-to-many marketing addressing complexity and networks and moving in the direction of balanced centricity (a network of stakeholders), service-dominant (S-D) logic merging goods and services marketing, and service science with a focus on efficient service system.

We must accept that new concepts and terms are fluid, fuzzy and dynamic. Even if we look back we find that established concepts and terms like "firm," "service," "value," "quality" and "market" remain fuzzy sets (Gummesson forthcoming a). We cannot quite grasp them, but we feel their presence and we are lost without them. In the process we may move in the direction of grand theory even if we will not reach all the way and find the ultimate truth.

DEFINING RELATIONSHIP MARKETING

Relationship marketing is usually defined as the opposite of transaction marketing and an approach to increase long term profitability through loyal customers. With increased customer retention, fewer resources need to be invested in acquiring new customers and marketing costs go down. Money may be needed to retain customers, but the net effect on revenue and profits is assumed to be favorable (Jackson 1985; Ballantyne 1994; Grönroos 1997, 2007).

Although this sounds like a sensible vantage point, reality works in mysterious ways. Relationship marketing – like many new ideas – came to be naively perceived as a panacea. It is not, but it has given relational dimensions a prominent place in marketing. They were missing in theory and education but were present in real-life marketing. Practitioners learn that relationships are crucial for success in business. In local markets, relationships are often close and personal, and in many cultures relationships are necessary antecedents to business. Despite our confession to competition as a driver of the economy, monopolies often exist in markets and certain brands dominate. In such cases firms may bully their customers as well as their suppliers; they are both captive. The bigger companies grew and the more they left their local roots, the more consumer marketing became mass marketing and employees were physically and mentally distanced from customers. Customer data were derived through statistical surveys, and especially consumers were de-personalized to scales, decimals, percentages, averages, staples and curves. In parts of business-to-business (B2B) marketing, the situation is different. Marketing and purchasing between companies remain more personal, and ongoing cooperation and sales negotiations are more in focus than advertising. For better and for worse, the Internet and other information technology (IT) have redesigned the stage for buying and selling and have given us new types of relationships.

These were glimpses of general observations. In practice, business is always context-controlled, and the variations and combinations of practices are multifarious. We are faced with a melting pot of influences that form extremely complex patterns. These cannot be understood and managed through old theories from marketing and economics that were created in a totally different environment and with reductionism as research strategy. Relationship marketing does not develop in a vacuum but is under the spell of technology, political decisions, social changes and other influences. Even if elements of the old can be incorporated – some things in life seem forever valid – we need new or revised theories.

As relationships are generic to life they also permeate marketing. My definition (Gummesson forthcoming b) is: "Relationship marketing is interaction in networks of relationships."

Relationships require at least two parties who are in contact with each other. A *network* is a set of relationships, which can grow and mutate into enormously complex patterns. *Interaction* signifies what is going on in the relationships and networks.

Put in this way my definition applies to all types of activity: Life is a network of relationships within which interaction takes place. Thus the definition will be helpful only if saturated with specific marketing content. To fill it up, this chapter reports a journey through the "destinations" listed in the introductory chronology. Each of the contributions offers insights, and my interpretation of these will be explained along the way.

Peppers and Rogers (1993) introduced the expression *one-to-one market-ing* (*1to1*). By its wording, one-to-one draws the attention to an individual supplier and an individual customer. This is contrary to anonymous mass marketing, which is stressed in marketing management and especially in consumer marketing.

In the wake of relationship marketing followed *customer relationship management*. My definition (Gummesson forthcoming b) is: "CRM is the values and strategies of relationship marketing – with special emphasis on the relationship between a customer and a supplier – turned into practical application and dependent on both human action and IT."

Sometimes CRM is presented as the basic concept including a new philosophy for marketing. I prefer to see relationship marketing as the overriding concept and CRM as techniques to handle customer rela-tionships in practice. Applications of CRM are more rooted in software than in human behavior, and I am anxious to emphasize the need for a high tech/high touch balance (see further Payne and Frow 2005; Buttle 2009).

TOWARD A GENERAL THEORY: THE NEW LOGIC OF SERVICE

Beginning to gather a critical mass of researchers in the late 1970s, a new tradition in marketing theory appeared: services marketing, or service management and marketing (Grönroos 2007). The latter expression emphasized interfunctional dependency and the avoidance of organiza-tional silos. Contributions from human resources, organization, opera-tions management, quality management and other areas were needed to put services marketing activities in context. This was supported by the discovery that service consumption often (but not always) takes place simultaneously with the customer's active participation in the production and delivery. The observation led to an innovation, *the service encounter*, as a platform for service providers and customers to build interactive relationships.

Differences between goods and services became the springboard for services marketing, and the differences were codified as big "truths." This may have been useful in its time to attract attention to services, but this preoccupation with differences has now become a burden. Some of it turned out to be academic rhetoric that was grounded neither in reality nor in logic. Unfortunately it is sticky and, despite new knowledge, it is repeated in both research articles and textbooks (see the critique by Lovelock and Gummesson 2004 and Gummesson 2007).

The new millennium started with a gradual change in our perception of what suppliers deliver and where and when service, value, quality, excellence and customer satisfaction are brought into being. Goods marketing and services marketing have now merged on a higher level of abstraction, "the new service marketing" (Gummesson forthcoming a). It prepares the ground for more general, valid and relevant marketing theory. Above all, three developments are turning the tide:

- *Service-dominant logic* merges goods and services into value propositions. The outcome of economic activity is perceived as service and value, no matter if it is based on what is traditionally called services or goods. S-D logic is defined through ten foundational premises (Vargo and Lusch 2008), which have recently been condensed into four axioms (Lusch and Vargo 2014: 15): 1) service is the fundamental basis of exchange; 2) the customer is always a cocreator of value; 3) all economic and social actors are resource integrators; and 4) value is always uniquely and phenomenologically determined by the beneficiary. These recast the roles of customers and suppliers and turn customers as well as other members of a network into active resources from having been treated in marketing theory as passive recipients. Summarized from Vargo (2009), S-D logic tackles markets as complex network structures, but value is always contextually determined ("value-in-context"). It is a synthesis of the best from service and relationship marketing and a rejection of irrelevant parts (see also Mele et al. 2010).
- *Service science* is a long term and global program run by IBM to create a ground for designing and maintaining efficient, trouble-free and innovative service systems (Spohrer and Maglio 2009). Service science has adopted S-D logic as its philosophy (Maglio and Spohrer 2008). The idea is also gradually to drop the concept of computer science, which is machine-centric, for service science, which is user-centric. Education and research, especially in schools of technology, had neglected service and customer aspects. Systems embrace everything – goods, services, software, technology, the human touch and so on – and form complex networks of relationships and interactions with numerous stakeholders involved. Business and government service systems are trouble-ridden. The more activities that constitute a system the higher the risk for failure. Specialists may deliver subsystems with internal consistency, but the subsystems may not add up as a concerted effort to fit customer or citizen needs.

The cost of sluggish and deficient systems is enormous, and as far as I know no one has ventured to calculate it. Service science has identified cities and universities as the most important and densest service systems. And the slogan is challenging: Create a smarter planet (Spohrer and Maglio 2009)!

- The expression "one-to-one" inspired me to name my extended relationships approach *many-to-many marketing*. Many-to-many is about individuals and individual organizations, although it recognizes that there are lots of them; yet they require individual attention. Many-to-many marketing is based on the application of network theory on marketing, putting emphasis on complex relationships and interaction. It is an extension of relationship marketing and aligns harmoniously with S-D logic and service science (Gummesson 2008). Many-to-many marketing will be explained in more detail later in the chapter.

My conviction is that relationship marketing, its variants and the added understanding of service are leading toward a paradigm shift in marketing.

THE 30 RELATIONSHIPS OF MARKETING: THE 30RS

My relationship marketing concept became broad at an early stage. It is based on a synthesis that was originally conceived in the early 1980s and has kept progressing ever since. In its complete form it first appeared in the 1990s with my book *Total Relationship Marketing*. The book is now in its fourth edition (Gummesson forthcoming b) and has been gradually expanded and revised to elaborate further on relational approaches to marketing.

Many of the contributions to relationship marketing concern single properties that have been found to influence success. Commitment and trust are among those that have been much discussed (Morgan and Hunt 1994), but the list can be made almost endless. In addition I have especially settled for the following properties: collaboration, power, longevity, dependence, importance, risk, uncertainty, frequency, regularity, intensity, adaptation, attraction, closeness versus remoteness, formality versus informality, transparency, routinization, content, and personal and social properties.

These were single properties. Real-life relationship marketing consists of innumerable composites of such properties adapted to innumerable and specific contexts. Therefore the philosophy of relationship marketing has to be converted into hands-on relationships to engender viable marketing and business planning. This has been done by identifying 30 relationships, the 30Rs, which embrace a mix of relationships between parties and relationship properties. The 30Rs can be used as a checklist in practical marketing planning and as ideas for research.

From the very beginning of developing the 30Rs, I felt that the two-party relationship between a supplier and a customer was inadequate; it did not acknowledge the complexity of the marketing context. Thus the extension to networks of stakeholders has progressively been given a central role and forms the basis for this following description of the 30Rs.

The 30Rs were originally a reaction to the 4Ps that still form the vantage point for much of marketing management. The relationships are 30 and not just 4, thus underscoring complexity. The yearning for simplicity had reduced marketing instead of condensing its very essentials.

The Rs started to brew in my head in the early 1980s. They were inductively derived from research, literature and my own experience. Note that they were first defined in the pre-Internet era. I'm happy to say – but also somewhat surprised – that what came out of it stays fit since the mid-1990s when the Rs became complete. I have only found reasons to redefine the content of some of them to adapt to new technology and other contemporary contexts but not to change them basically. This is an indication of validity and relevance – but not of perfection. Categorizing a complex marketing reality is demanding, as data are fuzzy and therefore categories are doomed to be fuzzy sets. I welcome constructive criticism of my 30Rs, meaning that you offer a more useful alternative.

The 30Rs are grouped on four levels. They are listed with a brief explanatory text in Tables 14.1–14.4. Each level will be presented below.

The first two levels encompass *market relationships*. They constitute the basis for marketing; they are externally oriented and apply to the market proper. Some of them concern relationships to both consumers and other organizations; others are focused on either consumers or are interorganizational relationships.

The first three market relationships are referred to as *classic* (R1–R3, Table 14.1). They are omnipresent in marketing theory and textbooks. With the exception of the first relationship between a supplier and a customer (R1) – which is the foundation of marketing – the Rs are not in ranking order. Their significance is always contextual and varies between companies, markets and specific situations. Many-to-many network dimensions are inherent in the classic relationships, although these have not been emphasized within the conventional relationship marketing literature. In R2 the dyad turns into a triad of the

Table 14.1   Classic market relationships

R1	The classic dyad – the relationship between the supplier and the customer	This is the parent relationship of marketing, the foundation cocreation of value.
R2	The classic triad – the drama of the customer–supplier–competitor triangle	Competition is a central ingredient of the market economy. It is a threesome of the customer, the current supplier and the supplier's competitors.
R3	The classic network – distribution	Traditional physical distribution and modern channel management, including goods, services, people, information and whatever consists of a network of relationships.

supplier–customer–competitor and in R3 into a multi-party network, the physical distribution network.

There are numerous variations in the application of these classic relationships. To bring the variations to the fore, the next set of relationships is labeled *special market relationships* (R4–R17, Table 14.2). For example, R4, relationships via *full-time marketers (FTMs)* and *part-time marketers (PTMs)*, puts emphasis on interfunctional dependency and that not only the designated marketing and sales people relate to customers and influence their perception of the seller. The close versus the distant relationship (R8) highlights the necessity of being close to the customer but also to others such as intermediaries and the media. Marketing textbooks give the impression that market research, usually statistical customer satisfaction surveys through ordinary post, the telephone or email and with standardized questions and answers, is adequate to understanding what is going on in the real world. In my view, surveys are only supplementary to the hands-on knowledge that you get in the field. Today the e-relationship (R12) permeates marketing. It has sometimes greatly improved customer–supplier interaction but sometimes raised an impermeable Berlin Wall between them; the customer cannot speak to a real person and clear up a problem. It has given rise to a new type of crime: efficiently and with limited risk mugging people without physical violence. This links to the last of the special market relationships, the criminal network (R17). Marketing and economics alike pretend that crime and corruption do not exist. Global organized crime especially is on the increase (Bagelius and Gummesson 2013). It upsets the functions of the market economy. Leaders of organized crime also go to business schools and learn systematic marketing and management. They see themselves as

Table 14.2   Special market relationships

R4	Relationships via full-time marketers (FTMs) and part-time marketers (PTMs)	Those who work in marketing, sales departments and customer service departments – the FTMs – are professional relationship makers. All others, who perform other main functions but yet influence customer relationships directly or indirectly, are PTMs. There are also contributing FTMs and PTMs outside the selling organization.
R5	The service encounter – interaction between customers and supplier	Traditionally production and delivery of services often involve the customer in an interactive relationship with the provider. In light of S-D logic the service encounter is broadened and the platform for cocreation of value; it is not limited to services in the traditional sense.
R6	The many-headed customer and the many-headed supplier	Marketing to other organizations, B2B, often means contacts between many individuals from the supplier's and the customer's organization.
R7	The relationship to the customer's customer	A condition for success is often the understanding of the customer's customer, and what suppliers can do to help their customers become successful.
R8	The close versus the distant relationship	In mass marketing, the closeness to the customer is lost and the relationship becomes distant, based on surveys, statistics and written reports.
R9	The relationship to the dissatisfied customer	It is common that dissatisfied customers experience a more intense relationship to a supplier than usual. The way of handling a complaint – the recovery – is often careless by providers, although it affects the quality of the future relationship.
R10	The monopoly relationship – the customer or supplier as prisoners	When competition is inhibited, the customer may be at the mercy of the supplier – or the other way around. One of them becomes prisoner.
R11	The customer as "member"	In order to create a long-term sustaining relationship, it has become increasingly common to enlist customers as members of various loyalty programs and clubs.
R12	The e-relationship	The electronic relationship, the e-relationship, represented by the Internet, email, social media, mobile telephony and other IT applications, is set against the h-relationship, the human relationship. The high tech/high touch balance becomes increasingly crucial in relationship marketing and CRM.

Table 14.2   (continued)

R13	Parasocial relationships – relationships to brands and objects	Relationships exist not only with people, but also with objects and mental images – symbols – such as brands and corporate identities.
R14	The non-commercial relationship	This is the relationship between the government sector, non-government organizations (NGOs), voluntary organizations and the commons, as well as activities outside of the official economy, such as those performed in families and between friends.
R15	The green relationship and CSR	Environmental and health issues and social responsibility in general have slowly increased in importance and are creating a new type of customer relationship through legislation, the voice of opinion-leading consumers and politicians, and changing behavior of consumers and citizens.
R16	The law-based relationship	A relationship to a customer is sometimes founded primarily on legal contracts and the threat of litigation.
R17	The criminal network	Organized crime is built on tight and often impermeable networks guided by an illegal business mission. Crime networks exist globally and are growing but are disregarded by marketing theory. These networks disturb the functioning of a market or industry.

business executives and are increasingly infiltrating legitimate business. The problem is their lack of citizenship and ethics treated as (R15) the green relationship and corporate social responsibility (CSR).

The next two types are *non-market relationships*, which influence the efficiency of market relationships. *Mega relationships* (R18–R23, Table 14.3) exist above the market relationships. They provide conditions for market relationships and concern the economy and society in general. Among these are R18 (social relationships, such as friendship and ethnic bonds), and R19 (mega marketing, such as lobbying, public opinion and political power). Although of utmost significance, mega relationships are little addressed in marketing textbooks and research.

Nano relationships (R24–R30, Table 14.4) are found below the market relationships; they are relationships inside an organization. Marketing is focused on the external environment, but the borderline between a firm's

Table 14.3   Mega relationships

R18	Personal and social networks	Personal and social networks often determine business networks. In some cultures, business is solely conducted between friends and friends of friends.
R19	Mega marketing – the real "customer" is not always found in the marketplace	In certain instances, relationships must be sought with governments, legislators, influential individuals and others in order to make marketing feasible.
R20	Alliances change the market mechanisms	Alliances mean closer relationships and collaboration between companies. Thus, competition is partly curbed, but collaboration is necessary to make the market economy work.
R21	The knowledge relationship	Knowledge can be the most strategic and critical resource, and knowledge acquisition is often the rationale for alliances.
R22	Mega alliances change the basic conditions for marketing	The European Union (EU) and the North American Free Trade Agreement (NAFTA) are examples of alliances above the single company and industry. They exist on government and supranational levels.
R23	The mass media relationship	The media can be supportive or damaging to marketing and they are particularly influential in forming public opinion. The relationship to media is crucial for the way they will handle an issue.

internal and external relationships is often thin, sometimes even erased. This is very obvious in the cocreation of value between suppliers, customers and other network stakeholders. All internal activities influence the externally bound relationships. Examples of nano relationships are the relationship between internal customers (R25), which are employees and organizational units. The relationship to owners and financiers (R30) is treated as a nano relationship here. When those with the wallet make short term decisions on the board of directors it is difficult to keep up a long term relationship marketing strategy. Therefore, make sure you have supportive owners and banks with a long term perspective.

The 30Rs have exposed the breadth and complexity of relationship marketing. The boundary between the market, mega and nano levels, and the external and internal relationships is fuzzy; it is a matter of emphasis. For example, the physical distribution network (R3) is part of a logistics flow, concerning internal as well as external customers.

Networks and many-to-many marketing have popped up every now

Table 14.4   Nano relationships

R24	Market mechanisms are brought inside the company	Through the introduction of profit centers in an organization, a market inside the company is created, and internal as well as external relationships of a new kind emerge.
R25	Internal customer relationship	The dependency between the different tiers and departments in a company is seen as a process consisting of relationships between internal customers and internal suppliers.
R26	Quality and customer orientation: the relationship between operations management and marketing	The modern quality concept has built a bridge between design, engineering, purchasing, production and other technology-based activities and marketing. It considers the company's internal relationships as well as its relationships to the customers.
R27	Internal marketing: relationships with the "employee market"	Internal marketing can be seen as part of relationship marketing, as it gives indirect and necessary support to the relationships with external customers.
R28	The two-dimensional matrix relationship	Matrices are the simplest form of networks and exist in all large corporations, and above all they are found in the relationships between product management and sales.
R29	The relationship to external providers of marketing services	External providers reinforce the marketing function by supplying specialized services in, for example, advertising, market research and distribution.
R30	The owner and financier relationship	Owners and other financiers partly determine the conditions under which a marketing function can operate. The relationship to them influences marketing strategy.

and then during our journey but will now dominate the landscape. The next stop of the journey exposes the importance of centricity in marketing: Who should be at the center of attention? It will be followed by a guided tour of complexity theory and the methodology that I favor: *case study research* in the novel form of *case theory*. It is followed by a definition of many-to-many marketing and an effort to offer a relational and expanded mix of the 4Ps, which are neither 4 nor Ps anymore, and the necessity to enter them into a network context. A real-world case concludes the chapter.

FROM ONE-PARTY CENTRICITY TO BALANCED CENTRICITY

In the 1950s and 1960s marketing management established itself as a discipline. A new type of reader-friendly textbooks started to come out. Early ones were Howard (1957), McCarthy (1960), who formulated the condensed 4P marketing mix, and Kotler (1967). The marketing mix consisted of strategies that could be applied to the planning and execution of marketing. Supportive techniques such as marketing planning, marketing research and segmentation grew in sophistication. The idea was to manage the market, including customers, intermediaries, competitors, the media and others. It was a one-sided approach with the supplier as King of Marketingland. Increasing understanding of customer needs, wants and behavior and how to adapt to and satisfy these led to the marketing concept and the ideas of market and customer orientation. The customer was declared the New King but more so in rhetoric than in practice. The Old King lingered on the throne, albeit with a more benevolent view of his subjects and a willingness to listen to them – but primarily on the Old King's conditions. Figure 14.1 illustrates the conceptual move from supplier to customer centricity, ending up in supplier-controlled customer centricity.

The old saying "The customer is always right" can mean at least two things: 1) the customer is cleverer than the supplier, which is sometimes true, sometimes not; and 2) if customers think they are right let them believe so and give them what they want. But the saying epitomizes an "us versus them" attitude and a fight for the throne. It is either–or; it is win–lose. If we make it both, we enter a different mode of thinking – dialog and interaction on equal, win–win terms – which is cocreation of value. It is the latter attitude that fits relational approaches.

Relationship marketing grew out of services marketing and parts of B2B marketing. In these the focus has primarily been on the dyad, the two-party relationship between a customer and a supplier, as shown in Figure 14.2. This focus has been productive by adding the relationship dimension. In my view it takes the lead over marketing management and the 4Ps, not by throwing them away but by positioning them on a lower level in marketing theory.

A reason why relational approaches have not been as successful as many of their advocates had hoped may be that they focus too much on the two-party relationship and customer centricity. This may not be realistic. Business and society consist of numerous stakeholders who all say "Put all the light on me!" Owners and investors have been successful in claiming that augmentation of shareholder value is the mission of business. Where

Three variations of one party centricity

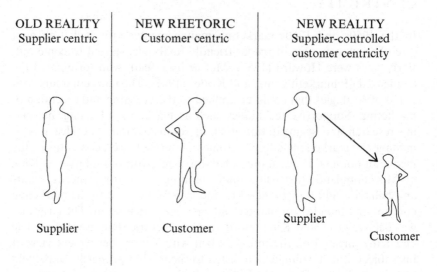

1950s–1970s:
TRADITIONAL AMERICAN MARKETING MANAGEMENT AND MARKETING MIX

Source: Adapted from Gummesson (forthcoming b); used with permission.

Figure 14.1   Supplier and customer centricity in marketing

Relationship centric marketing
Centered on <u>two</u> parties

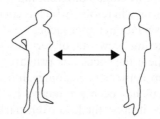

Customer   Supplier
1980s–PRESENT: RELATIONSHIP MARKETING,
CRM AND ONE-TO-ONE MARKETING

Source: Adapted from Gummesson (forthcoming b); used with permission.

*Figure 14.2   Two-party centricity: marketing focus on a win–win
relationship between customers and suppliers*

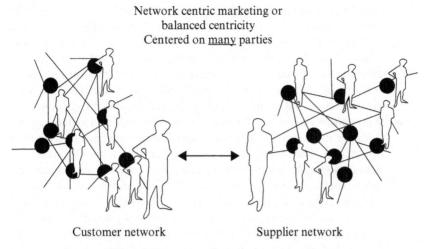

Network centric marketing or
balanced centricity
Centered on <u>many</u> parties

Customer network   Supplier network

2000s–PRESENT: MANY-TO-MANY MARKETING

Source: Adapted from Gummesson (forthcoming b); used with permission.

*Figure 14.3   Network centricity: networks meet networks, thus considering
multiple stakeholders*

trade unions are strong the demand for employee centricity is paramount. In Figure 14.3 network centricity or *balanced centricity* is introduced where multiple stakeholders are recognized. Networks meet networks. This multi-party approach translates into many-to-many marketing. Even if network or stakeholder icons are lacking on the conventional marketing screen, practicing managers are used to balance demands from customers, suppliers, intermediaries, employees, shareholders, governments and so on.

HANDLING MARKETING COMPLEXITY THROUGH CASE THEORY

Marketing and value creation through service systems are complex, and complexity should be an overriding issue in marketing. Above all I want to emphasize three aspects of complexity (Gummesson forthcoming a):

- *Recognition of the multitude of variables and the links and influences between them*. It includes the avoidance of non-productive oversimplification, such as: assumptions about customers being rational; all other variables staying "normal" (ceteris paribus); structuring a problem to fit a research technique (operationalization); and dropping disturbing findings (anomalies). Such assumptions reduce validity and relevance. We have to accept non-linearity and not flee into the safe house of academic linearity in which corners are cut for researcher convenience. In economics – belatedly, without considering extant research in marketing but with much hullabaloo – they have made an effort to crawl out of the box and introduce "behavioral economics."

● *Recognition of context.* We need general theories and general guide-lines for marketing, but the combination of strategies is invariably contextual. The strategies must be designed for a specific situation, actual customer behavior in targeted markets, competitor moves, infrastructural changes, political decisions and so on. When an issue is reduced to details and parts, an effort must always be made to place them in a systemic context. Even if we are not capable of comprehending the whole picture, we must at least feel the taste of honey. It further means that methodology claimed to be generally applicable to all social sciences has to be adapted to a marketing and management context.

● *Recognition of the only true constant in life: change.* Network theory was sometimes discarded as providing only static structure but is increasingly used for treating processes – changes in and of structures – as well. The behavior of companies, customers and the competition changes, new technology can make existing products obsolete, and so on. All this is part of everyday marketing. Then there are more dramatic changes in markets and the economy, such as the global financial meltdown that took off at full blast in 2008 and was still not put in order in 2014. We do not know as yet whether this is an irreversible discontinuity and paradigm shift, or whether things will go back to "normal" given sufficient time.

Complexity as a scientific domain has established itself in natural sci-ences and is slowly gaining ground in social sciences. With many-to-many we have arrived at the stage where complexity is being recognized in mar-keting. I have found that in social sciences case study research is the only widely used methodology that can handle complexity without imposing hosts of simplifying restrictions on a study. I have also found that the current use of cases for research can be improved in several ways, which has led up to the introduction of *case theory* (Gummesson forthcoming a). Of special interest here is the extension of the traditional case narrative, which is primarily based on words and to some extent on graphics and numbers, to include network theory, systems theory and fuzzy set theory in various degrees of sophistication.

Not all universities and journals accept case study research in marketing, and some consider statistical techniques such as surveys to be superior. The weakness with statistical techniques is that they cannot handle the complexity of service systems and the new service marketing logic. When results are hard to achieve, social sciences, including management and business, build their own universe of facilitating assumptions and convenience procedures. They quote each other, offering more of the same rather than development; it is quantity over quality. This guarding of the virginity of the mainstream gets institutionalized through ranking systems, funding and tightly regulated career paths. It may secure uniform quality inside the mainstream box, but it impedes breaking out of the box and thus impedes academic innovativeness and entrepreneurship.

The richness and complexity of relationships must come out in full bloom. In practical marketing, complexity has to be handled whether it fits preconceived ideas or not. It is about survival. My learning about complexity takes place in inductive case study research rather than through surveys and deductive hypotheses testing. Within case study research there are numerous ways of generating and processing data. I am not setting up the ideas of qualitative and quantitative against each other, as that is yet another categorization that impedes research. On the other hand, I find the application of quantitative techniques where they cannot deliver and the appointment of these techniques as superior to other techniques a shambles. Words and numbers form languages, and languages should be used when they apply and deliver.

Natural sciences are more daring than social sciences. Within *complexity theory* they have created a zoo of wild beasts that scientists try to domesticate. Among its yet untamed inhabitants are network theory, quantum theory, chaos theory, fractal geometry, autopoiesis (self-organizing systems) and several others. They have developed during the preceding hundred years in modern natural sciences and modern mathematics. They can be combined in accordance with the researcher's wishes in the pursuit of new insights. The new is adaptable to social life and, by the way, the categorization in natural sciences, social sciences and the humanities has been irrelevant and obsolete for a long time (Stacey 2007).

Complexity cannot be addressed without recognizing *simplicity*. In Western science these two are treated as opposites; it is either–or. I advocate both; complexity and simplicity are in interaction and continuously searching for an optimal or more realistically satisficing balance. In our personal lives and as business practitioners we have to find simple ways of muddling through based on incomplete information and limited understanding of a situation. Marketing managers need checklists and "the five keys to profitable marketing" to survive the day. The current problem with marketing theory on a midrange level (or "stuck-in-the-middle" level) and not striving toward grand theory is that overly simplistic formats like the 4Ps establish themselves and block our perception of reality. So we are looking for the balance between parts that we can overview and the whole picture, which we can't overview. My solution is that we accept both. Scholars should engage in long term basic research. They are not haunted by the demand for quick decisions and actions as the chief marketing executive is. To make things easier we need condensation, not reduction. Making a concept dense means packaging its essence into something more accessible but without losing information; reducing a concept means taking away information and diluting the concept.

Network theory offers a way of thinking in relationships and inter-action but also techniques for addressing complexity (Barabási 2002; Gummesson forthcoming b, forthcoming c). In its basic form, Figure 14.3 showed network graphics expressed as *nodes* and *links*. For example, a consumer node has a link to a supplier node. If there are more than two nodes and one link a network begins to emerge. Interaction takes place in the links, and the nodes influence and are influenced. It is a powerful tool to describe and analyze marketing. It even reflects how we think intuitively in practical life. Network theory can be used with different degrees of sophistication: verbal treatise (discussion or text), graphics (from sketches of nodes and links to computer generated diagrams), mathematical processing and computer simulation.

Many-to-many marketing is an application of network theory. Marketing is part of or a perspective on management, and to become effi-cient marketing should be seen in a management context; it's *marketing-oriented management* rather than marketing management. The Industrial Marketing and Purchasing Group (IMP), founded in Sweden, has addressed certain aspects of networks in B2B marketing since the 1970s (Håkansson et al. 2009). Other writers on relationship marketing have also broadened their view to a multi-party approach, for example Christopher et al. (2002) with "6 markets" and Morgan and Hunt (1994) with "10 part-nerships." The viable system approach (VSA) developed in Italy offers an effort to see a company in its systemic and complex reality. It concerns the total management of the company, but marketing is an integral part of the system and must be seen in its context (Barile and Polese 2010).

DEFINING MANY-TO-MANY MARKETING

Morsels of many-to-many marketing have been handed to the reader along our journey in Marketingland. Relationship marketing has limited itself to the two-party relationship between a customer and a supplier, although the 30Rs and some other models open up for a network view. Many-to-many takes the full step to multi-party relationships. It is defined in the following way (Gummesson forthcoming b): "Many-to-many marketing describes, analyzes and utilizes the network properties of marketing."

Many-to-many strategies stand out in several of the 30Rs, for example by showing that the service encounter includes many parties in interaction (R5); that the customer and the seller are many-headed (R6); that increasingly influential organized crime consists of networks (R17); that social and professional networks are important (R18); that relationships above the seller and buyer are influential (R19); that mega alliances change the basic conditions for marketing (R22); that marketing is dependent on other functions and has thus contributed to the interfunctional and inter-hierarchical dependency and a network between internal customers and suppliers (R25); and that quality has put the spotlight on the necessity to bridge the gap between technology, purchasing and marketing (R26). The first three Rs are market networks, the following three mega networks and the last two nano networks.

In B2B, two companies in a selling and buying negotiating stage are often represented by teams, many meeting many. Consumers purchase for personal consumption, but also for their families and dogs and cats, and they are influenced by advice from friends and the values of lifestyle groups to which they belong. A consumer network cocreates value with a retailer network.

Networks are largely ignored in marketing literature and education. The inner life of the organization is rarely treated as a network. Networks have primarily been treated in B2B marketing. But B2B is an antecedent to business-to-consumer (B2C) marketing. In the words of Gummesson and Polese (2009), "B2B is not an island." Or in line with the current theory, explicit in S-D logic, cocreation of value makes it appropriate to talk about consumer-to-business (C2B), stressing the consumer's role of operant resource.

There is further a growing interest in the interaction between customers, customer-to-customer interaction (C2C). This was once restricted to simultaneous physical presence. The telephone changed it during the twentieth century, and in last few last years the Internet, email and mobile technology have given rise to an expanded role for customers in marketing. C2C is most conspicuous in today's interactive websites and the social media.

All this is connected in endless networks – B2B2C2C2B2B ... – and the networks exist on market, mega and nano levels. The Bs and Cs have recently been further generalized to actor-to-actor interaction (A2A) (Lusch and Vargo 2014; Gummesson forthcoming b). Many-to-many marketing addresses the richness and variety of interaction in networks of relationships. Whether the customers are consumers, companies, governments or NGOs makes no difference. None thrives in isolation.

Even if networks have been treated in many sciences and in limited parts of marketing for a long time, it is striking how few footprints they have left in the 1000-page textbooks that claim generality. Even in B2B textbooks the acceptance is limited; networks are treated as special cases. In the literature on consumer marketing networks hardly exist. The connection between B2B and B2C is uncommon in the literature; it's just a snack to the welcome drink. In the future it is recommended that the A2A concept is used and that B2B and B2C/C2B are used solely as two of many dimensions of marketing but not as overriding categories.

Our journey started with a frugal concept of relationship marketing and midrange theory but keeps looking for the land flowing with milk and honey: grand theory. *The unique contribution of many-to-many marketing is the thesis that networks, which put relationships and interactions of a complex world into a dynamic context, are the basis of all marketing. Consequently it can be a contribution to grand theory development in marketing and management.*

A RELATIONAL AND EXTENDED MARKETING MIX

Relationship marketing and marketing management have not felt comfortable in each other's company. Should they be friends or foes, fight a hot or cold war, or just keep a neutral distance?

There is uncertainty and there is no easy way of categorizing marketing strategies. This is blatantly obvious if you look at the efforts so far. The 4Ps have become popular, although they are not the only effort to simplify the description of marketing (Grönroos 1997; Constantinides 2006). Can the 4Ps develop a working relationship with relationship marketing? Unfortunately too many advocates of relationship marketing are heavily programmed – even brainwashed – by the marketing mix paradigm. They cannot see the new and degrade relationships to a paragraph and a special case. The new is squeezed into the old box, like listing relationships under the P promotion. It is similar to squeezing digital technology into steam-engine mechanics.

Networks do not only consist of relationships person to person, organization to person or organization to organization. The nodes can represent whatever you want them to. Network theory and graphics will be used here to approach the complexity of the marketing mix.

Today marketing penetrates every corner of society and not just the market. Fast food chains establish themselves in hospitals and schools. Technology, shopping and consumption have become the meaning of life through experiences, adrenaline kicks and trendy brands. Music videos on TV tout such messages globally 24/7 and especially target the young. We now spend more money in the experience industry than on food. Andy Warhol said that the USA is "a country united, most of all, by commercialism," and Barbara Kruger's graphic image declared "I shop, therefore I am." The monumental buildings today are not cathedrals or royal palaces but shopping malls, arenas for sports and concerts, and airports.

Therefore it is not obvious when we are exposed to marketing. We have gone from 1P, price, which is the basis of neoclassical economics ("price theory"), to the marketing mix of 4Ps and even more Ps. The 4Ps are a huge improvement over the poverty of the 1P. Even if the 4Ps communicate in a popular way they are not complete. Complexity is made too simplistic, with limited validity, generality and relevance, and many are fooled into believing that the 4Ps offer the whole truth and nothing but the truth. You could not do that in rocket science; there is no pedagogical shortcut to flying to the moon.

Well, marketing is not rocket science. But shouldn't it be? Public pressure and legislation against tobacco promotion have prompted the industry to find smarter ways of exposing their products. In his mind-boggling book *Buyology*, Martin Lindstrom (2008) reports how neuroscience makes old "truths" in marketing stand out as embarrassingly stupid. His research shows that lung cancer warnings on cigarette packages and TV activate the smoker's reward and craving brain centers to urgently demand a cigarette. So, instead of being for the public best, the warnings promote the cigarette industry. Subliminal promotions such as logo-free advertising through colors and shapes and interior decorations of bars stimulate the consumer's desire for a specific cigarette brand more than the explicit messages. It does not mean that invasive and non-interactive advertising like TV spots – which consumers actively try to avoid – is dead. Lindstrom (2008: 43) illustrates a forcing attitude where sponsors of TV programs "are letting us know that it's futile to hide, duck, dodge, fast-forward, or take an extended bathroom break: they'll get to us *somehow*." The cigarette case shows that marketing may be more elaborate in application than theory and education admit. The complexity of the social universe is no less mysterious than the universe of the stars and planets. Marketing also needs rocket science.

Marketing strategies merge and can't be treated as stand-alones. The

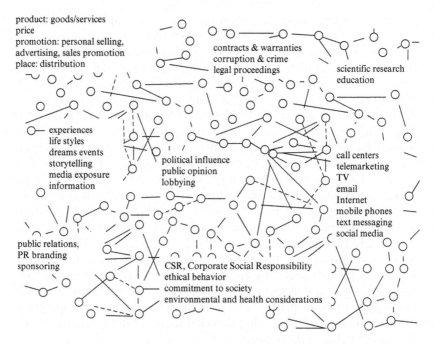

product: goods/services
price
promotion: personal selling,
advertising, sales promotion
place: distribution

contracts & warranties
corruption & crime
legal proceedings

scientific research
education

experiences
life styles
dreams events
storytelling
media exposure
information

political influence
public opinion
lobbying

call centers
telemarketing
TV
email
Internet
mobile phones
text messaging
social media

public relations,
PR branding
sponsoring

CSR, Corporate Social Responsibility
ethical behavior
commitment to society
environmental and health considerations

Source: Based on Gummesson (forthcoming b); used with permission.

Figure 14.4   *Today's "Ps" are neither Ps nor 4: numerous strategies interact in complex networks of relationships influenced by an extended relational marketing mix*

product is very much the pricing, promotion and place (distribution) as well. We will end our conceptual journey with a guided tour through an exhibition of "Ps." Figure 14.4 provides my best effort so far to add to our understanding of the complexity and context of marketing strategies. Even if it can be seen as a step forward there is a long way to go to formulate this into more valid and relevant grand theory. The expanded "Ps" lie on a network bed, which stresses the interrelationships between the strategies.

Originally the first P, product, was *goods,* and later *services* were added. Marketing makes many efforts to find a deeper meaning behind what we are buying and consuming. *Value proposition* has been advanced as a merger of goods and services and whatever is involved. We are also known to seek *experiences* and *dreams* through parties, diving in the Barrier Reef, or queuing up in the Louvre in Paris to see *Mona Lisa* for a brief moment. These choices are part of our *lifestyle.* The product can be an international *event* like the European Song Contest or a local exhibition of roses. The event is the product, but it is filled with promotional activities and sales offerings (food, drink, candy, souvenirs). Television shows are littered with commercial breaks, commercial symbols and product placement.

A product is also defined through *media exposure* and *storytelling*; we buy a story about something rather than the thing itself. For example, all stories about the love lives of celebrities build fame and sell tickets to theatres. The product is also *information* where websites and search engines such as Google have opened up new channels which are competing with or supplementing traditional news media.

The second P, price, is an intricate phenomenon. The classic economics supply and demand equilibrium only holds in special instances. In real life, pricing and getting customers to accept a price are a gamble involving costing, revenue, profit margins, volume, social influence, trickery, individual perceptions, expectations, inflation, competition, local conditions and so on. Prices also come in a multitude of different modes: fixed prices in supermarkets, negotiable prices in some stores, special agreements with loyal customers, exchanges and auctions to mention some of the more common. Today the pricing of hotel rooms and air tickets is partly computer-controlled and variable with supply, demand and the time of purchase. Customers are only partially aware of the mechanisms, and economic theory evades them.

The third P, promotion, once consisted of *advertising, personal selling* and *sales promotion*. Today it has become more sophisticated, as we have already discussed. Traveling by air is a core product, but today's airports are increasingly restaurants and stores that profit from our waiting for flights; we are captive customers, we have time to shop and sometimes there are price advantages because of taxes ("tax-free shopping"), and we have foreign currency left in our pocket. The purchasing becomes an integral part of the air travel. It is followed up in the aircraft with food and drink and special offers of products, all becoming integrated with the travel experience.

Advertising through the mass media and direct mail is supplemented by *public relations* (PR), with the aim of creating a positive image of a company. The messages are concealed in seemingly objective news reports and planted documentaries. There is mounting belief in *branding* and loading symbols with positive connotations. In a Formula 1 race the cars are covered by logotypes, and World Cup skiers are advertising pillars. Events are increasingly dependent on such *sponsorship*. A cultural or sports event gives the sponsoring companies an opportunity to expose themselves to the market and sometimes get into personal interaction with customers. They become associated with the event, and the glory of the winner of an Olympic gold medal is reflected on them.

On a mega level *politics, lobbying* and *public opinion formation* have established themselves as major marketing tools. They are used in honest and dishonest ways. Public opinion sometimes acts with common sense, sometimes not. For example, lobbyists can educate ignorant and stressed politicians, but they can also corrupt them and circumvent the democratic process to the benefit of their company or industry and to the detriment of customers, citizens and society. In a derogatory sense lobbyists are also known as "spin doctors."

Scientific research and *education* have received growing attention by companies as marketing opportunities. A long-existing case is the influence of the pharmaceutical industry over medical research. Scientists are dependent on their sponsorship, and the pharma industry needs the knowledge from research hospitals, but also to bask in the prestige of science, thus adding to its credibility in the public eye.

IT has given rise to *call centers*, which companies themselves run as customer contact and help desks or outsource to specialized providers. *Telemarketing* has entered into a new phase. These two operations require plenty of staff and add employment opportunities, but are equally dependent on IT; they are high tech/high touch. A *television program* could be a product but is today so full of advertising, banners and so on that are forced on you and may spoil the whole product. *Email, websites, mobile phones* and *text messaging* have redesigned the communication landscape. An avalanche of *social media* is offered, but many of these media have also turned into commercial platforms. The dissolution of the boundaries between telecom, television and computers is spawning a new world for marketers and customers. IT also causes problems. The *Internet* architecture is not designed to protect against dishonesty, and today a large share of the cost of a computer and its software goes to patching its unsafe service systems and continuously updating security software to curb abuse. Further, spam, pop-up windows and inventively transmitted advertising are intrusive elements, but they help finance digital service.

Contracts and *warranties* are big in B2B and often take up a major share of the negotiations about a complex sale; with some exceptions consumers are less active here. This is also closely related to the problems of *corruption* and *crime* in marketing, which may call for *legal proceedings*.

Finally, issues on *ethical behavior* in business, *commitment to society* and *environment and health* cause conflicts in the relationships between customers/citizens and suppliers. Unfortunately all too often businesses try to "solve" this through PR, with white-washing and green-washing as the core marketing strategy, rather than tackling the real problem.

It has been an effort to lay bare the complexity and interrelatedness of marketing strategies beyond the 4Ps. The categories are fuzzy by nature, and the categories presented here can be improved; this is just a beginning to free ourselves of the crude simplification of the 4Ps and set them in a network perspective, aligning them to the new logic of service and marketing.

A SUMMING-UP CASE

This chapter has taken us on a journey through the many concepts that constitute my Marketingland. Its purpose was to explore the evolution of relationship marketing and where it is heading. We visited the 30Rs, CRM and one-to-one and ended up in the complex interactive networks of many-to-many marketing. We visited supplier and customer centricity and the move toward balanced centricity. We toured marketing management and the 4P marketing mix to land in an extended relational mix. We found services on the map and stopped by a museum which exposed services marketing and management where goods and services were treated as two separate species. We moved to S-D logic where goods, services, software, information and what have you are embodied in knowledge and value propositions, the outcome being cocreated service involving customers, suppliers and other network members. Service science offered the sight of service systems in need of design and management on a substantially higher level of reliability. The whole journey was accompanied by relationships, networks and interaction. The itinerary became progressively more affected by IT and the new infrastructure of the Internet, email and mobile communication. Infrastructures – like roads, postal services or electricity grids – are networks. Today's IT is clearly both a technical and a social network.

It has been a conceptual journey, although the importance of practical relevance has been underscored. The rest of this summary consists of a complex case where the visited concepts have a role. It intends to make the concepts come alive in a context that we can relate to through our own experience. This should render a sense of the validity and relevance of the concepts and the necessity to address complexity through case theory. This will allow deeper understanding of complexity and dynamics.

The case comes from healthcare. It is rich and complex and concerns us all. In conventional – but unfortunately meaningless – terms, healthcare is a subsector of the service sector, which is a garbage can for all that does not fit the manufacturing and agricultural sectors (Gummesson 2007). Healthcare itself is extraordinary in its diversity. Each type of health service must therefore be examined on a substantive level and in minute detail until we sense its inner nature. Then, and only then, are we able to let our findings raise the level of generalization in marketing theory.

In 2009 the following event topped the news. A global epidemic, a pandemic popularly called swine flu, was spreading around the world. Its rapid spread added new dimensions to the influenza and the networks involved. In complexity theory, epidemic trajectories offer a generalized understanding of the course of events from the start, through the progress, and the sudden arrival of a tipping point, followed by termination. It provides an alternative to the conventional life cycle of products and the dissemination of information in the market that have been advanced in marketing management.

In September 2009 swine flu was approaching Europe and the USA from Asia and Mexico. Intense but confused preparations were made. Research so far had shown the flu to be mild, even milder than the common seasonal flu. Like all flu it could strike hard at some people, and deaths in the high risk groups of infants, the elderly and the chronically ill could occur. These were prime target groups for vaccination. This time people between 20 and 40 years of age were more severely affected than other groups, which caused insecurity and speculation in the medical network. There was a high risk of side effects for those who were already on heavy medication, as the synergy effects between their current medication and the vaccine were little known.

How does healthcare organize to receive, treat and vaccinate masses of people in the shortest possible time? The healthcare resource network is broad. It embraces the nano networks of doctors, nurses, laboratory staff, health administrations, and others who work in hospitals and clinics. In its core are market networks: consumers, patients and citizens, and their families and workplaces. Then there are suppliers of vaccines and medication and their intermediaries, who had to establish emergency logistical networks in collaboration with the mega networks of local, regional and national governments, politicians, and international organizations like the World Health Organization (WHO). The network boundaries are fuzzy, and the nano, market and mega designations rather refer to perspectives on an overriding network. The flu embraced numerous systems which should converge into a system of systems to match customer needs and behavior. But they usually only do so in a partially ordered way, leaving the customer in a troubled situation. This is a major concern of service science.

Healthcare is still ruled by the unrealistic postulate that the doctor is an expert and the patient ignorant, and that the doctor actively does something to the passive patient. Many-to-many marketing and S-D logic hold that the two are active resources cocreating service and value.

The flu was first found in pigs. This most likely reduced the sales of pork, although public authorities attested that there was no risk of infection if the pork was cooked. But could consumers trust the authorities and their experts? In the media experts spoke in all directions, offering a blend of information and noise. The confusion was accentuated when a reporter added a news twist to a story and editorial gnomes further twisted the content in headlines, one-liners and flashy pictures. The next day the story might go in another direction. Those who spoke had their special agenda, such as instilling trust in people to avoid panic. They might overtly or covertly represent pharmaceutical companies. Much of the research at university hospitals is directly or indirectly sponsored by commercial interests. Even if the funding is not explicitly conditional, there may be tacit agreements that are conducive to the sponsoring company's marketing but might not necessarily consider public responsibility.

Obviously marketing beckons in every corner of these networks of people and organizations. It is not known how the flu originated and why it did so at a specific moment. Two experts say that it leaked from a lab; the genetic combination could not have sprung up naturally. Could the flu have been planted by the pharmaceutical industry to create a market, or is this just conspiracy theory? "Big Pharma" is eager to sell vaccines and other medication. This cannot be achieved within the limited 4P mix. It must be handled through a many-to-many approach where specific networks and interactions are defined.

There was a lot of knowledge – which is the core of service – but there was uncertainty and ignorance and still decisions and action had to be taken. First, we were informed that we needed two shots of vaccine. Health authorities and others placed orders accordingly. Then it was claimed that one shot was enough, leaving the buyers with huge stocks of non-usable vaccine.

Time had not allowed the vaccine to be properly tested. After having studied existing reports one doctor concluded that 1) it was not proven that the swine flu vaccine had any protective effect at all and 2) it was proven that flu vaccines could have severe complications. Hallucinations, mental disturbances and cramps had been reported in children who had taken Tamiflu shots, and it may have caused five deaths in Japan. Even if knowledge about the virus gradually accumulated, the virus could suddenly mutate into a meaner version with unfamiliar properties. It left the field wide open for rumors, lobbying and public relations. It became imperative for suppliers to raise the media interest and make people demand vaccination as a citizen's right. Politicians were pressed by voters to allocate fresh money. The vaccine was in short supply, and delivery in time was uncertain. Related products were pain-killers and everything that could augment your immune system, such as vitamins, minerals and quality fruit and vegetables. Although healthcare is classified as services in official statistics, the healthcare service system is jam-packed with goods. It is the combination, the whole value proposition, that counts. It is cocreation of value where customers have a pivotal role by minding their hygiene and when ill avoiding public places. C2C interaction is part of the cocreation, as citizens can be supportive to each other in, for example, families.

According to the primitive interpretation of the free market forces and neoclassical economics, pharma companies should use the situation to overprice the vaccine. Pharma companies live in a competitive market economy. They develop and produce drugs and consequently they want hospitals and the public to buy at the highest possible price. In the spirit of relationship marketing and the cocreation of value this would jeopardize long term collaboration; it wouldn't be win–win. But pharma companies want life-time loyal customers; they want zero defection. The ideal customer is in need of one or several drugs regularly. So drugs should not cure but temporarily cause relief and keep the patient alive as long as possible. Some drugs are addictive and, when they are no longer needed to fight a disease, the patient is left with an addiction. Use turns into abuse, which unfortunately boosts the profits of drug sellers. A new R, the chemical relationship, could be added to the 30Rs. In a market economy, the pharma industry cannot live on developing drugs that cure quickly or are demanded only by small groups. An epidemic may be short lived, but it includes masses, which makes it interesting. Obviously the market economy is not a win–win solution if all stakeholders in the many-to-many network are considered. There is a need for balanced centricity, but the risk is great that supplier centricity and supplier-controlled customer centricity will take over.

In conclusion: *No marketing escapes interaction in networks of relationships.*

REFERENCES

Bagelius, N. and E. Gummesson (2013), "Criminal Marketing: An Inhuman Side of Business," in R.J. Varey (ed.), *Humanistic Marketing*, New York: Palgrave Macmillan.
Ballantyne, D. (1994), "Marketing at the Crossroads," Editorial, *Asia–Australia Marketing Journal*, 2(1) (August), 1–7.
Barabási, A.-L. (2002), *Linked: The New Science of Networks*, Cambridge, MA: Perseus.
Barile, S. and F. Polese (2010), "Linking the Viable System and Many-to-Many Network Approaches to Service-Dominant Logic and Service Science," *International Journal of Service Quality and Service Sciences*, 2(1), 23–42.
Buttle, F. (2009), *Customer Relationship Management*, 2nd edn., Oxford: Elsevier/Butterworth-Heinemann.

Christopher, M., A. Payne and D. Ballantyne (2002), *Relationship Marketing*, Oxford: Butterworth-Heinemann.

Constantinides, E. (2006), "The Marketing Mix Revisited: Towards the 21st Century Marketing," *Journal of Marketing Management*, 22(3–4), 407–38.

Grönroos, C. (1997), "From Marketing Mix to Relationship Marketing: Towards a Paradigm Shift in Marketing," *Management Decision*, 35(4), 322–39.

Grönroos, C. (2007), *Service Management and Marketing: Customer Management in Service Competition*, 3rd edn., Chichester, UK: Wiley.

Gummesson, E. (2007), "Exit *Services* Marketing – Enter *Service* Marketing," *Journal of Customer Behaviour*, 6(2), 113–41.

Gummesson, E. (2008), "Quality, Service-Dominant Logic and Many-to-Many Marketing," *TQM Journal*, 20(2), 143–53.

Gummesson, E. (forthcoming a), *Innovative Case Study Research in Business and Management*, London: Sage.

Gummesson, E. (forthcoming b), *Total Relationship Marketing*, 4th edn., London: Routledge.

Gummesson, E. (forthcoming c), "The New Service Marketing," in M.J. Baker and M. Saren (eds.), *Marketing Theory*, 3rd edn., London: Sage.

Gummesson, E. and F. Polese (2009), "B2B Is Not an Island!," *Journal of Business and Industrial Marketing*, 24(5–6), 337–50.

Håkansson, H., D. Ford, L.-E. Gadde, I. Snehota and A. Waluszewski (2009), *Business in Networks*, London: Wiley.

Howard, J.A. (1957), *Marketing Management*, Homewood, IL: Richard D. Irwin.

Jackson, B.B. (1985), *Winning and Keeping Industrial Customers*, Lexington, MA: Lexington Books.

Kotler, P. (1967), *Marketing Management*, Englewood Cliffs, NJ: Prentice Hall.

Lindstrom, M. (2008), *Buyology*, New York: Doubleday.

Lovelock, C. and E. Gummesson (2004), "Whither Services Marketing? In Search of a Paradigm and Fresh Perspectives," *Journal of Service Research*, 7(1), 20–41.

Lusch, R.F. and S.L. Vargo (2014), *Service-Dominant Logic: Premises, Perspectives, Possibilities*, Cambridge: Cambridge University Press.

Maglio, P.P. and J. Spohrer (2008), "Fundamentals of Service Science," *Journal of the Academy of Marketing Science*, 36(1), 18–20.

McCarthy, J.E. (1960), *Basic Marketing*, Homewood, IL: Richard D. Irwin.

Mele, C., T. Russo Spena and M. Colurcio (2010), "Co-Creating Value Innovation through Resource Integration," *International Journal of Quality and Service Science*, 2(1), 60–78.

Morgan, R.M. and S.D. Hunt (1994), "The Commitment-Trust Theory of Relationship Marketing," *Journal of Marketing*, 58 (July), 20–38.

Payne, A. and P. Frow (2005), "A Strategic Framework for Customer Relationship Management," *Journal of Marketing*, 69 (October), 167–76.

Peppers, D. and M. Rogers (1993), *The One to One Future*, New York: Currency/Doubleday.

Spohrer, J. and P.P. Maglio (2009), "Service Science: Toward a Smarter Planet," in W. Karwowski and G. Salvendy (eds.), *Service Engineering*, New York: Wiley.

Stacey, R.D. (2007), *Strategic Management and Organisational Dynamics*, London: Financial Times/Prentice Hall.

Vargo, S.L. (2009), "Toward a Transcending Conceptualization of Relationship: A Service-Dominant Logic Perspective," *Journal of Business and Industrial Marketing*, 24(5–6), 373–9.

Vargo, S.L. and R.F. Lusch (2008), "Service-Dominant Logic: Continuing the Evolution," *Journal of the Academy of Marketing Science*, 36(1), 1–10.

Index

TAM (technology acceptance model)
178, 187–8
'tangible service quality' (loyalty
program study variable) 197–8,
199, 201–3, 206, 207, 213
target marketing 4
targeting profitable customers 21
task conflict 277
'TB traveler' 158
TCE (transaction cost economics) 2,
224
team identification 216
'techno-inclined' consumers 187
technology
Indian adoption of 177–8, 180,
181–5, 187–8
and medical relationships 162–4
self-service technologies *see* SSTs
and service failure and recovery
142–3
and successful RM implementation
22
'technology readiness' 178, 186
'techno-prone' consumers 187
'techno-resist' consumers 187
'techno-savvy' consumers 187
Thailand 47
The House of God (book) 164–5
The Loyalty Effect (book) 3
The Theory of Moral Sentiments
(book) 249, 254
The Wealth of Nations (book) 254
therapeutic effects (source of service
negativity) 168
Thibaut, John 283, 284
third parties, use of 280
Thomasina, Mrs. (patient) 155–6,
164
tiered value propositions 106, 108–10,
115, 117
time frames, altering 286
time pressures (source of 'provider
wounding') 166
time saving benefits 35, 48
Tjosvold, Dean 279
Tombs, Alastair 63
Total Relationship Marketing (book)
306
TQM (total quality management) 2
transaction data 81–2

transaction marketing 21, 234–5, 236,
302
transaction-specific service recovery
137
TRI (Technology Readiness Index) 186
trust
Berry's trust-based relationships
model 17–21
'commitment and trust' perspective
225
and conflict 279
and CRP 27
and gratitude 257, 259
and loyalty programs 193
and opportunism 276
and relationship commitment 25
TSA (transaction-specific assets) 274
two-way communication 17–18

uncertainty 272, 274, 276
'unconvinced consumers' 187
unfairness 270, 271, 281–9, 290–91
United States 47
utility models 92

value equity 216
value-added process 119, 220–22, 223,
225, 226, 228
Van Doorn, Jenny 94, 96
Vargo, Stephen 10, 230, 231, 232–3,
234, 236, 240, 242, 244, 247, 305
Vázquez-Carrasco, Rosario 56–7, 61
Verhoef, Peter 81–2, 94, 96
Verma, Harsh 126–7
video links 163
vigilance (source of 'provider
wounding') 166
virtual revolution 3
volunteerism 164
VSA (viable system approach) 318

Wagner, Tillmann 65
Walker, Lauren 283, 284
Walker, Orville 198
Walker, Rhett 185–6
Wall Street Journal 290
Wall, J.A 278, 280
Wal-Mart (supermarket chain) 11, 223
Walton, Richard 278
Want Services 28